PAPA, PLUS JAMAIS !

# SURVIVRE À L'INCESTE

## Lucie G. Spear

**Le Chardon Bleu**

Cet ouvrage, le trenté-septième titre des éditions du Chardon Bleu et le deuxième de la collection VERITAS.

**Données de catalogage avant publication de Bibliothèque et Archives Canada.**

**Spear, Lucie G., auteure**
    **Papa, plus jamais! : survivre à l'inceste / Lucie G. Spear**

**(Veritas ; 2)**
**ISBN 978-2-923953-10-6 (couverture souple)**

    1. Victimes d'inceste—Réhabilitation. 2. Inceste. I. Titre.

RC560.I53S64 2013    616.85'836903    C2013-905310-7

\* \* \*

## DIFFUSION

### Les Éditions du Chardon Bleu

Courriel : edchardonbleu@yahoo.ca
Internet : www.chardonbleu.ca

ISBN 978-2-923953-10-6
© LES ÉDITIONS DU CHARDON BLEU 2013

Dépôt légal, Bibliothèque nationale du Canada

## AU SUJET DE L'AUTEURE

Le père de Lucie G. Spear l'a agressée sexuellement dès l'âge de neuf ans et jusqu'à quatorze ans. Lucie partage ici le cheminement qu'elle a parcouru pour recouvrer la santé; elle en profite pour nous parler de tout ce qu'elle a perdu à cause de l'inceste, à cause de ce lien de confiance que son père a brisé. Lucie montre aussi comment sa famille a su apprivoiser ce drame horrible et en ressortir grandie.

***PAPA PLUS JAMAIS ! SURVIVRE À L'INCESTE*** se veut un livre-guide très émouvant qui offre les techniques à suivre pour survivre à l'inceste et pour adopter des comportements sains et riches qui permettront aux victimes de reprendre leur vie en mains. Grâce à ce livre, les victimes du passé excluront à jamais l'inceste de leur avenir et protégeront leurs enfants et leurs petits-enfants de ce mal qui continue de faire des victimes silencieuses.

À lire absolument ! Que vous soyez une victime, un témoin, un parent ou toute autre personne dans le milieu de la santé et de la protection des enfants ! Le message d'espoir de l'auteure aidera toute personne touchée, de près ou de loin, par ce mal qui fait encore rage dans notre société.

«*À travers son récit, l'auteure démontre que l'inceste, quoique traumatique, n'a pas nécessaire-ment le pouvoir de déterminer la vie d'un(e) survivant(e). Son message d'espoir et de victoire atteste de la possibilité d'offrir un nouvel héritage aux générations futures.*»

LOÏS ALEXANIAN, PSYCHOLOGUE

Gatineau, Québec

## DÉDICACES

Je dédie ce livre à ma fille, à qui je dois ma survie; sans son amour, je n'aurais pu acquérir la force et l'énergie nécessaires pour transformer mon héritage. À elle, je dois ma vie et mon dévouement. Son amour m'a sauvée.

Cet ouvrage a pris naissance en raison de toi, mon amie très chère, « ma chum ». Toi et moi avons pu discuter de nos secrets les plus sombres et nous nous sommes réconfortées par notre amour et notre amitié. Tu es mon âme sœur, avec qui j'ai pu trouver la guérison; avec toi, j'ai complété ma mission. Je t'aime, chère amie, ton amitié me sera toujours précieuse.

Je le dédie aussi à mon compagnon de vie, mon amant, mon ami dévoué et attentionné. Il connaît mon cœur. Avec lui, je connais l'amour, le respect, le bonheur, le dévouement et la tendresse. Je suis privilégiée de l'avoir à mes côtés; son admiration me nourrit.

*J'offre ma compréhension et ma compassion à tous les survivants de l'inceste, ainsi qu'à tous ceux et toutes celles qui portent ce fardeau familial dans leur cœur. L'être humain cherche diligemment le chemin qui conduira vers l'art d'aimer et d'être aimé. J'offre ce livre à tous ceux et toutes celles qui ont le courage de transformer leur héritage.*

**Lucie G. Spear**

**TABLE DES MATIÈRES**

*Chère Lucie!*

*Quelle merveilleuse personne tu es! Je te félicite et t'admire.*

*Tout au long de la lecture de ton livre, j'ai admiré ta sagesse et ta bonté. Je suis certaine que tu es née avec tout ce qu'il y a de bon en toi. Je crois que tu es comme ta grand-maman que tu aimais tant. Les évènements tragiques que tu as vécus ont tenté de détruire toute cette bonté qui t'habite. Ton père n'a pu violer la beauté de ton être. Il l'a peut-être ternie ou voilée pour un certain temps, mais tu as su la retrouver, la restaurer, la rendre encore plus lumineuse.*

*Pourquoi fallait-il que ton cheminement soit si douloureux? On ne le saura sans doute jamais, mais comme tu le dis, c'est sans doute pour que tu deviennes la personne que tu devais être, la personne que tu es devenue. C'est sûrement aussi pour que tu aides d'autres victimes, et je suis certaine que c'est déjà commencé. Ton livre est tellement bien bâti. On y voit une grande sagesse, un grand désir d'aider. Pas de détails sordides, mais des explications sur les états d'âme d'une personne abusée et surtout des pistes pour retrouver la confiance et le bonheur. Tu t'es donné la peine de faire de nombreuses recherches. Ton livre est bien documenté, plein de belles citations et de judicieuses suggestions. Une victime qui te lira aura sans doute l'impression que tu la prends par la main et que tu l'entraînes tout doucement vers la lumière, vers la sérénité.*

*Je crois que mon chapitre préféré est le sixième, **Vos enfants n'ont plus à vivre avec l'inceste**. Il est bon pour tout le monde ce chapitre. C'est un programme de vie. J'ai relu les pages 137 et 138 qui me touchent et m'émerveillent à la fois. Elles me révèlent qui est Lucie, cette femme au grand cœur avec des valeurs qui me font t'aimer et t'admirer. Lors de notre rencontre, je t'ai vite perçue comme une personne aimable et chaleureuse, sympathique et agréable. J'ignorais ce que tu avais vécu. Tu as vraiment gravi tout un Everest! Lâche pas! Te voilà chef de cordée.*

*Je te félicite et te remercie d'avoir écrit ce livre. Je n'ose imaginer tout le courage que cela t'a demandé, mais imagine tout le courage qu'il va donner à d'autres victimes. Je suis très contente que Marc ait accepté de le publier en français : un précieux outil pour que ta mission continue.*

*Chère Lucie, tu connais l'impuissance des mots, mais je sais aussi que tu peux saisir tout ce que ces pauvres mots n'arrivent pas à communiquer. Si on souffre avec toi en lisant ton livre, on ressent aussi beaucoup de fierté, d'admiration et de reconnaissance.*

*Je te laisse avec un gros gros câlin. J'ai hâte de te revoir.*

*Colette*
*XOX*

## AVANT-PROPOS

Je vous avoue qu'au cours de ma vie j'ai rencontré peu de gens qui n'avaient pas, enfants, vécu une agression psychologique ou physique. Moi-même, j'ai été agressée sexuellement par mon père et, maintenant âgée de cinquante-neuf ans, je partage mon histoire en décrivant les étapes qui m'ont amenée à me guérir de cette blessure déshonorante qu'est l'inceste.

Ces agressions sexuelles, qui visent notamment les enfants impuissants à se défendre des assauts d'un parent, doivent cesser. En espérant prévenir cette souffrance chez les enfants, je désire partager, avec mes lecteurs, mes méthodes de guérison, ainsi que les répercussions de l'inceste sur ma vie et les effets traumatiques de l'inceste reçus en héritage.

Lorsque j'ai décidé d'écrire ce livre, j'ai opté pour une approche différente de celle de plusieurs livres déjà sur le marché traitant du même sujet. Je voulais que ma fille ainsi que mes lecteurs puissent recevoir mon message, sans avoir à visualiser par le détail mes agressions sexuelles. Selon les thérapeutes que j'ai interrogés, mon message se livre encore mieux si je n'exploite pas le voyeurisme.

J'ai décidé de ne révéler mon vécu qu'à une seule personne, mon premier thérapeute, que j'ai consulté il y a trente ans. Aucun autre être humain n'a à porter dans sa mémoire les détails d'une enfance aussi horrible et traumatisante. Je ressens une souffrance profonde lorsque j'écoute le récit d'une autre survivante; c'est donc pour cette raison que je préfère épargner à mes lecteurs les détails de mes sévices sexuels.

Cependant, je désire partager avec tous mes lecteurs mon cheminement vers la libération de l'ignorance et des effets de cette cruauté infligée aux enfants. Pour ma fille et ma descendance, j'ai créé un nouvel héritage : un héritage sans le poids de l'inceste.

Je partage :

- Ma transformation en un mieux-être.
- Qui de la famille était l'agresseur et qui en était conscient?
- Les conséquences du fardeau de l'inceste sur ma famille
- Les méthodes que j'ai utilisées pour me rééduquer comme parent
- Comment s'assurer que mes enfants ne propagent pas l'inceste?
- Promouvoir ce nouvel héritage.

Je connais plusieurs personnes, hommes et femmes, qui s'enterrent dans un silence écrasant autour de ce crime infernal qu'est l'inceste. Un passé incestueux paralyse un adulte si celui-ci ne cherche pas à se distancer de cet héritage toxique; une vie de sérénité et de bonheur est quasi impossible avec ce fardeau de silence.

Il m'a fallu une quarantaine d'années avant de comprendre que je n'étais aucunement responsable des actes que posait mon père sur ma personne ni des besoins quotidiens de mes frères et sœurs. C'était tout de même le devoir de mes parents de chercher le soutien et les ressources pour aider la famille à traverser ce traumatisme.

Ce que mon père a imposé à sa propre famille nous a tous diminués, déshonorés, humiliés, et blessés physiquement. Ma mère ainsi que mes frères et sœurs vivent avec ce passé crasseux tous les jours de leur vie. Mon père était très conscient de ses actes, mais il a quand même choisi d'agresser sexuellement ses enfants. Il a essayé d'imputer ses agissements à ses enfants, à notre mère, et même à sa propre mère. Je ne peux concevoir qu'un père de famille veuille blesser son propre enfant de cette façon. Je ne le comprends toujours pas! Quel monstre de parent lègue un tel héritage immoral à ses enfants, un tel fardeau de douleur? Notre père nous a tous handicapés; ce comportement perfide doit cesser. J'ai mis plusieurs années à constater le dommage et le retard que cette relation incestueuse avait causés à mon développement personnel.

Quant à moi, même si j'avais subi ces agressions sexuelles, je n'avais pas le droit de propager ce mal à mon enfant.

Certaines psychothérapeutes m'ont prévenue qu'en écrivant ce livre je ne serais aucunement populaire auprès des membres de la famille, des amis et même des collègues de travail; ces gens n'aiment pas admettre qu'il y a des enfants, si près d'eux, qui souffrent autant sous la garde de leurs parents. Qui peut leur en vouloir?

Moi aussi j'aimerais mieux ne pas voir ce crime infantile dans notre société. Et c'est donc pour cette raison que la vérité doit sortir. Écrire et contribuer à la cessation de ce crime social est le destin qui s'est tracé devant moi : je ne dois plus reculer. Mon cheminement a été ardu, acharné, et il me semble que j'ai mis beaucoup de temps à me libérer de ce fardeau; essayer d'alléger le trajet vers le mieux-être pour d'autres fait partie de ma propre guérison. La blessure est profonde et douloureuse. Toutefois, je ne peux garder le silence tant que ce comportement malsain et impur ne sera pas éradiqué de l'humanité.

Je voulais utiliser mon vrai nom, mais, après réflexion sur l'impact que ceci aurait sur les membres de ma famille, j'ai choisi un pseudonyme. Mon désir de dénoncer mon père en proclamant mon nom allait atteindre à la vie privée des autres membres de ma famille qui ont été victimes de l'inceste. Étant donné que j'ai choisi de ne pas exposer les détails des sévices exercés sur moi, j'ai aussi choisi de leur laisser à eux le droit de guérir en paix. Si vous êtes une victime de l'inceste, vous comprenez ce conflit intérieur. Je crois que la guérison se fait plus rapidement si chacun choisit sa propre manière de croître.

À l'âge de dix-sept ans, en 1971, j'ai juré que le chemin tortueux de l'inceste ne serait ni pour moi ni pour mes héritiers. Assise sur un banc du parc de la Confédération, à Ottawa, et remplie d'un sentiment de mal-aimée, j'implorais l'aide universelle de me guider dans l'apprentissage de l'amour et du bien-être. Ce jour est gravé dans ma mémoire comme un moment tournant de ma vie : c'était justement ce vent du changement qu'il me fallait pour survivre.

Depuis, fidèle à mon serment, j'ai choisi de promouvoir les valeurs dignes de la vie. Ma priorité demeure toujours de prendre les mesures nécessaires pour rétablir une succession saine, puissante et vigoureuse. Mon héritage est fondé sur l'amour, la générosité, le respect, l'honnêteté, la bonté, la tendresse et la compassion. Toutes ces vertus, j'avais à les apprendre par moi-même, car j'avais malheureusement été exposée et éduquée dans leurs contraires. Mon désir le plus fervent est que ces qualités éminentes veillent à la santé et au bien-être de ma descendance. Par le biais de ce processus, j'ai découvert ma force intérieure, mes compétences, et je me suis pénétrée de valeurs saines. J'écris donc ce livre pour léguer un héritage sain et bien informé à ma fille, mes petites-filles, ainsi qu'à toutes les victimes qui ont à surmonter ce traumatisme de l'inceste.

*« Nous pouvons tous évoluer, grandir et nous guérir nous-mêmes; cependant, la plupart d'entre nous avons besoin d'aide un jour ou l'autre. Nier ou minimiser l'agression empêche la croissance et la guérison. C'est là que le conseiller intervient. Le counseling est spécialement important lorsqu'un enfant a été trahi par un proche... »*

*Counseling en matière de violence sexuelle — Guide à l'intention des parents et des enfants*
Le Centre national d'information sur la violence dans la famille
Agence de la santé publique du Canada
www.phac-aspc.gc.ca/nc-cn

## PRÉAMBULE

De nombreuses victimes de l'inceste n'ont aucun intérêt à partager ce traumatisme et choisissent de garder le silence. Ces victimes, pour des raisons de tabous, de honte, de colère et de culpabilité, préfèrent ne pas recourir à la thérapie de peur d'être sévèrement jugées. C'est trop souvent, tragiquement, le cas.

Tout au long de l'âge adulte, j'ai essayé en vain d'oublier que j'en étais une victime. J'ai, jusqu'à l'âge de trente ans, survécu comme si l'inceste ne m'appartenait pas. J'ai souvent espéré qu'à la longue j'allais oublier les agressions sexuelles de mon père, mais ce n'était pas une attente réaliste. Il me fallait avant tout comprendre que cette forme d'agression marque les survivants à jamais et que je devais recourir à la thérapie professionnelle dans le domaine des agressions sexuelles pour cheminer vers un avenir sain et prospère.

Le passage suivant, tiré du guide *Counseling en matière de violence sexuelle* [1], de l'Agence de la santé publique du Canada, montre le travail qu'un conseiller peut offrir aux parents et aux enfants en matière de rétablissement :

*Un conseiller peut :*

- *Vous aider, vous et votre enfant, à aborder ce qui vous tracasse le plus, pas à pas, rendant ainsi l'expérience plus facile à traverser et moins effrayante. Notre réflexe naturel nous incite à « refuser de penser » à l'agression afin d'oublier ou même de nier son existence. C'est pourquoi tant d'adultes qui ont survécu à la violence sexuelle peuvent éprouver un grand nombre de problèmes ou de symptômes qu'ils ne comprennent pas.*

- *Vous aider, vous et votre enfant, à comprendre les sentiments complexes et confus ressentis pendant et après l'agression sexuelle.*

- *Vous aider, vous et votre enfant, à vous affranchir des effets du passé afin de profiter à l'avenir d'une vie plus heureuse.*

Dans le passé, il y a eu plusieurs éléments qui ont contribué au silence autour de l'inceste, tel que le manque de services et de ressources, les doctrines religieuses (le père était l'autorité absolue : conjointe et enfants devaient lui obéir), l'intimidation du père, l'humiliation et l'isolement. De plus, à cette époque, on ne croyait pas toujours les témoignages des enfants ou l'on minimisait leurs récits des faits. Même notre compréhension de ce qu'était l'agression sexuelle était vague ou mal interprétée.

L'article intitulé *L'agression sexuelle d'enfants*[2] publié par l'Agence de la santé publique du Canada (ASPC) définit l'agression sexuelle comme suit :

- *Il y a agression sexuelle d'enfant lorsqu'un adulte ou un adolescent se sert d'un enfant à des fins sexuelles, qu'il expose l'enfant à une activité ou à un comportement de nature sexuelle.*

*Le plus souvent, l'agression sexuelle comporte des attouchements; l'enfant peut être invité à faire ou à recevoir des caresses sexuelles.*

- *Les rapports sexuels, la prostitution juvénile et l'exploitation sexuelle dans la pornographie enfantine sont d'autres formes d'agression sexuelle.*

- *L'agression sexuelle est en soi de la violence affective qui, souvent, s'accompagne d'autres formes de maltraitance. C'est de l'abus de confiance et de pouvoir l'égard de l'enfant.*

- *L'agression sexuelle d'enfants est une infraction criminelle au Canada. Le Code criminel indique clairement les comportements illicites. La Loi sur la preuve au Canada définit les genres de preuves qui sont admissibles devant un tribunal. Ces dernières années, le Code criminel et la Loi sur la preuve au Canada ont tous deux été modifiés pour mieux protéger les enfants.*

Et, tirées du même texte, voici les raisons pour lesquelles un enfant ne révèle pas son agresseur :

- *Il y a des enfants agressés sexuellement dans toutes les classes sociales et communautés ethnoculturelles. L'enfant qui présente une déficience physique ou mentale est particulièrement susceptible d'être agressé sexuellement.*

- *L'enfant n'est pas en mesure de consentir de façon éclairée à une activité sexuelle, parce qu'il ne peut ni très bien comprendre un contact sexuel entre un adulte et un enfant ni en prévoir les conséquences, et parce que l'adulte abuse de sa situation d'autorité vis-à-vis de l'enfant.*

- *L'enfant isolé est le plus susceptible d'être agressé sexuellement. Il a peu de rapports avec des amis, des frères et soeurs ou des adultes en qui il peut avoir confiance. Certains agresseurs abuseront d'un enfant qui est déjà isolé. D'autres s'arrangeront pour isoler l'enfant en manipulant les gens et en tirant profit de situations. Parfois, l'enfant agressé sexuellement risque de s'isoler davantage parce qu'il se sent différent des autres ou qu'il a peur de ce que les autres vont penser.*

- *Le risque de traumatisme grave chez l'enfant est le plus élevé lorsque l'agresseur est un membre de la famille ou que l'enfant ne reçoit pas d'appui du parent non agresseur. Les conséquences à long terme sont également plus graves lorsque l'agresseur a recours ou menace de recourir à la force en commettant son agression, ou qu'il y a de nombreuses agressions sur une longue période.*

- *Comme il est mentionné plus haut, les enfants ont de la difficulté à rompre le silence. Dans l'univers de l'enfant, les adultes contrôlent la plupart des ressources et semblent tout* savoir. Lorsque l'agresseur profère des menaces contre l'enfant ou contre une personne que celui-ci aime, l'enfant ne doutera peut-être pas de la capacité de l'adulte de mettre ses menaces à exécution.

- Dans tous les cas, l'enfant veut parler de l'agression dont il est victime afin qu'elle cesse, mais souvent, il craint qu'on ne le croie pas ou qu'on ne le protège pas, ou il a peur de ce qui pourrait arriver s'il parle. Il est normal qu'un enfant attende un an ou plus pour parler de l'agression qu'il a subie. Il en parlera peut-être plus facilement si une autre victime signale une agression commise par le même contrevenant ou si on lui pose des questions directes au sujet d'agressions possibles.

- Surtout dans les cas d'inceste, lorsque l'agresseur est un proche parent, l'enfant ne parlera peut-être pas de sa situation avant d'avoir atteint l'âge adulte. Et même à cet âge, beaucoup de victimes gardent le silence. L'agresseur impose le secret et suscite chez l'enfant la crainte de détruire l'intimité et le sentiment de sécurité par ailleurs intact qu'inspire la famille.

- Il y a peu de preuves que beaucoup d'enfants font délibérément de fausses allégations ou qu'ils interprètent incorrectement un contact sain entre un adulte et un enfant comme une agression sexuelle. Dans les rares cas consignés où des enfants semblent avoir fait de fausses allégations, la cause en était habituellement de la manipulation de la part d'un adulte.

- Les fausses dénégations d'agression sexuelle (nier qu'il y a eu agression alors qu'elle a vraiment eu lieu) et les rétractations de déclarations d'agression (nier l'agression après avoir dit à quelqu'un qu'elle s'était produite) sont beaucoup plus courantes que les faux rapports.

- Parfois, les enfants se rétractent et retirent les allégations véridiques d'agressions. Cela n'a rien d'étonnant, puisque l'enfant craint spontanément les retombées qu'une divulgation aura sur la famille ou a peur qu'on ne le croie pas. Par ailleurs, il se peut que l'enfant se rétracte devant l'effrayante réalité que l'adulte agresseur a tellement plus de pouvoir.

- Lorsqu'un enfant agressé reçoit une aide professionnelle avant de témoigner en justice, ses déclarations sont plus susceptibles d'être claires et de refléter fidèlement le moment et les circonstances de l'agression. En outre, l'expérience est moins stressante lorsque l'enfant a reçu ce genre d'aide.

- Les enfants ne réagissent pas tous de la même façon à l'agression sexuelle. La manière dont les adultes réagissent à la divulgation par l'enfant influe grandement sur la perception que l'enfant aura de l'agression et du rôle qu'il y a joué. Le fait qu'on le croit et l'appui qu'il reçoit de sa famille peuvent l'aider *à surmonter l'épreuve et réduire certains effets perturbants de l'agression sexuelle.*

La plupart des auteurs d'agression sexuelle sont connus de leurs victimes et sont même des membres de leur famille (père, frère, sœur, mère, grands-parents, tantes et oncles). Parallèlement, les recherches et les statistiques des femmes-agresseurs sont disponibles depuis 1990. Val Young, auteur du livre *Women Abusers — A Feminist View (Female Sexual Abuse of Children)* [3], rapporte que jusqu'aux années 1990, les gens jugeaient que les agresseurs d'enfants étaient de sexe masculin. V. Young affirme que, même si les hommes sont plus susceptibles d'agresser les enfants, on ne peut plus négliger le fait que certaines femmes maltraitent aussi les enfants sexuellement.

Lors de mes recherches auprès des professionnels de la santé, conseillers et thérapeutes qui aident les victimes d'agressions sexuelles, j'ai été soulagée de constater qu'il existe maintenant plusieurs services et ressources disponibles aux familles faisant face à cette douloureuse épreuve de vie. L'Agence de la santé publique du Canada, Centre national d'information sur la violence dans la famille (ASPC/CNIVF) offre un répertoire de guides de traitement pour les enfants, les adolescents et les adultes qui sont victimes d'agressions sexuelles (se référer à l'annexe A). Ces ressources n'étaient pas encore développées lorsque je subissais les abus de mon père.

Je connais des victimes d'agressions sexuelles de ma génération qui n'entreprennent pas de thérapie, parce qu'elles présument ne pas y avoir droit, étant donné qu'elles étaient agressées dans leur enfance et que trop d'années se sont écoulées depuis. Elles présument que les traitements ne seront pas bénéfiques ou nécessaires à leur cheminement. Cette hypothèse me trouble. J'encourage plutôt ces gens à obtenir l'expertise et le soutien nécessaires afin de se créer une vie équilibrée, saine et heureuse. Si la honte, la rage, l'angoisse, la culpabilité et l'humiliation continuent de bouillonner à l'intérieur d'une personne agressée sexuellement, ces émotions s'amplifieront en toute probabilité et se transformeront en actes négatifs, qui seront ensuite transmis, sous une forme ou une autre, à leurs enfants ou à leurs proches.

En 1986, après avoir confronté mon père des souffrances qu'il avait imposées à sa famille, j'espérais que mes parents se joignent à mes frères et soeurs en thérapie familiale; mais ils ont refusé. Nous avons dû, comme dans le passé, nous distancer de nos parents et nous occuper nous-mêmes de notre guérison. Puisque nous n'avons pas entrepris la thérapie en famille et que ma mère demeure toujours avec mon père, j'ai dû choisir de ne plus fréquenter mes parents.

À la suite d'une rencontre avec la directrice du *Centre d'intervention en abus sexuels auprès de la famille* (CIASF), j'ai constaté que c'était possible pour une famille de bénéficier d'une thérapie de groupe; malheureusement, notre père, qui était la personne qui aurait dû assumer cette responsabilité, a choisi de se libérer de toute obligation.

En conséquence, notre famille s'est effritée et nous avons perdu contact. Nous aurions pu nous inspirer l'un et l'autre dans la compréhension, le soutien moral et l'affection, pour en sortir vainqueurs : c'est ce qui aurait dû être notre véritable héritage familial. Au lieu de cela, l'orgueil et la honte ont gardé mes parents muets à nos souffrances et à notre besoin de soutien.

J'ai travaillé avec plusieurs thérapeutes et conseillers spécialisés dans le domaine de la violence familiale et de la violence sexuelle, pour me permettre de survivre. Je peux rapporter qu'il y a une seule personne du domaine de la santé (science infirmière) qui m'a lancé assez durement : « *Reviens-en* ». Elle fut la seule personne de sa profession à ne pas saisir la souffrance des victimes de l'inceste et qui m'ait traitée avec autant de mépris; c'est irréaliste et cruel d'exiger d'un enfant victime de l'inceste d'ignorer cette épreuve horrible. Pour guérir de l'inceste, une personne doit être soutenue par des aidants formés pour épauler les victimes de l'inceste ou d'agressions sexuelles.

Chaque enfant réagit différemment à la violence. Certains enfants ne montreront pas de signes de traumatisme, tandis que d'autres auront des problèmes de comportement allant de l'anxiété de séparation au stress post-traumatique et même à la dépression. Le soutien et la thérapie sont essentiels pour aider les enfants à surmonter ce traumatisme associé à l'inceste. Augmenter les programmes de prévention, de sensibilisation, et d'éducation fera de l'inceste et des agressions sexuelles un crime du passé.

« *Et finalement, n'oublie jamais que ce qui est derrière toi et ce qui est devant toi n'est rien comparativement à ce qui est en toi* ».

**Robin S. Sharma**

*Le moine qui vendit sa Ferrari*

**CHAPITRE 1**

# MON CHEMINEMENT VERS UNE GUÉRISON ABSOLUE

À l'âge de trente et un ans, j'étais tourmentée par la rage, la dépression et la tristesse. Je sentais une force interne me pousser à me débarrasser de ce douloureux secret du passé. L'énergie que j'utilisais à contrôler mon environnement m'épuisait : j'étais toujours triste et déprimée. De plus, j'exhibais un complexe d'infériorité de la taille des montagnes Rocheuses. J'étais en dialogue constant avec cette voix intérieure qui persistait à vouloir se défendre et se libérer. Je voulais cette chose hors de moi. Je ne voulais plus m'identifier à l'inceste ou permettre à l'inceste de me définir.

J'étais mal à l'aise d'en parler à mes frères et sœurs, car, à cette époque, je pensais être la seule victime de mon père. Ce dernier m'avait avertie à maintes reprises de garder le silence, de n'en discuter avec personne, surtout pas avec ma mère. Je ne pouvais non plus demander l'aide de mes oncles ou mes tantes, de peur que le secret ne se rende aux oreilles de ma mère. Je ne pouvais pas non plus me confier à mes amies; quel enfant de neuf ans pourrait ou voudrait dévoiler une pareille action de son père? J'avais l'impression que j'étais la seule personne dans notre quartier à être agressée sexuellement.

Ce secret, je l'ai gardé jusqu'à l'âge de trente et un ans. Lorsque j'ai quitté la maison à l'âge de vingt-deux ans, c'était pour me marier. À ce stade-ci, je ne pouvais faire confiance à personne avec mon secret, pas même à mon conjoint. Je commençais tout juste à penser qu'il faudrait résoudre ce problème, mais je n'étais simplement pas prête ou en mesure de dévoiler mon secret. Pendant ce mariage qui ne dura que cinq ans, j'ai toujours gardé mon secret. Quelle relation peut durer avec ce genre de secret? Aucune, à mon avis.

La décision d'enfanter était unilatéralement la mienne; mon mari ne voulait pas d'enfant immédiatement. Comme de nombreuses femmes, j'ai vu l'arrivée de mon enfant comme une panacée. J'avais tort de supposer que mon enfant pouvait alléger ma situation ; un enfant n'est pas la réponse à tous nos besoins, loin de là. Un enfant doit avant tout grandir dans un environnement qui assure la sécurité, la santé, le bien-être et l'amour. J'avais l'impression, en enfantant, de combler un vide. Contrairement à mes attentes, le vide n'a pas disparu ; mais il s'est alourdi avec la crainte et la culpabilité. Élever mon enfant, alors que j'étais encore tellement déconcertée, me tourmenta pendant plusieurs années. Avoir un enfant avant d'entreprendre la thérapie appropriée aux victimes de l'inceste était irresponsable et égocentrique : j'ai mis plusieurs années à me pardonner cette imprudence.

À la suite de mon divorce, comme parent monoparental, je ne voulais pas que ma fille soit écrasée par mon traumatisme. Je décidai donc d'aller chercher de l'aide. La responsabilité d'élever un enfant est difficile et exigeante, même dans les meilleures situations conjugales. Maintenant, imaginez un parent angoissé avec un passé irrésolu qui choisit d'élever un enfant? Inévitablement, les sentiments de culpabilité, de peur et de traumatismes irrésolus émergent et ont un impact grave sur la vie de l'enfant. Au cours des premières années de ma fille, j'éprouvais énormément d'anxiété, de crainte et je me méfiais de tous ceux qui l'approchaient. J'ai toujours craint pour sa sécurité ; mais mon attitude était démesurée : j'étais toujours angoissée et stressée. Inconsciemment, je créais un environnement qui manquait de calme et d'harmonie. Ma propre expérience enfantine ne m'avait pas préparée à lui fournir un milieu auquel chaque enfant a droit.

Puisque j'avais choisi de me confier à personne de mon entourage, mon seul recours était d'obtenir de l'aide professionnelle. J'ai donc pris un rendez-vous avec un conseiller spécialisé en traitement des victimes de l'inceste et d'agressions sexuelles. Mais tout me semblait se dérouler trop rapidement. Avant ma première séance, la peur et l'anxiété m'ont saisie. J'avais un nœud dans l'estomac qui m'empêchait de manger. Toutes sortes de questions émergeaient. Qu'est-ce que je vais lui dire? Quelles réactions aura le conseiller devant mon histoire? Est-ce qu'il en sera répugné? Qu'est-ce qui se produira suite à ma rencontre? Est-ce que mon père sera accusé et envoyé en prison? Est-ce que le conseiller va me prendre ma fille? Toutes ces questions me rongeaient le cerveau et le cœur. J'ai failli annuler mon rendez-vous. Mais mon désir d'être une bonne mère pour ma fille m'a soutenue : par amour pour elle, je devais me débarrasser de ce secret infâme.

En 1964, je savais trop bien que je ne pouvais pas parler de l'inceste; le temps n'était pas venu où l'on ajoutait foi aux dénonciations des enfants contre leurs agresseurs. Il faut se souvenir aussi que les services pour les victimes d'agressions sexuelles commencèrent seulement à s'organiser dans les années 1980. Les prêtres, les autorités scolaires, les parents et les voisins n'avaient pas l'obligation d'avertir les autorités responsables des cas d'enfants maltraités. Ce n'est qu'en 1983 qu'on adopta une loi contre le viol au Canada et que les programmes de prévention contre la violence familiale ont fait leur apparition.

Léguer l'inceste à la génération suivante n'a jamais été une option pour moi. Il était indispensable que je dévoile le secret que notre père nous avait imposé. En août 1986, une vingtaine d'années après les agressions sexuelles, nous avons confronté notre père avec les souffrances qu'il nous avait fait subir. Tous mes frères et toutes mes soeurs se rassemblèrent pour la première fois, et discutèrent de ce secret de famille. À l'insistance du conseiller, nous devions nous assurer que notre père n'agresserait plus sexuellement aucune autre personne.

Aujourd'hui, il y a des processus établis et les enseignants, les infirmières, les médecins, doivent être vigilants et attentifs aux signes d'agressions sexuelles. Quiconque soupçonne l'agression sexuelle ou l'inceste doit avertir la police locale, le Centre de la petite enfance, l'hôpital ou le Centre national d'information sur la violence dans la famille. Il y a des professionnels responsables d'aider immédiatement les victimes : la sécurité et le bien-être des enfants sont leur priorité et leur responsabilité.

La section suivante est aussi tirée du guide de l'ASPC *Counseling en matière de violence sexuelle : Guide à l'intention des parents et des enfants* [4], et aide les victimes d'agressions sexuelles à en comprendre les effets à long terme :

- *Si vous avez été agressé sexuellement durant l'enfance, peut-être souffrez-vous depuis des années de problèmes qui ne s'atténuent jamais. Si vous avez maintenant des problèmes de drogue ou d'alcool, de fréquentes ruptures, une dysfonction sexuelle, des problèmes alimentaires, ou si pendant de longues périodes vous vous sentez coupé de la réalité, il est possible que la cause de tous ces problèmes soit liée à la violence sexuelle que vous avez subie dans votre enfance. Peut-être avez-vous été incapable d'en parler ou, si vous en avez parlé, vous a-t-on demandé d'oublier et de continuer à vivre comme si rien n'était arrivé.*

- *Souvent, les adultes qui ont mis de côté la violence sexuelle dont ils ont été victimes vont avoir une violente réaction physique et émotive au moment où un de leurs enfants est victime à son tour. Si cela vous arrive, il faudra peut-être que vous et votre enfant consultiez. Le counseling ne sert pas seulement à relater et à revivre les évènements pénibles du passé, mais bien aussi à adopter des stratégies qui vous permettront de faire face à votre détresse. Cela semble impossible à envisager ? Essayez plutôt de voir cette crise comme une chance de rapprochement inespérée pour votre famille.*

- *Même si vous n'avez pas été victime de violence sexuelle dans votre enfance, affronter l'agression infligée à votre enfant peut représenter le défi le plus important de votre vie. Vous devriez obtenir de l'aide auprès d'un conseiller pendant cette période.*

En outre, le guide décrit les méthodes d'un conseiller pour aider les adultes et les enfants à la suite d'agressions sexuelles (j'aurais grandement apprécié cette documentation avant mon premier rendez-vous de counseling).

*Un conseiller peut :*

- *Vous aider, vous et votre enfant, à aborder ce qui vous tracasse le plus, pas à pas, rendant ainsi l'expérience plus facile à traverser et moins effrayante. Notre réflexe naturel nous incite à « refuser de penser » à l'agression de façon à l'oublier ou même à nier son existence. C'est pourquoi tant d'adultes qui ont survécu à la violence sexuelle peuvent éprouver un grand nombre de problèmes ou présenter des symptômes qu'ils ne comprennent pas.*

- *Vous aider, vous et votre enfant, à comprendre les sentiments complexes et confus ressentis pendant et après l'agression sexuelle.*

- *Vous aider, vous et votre enfant, à vous affranchir des effets du passé afin de profiter à l'avenir d'une vie plus heureuse.*

Le premier rendez-vous avec votre thérapeute peut être difficile à affronter ; c'en était ainsi pour moi. S'ouvrir le cœur et partager, pour la première fois, votre secret le plus intime et douloureux peut être terrifiant. Pour moi, l'expérience fut presque insurmontable. Ma plus grande motivation était que je voulais me guérir pour ma fille. Je voulais être une mère bien « *dans sa peau* » afin d'être en mesure de fournir à ma fille un environnement sain, protégé et harmonieux. C'est pour cette raison que j'ai tenu à continuer en thérapie et à faire mon nouvel apprentissage.

Ma première séance de thérapie est mémorable. Puisque je voulais garder une certaine maîtrise sur le déroulement de ce rendez-vous, je m'étais munie d'une liste de consignes que le conseiller devait suivre. Ma liste comprenait plusieurs points que je voulais soulever avec le conseiller et, tout au début de la liste, j'avais formulé un avertissement personnel : s'il montrait de la répugnance ou du dégoût devant mon récit, je sortirais immédiatement de son bureau et il ne me reverrait plus jamais. J'avais une peur horrible qu'il me juge répugnante. Le conseiller a été très surpris de ma requête ; néanmoins, il s'y est plié. Il a probablement senti que c'était la seule façon dont je parlerais de mon passé. Au milieu de mon compte-rendu des faits, il a manifesté du dégoût ; mais ce dégoût était en réaction aux actes de mon père et non à moi. J'ai compris, à ce stade de notre rencontre, que le conseiller m'appuyait, que je pouvais donc lui faire confiance. À ce jour, je demeure reconnaissante de l'aide qu'il m'a apportée.

Une personne qui n'a pas été victime de l'inceste peut trouver incompréhensible que je me juge répugnante. Les parents influencent énormément la pensée de leurs enfants et ils peuvent les culpabiliser jusqu'à l'âge adulte. Mon père m'avait convaincue que j'étais responsable de ses agressions sexuelles -- il a même dit que c'était moi qui lui en faisais la demande. Comme plusieurs victimes de l'inceste, j'ai porté en moi cette accusation, sans en être consciente, jusqu'en thérapie.

Comme je l'ai dit dans l'introduction, je n'exposerai pas au public les détails crus des agressions sexuelles. Je veux que ma fille et mes lecteurs puissent lire mon livre sans subir les détails d'un récit perturbant. À mon avis, ces détails n'apportaient rien à l'objectif de ce livre : démontrer que nous pouvons nous libérer des traumatismes de l'inceste.

J'ai compris très tôt dans mon cheminement que je devais me guérir avant même d'aider les autres. J'ai dû conquérir la peur, l'humiliation, la honte et le manque d'estime de soi qui m'habitaient depuis mon enfance. Mais lutter contre ces états d'esprit, c'était pour moi escalader le mont Everest. C'était le début d'un voyage long et douloureux. Je me sentais tellement isolée et souvent je pensais ne jamais y arriver; le chemin de la guérison me paraissait insurmontable.

Lentement, mais sûrement, j'ai commencé à améliorer mon quotidien. J'ai transformé mon point de vue négatif en adoptant des réflexions et jugements positifs. J'ai choisi une manière d'être moins hostile envers les gens. J'ai compris qu'ils ne voulaient pas tous me faire du mal. Afin d'anéantir la mémoire-habitude qui était toujours présente dans mon psychisme, j'ai suivi les recommandations et les encouragements du thérapeute. J'ai lu plusieurs livres de progrès personnels et découvert de nouveaux champs d'études, telles que la philosophie, les plantes médicinales, les diverses croyances spirituelles. J'ai pratiqué le yoga, le tai-chi, le reiki. Pour entretenir un esprit joyeux et positif, je m'entourais de gens pleins d'entrain, et de divertissements amusants et sur un ton humoristique. Je n'avais plus peur de prendre des rendez-vous avec un conseiller professionnel, dans mes moments d'angoisse. J'avais de plus en plus confiance en moi. Chaque étape constructive et chaque enseignement augmentaient mes connaissances et m'aidaient à atteindre mon objectif premier : celui de me rétablir pour enfin retrouver la force de transformer l'héritage que m'avait légué mon père.

Cela peut sembler curieux, mais ma motivation la plus forte apparaissait lorsque je manquais d'enthousiasme pour l'une ou l'autre de mes activités. Dès que mon intérêt baissait, je réévaluais ma situation. J'entreprenais aussitôt soit une autre activité, soit une autre façon de penser ou d'agir. J'avais vécu avec tellement de pessimisme que je ne pouvais plus tolérer cette négativité destructrice. La vie, me disais-je, nous apporte assez d'embûches pour que nous n'en rajoutions pas. À ce jour, je maintiens une vie active et enthousiaste; ce mode de vie me convient à merveille : j'aime travailler, découvrir, m'amuser et rire. Je suis bien reconnaissante du travail que j'ai accompli.

L'un des plus grands obstacles à surmonter était ma faible estime de soi. Mon père avait égoïstement obligé ses enfants à grandir complètement dépourvus de confiance en eux et d'amour-propre. Pour venir à bout de cette attitude négative, je me suis inscrite comme étudiante à temps partiel à l'Université d'Ottawa ; jusque-là, je n'avais qu'un diplôme d'études secondaires commerciales. En entreprenant des études universitaires, j'entreprenais un défi que je m'étais toujours refusé.

À mon grand étonnement, j'ai obtenu une note scolaire supérieure à mes attentes. Je ne pouvais pas croire que j'avais si bien réussi. Je suis même retournée voir mon professeur pour la remercier de sa générosité. Elle a eu beau essayer de m'expliquer que j'avais bien mérité cette note pour mes rédactions, je ne pouvais pas croire, à ce moment-là, que je la méritais. Après des succès dans d'autres cours, j'ai enfin compris que je pouvais véritablement réussir à ce niveau d'enseignement supérieur. Cela explique que je puisse vous écrire aujourd'hui. Les avantages que j'ai retirés de ces nouvelles connaissances sont immenses.

Dès ma troisième consultation chez le psychologue, je lui ai fait part de ma volonté de venir en aide aux victimes de l'inceste. Je peux vous assurer que je n'étais guère prête à en aider d'autres à ce moment-là. Je n'avais pas encore compris combien de temps et d'énergie il me fallait pour guérir. Le psychologue m'a gentiment conseillé de prendre le temps de m'aider moi-même d'abord, car, expliqua-t-il, les traumatismes d'agressions sexuelles comportent plusieurs niveaux. Il a comparé ces niveaux à des pelures d'oignon. Une fois qu'une étape est résolue, d'autres émotions associées à l'inceste émergent et doivent être traitées et guéries avant de passer à la prochaine étape.

Ce conseil s'est avéré indispensable à mon cheminement vers la guérison. Je n'avais pas compris, au début de la thérapie, qu'il me faudrait plusieurs années avant de découvrir les différents niveaux de douleurs et les plaies qui habitaient mon corps, mon esprit, et ma spiritualité. Avec l'aide du psychologue, j'ai établi un programme plus réaliste pour me permettre d'assimiler les connaissances que j'acquérais dans le but d'atteindre mon objectif ultime : celui de transformer mon héritage.

Je connais plusieurs personnes, femmes et hommes, qui n'ont jamais bénéficié de thérapie ou de soutien aux agressions sexuelles qu'ils ont subies dans leur jeunesse. Selon les cas, l'humiliation, la peur de perdre son travail ou le jugement des autres empêchent une personne de parler des horreurs de son passé. Pour moi, essayer de résoudre ou de maîtriser seule tous les problèmes associés à l'inceste était impossible, car les arbres m'empêchaient de voir la forêt. J'avais besoin de consultation et de soutien appropriés pour ce lourd fardeau qui m'accablait jusqu'au cœur. Mon esprit ne cessait de fuir le passé. J'espérais toujours perdre la mémoire et noyer mon passé pour trouver l'harmonie et la sérénité. Maintenant, je sais que, sans thérapie, je n'y serais jamais parvenue. Le simple geste de consulter un psychologue et de m'en tenir à la thérapie conçue pour m'aider a nécessité un courage exceptionnel. Un bon conseiller comprend et respecte la souffrance physique et morale d'une victime de l'inceste et le courage qu'il lui faut pour revivre les horreurs du passé, les surmonter et aller vers l'avant.

C'est seulement lorsque j'ai fait face à la réalité de mon enfance que j'ai cessé d'essayer de fuir mon passé; il me fallait effectivement accepter que je fusse née d'un père pédophile. À cette phase de mon cheminement, une nouvelle attitude est née et un nouveau point de vue s'est avéré être un outil précieux dans le processus de mon développement. J'ai commencé à comprendre que je n'étais pas responsable de l'inceste, que c'est le pédophile qui l'impose à ses victimes. J'ai retrouvé un renouveau d'énergie. En écrivant ce livre, j'ai découvert et traité de nombreux aspects d'une jeunesse dysfonctionnelle. J'ai entrepris des recherches et me suis entretenue avec plusieurs personnes qui vivent ce traumatisme au quotidien. Je ne masque plus et ne fuis plus mes pensées. J'ai acquis un grand calme. Je pense souvent à aider les victimes de l'inceste à se rétablir. J'ai espoir que ce livre apportera aux victimes du réconfort et l'assurance qu'ils ne sont pas seuls à traverser ce chemin ardu. Et peut-être même que mon livre apportera un outil dont pourront se servir les conseillers en agressions sexuelles. Il est plus difficile pour la victime d'agressions sexuelles, qui n'a pas recherché l'aide de conseiller professionnel, de développer son plein potentiel, car celle-ci agit et décide d'après son traumatisme d'enfance. Il est impossible d'oublier ces agressions, mais il faut savoir qu'il est possible de ne plus s'identifier à cet enfant agressé. Le soutien et les avis professionnels aident les victimes à aller de l'avant et à atteindre un niveau de bonheur et de bien-être.

« *Personne ne peut retirer qui que ce soit d'où que ce soit. On s'en sort par ses propres moyens ou on y reste* ».

Alice Sebold

*Lucky*

CHAPITRE 2

# QUI ÉTAIENT LES GARDIENS DE CE SILENCE?

J'ai éprouvé de la difficulté à écrire ce chapitre en raison de *l'entente du silence* imposé à l'inceste. Le silence qu'on nous a obligé sur ce tabou est tellement enraciné que l'introduire au grand public m'effraie énormément. Écrire au sujet de l'inceste demande un courage et un sang-froid que je ne possédais pas. Ma voix intérieure me hurlait de me taire, de garder le silence et de n'en parler à personne… *« Surtout pas à ta mère, ou à tes frères et sœurs »*. Mais j'ai choisi de parler. J'ai fait taire la voix intérieure, car je reconnaissais dans cette voix la voix de mon père et j'avais découvert que l'inceste avait été le lot de plusieurs générations de la famille paternelle. C'était mon devoir, mon objectif, ma mission de mettre un arrêt aux agressions sexuelles des enfants.

Il y a quelques années, ma grand-mère paternelle m'avait confié qu'elle savait que certains de ses enfants étaient victimes/agresseurs d'actes incestueux. Elle était très malheureuse d'avoir, elle aussi, garder le silence. Je n'avais jamais été témoin d'autant d'amertume chez ma grand-mère. Elle avait porté ce secret toute sa vie, jusqu'à son décès. Aussitôt ce petit bout de récit terminé, elle n'a plus parlé et m'a priée de ne pas la questionner. J'ai conclu qu'elle savait que l'inceste avait terni sa famille et que mon père le faisait encore subir à ses enfants. Le sujet était donc clos, ma grand-mère ne voulait plus en discuter. Je crois que sa haine était en partie causée par son choix de garder le silence. Était-elle en colère de ne pas avoir affronté cette emprise incestueuse familiale? De voir ses petits-enfants endurer ce même avilissement?

Avant les années 80, les enfants (ainsi que les mères) n'avaient pas les ressources et l'appui nécessaires pour rapporter l'inceste, la violence ou les agressions sexuelles qui se produisaient dans leurs foyers. La plupart des livres ou manuels sur la prévention d'agressions sexuelles ont paru après 1980.

Lorsqu'un père ordonnait à un enfant de garder le silence, il écoutait; un point, c'est tout. Mon père a pratiqué la même emprise morale et physique sur mes frères et mes sœurs, qui ont aussi été ses victimes. Personne de la famille n'en soufflait mot; même pas entre nous, et surtout pas à notre mère. Nous avons été gardiens de ce silence, jusqu'en 1986, l'année où nous avons affronté notre père.

Un cas particulier d'une famille incestueuse m'a été rapporté. Ce récit m'angoisse quant à l'avenir de cette jeune famille. Vingt ans auparavant, deux enfants, un garçon et une fille, avaient été retirés de leurs parents, car ceux-ci les maltraitaient physiquement et sexuellement. Les enfants ont été placés dans une famille d'accueil, chez un couple bienveillant et dévoué. Quelques mois plus tard, le couple signala à la *Société de l'aide à l'enfance* que les enfants continuaient toujours les rapports sexuels entre eux. Les enfants ont donc été envoyés dans deux foyers d'accueil différents. Bien que la Société ait séparé les enfants à plusieurs kilomètres l'un de l'autre, le jeune garçon continuait toujours à poursuivre sa sœur. Je ne sais pas si ces deux enfants, maintenant adultes, ont reçu de la thérapie; mais on m'apprend qu'ils sont aujourd'hui eux-mêmes parents. Je frémis à la pensée de leurs jeunes enfants. Je ne peux qu'espérer que les parents ont reçu de l'aide et ont consulté pour éviter de propager l'inceste.

Les parents, les écoles, les services de sécurité et de protection, ainsi que les centres de services d'aide communautaires doivent être vigilants et informer la communauté de l'existence des programmes de sensibilisation contre l'agression sexuelle et l'inceste. Les enfants et les adolescents doivent savoir que le sexe entre frères et sœurs est un cas d'inceste. Si les frères et sœurs aînés forcent les enfants à se livrer à des activités sexuelles, ces agresseurs incestueux doivent être considérés comme des criminels.

À l'âge de neuf ans, je savais que mon père avait tort. Je n'avais pas les outils ou les ressources nécessaires pour obtenir de l'aide. Les gens de notre communauté ne discutaient pas de problèmes familiaux, et surtout pas de ceux qui touchaient à la violence. Ce silence et cet isolement, se sont révélés désastreux pour notre famille.

Lorsque j'étais adolescente, ma petite amie m'a confié que son père nourricier (mon oncle) essayait de la forcer à le caresser. Elle a rapporté sa conduite à ma tante, qui l'a durement giflée et traitée de menteuse. J'étais convaincue que nous ne pouvions pas nous fier aux adultes pour nous protéger. Avant les années 1980, les enfants maltraités n'avaient souvent pas de recours; ils ne pouvaient pas non plus dénoncer leurs parents abusifs sans crainte de représailles. La haine, l'humiliation, le rejet, le remords, la culpabilité et le dégoût font partie des réactions néfastes associées aux comportements des victimes de l'inceste. Les enfants victimes de ces agressions apprennent et retiennent à un très jeune âge, la douleur, l'intimidation, la malhonnêteté, la méfiance, la peur, l'insécurité, le non-respect, le manque d'estime de soi, l'intimidation et la soumission. Il leur faudra plusieurs années de thérapie (s'ils en reçoivent) pour retrouver leur bien-être et leur estime de soi.

Il y avait aussi plusieurs discussions dans ma famille, entre frères et sœurs, sur la question de savoir si notre mère était consciente de l'inceste. Au cours de mes recherches et entrevues, j'ai été surprise de découvrir que plusieurs victimes de l'inceste, agressées par le père, accusent et blâment la mère de ne pas les avoir protégés de leur père. N'est-ce pas aussi le rôle du père de protéger ses enfants? N'est-ce pas le rôle du père d'apprendre à ses enfants les bonnes valeurs humaines et sociales? Mon père était tellement manipulateur que je n'avais même pas connaissance qu'il agressait aussi certains de mes frères et sœurs (je ne l'ai su que beaucoup plus tard). Il avait une telle emprise sur nous! Nous n'aurions jamais osé parler de cela à notre mère, et encore moins en discuter entre frères et soeurs. C'est donc sur les épaules de mon père que je place la responsabilité de l'inceste. C'est le devoir de chaque génération d'améliorer sa progéniture; mon père a carrément refusé de participer à l'évolution et au bien-être de ses enfants.

Le rôle d'un père est de protéger ses enfants. Si, au contraire, il a choisi de maltraiter ses enfants, il doit en assumer les conséquences. La responsabilité de ce crime doit être assumée par la personne qui commet cet acte. Jeter le blâme à d'autres que lui-même est le genre de manipulation que mon père a toujours utilisé. Moi aussi j'ai été aveuglée et trompée par mon père. Lorsque, à l'âge de 14 ans, j'ai repoussé les avances de mon père, j'ai innocemment présumé qu'il s'était arrêté à moi. Malheureusement, il a fallu vingt ans pour que j'apprenne que d'autres de mes frères et sœurs étaient victimes de ses agressions sexuelles. Les pédophiles, ai-je appris beaucoup trop tard, savent particulièrement bien manipuler les enfants et leur entourage.

À un jeune âge, j'ai compris que les femmes étaient défavorisées et que, dans les années 1970, les femmes et les enfants étaient encore sous l'emprise d'une société patriarcale. À cette époque, plusieurs femmes étaient négligées ou totalement ignorées. Une conseillère que j'ai consultée a démystifié les contraintes sociales qui existaient lorsque la mère apprenait que le père avait agressé sexuellement leurs enfants. Ces femmes, essentiellement, se divisaient en trois catégories :

1) **La mère ne savait pas qu'elle devait protéger ses enfants** : la mère ne se doutait pas que les

enfants étaient en danger et par conséquent ne savait pas qu'elle devait les protéger.

2) **La mère ne pouvait pas protéger ses enfants en raison de contraintes sociales** : les droits, l'information et l'accès aux ressources lui étaient limités. La mère avait peu ou pas de pouvoir au sein de l'unité familiale puisqu'elle était elle aussi victime de violence. Les ressources internes et externes lui étaient refusées au sein d'une société patriarcale.

3) **La mère ne protégeait pas ses enfants** : elle savait que son partenaire agressait sexuellement ses enfants et parfois même était contrainte de participer à l'acte (dans ce cas, la mère généralement se place dans la catégorie précédente).

La structure sociale de mon époque et de celle de plusieurs générations précédentes accordait au père l'autorité absolue et le pouvoir de contrôler sa famille comme il le voulait. La mère devait donc se soumettre aux règles qu'imposait son mari, sans poser de questions. Les cliniques ou les centres pour secourir les femmes et les enfants victimes de violence familiale n'étaient pas encore établi. C'est seulement en 1977 que la *Loi canadienne sur les droits de la personne* institua la loi interdisant le harcèlement sexuel. Et c'est en 1983 que le Canada a adopté la loi contre le viol. Il n'y a vraiment pas si longtemps que notre société s'est attelée à la tâche de la prévention et de la cessation de la violence conjugale et des agressions sexuelles. Et, même si la loi a été promulguée, la transformation sociale peut prendre des décennies avant d'être assimilée dans les esprits et la culture.

Même dans les années 1980 et 1990, une femme ou un enfant qui tentait de dénoncer la violence faisait habituellement face à un système juridique sceptique qui était réticent à intenter des poursuites en raison de la difficulté à obtenir un verdict de culpabilité. Il était grand temps que les attitudes changent : de plus en plus, nous évoluons vers une société qui condamne les vrais criminels. Aujourd'hui, dans les cas d'agressions sexuelles, la sécurité des enfants devient prioritaire.

Il y avait d'autres membres de la famille de notre père qui savaient trop bien que nous vivions sous le toit d'un père incestueux. Par contre, je crois aussi qu'il y en avait parmi mes oncles et mes tantes qui ne s'en doutaient point. Ceux qui le savaient ne soulevaient jamais la question : ils préféraient que tous gardent le silence sur cette atrocité. À cette époque, il était plus important de protéger le maltraitant que de perdre la face.

Dans le passé, à chaque réunion de famille, j'étais très mal à l'aise. Leur silence oppressant, toujours aussi présent, me ramenait dans un passé non résolu. J'avais l'impression d'être l'invitée importune à ces évènements; peut-être que ma présence constitue pour eux, un reproche et un rappel de leur silence, ce silence qui avait contribué à perpétuer l'inceste dans notre génération. Il est très difficile pour une victime de l'inceste de recouvrer son bien-être lorsque la famille soutient ce crime du silence.

Mes frères et soeurs qui n'ont pas été agressés par notre père ont reçu un véritable choc lorsqu'ils ont appris ce qu'il nous avait fait subir. Sur les neuf enfants, cinq frères et sœurs avaient été agressés. Ils n'avaient jamais soupçonné l'inceste. Ils n'auraient jamais imaginé qu'un père pouvait faire tant de mal à ses enfants.

En août 1986, sur la recommandation du psychologue, nous avons affronté notre père et nous l'avons dénoncé à ceux et celles qui n'avaient pas été agressés. Ces derniers ne cessaient de m'interroger. Ils voulaient savoir comment ils ne l'avaient jamais su :

• Comment n'avons-nous pas vu ce qui se passait sous notre toit?

• Pourquoi vous a-t-il agressé et non pas nous?

Je ne pouvais leur répondre. Je ne pouvais qu'exprimer mon regret pour cette grande duperie, ce mensonge de toute une vie que notre père avait caché à tous et qui se perpétue encore après plus de 50 ans.

Pourquoi n'avons-nous pas tous été agressés? Une conseillère m'a expliqué que les prédateurs sexuels abusent des enfants les plus vulnérables : les enfants qu'ils peuvent contrôler, piéger, effrayer et forcer à la soumission et au silence.

Une autre personne savait que notre père nous maltraitait : c'était le prêtre du village, à qui il s'était confessé. Le prêtre lui avait simplement donné une légère tape sur la main en lui disant : « Ne fais plus ça ». Sachant ce que nous savons aujourd'hui des agressions sexuelles que les enfants ont souffert aux mains des prêtres, personne ne s'étonne de l'ignorance, de l'insouciance et surtout de la négligence criminelle du prêtre. C'était un complot cruel perpétué par ces violeurs d'enfants, dont le rôle était de sauvegarder et de protéger les femmes et les enfants. Cette irresponsabilité pénale envers les victimes de l'inceste est inacceptable et impardonnable.

Il y a deux ans, j'ai appris que mon père avait agressé sexuellement notre nièce lorsqu'elle était enfant; elle nous l'a déclaré à son trentième anniversaire. Le chagrin que j'ai ressenti à cette déclaration m'a fait pleurer pendant deux jours. La rage, l'humiliation, la peine, la culpabilité et la honte m'ont envahie avec une telle force que j'ai dû obtenir de l'aide psychologique pour gérer cette période douloureuse.

Les parents de ma nièce ne l'avaient jamais su avant le jour de ses 30 ans. Je ne savais pas comment je pouvais les aider. Tristement, comme par le passé, la famille ne s'est point soutenue dans cette épreuve et chacun a dû y faire face dans la solitude. Quelques jours plus tard, donc, j'ai rencontré une psychologue pour essayer de voir comment je pourrais démêler le tout et venir en aide à la famille de mon frère.

La première chose que la thérapeute a faite (la plupart des thérapeutes suivent cette procédure en prenant connaissance d'un cas de maltraitance) a été d'établir si les autres enfants étaient exposés à mon père. J'ai expliqué que ma nièce avait maintenant 30 ans et que notre père n'avait aucun accès à nos enfants. Mes frères et soeurs ne visitent pratiquement plus nos parents (j'explique cette relation plus en détail au chapitre 3) et ceux d'entre nous qui les visitent ne laissent jamais les enfants seuls avec leur grand-père. Les agressions sexuelles de notre nièce ont eu lieu avant que nous confrontions notre père. Elle serait la seule des petits-enfants à avoir été agressée.

La rencontre avec le thérapeute s'est déroulée ainsi :

**- Quel âge a votre père?**

- 81 ans.

**- Comment est sa santé?**

- Pas trop bonne, il est branché à une bonbonne d'oxygène en tout temps; il ne voyage pas, ne fait aucune sortie sans être accompagné. S'il doit faire des courses ou aller chez le médecin, ma mère et mon frère l'accompagnent. Il passe ses journées devant le téléviseur.

**- Maintenant, je vous pose cette question afin d'établir si votre père est en mesure de recommencer ses agressions sexuelles. Pensez-vous que votre père abusera de nouveau?**

Je suis troublée par cette question; je ne suis pas thérapeute, ou professionnelle dans ce domaine. Comment peut-elle me poser une telle question? Je finis par lui répondre :

- Je ne pense pas, mais je ne sais vraiment pas. Il n'a pas accès à nos enfants, mais je ne suis pas avec lui chaque minute de la journée. Je veux surtout savoir ce que je dois faire pour ma nièce; devrais-je le dénoncer, le rapporter à un policier ou à l'aide à l'enfance?

**- Savez-vous que si vous dénoncez votre père, votre fille, vos petites-filles et la famille entière devront faire face à la Cour et aux médias? S'il est incapable de recommencer, si vous pouvez garantir que vos enfants ne sont pas en péril, pensez-vous que vous devriez faire traverser cette épreuve à votre famille? Pourriez-vous laisser votre mère vivre ce stress, elle qui a été également traumatisée et qui a dû briser ses liens avec ses enfants et petits-enfants? Voulez-vous augmenter son angoisse et son stress? »**

Comment puis-je accepter de faire autant de mal à ma famille? Le cycle du silence est donc maintenu. Je suis envahie par la culpabilité.

Je lui réponds simplement :

-Non.

La rencontre terminée, je quitte son bureau, triste et déprimée. Heureusement que chaque séance de thérapie ne se termine pas ainsi. Je me sentais lâche de ne pas dénoncer mon père à la justice. Je n'avais pas, à mon avis, fait mon devoir envers ma nièce.

J'ai conclu (pour ma santé mentale) que c'était aux parents de prendre des mesures judiciaires pour défendre leur fille ? Mais l'incertitude me rongeait. Il me fallait faire quelque chose – on ne pouvait pas le laisser encore s'en sortir. Valait-il vraiment mieux que je me taise? La publicité, les médias, la Cour, tout cela serait tellement douloureux et stressant pour ma fille et sa famille; et puis, comment assujettir mon conjoint et les autres membres de la famille à ce cirque de publicité? Est-ce que ma nièce elle aussi était prête à affronter tous ces tracas? N'avaient-ils pas tous le droit à leur vie privée, à leur blessure, sans que le monde entier en soit témoin? Pourquoi soulever toute cette souffrance, cette honte et cet embarras? Étais-je craintive ou étais-je une bienfaitrice en épargnant à ma famille l'humiliation et la douleur?

J'ai plutôt décidé d'écrire ce livre. C'était ma façon de rendre justice à ma famille, particulièrement à ma nièce. Je veux qu'elle et tous mes lecteurs s'engagent à obtenir les soins nécessaires pour gérer le dommage causé par l'inceste; ces soins sont essentiels pour guérir de ce traumatisme infâme.

Même arrivés à l'âge adulte, nos enfants doivent être épaulés par les membres de leur famille, pour ne pas languir seuls dans ce silence destructif. Ce que je lègue à ma fille dans cette vie, ce ne sont pas nécessairement mes biens matériels, mais plutôt un héritage dont elle peut être fière : un héritage d'amour, de franchise, de respect d'autrui et d'harmonie, qui contribue à établir et à préserver le bien-être mental, physique et spirituel de tout être humain. Chaque enfant doit être respecté, aimé et honoré par chaque membre de sa famille : cet héritage est à la base de ce que chaque parent doit donner à ses enfants. Toute famille touchée par l'inceste doit s'unir dans le combat contre ce comportement si destructif et dénaturé.

Toute personne doit se soucier du bien-être des générations futures; il ne faut surtout pas penser qu'il est déshonorant de se soigner de cette violence sexuelle. On ne doit pas empêcher les gens d'obtenir l'aide et le soutien approprié; on doit l'envisager. Le survivant doit comprendre qu'il *NE DOIT PAS AVOIR HONTE — CE N'EST PAS LUI QUI EST RESPONSABLE!* Le vrai tort de nos communautés est de tolérer cette violence qui continue à protéger ces criminels. Si l'on soupçonne la présence de l'inceste dans une famille, c'est notre devoir d'intervenir, avec l'aide d'organisme tels que le *Centre d'aide et de lutte contre les agressions à caractère sexuel* (CALACS), le *Centre d'intervention en abus sexuels pour la famille* (CIASF) ou tout autre organisme responsable de la protection des enfants. C'est à tous de lutter contre cette violence qui continue de ronger nos communautés.

En conclusion, je peux dire que mon père nous a arrachés à toute la famille (incluant cousins, cousines, oncles, tantes), le plaisir des réunions de famille. L'ombre de celui ou celle qui savait, victime ou non-victime de l'inceste, plane toujours sur nos rencontres, malgré tous nos efforts pour dissiper le malaise. L'inceste a eu un impact si destructif sur nos familles que je ne vois pas le jour où nous allons nous réunir. J'espère que ce livre ouvrira les yeux et les coeurs des gens, de nos communautés et de nos gouvernements et contribuera à nous réunir et à rompre le silence qui ensevelit les victimes d'agressions sexuelles. Nous devons, tous ensemble, donner à nos enfants un héritage conçu dans l'amour, la sécurité et le respect d'autrui.

« *Ce n'est pas un signe de bonne santé que d'être bien adapté à une société profondément malade.* »

Jiddu Krishnamurti

**CHAPITRE 3**

# LES CONSÉQUENCES NÉFASTES DE L'INCESTE

De toutes les personnes que je connais, ma fille a été celle qui a perçu avec précision les effets que l'inceste a eus sur moi, mes frères, mes sœurs et ma mère. Elle semble avoir un sixième sens dans la démarche à adopter pour atteindre mon objectif, sans pour autant m'imposer un effort ardu ou faire naître de la culpabilité. Lorsqu'elle me proposait une marche à suivre, elle le faisait toujours avec une approche attentionnée et délicate; jamais pour me blesser ou me juger. Il n'est pas étonnant qu'aujourd'hui nous partagions une affection et un amour absolus.

Toute famille touchée par l'inceste doit, lorsqu'il s'agit du processus de guérison, traiter les effets néfastes de l'inceste. Les victimes doivent trouver l'équilibre de leurs propres cheminements vers le mieux-être et doivent aussi comprendre que d'autres, en particulier les membres de la famille qui n'ont pas été agressés sexuellement, souffrent aussi; ceux-ci doivent aussi recevoir du soutien.

Les effets de ce genre de violence envers les enfants touchent les hommes et les femmes différemment. Cependant, il existe des parallèles, comme le montre l'ASPC dans son dépliant : *Les survivants et survivantes adultes de l'abus sexuel dans l'enfance*[5] :

### *Similitudes entre survivants et survivantes*

- *C'est souvent une personne connue qui abuse des garçons et des filles, et la plupart du temps, le coupable est un hétérosexuel de sexe masculin. Ce dernier détient une certaine forme de pouvoir ou de contrôle sur la victime et occupe une position de confiance.*

- *Certains survivants peuvent souffrir de dépression, avoir peu d'estime de soi, se blâmer, être insatisfaits de leur vie, éprouver de l'anxiété, souffrir de dissociation (rupture entre l'esprit et le corps), avoir des difficultés relationnelles, avoir tendance à faire preuve de trop d'autorité ou d'une trop grande soumission, être incapables de se faire confiance ou de faire confiance aux autres, avoir des difficultés à définir en quoi consiste une sexualité saine, avoir des comportements autodestructeurs, notamment envisager le suicide ou tenter de se suicider, avoir des difficultés à gérer la colère, souffrir de maladies liées au stress, présenter des dépendances ou des troubles de l'alimentation ou passer à l'acte sur le plan sexuel.*

- *Dans le supplément sur la santé mentale de l'Enquête sur la santé en Ontario de 1990, 56 % des répondants et 56 % des répondantes ayant avoué avoir été victimes d'abus sexuel ont également fait état de violence physique.*

### *Préoccupations principalement féminines*

- *Il y a plus de risque que l'abus se produise à la maison et soit perpétré par une personne ayant des liens familiaux avec la victime.*

- *Les survivantes courent plus de risques de consommer trop d'alcool.*

- *Elles sont plus nombreuses à être de nouveau maltraitées à l'adolescence et au début de l'âge adulte.*

- *Elles ont plus de chances de recevoir de l'aide pendant le processus de guérison.*

- *Contrairement aux hommes, les femmes sont plus portées à résoudre leurs problèmes de tristesse et de dépression au cours des premières étapes du processus de guérison, tandis que leur colère ne semble émerger que plus tard.*

- *Les femmes semblent avoir plus de difficulté à se souvenir des détails précis de l'abus.*

- *Parmi les victimes d'abus sexuel dans l'enfance, les filles sont caressées plus souvent que les garçons.*

### Préoccupations principalement masculines

- *Les garçons sont plus souvent abusés par des professeurs, des entraîneurs ou des gardiens.*

- *Les garçons victimes d'abus sexuel par une personne de sexe masculin se préoccupent de leur identité sexuelle et craignent l'homosexualité. Les hommes abusés sexuellement dans l'enfance trouvent également plus difficile de définir leur rôle en tant qu'homme.*

- *Les survivants de l'abus sexuel de sexe masculin et leurs parents essaient plus fréquemment de minimiser les conséquences de l'abus sexuel.*

- *Les survivants de sexe masculin courent plus de risques de développer une toxicomanie.*

- *Les garçons sont plus souvent sodomisés que les filles.*

- *Les hommes éprouvent plus souvent de la colère et de la rage dans les premiers stades du rétablissement, et leur peine émerge en général plus tard.*

- *Les hommes sont plus nombreux à ressentir de l'impuissance et à avoir des fantasmes violents de vengeance.*

- *Les hommes sont beaucoup moins nombreux que les femmes à considérer leurs expériences sexuelles dans la première enfance comme un abus sexuel.*

- *La socialisation masculine, les réactions physiologiques différentes entre garçons et filles et les expressions de la sexualité déterminées par la culture peuvent faire que les garçons adoptent une attitude neutre ou positive au sujet de leurs expériences sexuelles. Cependant, les effets à long terme (p. ex., le manque d'estime de soi) sont négatifs.*

Les composants communs partagés tels que la dépression, l'autodestruction et les éléments uniques par exemple la différence entre leurs agresseurs et le processus de guérison utilisé aident à lier les deux groupes à reconnaître et respecter son individualité, lorsque celle-ci cherche à se réconcilier avec son passé.

Pour moi, les effets à court terme de la violence se sont manifestés deux ans après la cessation des agressions sexuelles; j'étais âgée de 14 ans. Dans les années qui ont suivi, j'ai vécu accablée par l'isolement et la dépression. Mon poids a grimpé jusqu'à 70 kilos, et à 1,5 mètre, j'étais obèse. J'ai détruit toutes les photos qui ont été prises au cours de cette période de ma vie. J'avais l'air d'une femme de 40 ans, pas d'une adolescente dans la fleur de l'âge. Je portais un grand châle bleu qui recouvrait pratiquement tout mon corps. Je coupais mes longs cheveux blonds très courts; je ne voulais être attrayante pour personne. Je me sentais tellement souillée et affreuse à l'intérieur que cette image se manifestait à l'extérieur. Pour la majorité des gens, l'adolescence est un rite de passage difficile, mais si, en plus une personne a été victime de l'inceste et essaie de traverser cette phase, la difficulté devient monumentale; c'est quasi insurmontable.

Les actions brutales et égoïstes de mon père m'avaient volé mon enfance et cet héritage incestueux allait m'emprisonner pour la vie. À l'école, j'étais effrontée et insolente avec mon professeur d'anglais jusqu'à ce qu'il m'envoie au bureau du directeur. En sortant de la classe, je tapais du pied et lui lançais des injures. Je suis convaincue que, s'il avait pu me gifler sans risquer son emploi, il l'aurait fait. Agir si démesurément contre une personne en autorité me procurait un semblant de pouvoir.

Ce comportement ne dura que pendant cette année scolaire. L'année suivante, c'est au couvent que j'ai poursuivi mes études secondaires. Le couvent était dirigé par des religieuses et une mère supérieure, qui ne tolérait aucune impertinence. Je n'ai été convoquée au bureau de la mère supérieure qu'une seule fois : c'était suffisant pour que je saisisse la politique de cet institut.

Comme beaucoup de jeunes filles d'âge scolaire, j'ai commencé à surveiller mon poids. J'ai consulté mon médecin pour obtenir des pilules amaigrissantes (oui, il m'a donné une ordonnance, sans broncher) et j'ai perdu 50 livres, en un rien de temps. Ce mode de vie n'était pas sain, car je me soutenais avec du café et des cigarettes. Mon corps me paraissait mieux, physiquement — mais je mangeais à peine. Je négligeais aussi mes besoins psychologiques. Voici une question tirée du livret de l'ASPC : *Counseling en matière de violence sexuelle : Guide à l'intention des parents et des enfants[6]* pour les survivants adultes qui n'ont pas reçu de thérapie psychologique ou de soutien comme enfant agressé.

**La violence sexuelle subie à l'enfance a-t-elle des répercussions dans ma vie d'adulte?**

> *Oui. Si vous avez été agressée sexuellement durant l'enfance, peut-être souffrez-vous depuis des années de problèmes qui ne s'atténuent jamais. Si vous avez maintenant des problèmes de drogue ou d'alcool, de fréquentes ruptures, une dysfonction sexuelle, des problèmes alimentaires, ou si pendant de longues périodes vous vous sentez coupé de la réalité, il est possible que la cause de tous ces problèmes soit liée à la violence sexuelle que vous avez subie dans votre enfance. Peut-être avez-vous été incapable d'en parler ou, si vous en avez parlé, on vous a demandé d'oublier et de continuer à vivre*

*comme si rien n'était arrivé. Souvent, les adultes qui ont mis de côté la violence sexuelle dont ils ont été victimes ont une violente réaction physique et émotive au moment où un de leurs enfants est victime à son tour. Si cela vous arrive, il faudra peut-être que vous et votre enfant consultiez.* (Voir le chapitre 4 pour de plus amples informations sur le counseling.)

*L'Association américaine de psychologie*[7] (*American Psychological Association*, APA) répond à une question fondamentale que la plupart des parents se posent : est-ce que leur enfant, qui a été agressé sexuellement, récupérera ? D'après l'APA, l'enfant qui est en mesure de se confier à un adulte grandit avec moins de traumatismes que les enfants qui ne révèlent pas l'abus. De plus, les enfants qui dénoncent leur agresseur peu après l'attaque seront possiblement moins traumatisés que les enfants qui révèlent les agressions beaucoup plus tard. Les enfants et les adultes qui ont été victimes d'agressions sexuelles infantiles confirment que le soutien familial, l'appui hors famille, l'estime de soi et la spiritualité deviennent des outils indispensables à leur rétablissement. Les victimes soulèvent l'importance de participer à des ateliers et des conférences sur l'exploitation des enfants, de se renseigner sur la prévention contre les agressions sexuelles

(Centre de ressources, programme communautaire), et de participer à une psychothérapie pour effectuer un retour plus rapide à une vie normale.

Les psychothérapeutes m'ont dit que chaque cas d'agression sexuelle ou d'inceste est différent, qu'aucun individu ne vit les mêmes symptômes ou les mêmes conséquences. Le traitement et la thérapie doivent être adaptés à chaque enfant ou à chaque famille. Je me souviens trop bien des effets destructeurs que l'inceste a eus sur les membres de ma famille. Nous avons confronté notre père il y a plus de 25 ans. Chacun a affronté cette épreuve séparément; nous avons entrepris les thérapies et les soins qui étaient appropriés à notre récupération et à notre survie individuelle. Puisque nous n'avons pas utilisé la thérapie de famille, aujourd'hui nous sommes bien dispersés et les rencontres familiales se font rares. Ce qui semble être notre point commun est un passé non résolu, toujours caché sous le silence. Nous luttons toujours seuls contre les effets nocifs de l'inceste.

Plusieurs caractéristiques négatives telles que la rage, la peur, le sarcasme, le manque de confiance, la culpabilité et le déshonneur (et la liste continue) me hantaient. Je trouvais difficile de m'engager dans le programme scolaire; l'effort pour surmonter mon complexe d'infériorité et ma lassitude me demandait une ardeur que je ne parvenais pas à trouver. Je ne réussissais pas très bien à l'école. Moi qui avais tant aimé l'école primaire! Dans les nouvelles matières et même pour trouver les réponses aux problèmes de mathématiques, j'avais du mal à obtenir la note de passage. Voici un exemple où l'inceste détruit l'inspiration, l'imagination et la joie de réussir chez l'enfant. L'unique passion qui m'offrait une porte de sortie de cette angoisse était l'art dramatique. Je pouvais me transformer en une héroïne forte et maîtresse d'elle-même, tenace et résolue.

Dans une misc en scène de la pièce *The Pen of My Aunt*, je jouais si juste le rôle d'un soldat que même la mère supérieure l'a remarqué et n'a pas tardé à me féliciter pour mon talent de comédienne. La mère supérieure était parcimonieuse dans ses compliments; alors ses éloges m'étaient d'autant plus valorisants.

La dépression ne faisait pas partie de mon vocabulaire, et je comprenais mal le sens de ce mot avant d'entreprendre une psychothérapie, à l'âge de 27 ans; c'était un état mental mal connu avant 1990. J'allais reconnaître beaucoup plus tard que, durant mes années scolaires, j'avais vécu une dépression.

Pendant plusieurs années suivant la cessation des agressions sexuelles, j'avais l'allure d'une personne indécise, inefficace et ternie. L'inceste m'avait confisqué mon aplomb, mon assurance, mon enthousiasme et ma joie de vivre. C'est seulement après la thérapie et le soutien que je me suis rendu compte de l'emprise ignoble qu'avait mon père sur moi; je n'étais que l'ombre de la personne que j'aurais dû être. Je ne possédais ni le courage, ni l'énergie, ni l'appui nécessaires pour affronter mon père. Sans vouloir l'admettre, je laissais mon père s'en tirer, se dérober. Je tournais le dos à ce crime ignoble. Les traumatismes associés à l'inceste et aux agressions sexuelles ne disparaissent pas simplement parce qu'une personne choisit de les ignorer. Ne pas obtenir les outils pour gérer les émotions et les effets traumatiques de l'inceste peut faire obstacle à toute tentative de la victime pour récupérer et reconstruire une vie normale, en sécurité.

Une triste conséquence de l'inceste est l'effritement de la cellule familiale. Lorsque les membres d'une famille choisissent de ne pas participer à une thérapie de groupe, la famille va probablement se fragmenter.

Un défi majeur pour notre famille est d'organiser une rencontre familiale pour célébrer un évènement, tels un mariage ou un anniversaire. Ce qui devrait être une occasion joyeuse est toujours obscurci par des émotions profondes. Chez nous, les enfants se divisent en trois groupes :

- Ceux qui participent à la rencontre, à condition que nos parents n'y soient pas;

- Ceux qui y viennent si nos parents sont invités, et

- Ceux qui n'assistent à aucune fonction familiale.

Il est difficile parfois pour un individu qui n'a pas été agressé sexuellement de saisir les conséquences ou les traumatismes qui perturbent les victimes de l'inceste. Par exemple, je connais deux mamans qui ont souffert terriblement à la suite de la mort de leur enfant. Un enfant était décédé à la naissance, l'autre à l'adolescence, dans un accident de voiture. J'éprouvais de l'empathie pour les deux mères, mais je me suis consciencieusement abstenue de dire que je comprenais leur perte. Je crois qu'il était plus important qu'elles réalisent que moi aussi je comprenais une perte inconsolable. Elles pouvaient reconnaître mon empathie, même si ma perte était bien différente des leurs — celle d'une âme violée. L'important était de reconnaître qu'elles souffraient sans relâche. Et il en va de même pour les victimes de l'inceste; cette perte est inconsolable, inoubliable et, j'ajoute, impardonnable.

Il est inconcevable pour les frères et soeurs qui n'ont pas été agressés de comprendre la raison pour laquelle ils ont été épargnés. Ils ont même de la difficulté à offrir de l'empathie ou du soutien à ceux et celles qui en ont été victimes. Les survivants sont souvent évités ou ignorés, car l'image de la « famille parfaite » s'est écroulée. Le fait qu'un père ait agi ainsi demeure insaisissable pour eux. La difficulté pour moi, après que le secret fut dévoilé, a été de me faire imposer « l'illusion » d'une famille idéale. Pour avancer, il me fallait ne plus accepter cette contrainte; l'inceste fait partie de mon héritage, un point c'est tout.

Aujourd'hui, c'est presque impossible pour moi, de m'entretenir avec les membres de ma famille qui insiste à maintenir *l'entente du silence.*

Si ma famille avait obtenu de la psychothérapie et le soutien approprié pour ce genre de traumatisme, je suis convaincue que nous aurions réussi à nous rapprocher et à recréer une unité au lieu d'être dispersés comme nous le sommes en ce moment. La famille se sépare non pas parce qu'il n'y a pas de ressources disponibles, mais parce qu'en vieillissant les enfants préfèrent garder le silence et vivre (tant bien que mal) avec leurs problèmes non résolus. Il y a une forte possibilité qu'ils craignent les médias ou n'aient plus la santé et l'énergie pour entreprendre une thérapie. Quoi qu'il en soit, les familles d'aujourd'hui ont l'avantage d'avoir les ressources disponibles. Les centres d'aide aux victimes d'agressions sexuelles offrent aux familles des soutiens, des méthodes préventives et de la protection pour les aider à guérir les perturbations déclenchées par l'inceste. Lorsque les agressions sont dénoncées, les enfants et les parents sont en mesure d'entreprendre immédiatement la thérapie pour avoir une vie saine et productive. Il n'y a aucune raison pour qu'on ne puisse offrir à nos enfants ces moyens de guérison.

Vu que la survie des enfants dépend entièrement de leurs parents, il est essentiel que les parents inculquent aux enfants des valeurs honorables et les guident avec un renforcement positif pour créer des citoyens responsables. Les conséquences de l'inceste sont tragiques pour toute la famille et la communauté. Une famille peut pratiquement surmonter n'importe quelle tragédie, mais dans le cas de l'inceste, la tragédie semble insurmontable, sans thérapie. La famille demeure souvent paralysée par l'humiliation, la colère, la confusion et l'anxiété. La dissolution de l'unité familiale est l'un des effets les plus néfastes de l'inceste.

Par exemple, il est rare aujourd'hui, comme je l'ai signalé plus haut, que la famille se réunisse. Plusieurs d'entre nous, y compris les petits-enfants et les arrière-petits-enfants, ne visitent plus mes parents. À l'époque de la dénonciation, mes parents n'ont pas eu recours à la thérapie familiale pour nous aider à franchir cette épreuve; alors, sans mes parents, nous avons dû faire notre propre cheminement pour traverser cette étape. Voilà le résultat de notre séparation d'eux jusqu'à aujourd'hui. Ceci veut dire que la plupart des enfants, du côté maternel et du côté paternel, n'assistent pas aux évènements familiaux. Ces fonctions incluent les mariages, les funérailles, les fêtes-anniversaires ou les fêtes nationales. Mes parents ne communiquent plus avec la majorité de leurs enfants, de leurs petits-enfants et de leurs arrière-petits-enfants. C'est un prix bien élevé pour avoir renoncé à la thérapie familiale.

Le livre « *Keeping Kids Safe – A Child Abuse Prevention Manual* » [8] de P. Tobin et S. Levinson Kessner, explique que les effets des agressions sexuelles ne sont pas destructeurs que pour la famille, mais aussi pour la communauté. Les effets sont onéreux, durables, gravés dans l'esprit de nos enfants et coûteux pour les citoyens : tant sur le plan économique que psychologique. Parfois, les gens ne s'en remettent pas. L'agression sexuelle affecte leur sexualité, leurs relations intimes et leur mode de vie. Par exemple, en étudiant le comportement des survivants-adolescents (p. ex., promiscuité sexuelle, prostitution, toxicomanie, délinquance, fugue, tentatives de suicide) les experts découvrent que leurs comportements sont souvent le résultat direct de l'agression sexuelle. Le coût pour la société des comportements délinquants est élevé.

Depuis les années 1960 jusqu'au jour où j'ai commencé ma thérapie dans les années 1980, j'ai gardé le silence sur l'inceste. Je vivais dans la peur : peur d'être menacée, jugée, blâmée et punie. Dénoncer mon père était pour moi une forme de trahison envers lui et les autres membres de ma famille. Mais la plus grande des peurs était que notre père soit emprisonné. Je me sentais tellement malsaine et angoissée. La peur me paralysait et m'empêchait d'aller de l'avant.

La peur peut être un facteur de motivation pour notre survie, mais peut également nous figer sur place. Si on ne fait pas face à ses craintes, d'autres peurs s'ajoutent aux évènements ou aux actions qui s'ensuivent. Affronter mes peurs est maintenant pour moi la meilleure façon d'amorcer la prochaine étape de mon cheminement.

L'article « *Les survivants et survivantes adultes de l'abus sexuel dans l'enfance* »[9], explique les raisons pour lesquelles les survivants tardent tant à parler des agressions sexuelles dont ils ont été victimes durant leur enfance.

> *Au Canada, on estime que la grande majorité des victimes d'abus sexuel tant de sexe masculin que féminin ne*

signalent pas l'abus sexuel. Certains survivants retardent le moment de dénoncer l'abus sexuel parce qu'ils craignent d'être menacés par l'agresseur, ont peur de ne pas être crus ou d'être blâmés et peut-être punis, se sentent coupables ou honteux ou veulent protéger leur famille et, parfois, l'agresseur lui-même. Parmi les autres inquiétudes, on peut mentionner l'impression d'être responsables de l'abus, le sentiment de confusion et de trahison attribuable à l'excitation physique ressentie pendant l'abus, la difficulté à trouver le moment idéal pour parler du passé et l'incapacité à reconnaître l'aspect abusif de l'abus sexuel, peut-être parce qu'on a amené les victimes à croire qu'il s'agissait d'un acte normal. On devrait encourager les victimes à ne pas confondre le caractère anormal de l'abus avec leur propre identité : l'abus était anormal, mais eux sont parfaitement normaux. Les personnes qui s'occupent des enfants devraient tenter d'être plus au fait des symptômes que présentent les survivants des deux sexes. Les familles, les médecins, les professeurs et les travailleurs des services de protection pourraient ainsi mieux reconnaître et signaler les cas d'abus sexuels fondés aux autorités compétentes.

J'ai du mal à comprendre les personnes qui maltraitent leurs enfants; c'est leur infliger une souffrance tellement destructive. Souvent, je souhaitais que mon père quitte le foyer ou meure tout simplement. J'imaginais que sa disparition résoudrait tous nos problèmes. J'allais par contre découvrir que la mort d'un père incestueux ne libère pas nécessairement la victime de son passé, surtout si celle-ci n'a pas résolu ses traumatismes incestueux avant la mort de son agresseur.

**« Il n'est jamais trop tard pour changer d'état d'esprit, mais une fois sur son lit de mort, ce n'est plus le moment de changer sa vie. » Sakyong Mipham**

Le père d'une amie agressée sexuellement par son père à partir de l'âge de neuf ans lui a laissé entendre qu'ils devraient tous les deux terminer leur relation incestueuse, car, disait-il, elle était maintenant trop âgée pour prolonger cette relation. Non seulement le père l'avait agressée sexuellement, mais il alourdissait sa honte en lui faisant endosser la responsabilité de l'inceste.

Dans ce cas-ci, les parents étaient divorcés depuis plusieurs années quand sa mère apprit que son ex-mari avait abusé de leur fille. Durant les années qui suivirent l'aveu de cette amie à sa mère, celle-ci l'a soutenue; mais ses deux frères ont préféré ne pas croire que leur soeur avait été agressée sexuellement par leur père; ils voulaient éviter d'en discuter complètement. Son père n'a même jamais voulu admettre ses torts. Sur son lit de mort, ses dernières paroles ont été: « Je n'ai rien à me reprocher dans cette vie, je ne regrette rien du tout».

J'étais tellement triste et en colère lorsque mon amie m'a fait part de ces dernières paroles. Je n'arrivais pas à croire que son père avait eu l'audace de lui lancer une pareille imbécillité. Même à son dernier souffle, il avait refusé carrément d'accepter la responsabilité d'avoir agressé sexuellement sa fille.

Ses frères connaissent maintenant la vérité, mais ils continuent de faire semblant que l'inceste n'a pas touché leur famille. Ils ne veulent pas admettre que leur père a commis ce crime contre leur sœur. En définitive, c'est elle qui se sent mal à l'aise d'évoquer le sujet et elle demeure donc seule à traverser les étapes nécessaires à sa libération.

Ne pas avoir le soutien de ses frères et soeurs est l'un des obstacles les plus ardus et isolants à traverser pour la victime de l'inceste : s'ils refusent de croire que l'inceste règne dans leur foyer, leur comportement aliène la victime et mène sûrement à la dissolution de la cellule familiale. Il est important que les autres membres de la famille, qui n'ont pas été agressés, se renseignent sur les méthodes qui peuvent aider les victimes à s'en sortir.

Celles-ci doivent être appuyées par leurs proches pour pouvoir guérir de leur traumatisme.

Reconnaître que l'inceste s'est produit offre aux victimes la preuve qu'on les croit et qu'elles n'en sont pas responsables. De plus, le soutien des autres membres de la famille favorise la transparence, l'honnêteté, la communication, le réconfort et la force de reconstruire le noyau familial.

J'ai dû développer certaines aptitudes au sein de ma famille pour assurer ma survie et mon rétablissement. Chacun, individuellement, a trouvé la méthode qui lui convenait le mieux pour se remettre de son traumatisme.

Ma mère venait d'une famille de sept enfants où l'agression sexuelle ne s'était jamais produite; elle se trouvait mal renseignée pour aider ses enfants à traverser les traumatismes associés aux agressions sexuelles. Lorsqu'elle a été avisée de l'inceste, ma mère a été désorientée, troublée et blessée de ne pas être en mesure de soutenir ses enfants; certains de mes frères et sœurs lui reprochaient de ne pas les avoir protégés; malheureusement, elle a choisi de ne pas obtenir l'aide nécessaire pour appuyer ses enfants.

Ma mère n'a jamais été à l'aise de parler de sexe. Sa timidité et sa gêne étaient omniprésentes le jour où elle a voulu parler du cycle menstruel avec moi. Lors de notre première (et dernière) discussion à ce sujet, la conversation s'est déroulée ainsi :

Sans me regarder, elle m'a demandé timidement :

*- Est-ce qu'il y a des grandes filles dans ta classe?*

*- Oui, maman,* que je réponds promptement pour l'encourager à parler. *Il y en a de très grandes, beaucoup plus grandes que moi, et deux très petites, exactement comme moi.*

*- Ce n'est pas ce que je veux dire, Lucie,* continue-t-elle, un peu exaspérée. *Ce n'est pas de la grandeur que je parle, mais plutôt s'il y en a qui ont commencé leurs périodes.*

*- Oh, tu veux dire, si elles sont menstruées ou non? Oui, il y en a qui ont commencé, mais pas moi.*

Ma mère m'a offert un petit livre qui explique le cycle menstruel et a dit :

*- Tu dois lire ce livre et partager le contenu avec tes soeurs. Si tu as des questions, reviens me voir.*

*- D'accord, Maman,* ai-je dit simplement.

J'ai quitté sa chambre ne sachant pas que ce serait l'unique discussion qu'on aurait sur le sexe. Ce n'est pas étonnant, car à cette époque l'éducation sexuelle était très limitée, même dans nos écoles. Son malaise avec le sexe a contribué à mon silence et au fait que je ne me suis pas confiée à elle sur les agressions sexuelles de mon père. Il était parfaitement conscient de sa gêne et il l'a utilisée pour satisfaire ses désirs égoïstes et criminels.

Il est difficile d'imaginer que notre mère ne savait pas ce qui se passait sous son nez, mais mon père nous agressait toujours lorsqu'elle travaillait hors de la maison ou faisait ses épiceries. Il avait toujours une allure si innocente et paternelle avec nous lorsqu'elle était présente. Et il faut savoir l'Église catholique encadrait assez sévèrement les mères des années antérieures à 1970. Une amie me racontait qu'un prêtre avait refusé de lui donner l'absolution parce qu'elle n'avait pas enfanté après 4 ans de mariage. Les prêtres se faisaient un devoir de visiter chaque famille pour dicter aux parents le nombre d'enfants qu'ils devaient engendrer. Certains prêtres imposaient à la femme de permettre à son mari de la féconder aussitôt après un accouchement. D'après les prêtres, la femme n'était pas maîtresse de son corps et ne devait jamais renoncer à ses devoirs d'épouse. Les prêtres poussaient les femmes au bord de l'épuisement; elles étaient contraintes à élever un nombre d'enfants au-delà de ce que la plupart des femmes pouvaient gérer ou tolérer.

En 13 ans, ma mère a donné naissance à neuf enfants à terme : quatre filles et cinq garçons. À cette époque, les frères et les sœurs plus âgés avaient la responsabilité de s'occuper des plus jeunes, sans protester, sans se plaindre et sans poser de questions.

Un des tournants marquants de ma vie eut lieu à l'âge de neuf ans. Dans l'échelon familial, je suis la troisième, mais l'aînée de quatre filles. Par conséquent, en vertu de la tradition canadienne-française (ou de chez nous), c'est l'aîné des garçons et l'aînée des filles qui prenaient la relève de la mère pour les soins des plus jeunes.

En mai 1965, lorsque ma mère est revenue de l'hôpital avec le dernier garçon, j'accourus à la porte pour l'accueillir et lui demander de me donner mon petit frère. À partir de ce jour, mon frère devenait ma pleine responsabilité. Chaque jour, je veillais à sa toilette, la préparation de ses repas, ses randonnées, sa sécurité. Quand il a fréquenté l'école, je m'assurais qu'il était proprement vêtu et qu'il faisait ses travaux scolaires.

Je le surveillais surtout si mon père le réprimandait; je me plaçais devant lui, comme un bouclier, ce qui obligeait mon père à reculer. Ma mère regardait cette scène toujours avec étonnement parce que je ne laissais jamais mon père l'approcher. J'avais tellement peur qu'il abuse de lui aussi. J'ai appris beaucoup plus tard que mon père avait abusé de certains de mes autres frères et sœurs, et qu'eux aussi auraient bénéficié de ma protection.

Depuis mon adolescence, je me répétais constamment cet engagement : « je ne maltraiterais jamais mes enfants, je ne les agresserais jamais sexuellement et je ne lèguerais pas ce crime infâme à ma descendance ». Ce serment a probablement changé mon destin, car P. Tobin et S. Levison Kessner [10] expliquent que les enfants victimes de violence sont plus susceptibles de devenir des agresseurs (dans une étude, 81 % des agresseurs adultes ont été abusés comme jeunes garçons) et que plusieurs femmes victimes de l'inceste choisissent inconsciemment des hommes qui molesteront leurs enfants. Je crois que j'aurais eu ce destin si je n'avais pas entrepris de transformer mon héritage. À deux reprises, deux camarades de classe m'ont harcelée pour un tête-à-tête que je refusais farouchement; j'ai même dû donner un solide coup de poing dans l'estomac de l'un d'eux qui ne semblait pas comprendre mon refus. Plus tard, j'ai appris que tous deux avaient molesté leurs enfants.

Les effets néfastes de l'inceste sont monumentaux, s'étendant souvent sur plusieurs générations. Aujourd'hui, heureusement, il existe des centres comme le *Centre d'intervention en abus sexuel auprès de la famille* [11] (CIASF) qui fournit des services spécialisés pour tous les membres d'une famille incestueuse. Le Centre soigne les enfants à partir du jeune âge de trois ans, ainsi que les adultes ou les adolescents qui les agressent. Le Centre offre de la thérapie et de l'appui aux agresseurs afin de réduire la probabilité de récidive. Les services fournis par le CIASF sont si bénéfiques aux familles que des pays tels le Chili, la Belgique, ainsi que plusieurs villes du Québec ont fait l'acquisition du programme de cet organisme. Voici quelques-uns des objectifs du CIASF :

- *Développer et offrir des services adaptés pour réduire l'incidence de l'agression sexuelle à l'égard des enfants.*

- *Contrer l'agression sexuelle en enrichissant les connaissances des personnes, des organismes et des partenaires au sujet de cette problématique.*

- *Offrir un lieu d'accueil, d'aide et de réconfort permettant de surmonter les difficultés liées à l'agression sexuelle et de briser l'isolement.*

Les services de ce Centre apportent de l'espoir aux familles qui normalement seraient impuissantes à se remettre d'un tel traumatisme. Malheureusement, ma famille, comme la plupart des familles des générations précédentes, n'a pas eu accès à ce genre de services spécialisés.

Ce ne sont pas tous mes frères et sœurs qui ont été agressés sexuellement, mais cela ne signifie pas qu'ils ne sont pas victimes de l'inceste. Lorsque nous avons dénoncé mon père, les frères et soeurs qui n'avaient pas été agressés sexuellement ont été profondément blessés; ils éprouvaient de la honte et de la colère et ne pouvaient croire qu'ils étaient les enfants d'un père incestueux. Ils ne pouvaient non plus comprendre pourquoi ils avaient été épargnés.

Selon les thérapeutes que j'ai consultés, la raison pour laquelle notre père ne nous a pas tous agressés est que, dans la plupart des familles, les enfants communiquent et se confient à l'un ou l'autre de leurs parents. Les enfants qui n'étaient pas victimes de l'inceste étaient probablement plus près de ma mère. La conséquence tragique d'avoir fait confiance à notre père était donc qu'il maltraitait les enfants qui, avant les agressions, comptaient sur lui pour leur protection et leur bien-être.

Cette trahison a eu des effets désastreux sur ma personne. Comme jeune maman, j'avais décidé d'élever une enfant seulement, même si j'avais toujours espéré en avoir trois. Je portais un bagage lourd de culpabilité, de honte et de tous les autres traumatismes associés à l'inceste, trop nombreux pour les énumérer ici. Je savais qu'avoir un seul enfant (comme la plupart de mes frères et sœurs) était la décision la plus charitable que j'aie pu choisir pour ma fille et moi-même. Je n'avais aucune idée du travail que je devais entreprendre pour recouvrer la santé.

La plupart des parents veulent tout ce qu'il y a de mieux pour leurs enfants : être le meilleur parent possible et enrichir leur vie. Mais j'avais du mal à envisager cette énorme responsabilité d'élever mon enfant. Je ne savais même pas qu'il existait de la thérapie et des services de soutien pour les victimes de l'inceste. Pour éviter de donner naissance à d'autres enfants, après la naissance de ma fille, j'ai subi une ligature des trompes à l'âge de 27 ans. Mes sœurs et mes frères ont aussi choisi de se faire opérer après la naissance de leurs enfants. Je suppose que cette coupure de notre cycle reproductif, c'était une forme d'approche subliminale pour mettre fin à un héritage incestueux.

Afin de me libérer des chaînes de l'inceste, j'ai écrit trois lettres : une à mon père, une à ma mère, comme un dernier adieu, et une adressée à ma nièce, à qui je dois ce livre, et pour lui faire mes excuses.

Ces lettres bouclent le cycle de ma guérison : elles font connaître aussi, à mes lecteurs et lectrices, les sentiments aigus qu'éprouve une survivante de l'inceste. J'espère que les familles incestueuses seront encouragées à entreprendre une psychothérapie et à obtenir le soutien nécessaire pour prévenir et empêcher l'inceste de se propager à d'autres générations. La lettre à mon père démontre que le fardeau de l'inceste déforme et ralentit la croissance naturelle de l'enfant et demeure à jamais dans l'esprit et le cœur de l'adulte survivant.

## Lettre à mon père

Père,

Je t'écris pour une première et dernière fois. Il faut t'expliquer la cruauté que tu nous as tous fait endurer, dans le silence. Tu n'as songé qu'à toi. Tu as en effet légué un héritage dévastateur qui engendre la dépression, la tristesse, l'isolation, la honte, la douleur, l'humiliation, la culpabilisation, et je n'en nomme que quelques-unes de ces répercussions malsaines qui nous accablent encore après tant d'années. Tu es égoïste d'avoir donné à tes enfants un héritage incestueux.

Tu sais que les agressions sexuelles que tu as infligées à tes enfants demeurent avec nous le reste de nos vies. Ceux et celles qui ont été épargnés de ton viol ne peuvent concevoir que leur père ait commis des actions aussi basses. Comment as-tu pu penser que tes actions n'auraient pas de conséquences? Tu étais pourtant assez intelligent pour le *concevoir. Aujourd'hui, tu mènes ta vie comme si rien ne s'était passé et comme si tu n'avais pas à t'en repentir. N'as-tu aucun regret?*

*Tu dois bien savoir qu'un enfant n'oublie jamais qu'il a été abusé sexuellement. La mémoire de ces abus est enracinée chez l'enfant pour la vie — même à l'âge adulte. Je ne comprends toujours pas pourquoi tu as blessé tes enfants et ta petite-fille de cette façon. Personne ne peut comprendre ou accepter un tel geste. Tu te caches encore derrière « la jupe » de notre mère, comme si elle pouvait te protéger contre les conséquences de tes actes. Ne pense surtout pas que tu nous es invisible, ou que nous pouvons t'oublier.*

*Malheureusement, nous avons été élevés par un père menteur, sournois, malhonnête, trompeur, lâche et borné. Lorsque j'étais enfant, chaque jour j'espérais que tu disparaisses, que tu nous quittes ou simplement que tu meures. Mais à cause de ta nature égoïste, nous avons eu à endurer tes agressions sexuelles pendant plusieurs années. Ton espèce n'est pas bienvenue dans notre cercle familial — ni aujourd'hui ni jamais. Par tes actes, tu as toi-même renoncé à l'unité familiale, car dans une famille on se respecte et on s'entraide. Je ne peux pas parler pour mes frères et sœurs; mais moi, je n'ai gardé aucun bon souvenir de toi. Tout ce* que je me rappelle de toi, c'est la souffrance du calvaire ignoble que tu m'as fait vivre.

Tu as enlevé à notre famille toute possibilité et tout espoir de nous unir ou de partager un vécu harmonieux. Tu as désuni la famille à jamais. Nous avons dû, par mesure préventive, ignorer ton existence. Est-ce ce que tu voulais? Molester tes enfants, que pensais-tu? Qu'on l'oublierait? Toi, l'as-tu oublié? Je ne peux consentir à ensevelir cet héritage destructeur que tu nous lègues. Cet héritage est tristement partagé avec notre mère. Toutes ces années, tu nous obligeais à lui mentir, tu as fait de nous tes complices débauchés, trop innocents pour savoir ce que nous faisions — tu me fais honte.

N'as-tu pas songé à ta progéniture? As-tu cru que tes actions n'affecteraient pas ta relation avec tes enfants, tes petits-enfants et tes arrière-petits-enfants? Comprends-tu maintenant que c'est à cause de tes agressions sexuelles que la famille ne se réunit plus aux anniversaires, aux baptêmes, aux fêtes nationales, aux funérailles, aux mariages? Nous ne te célébrons plus à la fête des Pères ou la fête des Grands-parents; tu n'as aucun droit à ces rôles prestigieux. Je suis une grand-mère et n'éprouve que du chagrin lorsque je ne peux célébrer ces fêtes avec toi. Ce n'est pas censé être comme ça. Aucun de tes enfants ne te veut autour *de leurs enfants. Nos enfants ne peuvent pas visiter leur grand-mère à cause de toi. Tu me fais tellement pitié!*

*C'est ce que tu nous lègues. Tu as essayé de blâmer ton père, ta mère, les prêtres, ton épouse et même nous, les enfants que tu maltraitais. Mais tu dois accepter l'imputabilité de tes fautes, de tes actes. Toi seul es responsable de cet héritage incestueux. Tu n'avais aucun droit de me salir ainsi. C'était à moi de décider avec qui je partagerais les parties les plus intimes de ma personne. Tu m'as ôté cette option lorsque tu m'as violée. Perdre ma virginité entre tes mains a été la plus grande perte de ma vie.*

*Tu sais très bien que tu aurais pu prendre une autre direction; mais tu as choisi de faire l'autruche. Imagine un moment, si tu avais suivi une psychothérapie au lieu d'accabler ta famille avec tes manières perverses. Comme nos vies et nos relations auraient été différentes!*

*Tu savais ce que tu devais faire. C'était ton devoir comme parent de donner à tes enfants une vie à l'abri de l'inceste. Ton devoir de père était de nous sécuriser, de nous protéger, obligation de base pour un parent. N'était-ce pas évident pour toi lorsque tu as pris ton rôle de père? C'était de l'ignorance voulue!*

*Aujourd'hui, j'ai réussi à modifier mon héritage avec l'amour, la générosité, la compassion, l'honnêteté, la sagesse et la dignité.*

*Ma descendance jouit d'une progéniture conçue dans le respect et le bien-être d'autrui. Ces attributs anéantiront l'héritage incestueux que tu nous as égoïstement transmis.*

*Je ne vois aucune autre façon de terminer cette lettre qu'en te disant que je suis profondément attristée de tes choix.*

**Note au lecteur :** L'important n'était pas que mon père lise cette lettre. L'important, c'était de me libérer de ma souffrance en l'écrivant. J'y suis parvenue, comme vous le constaterez à la fin de ce livre.

## Lettre à ma mère

*Maman,*

*Cette lettre a pour but de t'expliquer les raisons pour lesquelles je ne peux plus te rendre visite. Ce choix n'a pas été facile. C'est pour l'amour et le respect de ma fille et de mes petites-filles que j'ai dû prendre cette décision.*

*Une autre tragédie est encore liée à notre père incestueux. Notre nièce (ta petite-fille) est une autre de ses victimes; il l'a aussi agressée sexuellement lorsqu'elle était enfant. Cette nièce, comme nous d'ailleurs, a attendu d'être adulte avant de révéler ces abus. J'éprouve tellement de colère et de tristesse à la pensée des traumatismes qui maintenant l'accaparent elle aussi. Tu peux comprendre l'enfer que traversent ses parents à la suite de cette déclaration. La rage, l'angoisse, la culpabilité, la douleur de ces parents sont insupportables. Ton mari a encore égoïstement abusé de ce qu'il y a de plus sacré : la confiance d'une enfant.*

*Je partage leur chagrin, car je connais trop bien le calvaire que ma nièce doit vivre pour s'en remettre. Ce qui est le plus pénible, c'est que si nous l'avions dénoncé avant qu'il l'agresse nous lui aurions épargné cette écoeuranterie. Cet homme n'est pas digne d'être un père, un grand-père ou même ton conjoint. Cet homme* représente tout ce qui est malhonnête, cruel, haineux, pervers, sournois.

Maman, tu ne mérites pas de faire partie de cette existence infâme. Malheureusement, sans que je puisse comprendre, tu as choisi de demeurer à ses côtés. En 1986, la famille aurait effectivement bénéficié des services et soutiens offerts par ta psychologue, mais tu as choisi de ne pas avoir recours à cette thérapie pour nous. Nous avons donc dû, comme dans notre enfance, subir notre sort, sans le soutien de nos parents. C'est ce qui nous empêche de te voir aujourd'hui — on n'a toujours pas ton soutien.

Grâce à la thérapie et à son soutien, j'ai pu léguer un nouvel héritage à ma fille et à mes petits-enfants.

J'aurais aimé, Maman, que tu aies une meilleure vie.

## Lettre à ma nièce

*Ma chère nièce,*

*Les lettres que j'ai écrites à mon père et à ma mère, tes grands-parents, ont pour but de dévoiler, une fois pour toutes, ce secret ignoble de l'inceste; ce crime qui persiste depuis plusieurs générations et qui existait avant même que toi ou moi soyons de ce monde. J'aurais souhaité avoir écrit ce livre avant ta naissance, car tu n'aurais pas eu à supporter le poids de l'inceste sur tes jeunes épaules. Je ressens beaucoup de tristesse pour toi, chère nièce. Jusqu'à maintenant, j'étais incapable de mettre des mots sur les sentiments et les pensées qui alourdissaient mon coeur; mais tout a changé lorsque j'ai appris que ton grand-père t'avait toi aussi agressée sexuellement. Malheureusement, il m'a fallu ce « coup de pied au cœur » pour réagir. Grâce à ton courage à dénoncer ton grand-père, tu m'as donné la force et le courage d'écrire ce livre afin que lui et ses semblables comprennent les souffrances qu'ils causent à leurs familles. La voie qu'a choisie ton grand-père était assurément tordue et t'a remplie d'amertume; ce n'est pas du tout ce que nous, tes parents, tes tantes et tes oncles voulons t'offrir. L'inceste doit être balayé de notre société, de nos familles; il faut cesser de le transmettre à nos descendants. J'espère que cette lettre et ce livre t'apporteront du réconfort, du soutien et l'assurance que je suis ici pour toi.*

*Affectueusement, tante Lucie*

**« *Le counseling ne sert pas à relater et à revivre les évènements pénibles, mais bien à adopter des stratégies qui vous permettront de faire face à votre détresse.* »**

*Counseling en matière de violence sexuelle*

*Guide à l'intention des parents et des enfants*

L'agence de la santé publique du Canada

**CHAPITRE 4**

# LES SURVIVANTS ET SURVIVANTES DE L'INCESTE DOIVENT SE RÉÉDUQUER DANS LEUR RÔLE PARENTAL

Je ne possède aucune formation professionnelle qui me permet de conseiller les parents sur la meilleure façon d'élever leurs enfants, surtout si ceux-ci sont des survivants et survivantes de l'inceste, car je n'ai pas reçu une orientation adéquate de nos propres parents. Toutefois, je peux parler de mon approche pour devenir un parent respectueux et digne d'élever des enfants. À l'adolescence, j'ai constaté que je devais chercher ailleurs pour trouver des parents qui m'offriraient des valeurs saines et équilibrées. J'ai eu la chance d'être gardienne d'enfants chez deux familles. Ces parents guidaient leurs enfants dans l'amour, l'harmonie, avec une éthique basée sur le respect des droits d'autrui. J'ai suivi ce modèle de parents, car je réalisais que ce n'était pas tous les parents qui maltraitaient leurs enfants. Ces parents sont donc devenus mes mentors et mes bienfaiteurs; grâce à eux, j'ai eu le « coup de pouce » pour apprendre à être un bon parent.

Je crois qu'être parent est un des rôles les plus difficiles. Il y a peu de parents qui ne sont pas frappés par l'énorme responsabilité qui apparaît à la venue d'un nouveau-né. Cette réalisation ne m'est malheureusement venue qu'après la naissance de ma fille. Même si, en grande partie, j'avais élevé mon jeune frère, rien ne m'avait préparée pour le stress et l'angoisse que j'éprouverais à l'égard de ma fille. J'aurais souhaité avoir reçu une formation telle que l'éducation de la petite enfance avant de mettre au monde un petit être qui avait de si grands besoins. J'aurais sûrement profité de cet apprentissage. Faute de cet apprentissage, ce fut une lutte continuelle entre donner à mon enfant tous les soins nécessaires pour son quotidien et simultanément travailler à surmonter mes propres traumatismes. J'aurais pu fournir à ma fille un environnement plus calme, si j'avais compris les conséquences physiques et psychologiques de l'inceste. Je conseille à tous les parents, surtout ceux qui sont survivants d'agressions sexuelles et de violence, de suivre une thérapie pour obtenir du soutien,

AVANT d'avoir des enfants. Chaque enfant a le droit de naître dans un milieu enrichissant et serein.

Maintenant, il est beaucoup plus facile pour moi de voir quelles méthodes j'aurais pu utiliser pour ne pas affecter inconsciemment ma fille avec mon fardeau émotif. Je ne regrette pas de l'avoir mise au monde; au contraire, elle m'apporte son amour, sa générosité et sa joie de vivre. C'est une personne belle et bienveillante qui a été une alliée formidable; je lui en serai toujours reconnaissante.

Je regrette par contre de n'avoir pas reçu le soutien et les traitements appropriés aux survivants de l'inceste. Il est dit qu'on ne doit rien regretter dans la vie; mais, d'après moi, il est pratiquement impossible de vivre une vie sans regret. Il faut être cloîtré dans un monastère lointain et ne jamais communiquer avec qui que ce soit, pour ne pas avoir de regrets. J'ai des regrets, mais je redonne à ma famille et à la société de façon à ne plus accumuler de regrets. Il y a un apprentissage nécessaire au développement de l'enfant et son développement est plus facile s'il n'y a pas la lourdeur traumatique des parents. Il est certain que j'aurais préféré être une maman sereine, mais aujourd'hui cette expérience a fait de moi une grand-maman dévouée, engagée et bien équipée pour véhiculer la joie, l'amour et la sagesse.

J'ai dû accélérer ma thérapie psychologique pour guider ma fille vers l'épanouissement que je souhaitais pour elle, comme parent. Mon angoisse pour sa sécurité était démesurée; je la surprotégeais au point de lui causer de l'anxiété. Ma fille a quand même exprimé sa gratitude à plusieurs reprises, reconnaissante du fait que je ne lui aie pas légué mon héritage. Elle ne me reproche aucunement cette période de ma croissance. Être une survivante de l'inceste m'a conscientisée à l'importance du rôle parental. J'étais vigilante et attentive aux gens qui pouvaient blesser mon enfant. Je ne confiais ma fille à personne. Quoique cette vigilance puisse être parfois exagérée, avec le soutien thérapeutique, le parent peut arriver à trouver l'équilibre. Quoi qu'il en soit, je ne crois pas qu'une victime de l'inceste ne puisse jamais cesser de surveiller l'entourage de son enfant.

Je cherchais toujours avec inquiétude le moment propice pour parler à fille des dangers de l'inceste. Était-il nécessaire d'exposer mon enfant à ce passé sordide? Quand? Comment? Devais-je même me confier? Les questions que je me posais étaient: quelles réactions aura ma fille lorsqu'elle apprendra que son grand-père m'a agressée sexuellement? Est-ce qu'elle va me repousser? Être dégoûtée? Va-t-elle être fâchée parce que je ne me suis pas confiée plus tôt? Comment me jugera-t-elle? Les survivants de l'inceste doivent considérer toutes les facettes de ce dilemme. La détresse et l'inquiétude du parent quant à cette tâche ardue se comprennent, mais le counseling peut faciliter cet échange. Voici ce que conseille l'ASPC dans sa publication intitulée : *Le Counseling en matière de violence sexuelle. Guide à l'intention des parents et des enfants[12] :*

> *Le counseling ne sert pas à relater et à revivre les évènements pénibles, mais bien à adopter des stratégies qui vous permettront de faire face à votre détresse. Cela semble impossible à envisager? Essayez plutôt de voir cette crise comme une chance de rapprochement inespérée pour votre famille. Même si vous n'avez pas été victime de violence sexuelle dans votre enfance, affronter l'agression infligée à votre enfant peut représenter le défi le plus important de votre vie. Vous devriez obtenir de l'aide auprès d'un conseiller pendant cette période difficile, cela aidera votre enfant à poursuivre son traitement.*

Par contre, plusieurs adultes, nés de parents victimes de l'inceste, me confirment qu'elles n'étaient pas étonnées de découvrir que leur mère ou leur père avait été maltraité ou agressé sexuellement.

Elles avouent que leur parent subissait plusieurs traumatismes, tels la dépression, l'alcoolisme, le stress et l'angoisse aigus, tous associés à l'inceste.

Une amie, survivante de l'inceste, s'interroge sur les démarches à suivre avant de confesser à ses adolescents que leur grand-père l'a agressée sexuellement, durant son enfance. Il y a certes plusieurs considérations auxquelles le parent doit songer avant de le dévoiler. Avant tout, la priorité est de s'assurer de la sécurité de ses enfants. Quelle est la relation des enfants avec ce grand-parent? Celui-ci a-t-il accès à ces enfants?

Toutefois, si le parent peut garantir la sécurité des adolescents, comme dans ce cas (le grand-père étant décédé), la survivante peut choisir de ne pas faire de confidences à ses enfants immédiatement, car découvrir que leur grand-père molestait leur mère peut être horrible à absorber pour eux. Néanmoins, la survivante songe à partager son secret avec ses enfants, car ceux-ci s'interrogent sur la raison pour laquelle leur mère suit de la thérapie psychologique régulièrement. Mais avant de le dévoiler, la mère doit se prévaloir sagement des conseils de son thérapeute sur la façon d'aborder le sujet. En apprenant à répondre à leurs questions et à prévoir leurs réactions, la mère sera en mesure de mieux en discuter avec eux et la famille pourra s'épauler au besoin.

Il faut comprendre que chaque cas est unique et que les conseils et le soutien thérapeutique sont indispensables si on veut rendre cette tâche plus abordable. Dans mon cas, par exemple, j'ai dû tout dévoiler à ma fille à ses quatorze ans, car il y avait toujours une possibilité que son grand-père prenne avantage d'elle durant nos rencontres familiales. La Loi sur les agressions sexuelles d'enfants prescrit que la protection de l'enfant est prioritaire; sa protection doit être garantie. Si le père est l'agresseur, la mère est responsable d'assurer un environnement sécuritaire à ses enfants; elle doit alerter les policiers ou l'agence contre la violence infantile immédiatement afin d'assurer leur protection. Si elle néglige cette responsabilité, les enfants seront sortis de ce milieu et logés dans une famille d'accueil. Dans les cas où c'est la mère qui maltraite les enfants, le père a la même responsabilité juridique pour s'assurer que ses enfants sont protégés. Le bien-être et la sécurité des enfants demeurent la principale préoccupation des tribunaux.

À l'adolescence, j'ai été capable d'arrêter les agressions de mon père. Mais, contrairement à ce que j'avais imaginé, cet arrêt ne m'a pas totalement soulagée; je n'avais pas pris conscience des traumatismes associés à l'inceste et je n'étais pas préparée à en envisager les effets. J'étais malheureuse, colérique, obèse, accablée par un complexe d'infériorité et une faible estime de moi. Si je voulais survivre et sortir de ce trou noir, il était essentiel que je change et que j'améliore mon image de la vie.

La seule ressource disponible à cette époque était de fréquenter des familles dont les enfants étaient heureux et aimés. Je devais être proche de parents bienveillants et cette proximité devenait mon objectif de survie. J'ai eu la chance d'être employée par deux familles chaleureuses du voisinage pour la garde de leurs enfants; j'ai aussi eu la chance de fréquenter un enseignant de mathématiques qui m'a prise sous son aile. Ces trois familles, de classe moyenne, travaillaient vaillamment pour nourrir, habiller et éduquer leurs enfants. Ces enfants n'étaient ni giflés ni agressés. Peu importe la pression que ces parents subissaient, ils créaient un environnement respectueux, rempli d'amour et de compassion. Ces familles ont contribué grandement à ma guérison.

De ces trois familles, j'ai appris, sans qu'elles le sachent, les compétences parentales nécessaires. Marquée par leur exemple, j'ai élevé plus tard ma propre fille dans l'amour et la dévotion que ces parents m'avaient enseignés. Aujourd'hui, je suis très fière d'elle, car ma fille est une maman chaleureuse, travaillante et elle inspire à ses enfants le respect d'autrui, l'amour et le partage. Je suis privilégiée et ne peux être plus reconnaissante.

Même que ces couples démontraient une union conjugale solide, moi, il m'a pris du temps à trouver un copain en qui je puis faire confiance. Comme mon père n'a pas été le modèle d'époux fidèle et respectueux, j'avais du mal à faire confiance aux hommes. Après l'échec de deux mariages, j'ai demandé l'aide d'amis et de la famille, pour m'aider à trouver un bon partenaire : un homme, avec qui je puis partager mon vécu, sans l'effrayer! Heureusement, j'ai trouvé ce bijou d'homme, avec qui je niche amoureusement depuis 16 ans.

Mon compagnon me prête toujours une oreille attentive. Son amour et sa compréhension m'ont aidée à affronter les effets nocifs d'une famille dysfonctionnelle. Nous avons, l'un pour l'autre, le plus grand des respects. Je l'aime profondément et je suis reconnaissante de son amour. En plus d'être un partenaire attentionné, il est un père dévoué à son fils et à ma fille; mes petites-filles l'ont adopté comme leur grand-père. Quand je suis témoin d'une discussion entre lui et ma fille, que ce soit sur des voitures ou sur les finances, ils sont tellement bien synchronisés que j'en oublie qu'il n'est pas son père biologique. Je suis très heureuse de ce que nous partageons; c'est ce qu'une famille doit acquérir et ce dont elle peut jouir.

Si j'ai pu bâtir des relations saines et fructueuses avec mon compagnon, ma fille, mon gendre et mes petites-filles, c'est grâce au travail considérable que j'ai fait en thérapie pour surmonter les dommages que l'inceste m'avait légués. Le confort, la stabilité, le dévouement et l'amour qui m'entourent m'apportent finalement la paix, la joie et la sérénité. Cette victoire est d'autant plus exceptionnelle qu'elle anéantit les blessures occasionnées par un père abusif.

> **« Un enfant bien informé a plus de chances de ne pas devenir une victime. Apprenez-lui à trouver des solutions en gardant la tête froide. Écoute-le, il vous écoutera; parlez-lui, il vous parlera; respectez-le, il se fera respecter. »**

*Te laisse pas faire! Les abus sexuels expliqués aux enfants.*

Jocelyne Robert

CHAPITRE 5

# HONORONS NOS ENFANTS - PRÉVENIR L'INCESTE ET LES AGRESSIONS SEXUELLES

Le quatrième commandement de la religion catholique romaine dit : « *Tu honoreras ton père et ta mère* ». J'implore toutes les sectes spirituelles d'ordre religieux et les groupes séculiers de modifier leurs livres souverains et d'inclure une nouvelle prescription : « Honorez vos enfants ». Ou plutôt, afin d'inclure l'ensemble des êtres vivants : « Honorez tous les êtres vivants ».

C'est dans notre intérêt à tous de protéger nos enfants contre la souffrance et la détresse causées par les agressions sexuelles. Mettre fin à cet enfer produira assurément des enfants altruistes, respectueux et confiants.

J'ai reçu une des plus précieuses leçons de vie et je dois rendre hommage à ma fille. L'évènement s'est produit dans l'année où nous (mes frères et sœurs) avons confronté notre père. Peu de temps après cette confrontation, j'ai remarqué que ma fille pleurait chaque fois que je n'étais pas dans son champ de vision.

Ce n'était pas son comportement habituel, car elle était généralement une enfant heureuse et joyeuse. J'ai consulté un psychologue qui m'a fait comprendre que, bien que nous n'ayons pas eu nos discussions entourant l'inceste en sa présence, elle avait quand même été plongée dans toutes ces émotions fortes qui imprégnaient l'air autour d'elle : la honte, la peur, la culpabilité, la rage, les remords, l'humiliation, la tristesse. Elle n'était simplement pas équipée pour gérer toutes ces émotions négatives. Sans en être consciente, j'empiétais sur sa sérénité et sa tranquillité d'esprit. J'ai compris que mes émotions, positives ou négatives, pouvaient facilement être transmises à mon enfant. Avec l'assaut de toutes ces émotions et ces réactions autour d'elle, ma fille a réagi de la seule façon qu'elle avait à sa disposition pour communiquer avec moi : elle a pleuré. Cette leçon s'est avérée être un tournant dans ma vie et dans mon approche pour toutes nos discussions *mère-fille*. La thérapie familiale et le soutien d'un conseiller nous auraient été grandement bénéfiques pendant cette période.

Je ne prétends pas que c'est facile pour ma fille de vivre avec l'histoire de ma famille. Malgré tout, nous avons réussi à cultiver une relation honnête, sereine, vertueuse et respectueuse. J'ai confiance en son jugement; elle est d'une sagesse au-delà de son âge. Ma fille se dit fière de mon cheminement thérapeutique; son soutien et son amour sont la force qui m'a poussée à me débarrasser de mon sale héritage.

Comme j'aurais aimé être dans un meilleur état d'esprit et de cœur avant sa naissance! Aujourd'hui, je travaille diligemment à prévenir et à empêcher que ce comportement inhumain se produise chez les futures générations. Je contribue à assurer une destinée saine et sans danger pour tous les enfants. Une existence comblée d'amour, de respect, de compassion et de bien-être.

Comme je l'ai dit plus haut, j'ai dû avertir ma fille d'une possible agression incestueuse de son grand-père lorsqu'elle était âgée de 14 ans. J'avais toujours peur que mon père lui fasse des avances et que, ne sachant pas comment réagir, elle devienne une autre de ses victimes. Je la surprotégeais lorsqu'elle était jeune et je ne permettais pas qu'elle soit seule avec lui. Mais, comme les adolescents tolèrent mal la supervision parentale, je craignais que sa quête naturelle d'indépendance puisse la rendre vulnérable à ces attaques. J'étais très angoissée à l'idée d'en discuter avec elle; je craignais son rejet, son dégoût à la suite d'une telle révélation.

L'incrédulité fut sa première réaction, mais elle a rapidement pris le rôle de protecteur; elle m'a prise dans ses bras et nous avons pleuré ensemble. Depuis ce jour, elle ne s'est jamais approchée de son grand-père et était toujours sur ses gardes en sa présence. Sa cousine, cependant, n'a pas eu cette chance.

J'ai continué à rendre visite à mes parents pendant plusieurs années après avoir confronté mon père. Cela est souvent difficile à comprendre pour les personnes hors de ce milieu, mais j'y allais pour appuyer mes frères et mes sœurs qui voulaient maintenir le noyau familial. Je me reprochais toujours de ne pas les avoir protégés. Malgré l'aide thérapeutique, j'ai été enchaînée par cette culpabilité pendant de nombreuses années.

À cette époque (1986), je ne voyais aucune possibilité de rompre les liens avec ma famille, même si mon père était présent à ces réunions. Ma loyauté envers mes frères et soeurs était profondément enracinée.

En 2009, vingt-trois ans après la dénonciation de l'abus, j'ai mis fin à ma relation avec mes parents. Cette rupture était très pénible pour moi, car cette décision engendra aussi une séparation avec les membres de la famille, qui continuaient à les fréquenter.

De plus, maintenir un contact avec mes parents, semait de l'incertitude dans mon rapport avec ma fille; elle ne pouvait comprendre la raison pour laquelle nous persistions tous à protéger un pédophile. J'ai finalement décidé de ne plus sanctionner ce drame maléfique lorsque j'ai appris que ma nièce avait été agressée par mon père.

Je présume que, si ma mère avait choisi de ne pas demeurer avec mon père après la confrontation, aucun des enfants n'aurait entretenu une relation avec lui. Aujourd'hui, elle est âgée de 83 ans, elle demeure toujours avec lui, et presque aucun de ses enfants ne la visite. Quelles que soient ses raisons pour demeurer avec notre père, moi j'ai dû faire d'autres choix pour avancer.

Est-ce que la thérapie de groupe aurait aidé notre famille? Mes parents m'ont bien déçue lorsqu'ils ont refusé le soutien thérapeutique pour nous aider à récupérer. J'espérais qu'ils nous aident à traverser les étapes de recouvrement. J'aurais voulu que mon père se charge lui-même de trouver une façon de nous aider. C'était lui qui était la cause de notre drame; selon moi, il lui revenait de le rectifier. S'il avait pris l'initiative d'obtenir du soutien et de la thérapie, le résultat pour notre famille aurait sans doute été différent. Au lieu de vivre ce cheminement en solitaires, nous aurions eu des thérapeutes pour nous aider à progresser, en famille. Malheureusement, la famille demeure fractionnée, car notre noyau familial n'a pas survécu à ce processus individuel.

Je ne réalisais pas qu'entretenir un lien avec mes parents empiétait sur ma santé physique et mentale, ainsi que sur ma liberté de faire mes propres choix. Il fallait que je me libère des griffes de l'inceste : me libérer des souvenirs douloureux, de la culpabilité, de la honte, du fardeau des responsabilités oppressives, de mon complexe d'infériorité et de ma faible estime de moi. Bref, maintenir ce lien parental dysfonctionnel m'enchaînait au passé et m'empêchait d'aller de l'avant.

Le dernier éclairage à apporter à ce macabre récit est que j'entretenais un lien avec mes parents pour que ma fille connaisse ses grands-parents. Je croyais que ce n'était pas juste de ma part de la séparer de sa grand-mère. D'ailleurs, pensais-je, en brisant le lien avec ma mère, est-ce que je n'allais pas causer un impact négatif sur la relation avec ma fille? Je ne savais plus quoi faire; je voulais me séparer de mes parents, mais je ne savais pas comment parler de mes préoccupations avec ma fille. J'ai décidé de m'adresser à mon gendre; je lui ai confié mes peurs et mes angoisses; si je me séparais de mes parents, ma fille voudrait-elle aussi rompre avec moi? Il m'a rapidement rassurée en m'affirmant que cela ne serait pas le cas. Il a même été très surpris que je réagisse ainsi. Il m'a doucement fait comprendre que je n'avais pas été le même parent que mon père et ma mère; je n'avais pas abusé de ma fille.

J'ai pris mon courage à deux mains et j'ai annoncé à ma fille que je voulais briser le lien avec mes parents, tout en lui expliquant les raisons de ma décision. Elle m'a confié qu'elle avait l'impression qu'en gardant contact avec mes parents j'acceptais le comportement de mon père. Elle ne pouvait pas faire confiance à mon jugement. J'ai donc écrit à mes parents pour mettre fin à notre relation. Aussitôt les lettres écrites, j'ai été soulagée d'un poids considérable de culpabilité. Je n'avais pas réalisé que j'avais pris sur moi la responsabilité de l'inceste. Tous mes frères et sœurs n'étaient pas d'accord avec ma décision. C'était mon choix de ne plus porter sur mes épaules la responsabilité de ce que mon père m'avait fait vivre. En réalité, je n'étais pas responsable et le fait de rompre le lien avec mes parents nous a tous libérés de l'inceste : ma fille, mes petites-filles, mon gendre et mon compagnon. Nous avons finalement tourné la page.

Une fois cette étape franchie, j'ai approfondi mes connaissances en recherchant les ressources maintenant à ma disposition. J'ai étudié les statistiques et les résultats provenant des analyses sur les répercussions de l'inceste. J'ai obtenu une quantité substantielle d'informations, j'ai reçu beaucoup de soutien et d'encouragements des membres de ma famille, d'amis, de bibliothécaires, ainsi que de thérapeutes de centres qui traitent les victimes de l'agression sexuelle et de la violence familiale. J'étais peu au fait des services offerts par ces centres, mais j'étais encore plus surprise de découvrir les méthodes des thérapeutes. J'ai rencontré des personnes dévouées, renseignées, compréhensives, calmes et attachantes. Je me sentais tout à fait à l'aise en leur présence. Je sais aujourd'hui qu'il existe du soutien et des thérapies adaptées aux familles ou aux personnes qui sont ou ont été victimes de l'inceste : grâce à ces services, victimes et agresseurs peuvent aujourd'hui se rétablir.

De nos jours, plusieurs professionnels (thérapeutes, policiers, enseignants, administrateurs de la santé) ont reçu une formation en prévention d'agressions sexuelles et de violence familiale. Sans soutien thérapeutique, l'agresseur sexuel ne cesse pas d'être un prédateur astucieux, même s'il a été accusé et jugé coupable.

Par contre, j'étais offusquée d'apprendre qu'il n'y a pas de centre en Ontario qui traite avec toutes les membres de la famille incestueuse en même temps. Pour trouver un tel centre, il faut aller au Québec. C'est le *Centre d'intervention en abus sexuel auprès de la famille* (CIASF). Ce Centre est considéré comme un leader mondial en thérapie de groupe familial pour les victimes et pour leurs agresseurs.

À son ouverture (1987), avec peu de financement, le CIASF offrait du counseling aux mères d'enfants maltraités et aux pères qui abusaient ces enfants. Son objectif premier était d'arrêter les agresseurs récidivistes et de responsabiliser les mères pour la protection de leurs enfants. Au fur et à mesure que le CIASF démontrait que ses services de counseling produisaient de bons résultats, le financement s'est accru et le Centre a pu offrir des services thérapeutiques directement aux victimes d'agressions sexuelles : d'abord aux adolescents, puis aux enfants dès l'âge de trois ans.

Malgré la nécessité du CIASF, le financement demeure toujours une lutte; un programme, conçu pour s'attaquer au problème des agressions sexuelles entre enfants, a dû être coupé en raison du manque de financement. Il est prouvé que, sans aide ni intervention, certaines victimes de l'inceste vont grandir et devenir elles-mêmes des agresseurs. Un peu d'investissement, dès maintenant, aiderait les futures générations à vivre sans la douleur de la violence sexuelle et de l'inceste. C'est donc, à tous les membres de la communauté, et non seulement aux personnes impliquées, que relève la responsabilité de nous assurer que les victimes ainsi que les agresseurs reçoivent les soins nécessaires pour leur guérison.

À la suite de ma visite au CIASF, j'ai compris que les membres de ma famille auraient bénéficié du counseling de groupe; mon père aurait reçu le soutien approprié pour bien voir les conséquences de son crime. En 1986, lorsque l'inceste a été étalé au grand jour, ma mère s'est rendue en consultation. On lui a conseillé de quitter son mari immédiatement. C'était un mauvais conseil pour ma mère, car son but premier était de garder sa famille unie. Je crois que la thérapeute n'avait pas bien conseillé ou compris ses besoins en essayant de séparer ma mère de mon père. Ma mère aurait voulu que l'on traverse cette épreuve tous ensemble. Elle n'est donc plus retournée consulter.

Se débarrasser d'un héritage incestueux exige des efforts, de la persistance, de la tolérance et une approche unique pour chaque famille et chaque individu. Aujourd'hui, le CIASF fournit du soutien de groupe, favorise les prises de conscience et donne de la formation à tous les membres de la famille pour que la guérison puisse se faire, pour que les victimes ne soient plus contraintes de choisir entre le silence et la perte du lien familial. Quel bien ce type de soutien aurait fait à ma famille!˙

Mes objectifs actuels sont :

- d'épargner aux enfants les souffrances de l'inceste,

- de soutenir les survivants dans leur cheminement vers la guérison, et

- de raconter mon histoire de survivante aux thérapeutes, aux travailleurs sociaux, aux membres du système juridique et aux membres des gouvernements, pour qu'ils sachent ce dont a besoin une victime de l'inceste pour recouvrer la santé.

Donner son appui à un centre tel que le CIASF permet d'aider tous les membres de la famille, y compris les agresseurs. Ceux-ci reçoivent du soutien et un apprentissage pour vivre respectueusement dans une communauté : sans violence et sans abus.

J'ai connaissance de frères et sœurs qui avaient des relations sexuelles, ainsi que d'adolescents qui agressaient sexuellement leurs petits frères et petites soeurs. Il est donc essentiel pour les parents de ne pas se fermer les yeux sur le fait qu'il existe possiblement dans leur famille des adolescents/enfants qui abusent des autres enfants. Il faut être conscient de cette possibilité et faire prendre conscience à tous les membres de sa famille, adolescents et enfants, du fait que l'exploitation sexuelle est un crime inacceptable dans notre société. Nous voulons tous que nos enfants deviennent des citoyens responsables et bienveillants; il ne faut donc pas hésiter à offrir à nos enfants les services, l'appui, l'éducation, et les thérapies nécessaires pour mettre fin aux agressions sexuelles. Votre bibliothèque municipale ainsi que l'ASPC du Canada offrent une multitude de manuels pour aider les parents à guider leurs enfants hors de l'inceste.

À l'âge de quatorze ans, bien que je n'aie jamais entendu l'expression « survivante de l'inceste », je savais que j'étais une victime d'agressions sexuelles et je ne voulais pas le demeurer. J'ai donc trouvé différents moyens pour me sortir de cette détresse infernale, entre autres, grâce à mes contacts avec des parents-bienfaiteurs de mon quartier, dont j'ai parlé plus haut. J'ai quitté la maison à l'âge de 22 ans, comme jeune épouse. Ce n'est pas la meilleure des raisons pour partir de la maison familiale, mais c'était le seul choix que je pensais avoir à cette époque. C'est à ce moment-là que j'ai aussi commencé à consulter un psychologue. Ce n'est que lorsque je suis devenue mère que j'ai dévoilé à mon psychologue que j'avais été agressée sexuellement par mon père. Il avait probablement déjà deviné, vu nos discussions; mais il ne m'avait pas poussée à en parler avant que j'y sois prête. Durant les différentes phases thérapeutiques, j'ai découvert l'outil qui s'avérerait essentiel à mon recouvrement : l'enthousiasme. Je trouvais que pour accélérer ma transformation, l'enthousiasme était le meilleur outil pour « aller de l'avant ». (Dans le prochain chapitre, j'explique davantage les méthodes que j'ai utilisées pour récupérer).

Il existe plusieurs membres dans votre communauté qui sont formés pour prévenir et assister les personnes souffrant d'agressions sexuelles ou de violence familiale. On peut trouver des services, tels que ceux offerts par le CIASF, des manuels, des guides et des livres de référence pour renseigner les adultes et les enfants sur la prévention des agressions sexuelles (annexe A). Signaler aux autorités appropriées un cas de délit sexuel est la responsabilité de tous les citoyens. Chacun doit se renseigner et contacter les personnes de sa communauté responsables de la prévention et du soutien des enfants et des adultes agressés sexuellement.

Voici une liste des personnes de votre communauté formées pour vous fournir ce soutien et ces mesures préventives :

- Conseillers scolaires, travailleurs sociaux et infirmières
- Policiers
- Membres du clergé

- Psychothérapeutes

- Membres des centres d'intervention en cas d'abus et de violence familiale

- YWCA et YMCA

- *Le réseau enfants retour Canada* (www.enfantsretour.ca)

- *Centres d'aide et de lutte contre les agressions à caractère sexuel* (www.calacs.ca)

- *Jeunesse j'écoute* (www.jeunessejecoute.ca) (1-800-668-6868)

- *Société de l'aide à l'enfance d'Ottawa* (SAE) (www.casott.on.ca)

- *Centre des enfants, des familles et le système de justice* (www.lfcc.on.ca)

Par exemple, la *Société de l'aide à l'enfance* (SAE) a pour objectif d'assurer que les enfants reçoivent la sécurité et les soins nécessaires de leurs parents. Si vous connaissez un ou des enfants qui sont maltraités, un appel téléphonique à la SAE apportera une aide immédiate à un enfant victime d'abus ou de négligence. C'est un agent de la SAE qui répond à votre appel et qui est responsable de l'enquête et de la gestion des cas d'enfants agressés.

« Il vaut mieux prévenir que guérir! » Ce principe de base demeure aussi vrai et peut être mis en pratique dès aujourd'hui comme le conseille Jocelyne Robert dans son livre « Te laisse pas faire! Les abus sexuels expliqués aux enfants »[13]; elle présente aux parents un ensemble de conseils à donner à leurs enfants pour bien les outiller contre les agressions sexuelles et l'inceste. En voici quelques extraits :

➢ *L'ENFANT DOIT SAVOIR :*

  o *Qu'il ne doit pas accepter des promesses et des cadeaux offerts par une personne qui lui propose de la suivre, homme ou femme, ou qui sollicite son aide; il ne doit même pas s'approcher d'une voiture pour répondre aux questions d'un automobiliste égaré;*

  o *Que le prédateur sexuel a souvent l'air normal et gentil;*

  o *Qu'il doit se méfier d'un individu qui recherche des situations de rapprochement physique avec lui;*

  o *Où et à qui s'adresser en cas de besoin pour être aidé.*

➢ *L'ENFANT DOIT AGIR :*

o *En s'éloignant dès qu'une situation lui semble louche;*

o *En racontant, à une personne de confiance, ce qui lui est arrivé;*

o *En allant, en votre absence, demander l'aide des personnes que vous lui avez recommandées.*

➢ *L'ENFANT DOIT COMPRENDRE :*

o *S'il ne comprend pas le pourquoi de la prudence, l'enfant aura tendance à dramatiser en s'inventant un cruel « monstre sexuel » qui n'a rien à voir avec le pédophile « affectueux ». Par ailleurs, si vous ne lui expliquez pas pourquoi il doit refuser les bonbons d'un étranger, il croira que c'est parce que les sucreries donnent des caries ou encore que ces friandises sont empoisonnées.*

o *Fournir des outils de prudence et de discernement à l'enfant, c'est un peu comme le faire vacciner. Cela ne l'empêche pas d'être en contact avec le virus ou la maladie, mais ça lui permet d'y résister.*

> ❋ *Documentez-vous et éduquez votre enfant à la sexualité d'abord.*
>
> ❋ *L'enfant est une personne à part entière, non un adulte en miniature.*
>
> ❋ *Respectez son âge, sa pudeur...*

J. Robert souligne certaines caractéristiques de l'agresseur familial (parent incestueux), l'agresseur familier (le pédophile), l'agresseur inconnu (pervers sympathique), et l'agresseur masqué (prédateur électronique).

## *L'AGRESSEUR FAMILIAL : POUR EN FINIR AVEC LE PARENT INCESTUEUX*

Voici quelques-unes des caractéristiques du parent incestueux :

- *Intérêt singulier à l'endroit des enfants;*
- *Favoritisme marqué envers un enfant de la famille;*
- *Rigidité excessive des méthodes éducatives;*
- *Propos contradictoires ou réponses évasives sur les malaises physiques de l'enfant (irritations, inflammations...) ainsi que sur ses troubles affectifs et psychologiques (stress, peur, déroute...);*

- *Emploi de moyens étonnants, déraisonnables ou démesurés pour éduquer et prendre soin de l'enfant;*

- *Consommation de pornographie juvénile (cette caractéristique n'est pas spécifique de l'agresseur familial).*

## L'AGRESSEUR FAMILIER : POUR EN FINIR AVEC LE PÉDOPHILE « AMI »

*L'agresseur « ami », c'est souvent l'entraîneur sportif, le chef scout, le gardien, le moniteur, etc. En raison même de la confiance qu'on lui témoigne, l'enfant est plus exposé à sa ruse. Il n'est pas rare qu'il envoûte d'abord les parents. Une mère monoparentale pourra croire qu'il incarne la figure masculine idéale dont son fils a besoin. Présent, disponible, à l'écoute, compréhensif, dévoué et serviable, il s'intéresse au progrès de l'enfant et lui consacre une grande attention. Si l'ami adulte de votre enfant est une sorte de saint, presque trop parfait pour être vrai, vigilance s'impose. Au-dessus de tout soupçon, il est souvent très respecté dans son milieu. Quand on y regarde de plus près, c'est souvent un grand enfant lui-même.*

Le parent est dans son droit de s'assurer du comportement de chacune des personnes (adultes/adolescents) en contact avec son enfant. J. Robert précise :

- *Ne présumez pas que les organismes s'en sont occupés;*
- *Rencontrez les personnes responsables des groupes qu'il fréquente;*
- *Informez-vous des méthodes de sélection du personnel, salarié ou bénévole;*
- *Exigez des références chaque fois que vous retenez les services d'un adulte pour s'occuper de votre enfant;*
- *Ne vous gênez pas pour demander les numéros d'assurance sociale et de permis de conduire. Une personne sans antécédent judiciaire ne sera pas embarrassée par ces demandes;*
- *Sachez être attentif aux changements d'attitude de votre enfant.*

---

* *Un enfant bien informé a plus de chances de ne pas devenir une victime.*
* *Apprenez-lui à trouver des solutions en gardant la tête froide.*

---

> ✳ *Écoutez-le, il vous écoutera; parlez-lui, il vous parlera; respectez-le, il se fera respecter.*

## L'AGRESSEUR INCONNU : POUR EN FINIR AVEC LE PERVERS SYMPATHIQUE

L'agresseur inconnu n'est pas habituellement connu de l'enfant, soutien J. Robert; une personne apparaît soudainement sur la route de votre enfant, dans sa belle voiture ou dans un parc; c'est l'homme ou la dame qui a perdu son chien et demande de l'aide aux enfants pour le retrouver; c'est l'adolescent amusant, qui présente aux enfants de nouvelles bagatelles électroniques. J. Robert rappelle aux parents les points essentiels à partager avec leurs enfants à l'égard de l'agresseur inconnu :

- *Défendez-lui de se trouver seul dans une foule ou dans un lieu isolé.*

- *Rappelez-lui qu'il ne doit jamais se laisser tenter par un cadeau ou une promesse de récompense. Que ces gâteries, tout comme les mauvais secrets, sont des présents empoisonnés.*

- *Formez au besoin avec vos voisins des groupes de solidarité : en notant les suspects, en partageant vos inquiétudes, en avertissant les policiers.*

- *Faites tout ce que vous pouvez pour que votre enfant ne se trouve pas au mauvais endroit au mauvais moment.*

## L'AGRESSEUR INCONNU : POUR EN FINIR AVEC LE PRÉDATEUR ÉLECTRONIQUE

J. Robert nous avertit que le prédateur électronique « *surfe* » *sur une quantité incroyable de matériel pornographique infantile, se procure des images qui nourrissent son érotisme tordu et s'y fait conforter dans sa déviance par les groupes de soutien aux pédophiles. Ceux-ci y décrivent, incognito, leurs fantasmes, s'encouragent mutuellement à assouvir leurs désirs, échangent leurs tactiques manipulatrices pour créer le contact avec l'enfant, puis pour obtenir audience auprès de lui.* » Ce paragraphe fait frissonner de terreur tout parent désireux de protéger son enfant de ces prédateurs invisibles. Voici donc quelques conseils du même auteur :

* *Si possible, bloquez à votre enfant l'accès des sites contenant de la pornographie, de la violence, de la pédophilie.*
* *Faites en sorte de placer l'ordinateur dans la salle familiale, surtout si votre enfant est âgé de 6 à 12 ans.*
* *Exigez qu'il ne transmette jamais ses coordonnées, pas même son nom, sans votre permission.*

Que feriez-vous si votre enfant vous confiait qu'il a été agressé sexuellement? Tout d'abord, il faut le croire, car il est rare l'enfant qui mentira à ce sujet. Il y a vingt ans, les parents ne croyaient pas toujours les enfants qui rapportaient ce crime. Aujourd'hui, les gens sont plus renseignés sur ce genre de comportement et vont encourager l'enfant à en parler. L'appui des membres de la famille est essentiel à l'enfant, pour que celui-ci ne vive pas l'isolement ou la culpabilité en dénonçant son agresseur. J. Robert résume ce qu'il faut faire si un enfant dévoile un abus :

* *Gardez votre calme.*
* *Prenez du temps pour parler avec l'enfant; informez-vous de ses préoccupations et de ses soucis.*

✳ *Encouragez-le à se confier, comme il le ferait s'il s'était fait voler son vélo.*

✳ *Écoutez-le attentivement s'il vous dit qu'il n'aime pas la personne à qui vous le confiez ou s'il décrit un abus indirectement : « Un de mes amis m'a raconté que... »*

✳ *Tentez de démêler les faits.*

✳ *Évitez les conclusions hâtives qui le bouleverseraient davantage.*

✳ *Encouragez-le à en parler sans le brusquer.*

✳ *Utilisez les mêmes mots que lui pour en parler.*

✳ *Tentez délicatement de lui faire préciser les faits s'il en parle de manière vague.*

✳ *Évitez les jugements et les reproches.*

✳ *Montrez que vous le comprenez. L'attitude de la première personne à recevoir la confidence est déterminante dans le processus de guérison de l'enfant. **C'est à ce moment précis que commence à se rétablir sa capacité de confiance en l'adulte.***

✳ *Rassurez-le en lui disant qu'il a bien fait de vous en parler.*

✳ *Affirmez qu'il n'est aucunement responsable. L'enfant, pour donner un sens à cet évènement, pourra croire que c'est arrivé par sa faute, qu'il est puni pour ses inconduites, réelles ou imaginaires.*

* *Offrez-lui votre protection, promettez-lui de l'aider, **et tenez cette promesse**.*

* *Signalez le cas à la Direction de la protection de la jeunesse (DPJ) si l'abus a lieu à l'intérieur de la famille et aux autorités policières si l'abus est extrafamilial.*

J'avais toujours du mal à écouter le récit d'une victime de l'inceste ou d'agressions sexuelles, particulièrement venant d'un enfant. Mais, avec ces lignes directrices, je suis maintenant mieux équipée pour être à l'écoute et pour guider la victime vers la protection et le soutien appropriés.

Il est pénible d'envisager l'idée de prévenir nos enfants contre la possibilité qu'ils soient agressés sexuellement; plus pénible encore si l'agresseur est un membre de la famille. Il faut outiller nos enfants avec les meilleures techniques de protection sans causer de torts ni de panique. Il importe aussi d'employer une méthode appropriée à l'âge de l'enfant lorsqu'il dénonce son agresseur. Il faut aussi dépasser le malaise profond qu'on ne peut s'empêcher d'éprouver dans de telles situations si on veut que nos enfants soient protégés contre la violence physique et sexuelle. Nous pouvons espérer qu'avec la sensibilisation du public, l'éducation et les programmes de prévention et de soutien contre les agressions sexuelles, nous pourrons voir le jour où l'inceste et les agressions sexuelles ne seront plus des composants de notre société.

# « *Nous n'héritons pas de la Terre de nos ancêtres, nous l'empruntons à nos enfants.* »

Antoine de Saint-Exupéry

**CHAPITRE 6**

# VOS ENFANTS N'ONT PLUS À VIVRE AVEC L'INCESTE

Qu'est-ce que l'on doit faire maintenant? Que peut faire un survivant de l'inceste pour mettre en place ce nouvel héritage? Comment peut-on s'assurer que l'inceste ne se produira plus dans les générations à venir? Il est impossible de contrôler les gestes des autres; mais quant à moi, je me suis donné comme objectif de rompre le silence qui entoure l'inceste. J'ai, par ma persistance et mes efforts, surmonté les effets de l'inceste, et j'ai pu changer ma vie pour que cette affliction ne soit pas transmise à mon enfant. Il revient à chaque survivant de choisir : soit propager l'inceste, soit apporter les changements qui lui offriront une vie saine, responsable et honorable.

J'ai créé, pour moi-même, une affirmation quotidienne afin de me concentrer sur mon objectif :

> **« J'ai réussi à ne pas propager l'inceste. J'ai complètement transformé le destin de ma descendance. Je prends les mesures nécessaires pour me construire**

**et m'éduquer afin d'apporter un nouvel héritage aux miens. Je suis bienveillante, saine d'esprit et de cœur. Mon héritage est bâti sur l'amour, le respect, la confiance en soi, la compassion, la communication, la bonté, la bonne volonté et la non-violence. Les chaînes de l'inceste ne font plus partie de mon héritage, de notre héritage. »**

À l'âge de 12 ans, j'avais dit à ma grand-mère maternelle que je serais aussi grande en sagesse qu'elle lorsque j'atteindrais mes 14 ans. Elle m'avait souri tendrement et avait acquiescé sans mot dire. Elle était la meilleure grand-mère que j'aurais pu espérer dans ma vie. Elle est décédée il y a plusieurs années et je peux encore sentir son regard rempli d'amour et de bonté sur moi. Son cœur d'or a été mon héritage; cette bonté, comme grand-mère, je la transmets à mes petites-filles. J'aimerais bien être avec ma fille lorsqu'elle deviendra grand-mère. Quel beau cadeau d'amour à léguer! Ce que je lègue à ma fille et à sa petite famille, c'est ce que j'avais espéré pour moi. Ç'a été ma façon d'effacer l'héritage que m'avait légué mon père. Ma victoire a été de m'assurer qu'aucun de mes enfants ou petits-enfants n'endurerait la souffrance que mon père m'avait fait subir.

Pour me donner ou reprendre la force et le pouvoir qui m'avaient été si cruellement volés, je me suis promis, à l'âge de 17 ans, de rebâtir ma vie. Cette promesse est devenue l'objectif de ma survie. Je voulais apprendre à bien aimer. Je voulais trouver la façon saine d'aimer et d'être aimé. Depuis ce jour, avant chaque grande étape ou décision de vie, je me pose la question suivante : « Pour ce que je m'apprête à faire (soit pour moi-même, soit pour d'autres), est-ce que mon geste, ma parole ou ma pensée sont aimables, sincères, et essentiels à l'attente de mon objectif? » Avec cette question souvent méditée, j'ai transformé un héritage de haine, de trahison, de confusion, de frustration, d'abus et de malhonnêteté *en un héritage d'amour, de sincérité, d'honnêteté, de prospérité et de bonté.*

L'un de mes plus grands défis a été de remettre la responsabilité de l'abus sur les épaules de mon père. Cette déclaration peut sembler étrange; mais mon père, tout comme le père de l'amie dont je parle au chapitre 3, nous ont tous deux rendues responsables de leurs agressions. J'ai donc dû prendre du recul de la famille afin de démêler la culpabilité et la confusion qui s'étaient accrochées à moi.

Pour y réussir, j'ai consulté un thérapeute spécialisé dans les cas d'agressions sexuelles, qui me fournirait une vision objective de ma situation familiale. J'en avais consulté deux avant d'en trouver un avec qui j'étais à l'aise. Je crois que c'était la première fois que je me donnais la permission d'être sélective. Il faut beaucoup de travail pour effacer les traumatismes associés à l'inceste. En choisissant le conseiller qui me convenait, j'ai ressenti immédiatement que j'avais le contrôle de ma guérison. Par le biais de la thérapie, j'ai appris à être ma meilleure amie.

C'est d'une importance primordiale pour le cheminement vers votre bien-être de choisir un thérapeute ou une conseillère formée dans le domaine de la violence familiale. Car les conséquences de ne pas avoir été bien avisé pourraient retarder ou même empêcher votre guérison. Donc, assurez-vous que votre choix de thérapeute vous convient, à vous.

Entre les rencontres avec mon thérapeute, dans ces intervalles de quelques semaines ou de quelques mois, j'essayais d'analyser le bien que la thérapie m'avait fait; je prenais le temps d'intégrer les méthodes suggérées par le thérapeute. Ces périodes de réflexion m'aidaient à me découvrir mentalement, spirituellement et physiquement. J'ai compris, parce que mon corps avait été violé sans mon consentement et, plus précisément, sans que j'aie eu la capacité d'empêcher mon père de me blesser, que les souvenirs de ce mal étaient logés dans différentes parties de mon corps.

J'ai suivi des méthodes d'entraînement qui s'intégraient favorablement à mon physique, mon caractère et ma philosophie de la vie. Par exemple, j'ai appris que la méditation et les exercices de yoga pouvaient réaligner les sept chakras correctement. Le chakra qui me posait le plus grand problème était le chakra *Mulâdhâra* ou *Le Centre de la Base*. Ce chakra est situé à la base de la colonne vertébrale. Depuis l'adolescence jusqu'à la quarantaine, une mauvaise digestion, des brûlures d'estomac et la constipation mettaient mon corps à l'épreuve quotidiennement.

Grâce aux diverses méthodes de traitement, tels qu'un bon régime alimentaire, le yoga, le jogging, la méditation, l'acupuncture, les produits naturopathiques, les affirmations positives, j'ai réussi à soulager mon corps des émotions et pensées envahissantes du passé. Ces méthodes utilisées à différentes étapes de mon cheminement vers la récupération redonnaient à mon corps et à mon esprit l'énergie dont j'avais besoin pour élever mon enfant, faire mon travail et recréer un nouvel héritage pour le bien de ma descendance.

Je me suis libérée des traumatismes associés à l'inceste qui s'étaient logés dans les différentes parties de mon corps. Essentiellement, j'ai pris connaissance des réactions et attitudes qui m'habitaient, telles que la nervosité, la timidité, les crises d'anxiété, la méfiance, l'intolérance, la faible estime de moi, l'hostilité, la rudesse, la vengeance. Mon comportement le plus autodestructeur était mon besoin d'amour; je voulais que les autres m'aiment avant même que je m'aime moi-même. Tous ces comportements et ces émotions devaient être reconnus et acceptés pour être enfin modifiés. Avec les traitements, j'apprenais à me prendre en main — à gérer toutes les facettes de mon existence physique, mentale et spirituelle.

En plus de soigner mon corps et mon esprit, j'ai dû trouver une nouvelle voie spirituelle autre que la religion catholique. Il a fallu que je renonce même à participer aux messes hebdomadaires, car ces cérémonies me rendaient anxieuse et aigrie. Certains prêtres catholiques ont été liés aux agressions sexuelles d'enfants pendant plusieurs décennies et, en participant à leurs rituels religieux, j'avais l'impression d'accepter ou de soutenir leurs comportements.

À l'âge de 17 ans, ma quête d'une nouvelle philosophie spirituelle m'amena à étudier une myriade de livres sur la spiritualité, le paganisme, le bouddhisme et la méditation Vipassana. J'ai également eu recours aux traitements alternatifs comme le reiki, l'acupuncture, la massothérapie et la naturopathie, au lieu de prendre les médicaments prescrits. J'ai même suivi les enseignements d'une secte spirituelle dont j'ai appris les exercices contemplatifs pour améliorer ma concentration et retrouver mon équilibre. Je ne craignais pas de m'exposer à tout cela pour effacer les traumatismes de mon passé. Il n'y eut que quelques personnes dans mon entourage pour me taquiner, mais jamais méchamment, à propos de tout cet apprentissage que j'entreprenais. Je prenais leurs taquineries en souriant, parce que j'étais sûre que ma santé et mon esprit s'amélioraient. J'étais partie pour la plus grande mission de ma vie et je m'accordais la liberté de choisir le mode de guérison que je jugeais approprié à cette phase de ma récupération.

Comme je l'avais prévu, ces méthodes d'apprentissage m'ont aidée à avancer et à enrichir ma vie et la vie de ceux que j'aime. Je maintiens toujours mes rencontres avec une thérapeute lorsque mon quotidien devient trop tumultueux. Pour moi, il n'y a aucune honte à s'assurer que la tête et le coeur sont en bon état. Le but de ces rencontres est de m'aider à prendre grand soin de moi pour mieux vivre et mieux aimer mes proches. Après tout, on ne décerne pas de médaille de bravoure à ceux qui souffrent inutilement. Je veille à toujours choisir le thérapeute professionnel qui convient à l'étape où je suis rendue dans mon cheminement; je me dois d'être à mon aise durant ces rencontres pour en tirer le plus grand profit.

Pour que la thérapie m'apporte les résultats espérés, j'arrive toujours avec une liste de questions déjà préparées. Durant la rencontre, je prends le temps de noter, si nécessaire, les points saillants de notre échange. Pourquoi faire cet exercice avant la rencontre? Pour moi, ce petit devoir me donne une direction et de la concentration sur les points importants de ma guérison. Ces notes me permettent de ne pas oublier les questions essentielles à traiter et de souligner au thérapeute mes préoccupations du moment.

Je comprends mieux maintenant pourquoi je ne peux travailler que sur quelques difficultés à la fois. J'ai compris l'importance de la confiance absolue en son thérapeute après qu'une amie m'eut confié que pendant dix années de thérapie elle n'avait jamais pu dévoiler à son psychologue que c'était son père qui l'avait agressée sexuellement... elle avait attribué ce crime à son voisin. Peut-être ne pouvait-elle pas parler de sa situation en raison d'un malaise particulier ou n'était-elle pas assez confiante en son thérapeute pour lui dévoiler sa véritable situation. Quelles que soient ses raisons, sa thérapie lui a coûté très cher en raison des nombreuses années supplémentaires qu'elle a dû y consacrer.

Quant à moi, je m'étais alloué moins de temps pour ces séances thérapeutiques, mais plus de temps pour d'autres méthodes alternatives de santé (yoga, contemplation, etc.). J'avais toujours le même but en tête — il fallait me guérir le plus effectivement et économiquement possible et intégrer les changements nécessaires, pour me permettre de créer pour ma fille, un héritage débarrassé de l'inceste et de ses effets nocifs. Lorsque j'ai entrepris de me soigner, j'ai veillé à obtenir les soins les mieux adaptés à ma situation – c'était indispensable pour ma santé mentale. Le temps était venu de lever le masque sur le crime de mon père. Durant mon rétablissement, j'ai travaillé avec trois thérapeutes différents; chacun a contribué à mon cheminement vers une vie plus saine et plus heureuse.

Avec le temps, j'ai constaté qu'avoir bien choisi ma thérapie et mes thérapeutes avait porté ses fruits. Je m'affirmais davantage. Je retrouvais une force intérieure que j'avais perdue. J'étais moins dépressive et moins triste. Je menais ma propre barque vers une vie plus saine et plus attrayante. Je prenais conscience de tout ceci pendant mes moments de réflexion.

J'ai dressé une liste de quelques-unes des activités qui ont contribué à mon bonheur, à ma croissance et à mon moral pendant cette période de retour à la santé.

**Mes activités pour maintenir un esprit sain :**

- Méditer quotidiennement (pour faciliter la méditation, voir la référence pour les livres à l'Annexe B de William Hart, Steve Hagen, Phillip Moffitt, et Sakyong Mipham).
- Participer à une classe de tai-chi
- Faire des randonnées
- Cuisiner
- Aller à l'opéra
- Recevoir des amis
- Voyager en train, en avion, en auto
- Nourrir les oiseaux
- Amuser mes petites-filles
- Jardiner
- Écrire
- Témoigner de la reconnaissance
- Répandre l'amour

Grâce à ces activités, je suis heureuse. Je ne pouvais soupçonner la force et l'énergie qui étaient en moi pour apporter tant de changements à mon destin. Ce processus de guérison que je m'étais façonné a fait que j'ai pu relever les défis de mon cheminement; toutes mes luttes et mes efforts en ont valu la peine.

Lorsque l'harmonie règne dans son milieu, il est plus facile d'être créatif et d'inventer des moyens d'améliorer sa vie quotidienne. Pour moi, le jardinage embellit mon entourage, l'écriture m'aide à inspirer d'autres personnes. Toutes mes activités m'aident à être saine et équilibrée. Je m'aime mieux lorsque je suis dynamique et enthousiaste.

Je crois que mon nouvel héritage a fait de moi une personne bien intentionnée. Mes épreuves m'ont donné une compréhension de la souffrance humaine et m'ont fait découvrir ma force intérieure. J'ai mis au point plusieurs techniques qui me permettent de me libérer sainement de vieux traumatismes qui resurgissent à l'occasion.

Pourquoi ne pas demander à notre gouvernement de créer une journée de sensibilisation spécifiquement pour les survivants de l'inceste; des châtiments plus sévères pour les agresseurs sexuels? Nous devons exiger, pour l'amour de tous nos enfants, une société où l'inceste et les agressions sexuelles ne sont aucunement tolérés, où nous ne sommes plus silencieux et passifs devant la souffrance infligée à nos enfants. Il faut être vigilants, à l'écoute et prévoyants — en tout temps. Nous devons insister pour que notre société traite les enfants avec amour, dévouement et bienséance. C'est notre droit et notre devoir.

Comme êtres humains, nous choisissons, si nous le voulons, de grandir et d'évoluer. La vie n'est certainement pas pour les lâches. Plusieurs enseignants, conseillers et mentors m'ont inspirée et j'en suis reconnaissante. Malgré mon enfance dénaturée, mes expériences de vie et mes méthodes de rétablissement m'ont apporté la compassion, la compréhension, le respect et, surtout, l'amour.

Souvent, les gens me demandent si j'ai pardonné à mon père sa conduite. Oui, j'ai pardonné à mon père lorsqu'il m'a demandé le pardon. Mais je vous avoue que j'étais bien perplexe par cet échange; c'est comme s'il me demandait que je l'acquitte de sa peine.

Après réflexion, je ne crois pas que c'est même en mon pouvoir de lui pardonner. Je ne sais pas au juste qui peut lui accorder ce pardon, mais cette responsabilité n'est pas la mienne. Ce que je sais, c'est que pour me permettre d'avancer dans la vie, il fallait d'abord que je ME pardonne.

D'une autre part, je n'ai jamais songé à me venger de mon sort sur mon père. L'éducation contre l'ignorance était mon moyen de me défendre. Écrire ce livre est ma façon de combattre l'ignorance qui permet une société de prétendre que l'inceste n'existe pas dans nos familles.

Je savais, très jeune, que tout acte de vengeance ou de haine envers mon père m'aurait maintenue près de lui et m'aurait empêchée de guérir et de tourner la page. Mon but premier n'était pas là. Il était de transformer mon héritage et d'éradiquer l'inceste de la société.

Des défenseurs comme l'honorable Muriel McQueen Fergusson, Madeleine Delaney-LeBlanc, le docteur Peter Jaffe, Rona Brown et le docteur Donald G. Dutton, sont de ceux qui ont accompli d'innombrables réalisations dans la prévention de la violence familiale. Ils ont travaillé sans relâche à la prévention et à l'élimination de la violence familiale. Pour vaincre la brutalité entre êtres humains, il nous faut intensifier la sensibilisation et la compréhension de ce problème mondial. De plus, il faut soutenir et encourager les victimes et les survivants à dénoncer leurs malfaiteurs. J'espère qu'ensemble nous pourrons mettre fin à cette grande souffrance humaine. J'ose espérer qu'un jour tous les êtres humains auront évolué et aspireront à une société sans cruauté, ni maltraitance, ni ignorance.

J'ai amorcé mon parcours de guérison comme adolescente qui luttait contre les chaînes d'un héritage incestueux et j'ai transformé mon héritage avec succès. Il est pertinent que je termine ce livre par un poème que j'ai écrit pour ma fille il y a plusieurs années...

*Ma première leçon d'amour*

*Suite à maintes leçons faillies*
*Je m'étais ensevelie dans une furie.*
*Alourdi par un corps et un esprit fatigué*
*J'ai tout de même donné naissance à ma fille aînée.*
*Elle pouvait donner tant d'amour*
*Sans en exiger en retour.*
*Son amour a illuminé ma vie*
*Et a été la source éternelle de ma survie.*
*Grâce à sa naissance*
*Je baigne maintenant dans la reconnaissance.*

Chapitre 7

# Références

1. Agence de la santé publique du Canada/Centre national d'information sur la violence dans la famille (CNIVF). *Counseling en matière de violence sexuelle. Guide à l'intention des parents et des enfants*. 2008, (p. 5).

**Tous les guides de l'Agence de la santé publique du Canada sont offerts au site Web : http://www.phac-aspc.gc.ca/ncfv-cnivf/nfntsabus-fra.php. Courriel : national_clearinghouse@hc-sc.gc.ca.**

2. Agence de la santé publique du Canada/CNIVF. *L'agression sexuelle d'enfants*. 1997, (pp. 3-4).

3. Young, Val. (1994). *Women Abusers: A Feminist View. Female Sexual Abuse of Children*. New York: Guilford Press. 1994, (pp. 100-114).

4. Agence de la santé publique du Canada/CNIVF. *Counseling en matière de violence sexuelle. Guide à l'intention des parents et des enfants*. 2008, (pp. 4-5).

5. Agence de la santé publique du Canada/CNIVF. *Les survivants et survivantes adultes de l'abus sexuel dans l'enfance*. 2002, (pp. 3-5).

6. Agence de la santé publique du Canada/CNIVF. *Counseling en matière de violence sexuelle. Guide à l'intention des parents et des enfants*. 2008, (pp. 4-5).

7. American Psychological Association. *Understanding Child Sexual Abuse: Education, Prevention, and Recovery*. http://www.apa.org/pubs/info/brochures/sex-abuse.aspx. 2010, (p.8).

8. Tobin, Pnina. & Levinson-Kessner, Sue. *Keeping Kids Safe - A Child Sexual Abuse Prevention Manual*. Alameda, CA : Hunter House. 2002, 192 pages.

9. Agence de la santé publique du Canada/CNIVF. *Les survivants et survivantes adultes de l'abus sexuel dans l'enfance*. 2002, (p. 3).

10. Tobin, Pnina. & Levinson-Kessner, Sue. *Keeping Kids Safe - A Child Sexual Abuse Prevention Manual*. Alameda, CA : Hunter House. 2002, 192 pages.

11. *Centre d'intervention en abus sexuels pour la famille*. www.ciasf.org. 92, boul. St-Raymond, Gatineau, QC.

Téléphone : 819.595.1905 ou, sans frais, le 1.888.368.7243. Adresse courriel : info@ciasf.org.

12. Agence de la santé publique du Canada/CNIVF. *Counseling en matière de violence sexuelle Guide à l'intention des parents et des enfants.* 2008, (p. 3).

13. Robert, Jocelyne. *Te laisse pas faire! Les abus sexuels expliqués aux enfants.* Montréal : Les Éditions de l'Homme. 2005, 112 pages.

## Ressources utiles

Berry, Joy, W. *Abus sexuel : Avertir les enfants du danger c'est déjà les protéger.* Québec : Jean-Paul Saint-Michel. 1996, 56 pages.

Brillon, Pascale. *Se relever d'un traumatisme – Réapprendre à vivre et à faire confiance.* Montréal : Les Éditions Québécor. 2010, 272 pages.

Foucault, Pierre. *L'abus sexuel – l'intervention.* Montréal : Les Éditions Logiques. 1990, 132 pages.

Lamarche, M., Danheux, P. et Tibo. *Apprends à dire non : Se protéger des agressions.* Montréal : Éditions de l'Homme. 1993, 63 pages.

**Annexe A**

**Voici quelques livres pour aider les parents à préparer leurs enfants à se protéger et à dialoguer avec eux à propos de situations à risques d'agressions sexuelles**

- Boegehold, Betty. *Pourquoi faut-il parfois dire non? Un livre sur la protection*. France : Deux Coqs D'or. 1986, 32 pages.

- Justice du Canada. *Le secret du petit cheval*. Lien pour obtenir cette publication : http://publications.gc.ca/site/fra/83923/publication.html. 1999, 15 pages.

- Lenain, Thierry. *Touche pas à mon corps, Tatie Jacotte!* Montréal : Éditions Les 400 coups. 1999, 32 pages.

- Robert, Jocelyne. *Full Sexuel...La vie amoureuse des adolescents*. Montréal : Les Éditions de l'Homme. 2002, 192 pages.

- Robert, Jocelyne. *Parlez-leur d'amour...et de sexualité*. Montréal : Les Éditions de l'Homme. 1999, 192 pages.

- Robert, Jocelyne. *Te laisse pas faire! Les abus sexuels expliqués aux enfants*. Montréal : Les Éditions de l'Homme. 2005, 112 pages.

**Les guides suivants, en document PDF, sont offerts par l'Agence de la santé publique du Canada au site Web :** *http://www.phac-aspc.gc.ca/ncfv-cnivf/nfntsabus-fra.php*

***Les adolescentes victimes de violence sexuelle : Guide à l'intention des adolescentes***

- Conçue pour les adolescentes qui ont été victimes d'agressions sexuelles, cette brochure donne un aperçu de la violence sexuelle et de ses effets, en insistant sur le récit d'adolescentes qui en ont été victimes. Elle explique quelles sont les lois sur la délinquance sexuelle et précise ce qu'il est possible d'accomplir grâce au counseling et aux groupes de soutien. 2008, 19 pages.

***Les adolescents qui ont été agressés sexuellement: Guide à l'intention des adolescents***

- Conçue pour les adolescents qui ont été victimes d'agressions sexuelles, cette brochure donne un aperçu de la violence sexuelle et de ses effets, en insistant sur le récit d'adolescents qui en ont été victimes. Elle explique quelles sont les lois sur la délinquance sexuelle et précise ce qu'il est possible d'accomplir grâce au counseling et aux groupes de soutien. 2008, 19 pages.

*Les agressions sexuelles : Que se passe-t-il lorsqu'on en parle?*
*Guide à l'intention des enfants et des parents*

- Cette brochure est conçue pour aider les enfants qui ont
  été victimes de violence sexuelle. Elle explique pourquoi
  l'enfant doit en parler et à qui il doit en parler. Elle précise
  les réactions que peuvent avoir les membres de la famille
  et ce que les travailleurs sociaux et les policiers font
  lorsqu'on leur signale une agression sexuelle. Elle décrit
  brièvement la procédure judiciaire lorsque le cas est porté
  devant un tribunal.  2008, 13 pages.

*Les agressions sexuelles entre frères et sœurs : Guide à*
*l'intention des parents*

- Cette brochure a été écrite pour les parents qui veulent
  comprendre ou empêcher la violence sexuelle entre frères
  et sœurs dans leur propre famille ou y mettre un terme.
  Elle explique quelques-uns des facteurs qui contribuent à
  la violence sexuelle entre frères et sœurs et décrit ses
  effets sur les victimes.  2008, 18 pages.

*Counseling en matière de violence sexuelle : Guide à l'intention*
*des enfants et des parents*

- Cette brochure, destinée aux adultes, explique comment le counseling peut les aider à se remettre d'une agression sexuelle, selon qu'ils en sont l'auteur ou la victime. Elle décrit les effets des sévices sexuels et identifie le rôle des conseillers et des membres de la famille pour aider à surmonter cette pénible expérience. 2008, 12 pages.

*Les enfants sexuellement agressifs : Guide à l'intention des parents et des enseignants*

- Cette brochure évoque les étapes du développement sexuel normal et explique comment reconnaître et faire face au comportement sexuellement agressif des enfants. Elle fournit des réponses aux questions les plus courantes sur la violence sexuelle et le comportement sexuel inadéquat. La brochure explique comment les parents, les enseignants et les autres peuvent aider un enfant sexuellement agressif. 2008, 12 pages.

*Les filles victimes de violence sexuelle : Guide à l'intention des très jeunes filles*

- Cette brochure décrit les expériences et sentiments de sept filles qui ont été victimes de violence sexuelle. Elle insiste sur le fait que les sévices sexuels sont néfastes. La brochure explique comment obtenir de l'aide et ce à quoi il faut s'attendre après la divulgation de la violence. 2008, 13 pages.

***Les hommes qui ont été victimes de violence sexuelle durant l'enfance : Un guide à l'intention des hommes***

- Cette brochure porte sur certaines des questions les plus fréquentes des hommes qui ont été victimes de violence sexuelle pendant leur enfance. Elle fournit des indications sur l'identification des sévices sexuels, les moyens pour obtenir de l'aide et ce qu'il faut attendre du counseling. Elle donne aussi des conseils sur la manière d'annoncer à son conjoint qu'on a été victime de violence sexuelle. 2008, 17 pages.

***Les jeunes garçons victimes de violence sexuelle : Guide à l'intention des jeunes garçons***

- Cette brochure décrit les expériences et les sentiments de sept garçons qui ont été victimes de violence sexuelle. Elle insiste sur le fait que les sévices sexuels sont néfastes. La brochure explique comment obtenir de l'aide et ce qu'il faut attendre d'un parent ou d'un conseiller en la matière. 2008, 16 pages.

***Lorsque notre conjoint ou conjointe a été victime de violence sexuelle durant l'enfance : Guide à l'intention des conjoints***

- Conçue pour les conjoints de ceux qui ont été victimes d'abus sexuels lorsqu'ils étaient enfants ou adolescents, cette brochure évoque les effets des sévices sexuels sur le conjoint ainsi que sur la relation de couple. Elle fait le point sur divers sujets à l'aide d'une série de questions et de réponses ainsi que de vignettes personnelles. 2008, 19 pages.

***Manuel de pratique sensible à l'intention des professionnels de la santé – Leçons tirées des personnes qui ont été victimes de violence sexuelle durant l'enfance***

- Ce guide est conçu pour aider les professionnels de la santé à répondre aux besoins des adultes survivants d'abus sexuel pendant l'enfance. Il offre des renseignements de base sur les abus sexuels pendant l'enfance et explique en quoi ces abus peuvent nuire aux rencontres avec  tout professionnel de la santé. Les principes et les directives sur la pratique sensible présentés dans le guide sont le fruit d'un dialogue entre des survivants et des professionnels de la santé et exposent à grands traits des conseils complets et pratiques que tout professionnel de la santé peut appliquer dans le cadre de la pratique clinique. 2009, 142 pages.

**Répertoire des services aux survivantes et survivants adultes de violence sexuelle à l'égard des enfants**

Ce répertoire présente une liste de programmes qui répondent aux besoins des survivantes et survivants adultes de violence sexuelle à l'égard des enfants. Les organisations offrent du counseling en groupe et individuel à l'intervention d'urgence et individuelle. Chaque inscription indique si les services sont destinés aux femmes, aux hommes ou aux enfants, si des frais sont exigés et si ces services sont offerts en français et en anglais. 2009, 119 pages.

**Annexe B**

Les livres suivants m'ont aidée à franchir les étapes d'une position de victime de l'inceste à une survivante de l'inceste.

**<u>Livres pour promouvoir la guérison personnelle</u>**

Arrowsmith-Young, Barbara. *The Woman Who Changed Her Brain*. New York: Simon & Shuster. 2012, 261 pages.

Beattie, M. *Codependent No More: How to Stop Controlling Others and Start Caring for Yourself.* Minnesota: Hazelden Foundation. 1996, 254 pages.

Bradshaw, John. *Creative Love: The Next Great Stage of Growth.* New York: Bantam. 1992, 374 pages.

Byrne, Rhonda. *The Secret.* New York: Beyond Words Publishing. 2006, 198 pages.

Carnegie, Dale. *How to Win Friends*. New York : Simon & Schuster. 1981, 260 pages.

Carroll Moore, Mary. *How to Master Change in Your Life: Sixty-Seven Ways to Handle Life's Toughest Moments.* Minneapolis, MN: Eckankar. 1997, 368 pages.

Eden, Donna. & Feinstein, David. *Energy Medicine*. New York: Penguin Putnam. 1998, 378 pages.

Feinstein, D. & Krippner, S. *The Mythic Path*. Santa Rosa, CA: Energy Psychology. 2006, 326 pages.

Muni, Swami Rajarshi. *Yoga, the Ultimate Spiritual Path*. Minnesota: Llewellyn. 2001, 184 pages.

Myss, Caroline, Ph.D. *Anatomy of the Spirit: The Seven Stages of Power and Healing*. New York: Three River Press/Crown Publishing Group. 1996, 302 pages.

Peck, Scott. *A World Waiting to Be Born: Civility Rediscovered*. New York: Bantam. 1993, 366 pages.

Pinkola Estés, Clarissa. *Women Who Run With Wolves: Myths and Stories of the Wild Woman Archetype*. New York: Random House. 1992, 520 pages.

Robinson, Ken. PH.D. & Aronica, L. *The Element: How Finding Your Passion Changes Everything*. New York: Penguin Group. 2009, 274 pages.

Sams, Jamie & Carson, David. *Medicine Cards*. New York: St. Martin's Press. 1999, 246 pages.

Stern, Ellen Sue. *La femme indispensable*. Montréal : Les Éditions de l'Homme. 1989, 296 pages.

Tolle, Eckhart. *A New Earth: Awakening to Your Life's Purpose*. Canada: Penguin. 2006, 313 pages.

Tolle, Eckhart. *The Power of Now: A Guide to Spiritual Enlightenment*. Vancouver, B.C.: Namaste Publishing. 2004, 236 pages.

## Livres qui favorisent les bonnes valeurs humanitaires

Chopra, Deepak, M.D. *Ageless Body, Timeless Mind: The Quantum Alternative to Growing Old*. New York: Three River Press. 1993, 342 pages.

Chopra, Deepak, M.D. *Reinventing the Body, Resurrecting the Soul*. New York: Random House. 2009, 287 pages.

Craig, Sidney D. *Raising Your Child, Not by Force but by Love*. Philadelphia, PA: Westminster Press. 2003, 190 pages.

Faber, Adele. & Mazlish, Elaine. *How to Talk So Kids Will Listen & Listen So Kids Will Talk*. New York: Avon Books. 1999, 286 pages.

Hay, Louise. L. *You Can Heal Your Life*. Carlsbad, CA: Hay House. 1999, 267 pages.

Holmes, Ernest. *How to Change Your Life*. Florida: Health Communications. 1999, 317 pages.

Katie, Byron. *Loving What Is: Four Questions That Can Change Your Life*. New York: Random House. 2002, 322 pages.

Price, John Randolph. *The Abundance Book.* Carlsbad, CA: Hay House. 1987, 96 pages.

**Livres qui nous libèrent et nous ressourcent**

Altea, Rosemary. *Proud Spirit.* New York: Eagle Brook. 1997, 267 pages.

Avery, Mike. *The Secret Language of Waking Dreams.* Minneapolis: Eckankar. 1992, 137 pages.

Caponigro, Andy. *The Miracle of the Breath.* Novato, CA: New World Library. 2005, 316 pages.

Chödrön, Pema. *The Places That Scare You: A Guide to Fearlessness in Difficult Times.* Boston: Shambhala/Random House. 2002, 140 pages.

Coelho, Paulo. *By the River Piedra I Sat Down And Wept.* New York: HarperCollins. 1996, 210 pages.

Coelho, Paulo. *The Alchemist.* New York: HarperCollins. 1995, 177 pages.

Coelho, Paulo. *The Valkyries: An Encounter with Angels.* New York: HarperCollins. 1995, 245 pages.

Confalonieri, Pierluigi. *The Clock of Vipassana Has Struck.* Seattle: Vipassana. 1999, 256 pages.

Cyr, M. *Que la force d'attraction soit avec toi.* Montréal: Les Éditions Transcontinental. 2007, 144 pages.

Dalai Lama (His Holiness the) & Chan, Victor. *The Wisdom of Forgiveness.* New York: Berkley Publishing. 2004, 266 pages.

Dalai Lama (His Holiness the) & Cutler, H.C., M.D. *The Art of Happiness: A Handbook for Living.* New York: Penguin Putman. 1998, 322 pages.

Dalai Lama (His Holiness the). *Ancient Wisdom, Modern World: Ethics for the New Millennium.* London, UK: Abacus/Time Warner. 2003, 246 pages.

Davis, James. *The Rosetta Stone of God.* Minneapolis: Eckankar. 2000, 289 pages.

Gawain, Shakti, *Creative Visualization.* New York: Bantam. 1985, 127 pages.

Hagen, Steve. *Buddhism Plain & Simple: The Practice of Being Aware, Right Now, Every Day.* New York: Random House. 1997, 161 pages.

Hagen, Steve. *Meditation Now or Never.* New York: HarperCollins. 2007, 200 pages.

Hart, William. *The Art of Living: Vipassana Meditation as Taught by S.N. Goenka.* New York: HarperCollins Publishers. 1987, 167 pages.

Hughes-Calero, Heather. *The Golden Dream.* Carmel, CA: Coastline Publishing. 1987, 294 pages.

Hughes-Calero, Heather. *The Sedona Trilogy – Tome 1 to 3.* Carmel, CA: Coastline Publishing.

- **Tome 1**: *Through the Crystal.* 1985, 139 pages.

- **Tome 2:** *Doorway Between the Worlds.* 1985, 159 pages.

- **Tome 3:** *Land of Nome.* 1985, 157 pages.

Hughes-Calero, Heather. *Women Between the Wind.* Carmel, CA: Coastline Publishing. 1990, 156 pages.

Mipham, Sakyong. *Ruling Your World: Ancient Strategies for Modern Times.* New York: Morgan Road Books. 2005, p. 210.

Moffitt, Phillip. *Dancing with Life: Buddhist Insights for Finding Meaning and Joy in the Face of Suffering.* New York: Rodale. 2008, 309 pages.

Newton, Michael Ph.D. *Journey of Souls: Case Studies of Life between Lives.* St. Paul, Minnesota: Llewellyn publications. 1996, 280 pages.

Redfield, James & Adrienne, Carol. *The Celestine Prophecy: An Experiential Guide.* New York: Warner Books. 1995, 284 pages.

Redfield, James. *The Celestine Prophecy : An Adventure.* New York: Warner Books. 1993, 246 pages.

Redfield, James. *The Tenth Insight: Holding the Vision.* New York: Warner Books. 1996, 236 pages.

Revel, Jean-François & Ricard, Matthieu. *The Monk and the Philosopher.* New York: Random House. 1999, 351 pages.

Ricard, Matthieu & Xuanthuan, Trinh. *L'infini dans la paume de la main.* Paris : Édition Club France-Loisirs. 2001, 399 pages.

Ricard, Matthieu. *Happiness : A Guide to Developing Life's Most Important Skills.* New York: Hachette. 2006, 282 pages.

Ricard, Matthieu. *La Citadelle Des Neiges.* Paris : Édition France Loisirs. 2005, 111 pages.

Ricard, Matthieu. *Monk Dancers of Tibet.* Boston: Shambhala Publications. 2003, 125 pages.

Rinpoche, Yongey Mingyur & Swanson, Eric. *The Joy of Living: Unlocking the Secret & Science of Happiness.* New York: Harmony Books, Random House. 2007, 272 pages.

Rinpoche, Sogyal. *The Tibetan Book of Living and Dying.* New York: HarperCollins. 1993, 441 pages.

Sharma, Robin S. *The Monk Who Sold His Ferrari: A Spiritual Fable about Fulfilling Your Dreams and Reaching Your Destiny.* Toronto: HarperCollins Publishers. 1997, 198 pages.

Sharma, Robin S. *Who Will Cry When You Die? Life Lessons from the Monk Who Sold His Ferrari.* Toronto: HarperCollins Publishers. 1999, 225 pages.

Spalding, Baird T. *Life and Teaching of the Masters of the Far East (volume 1 to 6).* Camarillo, CA: DeVorss Publishing. (À partir de 1964 à 1996, l'auteur a publié 6 tomes dans cette série. Il y a environ 200 pages par tome).

Zukav, Gary. *The Seat of the Soul.* New York: Simon & Shuster. 1990, 256 pages.

## Livres pour apprendre à écrire ton histoire

Bettelheim, Bruno. *Psychanalyse des contes de fées.* Paris: Robert Laffont. 1976, 403 pages.

Burdette Sweet, Robert. *Writing Towards Wisdom: The Writer as Shaman.* Carmichael, CA : Helios House Publisher. 1990, 183 pages.

Demers, Dominique & Bleton, Paul. *Du petit Poucet au Dernier des raisins.* Boucherville, QC :Éditions Québec/Amérique Jeunesse. 1994, 253 pages.

Hughes-Calero, Heather. *Writing as a Tool for Self-Discovery.* Carmel, CA: Coastline Publishing. 1988, 125 pages.

Klausen, Henriette Anne. *Writing on Both Side of the Brain: Breakthrough Techniques for People Who Write.* San Francisco: Harper Collins. 1987, 143 pages.

Seuling, Barbara. *How to Write a Children's Book and Get It Published.* New York: Macmillan Publishing. 1991, 214 pages.

Williamson, Serena. Ph.D. *Write That Book: Guiding You from Inspiration to Publication.* Ottawa, ON: Book Coach Press. 2004, 127 pages.

**Par amour pour l'apprentissage**

Edwards, Betty. *Drawing on the Right Side of the Brain.* New York: Putman Publishing. 1989, 254 pages.

Gagnon, Yves. *Le jardin écologique.* Saint-Didace, QC : Les Éditions Colloïdales. 1993, 269 pages.

Gelb, Michael J. *How to Think Like Leonardo da Vinci: Seven Steps to Genius Every Day.* New York: Random House. 2004, 317 pages.

Hale, Gill. *How To Feng Shui Your Garden.* London, UK: Hermes House. 2000, 96 pages.

Lewis Paulson, Genevieve. *Kundalini Yoga and the Chakras: Evolution in This Lifetime.* Woodbury, MN: Llewellyn Publications. 2005, 222 pages.

Rossback, Sarah & Yun, Lin. *Living Color Master Lin Yun Guide to Feng Shui and The Art Of Color.* New York: Kodansha America. 1994, 173 pages.

Stein, Diane. *Essential Reiki: A Complete Guide to an Ancient Healing Art.* Berkeley, CA: The Crossing Press. 1995, 156 pages.

Stein, Rebecca L. & Stein, Philip L. *The Anthropology of Religion, Magic, and Witchcraft.* New York: Kensington. 2002, 336 pages.

Whitaker, Hazel. *Numerology: A Mystical Magical Guide.* Vancouver: Lansdowne. 1998, 79 pages.

*Mise en page : Pierre Arvisais*
*Gatineau (Québec) Canada*

*ISBN 978-2-923953-10-6*


*Imprimé sur papier contenant des fibres post-consommation, à*
*l'Imprimerie Gauvin*
*Gatineau (Québec) Canada*

For Alan and Oliver

# CONTENTS

# ACKNOWLEDGEMENTS

Several patient souls have encouraged me on this, my third Mallorcan odyssey. They include my ingenious legal-eagle nephew Alexander, long-standing friend Sari Andreu (aka Catalina), Professor Adrian Lister from the Natural History Museum in London and Roger Katz from Hatchards Bookshop. I am hugely grateful for the kind support of Pere and Margarita Serra of the Serra Newspaper Group, Ignacio Vasallo of Turespaña, Jelle Reumer, director of The Rotterdam Natural History Museum, Carolina Constantino of Museu Balear de Ciències Naturals, Joan Bolart Xarrié, Jackie Waldren and Lluc Garcia, editor of the Sóller newspaper. Thanks too must go to Karolyn Shindler for her inspirational biography about Dorothea Bate, entitled *Discovering Dorothea*. I would also like to give a special mention to the commissioning editor, Jennifer Barclay, and the editorial team at Summersdale for having given me the opportunity to weave my tale.

Finally, my deepest gratitude goes to our local Mallorcan community for having welcomed Alan, Ollie and me so warmly to Sóller's golden valley.

# ABOUT THE AUTHOR

As a freelance journalist, Anna Nicholas has contributed to titles such as the *Financial Times*, *The Independent*, *Tatler*, the *Daily Express* and the *Evening Standard* and contributes a monthly column to the magazine *Spain*, and a weekly column to the *Majorca Daily Bulletin*. She is a fellow of the Royal Geographical Society and has been an international invigilator for Guinness World Records. Together with explorer Colonel John Blashford-Snell she has also organised an expedition to carry a grand piano to the remote Wai Wai tribe in South America, which was the subject of a BBC TV documentary.

# AUTHOR'S NOTE

Most of the local vernacular used in this book is in the Mallorcan dialect. Although Mallorcan is derived from Catalan and is believed to have been spoken for more than five or six centuries, it varies greatly when written. During the Franco era, Mallorcan was forbidden in Balearic schools and this has made it an oral language, reliant on Catalan when transcribed to print because no dictionary in Mallorcan exists. Today, Catalan is the main language used in Mallorcan schools with the Mallorcan dialect being spoken in the street and in the home. The vocabulary and spelling often varies greatly from village to village in Mallorca. I have taken advice from local language experts and so hope to have accurately transcribed the Mallorcan language to print. However, I apologise unreservedly to any fervent linguists who may care to differ!

# ONE

# SHOOTING STARS

'CUTTTTTT...!'

My eyes ping open. A clutter of raised voices assails my ears, one high-pitched and feverish, another thunderous and the last plaintive. Now what? Can't I enjoy five minutes' shut-eye, my first since the crack of dawn, without World War Three breaking out? I'm beginning to wonder if my sole role on this gruelling film shoot is as a one-woman peacekeeping taskforce. Squinting up from my sun lounger at a sky the colour of washed denim, I try to contemplate what kind of drama is unfolding at the poolside. Perhaps Anastasia has broken her little toenail or lost her eyeliner or, worse, Greedy George has hidden her vodka glass. An elegant falcon glides overhead, caught on a whisper of briny breeze, then in one swift move dives seawards and is gone. I have been hanging about the hotel gardens since 6 a.m., watching the sky turn from dusky rose to pale blue, and wondering when my torment will end. This was supposed to have been a one-day wonder but unless the shoot is wrapped up within the hour, we'll be back here again tomorrow morning. A huge form suddenly blocks out the sun. It's Greedy George. George Myers, to be exact, an old client who wafts between an ever-so-chic three-story affair in South Kensington and a brownstone apartment block on New York's Upper East Side. Now he's in Mallorca, crowding my space.

'There you are!' he booms. 'Shirking in the sun?'

I scrabble to sit upright. 'Actually, I was hoping to have five minutes' peace. Thought you could manage the last shot without me.'

He slaps my shoulder. 'Come on, guv, this Smirnoff babe is doing my head in. Nick says he's never had such a difficult time directing an ad and he's worked with some of the world's most painful supermodel divas. I mean who the F does she think she is?'

'What's her problem now?'

'Lazy cow won't dive in the pool for the last shot.'

'Probably doesn't want to get her hair wet.'

'Yeah, well, at ten grand a day, she should be willing to drown in chocolate.'

'Keep your fantasies to yourself,' I grunt.

Some distance away, beyond a small crop of lemon trees, a bronzed gazelle with black roots and tumbling blond locks is strutting about the vast patio surrounding the pool with a mobile phone suctioned to her ear.

'She doesn't look happy.'

'I don't give a monkey's. I'm paying her to get her togs off and flog the goods.'

'All the same, we don't want to upset her. Dannie will be angry.'

He pulls a face and snorts loudly. Dannie, or rather Daniella Popescu-Miller, is another client who also hangs out in New York when she's not flitting back to Mayfair to bully the staff over at the Berkeley Hotel where she's a frequent guest. She runs Miller Magic Interiors from Trump Tower and, wearing her Romanian heritage like a badge of honour, proudly informs me that she's a descendent of Dracula. When George suggested doing an advertising shoot for his company, Havana Leather, here in Mallorca, he foolishly asked Daniella for advice about models. She suggested Anastasia Mirnov, a Russian supermodel and close friend. Knowing how dysfunctional most of Dannie's friends are, I vehemently opposed the idea, just as I had opposed the idea of George coming to my neck of the woods to film his new ad.

Ever since settling in rural Mallorca with my family, I have relished the freedom of being able to keep apart two vastly different worlds for life and work. It has been easy to hop back to London every few months to handle client work at my Mayfair-based public relations company, and then return to relative sanity in the mountains of Mallorca. The thought of these two worlds colliding here on my home turf initially filled me with dread. Greedy George is demanding at the best of times, and any contact of Dannie's, my spoilt and neurotic interiors client, would inevitably spell trouble. As it transpired I failed to halt proceedings, even weakly setting up the entire shoot at Aimia Hotel in the Port of Sóller, owned by some good Mallorcan friends. Not only have they generously offered us a couple of mornings to shoot the new advert by their stunning pool, but have also kept George and the highly strung Anastasia frequently supplied with shots of iced vodka and beluga caviar. By contrast, Nick, the shoot director, and I have stuck to strong espressos in the hope of keeping ourselves on the ball while filming in the early morning.

George is hovering over me like an excitable orang-utan. 'Can you go and talk to Smirnoff?'

I groan.

'Come on! That's what your job's all about, isn't it? Schmoozing people.'

'Oh, be quiet.'

It's always intrigued me that no matter how utterly rude I am to George he always comes back for more. The man must be a complete masochist.

I get up and stretch my back while he stands glowering at an equally glowering sun. There's nothing for it. Diplomatic negotiations are needed. As I make my way through the walled garden towards the pool, I spot Cristina, one of the hotel's owners, heading towards me. She is full of smiles.

'How's everything going?'

'Fine. Just another hour should wrap it up.'

She looks at her watch. 'That should be OK. The guests know the pool is out of action till ten.'

She offers to fetch me another espresso, which I hastily accept. Anastasia is now kneeling on a towel, her head bent over a vast Louis Vuitton branded handbag. Her face is lost in a sea of tumbling blond hair. She looks up when I approach, sweeping her mane back and offering me a well-rehearsed pout.

'George is pig.'

'He's a little stressed, Anastasia. I'm sure he didn't mean to upset you.'

'Listen, darlink, when I say to Dannie I come do shoot, I don't agree dive in pool. My agent only agree sitting on leather loop and sun lounger.'

I glance at the big black leather ring floating on the surface of the azure water and wonder, not for the first time, who in their right mind would buy one.

'Look, it's the very last take.'

'I can't.'

I try to reason. 'Are you frightened to dive in?'

She hisses like an angry viper. 'Me? Frightened to dive? Please! I am in Soviet junior swim squad when only eight year old. No, if I dive, hair turn green.'

This I hadn't anticipated. 'What on earth do you mean?'

'Much bleach in hair always go green in chlorine. Later this week I have big *Vogue* shoot in Moscow but not with green hair.'

Cristina wanders over with a small tray. I reach for the coffee gratefully.

'Darlink, get waiter bring me a little iced vodka, yes?' says Anastasia sweetly.

Cristina smiles and gives me a surreptitious wink. '*No problema.*'

She walks off in the direction of the hotel along one of the winding paths flanked by pink and white oleander blooms. A few guests are emerging, wrapped in white bath robes and clutching beach towels. They head for the teak sun loungers, eager to claim their creamy parasol and patch of paradise closest to the pool. Nick is standing by the al fresco bar some feet away, taking comfort in a cigarette. He seems lost in his own thoughts.

'But lots of women swim in chlorinated pools with dyed hair without it turning green.'

'Yes, yes, but I have much bleach and many time in pool.'

I shake my head wearily, drain my coffee and place the cup on a small wooden table.

'Let me speak with Nick.'

Anastasia rumbles around in her bag with long painted talons and fishes out a packet of Russian cigarettes and a huge gold and diamante lighter. She shrugs and flutters her spidery false eyelashes. 'Go talk with him but I won't dive.'

I stroll the length of the pool, past the patio and towards the bar. Nick grinds the butt of his cigarette under his shoe and gives me a resigned expression.

'Tell me the worst.'

'She thinks her hair will turn green if she dives in to the pool. Can't we just stick a swimming cap on her head?'

'Sure, that'll make a great shot,' he says, flatly. 'Very aesthetic.'

'So, what's the solution? We've got less than an hour to do this.'

He sighs deeply. 'That woman's a bloody nightmare. OK, we'll forget the diving shot. Let's just do a final cut to her floating on the leather lilo.'

'Could her hair really turn green?'

'Yep. Peroxide and chlorine don't mix. It's because of the copper traces in the water but that's nothing. I was on a shoot in the desert where the model's hair came out in clumps after a perming session.'

'Did you put her in a wig?'

'Didn't have any. We dressed her up in sheik headdresses. Looked pretty cool, believe it or not.'

He fumbles for another cigarette in his jacket pocket.

'Some models swear by tomato ketchup.'

'What's that got to do with anything?'

He lights up. 'Removes green staining in dyed blonde hair. We could suggest it to Anastasia?'

'Don't even go there,' I growl.

We saunter back to the pool, where Anastasia is drawing heavily on her cigarette while the film crew stands around aimlessly awaiting a decision. George, accompanied by a waiter, is bounding towards us.

'Who is the vodka for, sir?'

18

George directs him to Anastasia. 'Er, it's for Miss Smirnoff here.'

She rounds on him with fury. 'It's Mirnov, not Smirnoff. You remember nothing.'

George smothers a smile. 'Sorry, can't think why I keep getting it wrong.'

I poke him in the back. 'I've some good news. Nick's come up with a bit of a brainwave for the final shot. We're going to have Anastasia floating serenely on the lilo.'

'What about her diving into the leather loop?' quizzes George.

'No, we think this will be a more powerful image,' Nick replies smoothly.

Anastasia sniffs and gives a watery smile, no doubt emboldened by the shot of vodka. 'Is good with me.'

George knits his eyebrows together. 'But...'

I grab his arm and drag him away while Nick rounds up his crew and begins setting up the shot.

When we're a good distance away I explain the delicate matter of Anastasia's green hair to George. He stares at me for a second and then guffaws loudly. 'We could always rename her the Green Goddess.'

'Or we could forget all about it, finish the shoot and get Anastasia on a plane to Moscow by tonight.'

He gives me a crocodile smile. 'You're right, guv, and I save myself another ten grand fee and the cost of a day's shoot.'

'Exactly.'

He claps his hands together. 'Isn't your mate Catalina cooking us paella tonight?'

'She certainly is, so let's just wrap everything up and then you can have a relaxing day here at the hotel.'

'I'll drink to that.'

We walk back slowly towards the pool. I touch the sleeve of his linen shirt.

'Now be nice and don't make any silly jokes about her green hair, alright?'

'Of course not, guv.'

Like a beached mermaid, Anastasia is already lying voluptuously on the lilo in a microscopic tangerine bikini, her lean legs stretching out in the sun like toasted toothpicks. The lilo bobs gently to and fro on the dazzling water as George smiles down at her with a mischievous grin. Then, just as the cameras roll, he stands defiantly at the edge of the pool and breaks into a painful rendition of 'Greensleeves' at the top of his voice.

Alan, my Scotsman, is standing in the front garden, a fat cigar, a *puro*, gripped tightly between his teeth as he pulls violently at a clump of weeds. His shirt is damp with sweat. A profusion of lavender and white plumbago form a dazzling ring around his legs as he works and, from high in the rocky walls, water trickles softly into the pond. Our old, gnarled olive tree that sits in the centre of the lawn looks weary and its few remaining leaves droop in the heat, yet it has a nobility and robustness about it. After all, it has survived several hundred years of similar drought during long Mallorcan summers. Alan looks round as the car sweeps by, churning up the gravel before coming to rest in the courtyard. He potters over to greet me.

I lean out of the driver's window. 'Glad to see you're still keeping the *puro* industry going strong.'

He waves the cigar in the air a tad sheepishly. 'This is the first one I've had since you left this morning.'

I raise my eyebrows a fraction, just so that he knows I'm on to him.

'Anyway, how did the shoot go?' he asks, quickly changing the subject.

'Better not ask. Suffice to say that Anastasia Mirnov is happy to be heading back to Moscow.'

'I take it George was his usual ebullient self?'

'Worse than ever.'

He laughs. 'Come on, I've got just the thing to cheer you up.'

I clamber out of the car and stretch my arms. The facade of the *finca*, our old stone house, is now covered with shrivelled, thirsty creeper. Small geckos claw on to the dry rocks and then, like miniature abseilers with invisible ropes, gradually descend the wall, darting into any number of cool and dark crevices. The *finca* is at its best when it sports its spring coat, drowning in a mass of soft green leaves, but now it is the dry season. Time is elastic here in the mountainous Sóller Valley, and life is about accepting each new season and the changes it brings. It's best to be philosophical and adopt a more *mañana* attitude, which is summed up in my favourite little Mallorcan expression, *poc a poc* – little by little. My memory trawls back to the time when we first bought the house. In those days our *finca* was an unloved ruin and it took us five long years to restore it from a distance. I can hardly believe that the ragged gardens and orchard which were once home to discarded chicken coops, builders' refuse and limp, dying trees are now an abundance of colour and a picture of health. We still have more improvements to make but we have come a long way.

'Are you coming?' The Scotsman is growing impatient.

I follow him across the gravel courtyard, the fiery ball of the sun pursuing our every step as we head down the stone steps into the orchard. We have just finished the last crop of oranges so the twenty or more scattered trees stand self-consciously in the arid soil like undressed scarecrows, bereft of fruit and zest. By contrast, the lemons are still going strong and the trees are heavy with golden orbs. I breathe in their citrus perfume as we pass. Alan strides through the orchard, brushing past the long, sun-scorched grass and an unruly bush of vermilion oleander en route to his vegetable patch. He pauses briefly at the side of one of the gravel paths to admire a clump of cardoons, their giant thistles thrusting into the sky. No doubt they remind him of his beloved Scotland. He reaches the neatly laid out vegetable patch where a battered old straw pannier is lying in its midst, overflowing with a mound of beetroots.

'Aren't they beauties?' he says proudly.

'Gosh, that's some cache.' I wipe the sweat from my forehead and bend down to pick up a few muddy specimens. They are massive and sprouting dark green stalks and leaves.

'Perhaps you can do a dish for tonight?'

'Catalina's got the paella in hand so I suppose I could do some sort of beetroot starter… maybe with baby broad beans?'

'Perfect,' he beams. 'I'll carry them into the house.'

He sweeps the beets back into the bag and lifts it on to his shoulder. A few feet away the chickens in the corral are clucking throatily. Salvador, our disdainful cockerel, is strutting about looking hot and bothered. He pecks listlessly at some grain and has an irritable scowl on his face.

'I think he's suffering with this heat, poor old boy.'

Alan shrugs. 'He can always cool off with the girls in the hen house.'

'What, a *macho* like him? He'd much rather prance about the corral proving to his harem what a good catch he is and showing off his plumage.'

Beyond the corral is a clutter of wild brambles, weeds and assorted trees that we are currently clearing to make way for a small cattery. An abandoned digger skulks in among the trees and a mountain of weeds and old decayed branches have been swept up at the side of a metal skip. This uncared-for piece of terrain was recently sold to us by some local Mallorcans and our intention is to create a rural holiday retreat for cats. It has taken determination and perseverance to get this far and yet we still face more bureaucracy.

'Where are the guys?' I ask.

Alan rubs his chin. 'They'll be back tomorrow. They can only work on the site early in the morning now because of the heat.'

'I suppose they'll down tools completely in August.'

'Yep, afraid so, but they'll be up and running again in September.'

Orlando, one of our cats, slips out from behind a terracotta pot and shadows us. He often lurks near the corral, avidly watching the daily activities of the hens as if they were lead parts in some entertaining TV soap. He only averts his gaze when he hears the distant tinkle of his metal dish being refreshed with more food. We walk up the stone steps to the back patio and garden. The kitchen doors and windows are flung open and sprawled outside on the shaded patio are our other two felines – Inko, the queen of the household, and Minky, Orlando's twin. It has taken Inko, our part-Siamese, some time to accept the arrival of the twins and she still regards them with utter contempt. Whenever one of them dares to make an approach, she thumps her stumpy knot of a tail against the floor and hisses with all her might. Alan steps over Minky.

'I'd like to come back as a cat in my next life.'

'Be careful what you wish for.'

He yawns. 'Thinking about it, I suppose it's not so great when your manhood's stripped from you without a by-your-leave.'

The twins are off to the vet to be neutered soon and this has caused some angst, not least because our maverick Mallorcan friend, Pep, insists we are cruel savages for doing so. The feral population is fast growing in our part of the mountains and so stray cats are regularly culled to keep numbers down. We'd rather avoid adding to the moggy death toll.

Alan dumps the pannier on the kitchen table and fetches us both a glass of cool lemon juice from the fridge.

'What's Ollie up to?' I ask.

'Doing his summer project work. Something about the solar system but it's all in Catalan so I can't understand much.'

As if on cue, our eleven-year-old son appears barefooted in the *entrada,* our spacious entrance hall that serves as a living room, wearing a pair of crumpled shorts. He twiddles a pen between his fingers. 'Did you know that a shooting star is really just a burnt-out meteorite?'

'I do now.'

He turns to me impatiently. 'Apparently, July and August are when you see the most shooting stars so can we set up the telescope in the garden?'

Our friend Victoria Duvall has given Ollie the enormous astronomical telescope that previously occupied a space in her house.

'Good thinking,' says the Scotsman enthusiastically. 'We'll spend every night stargazing.'

Ollie gives his father a cool stare. 'Yes, but don't expect to see shooting stars every night.'

Alan nods. 'No, indeed. Anyway, how's the project going?'

Ollie puffs out his cheeks. 'I don't see why we have to do homework in the summer holidays.'

Having completed one year at Llaut, a new Spanish school near the island's university, Ollie has had to get to grips with learning in Castilian, which is spoken in most parts of the Spanish Peninsula, and Catalan, the language of Cataluña and also the Balearic Islands. A further complication is that Mallorcans add their own special twist to Catalan, using vocabulary distinct to the Balearic Islands, so what is taught in Mallorcan schools is not necessarily what is spoken at home. Consequently for a foreign child, learning in the Mallorcan school system is particularly challenging. Prior to joining Llaut, Ollie attended a British school in Palma where English was the first language, so embarking on a curriculum taught in two new languages simultaneously has been tough. Still, there are compensations; he can now curse in Spanish with his classmates and hurl insults in the local vernacular, which he knows his parents can't easily follow.

I try reasoning with Ollie. 'You've got three whole months of holiday so just think how bored you'd be without homework.'

'If I had a Wii and a PS2 I wouldn't be.'

Alan studies him. 'What in heaven's name is a wiwi? It's not one of those wretched playboy things, is it?'

Ollie shakes his head in frustration and, muttering in Mallorcan, stomps off to his room.

'It's that interactive TV thingy,' I say, trying to sound knowledgeable. 'All his chums have them apparently.'

'Good for them but we're not having any truck with that nonsense. There's nothing to beat reading books and walking in the mountains.'

He lugs the pannier of beetroots over to the sink and begins to run the tap. I walk out on to the patio and watch the light playing on the surface of the swimming pool. It's a glorious day and the Tramuntana mountains which overlook our terrain are bathed in golden light. High up in the hills, *fincas* glint like small diamonds as the sun kisses their glass window panes, reflecting sharp light across the valley. There's a braying from a nearby field and the sound of a donkey pawing the ground. Mingled with the clucking of our hens is the gentle tinkle of bells. Our neighbour, Rafael, has recently taken delivery of some young sheep, all of whom are sporting bronze neck bells that clang gently as they graze.

'So,' says Alan, emerging from the kitchen with a pair of secateurs in his hand. 'How many of us are there for supper?'

'Eight, including George.'

'At least we can eat outside. By the way, when's he leaving for London?'

'Hopefully tomorrow sometime but he was talking about staying on to see Sa Mostra.'

Once every year, dance troupes from around the world congregate for a week in the heart of Sóller, our local market town, to take part in Sa Mostra. It is a lively and colourful event with al fresco dance demonstrations during the day and every evening. The town's folk dancing group gets involved and it is always fun to see neighbours and shopkeepers out of context wearing traditional Mallorcan costumes and sashaying graciously and joyously about the stage in the *plaça*. Often they'll invite spectators to come up and join them on the dance floor and it surprises me how gregarious tourists become when away from home, skipping and clapping in happy abandonment in front of live audiences. In all honesty, they probably don't get much of an opportunity back home in their local shopping centres. Much as I'd like George off the island, it would be a pity for him to miss such a wonderful occasion.

'Maybe we can all go tomorrow night?' says Alan. 'I think Pep mentioned that Juana would be dancing. George and Pep would get on like a house on fire.'

Our good friends, Pep, Juana and their son, Angel, always throw themselves wholeheartedly into every fiesta and we tag along with them to most local events. When we first moved here it was extremely helpful to have Mallorcan friends who spoke fluent English, although now we get by well enough save for a few linguistic gaffes. I'm not sure whether putting Greedy George and Pep together is necessarily a good thing, both being complete exhibitionists and having a puerile sense of humour.

'Are you sure that's wise?'

The Scotsman smirks. 'Yes, I think it will be highly entertaining to see how they spark each other off. I shall suggest it to Pep.'

'On your own head be it.' I look at my watch and give a little shriek. 'Damn. I promised to email Rachel that PR proposal by lunchtime and it's already noon.'

'You'd better get your skates on then,' he warns. 'And don't forget you've got to get your column off this afternoon.'

The weekly column which I've been penning for the local British newspaper, *The Majorca Daily Bulletin*, offers snippets and comments on London and international news. I shake off my sandals and plod up the staircase to my office eyrie. The marble is dry and cool beneath my feet.

'Don't let anyone disturb me,' I call to Alan.

'Of course not. No one's going to be here till seven tonight.'

I barely reach the top step when the front door crashes open.

'*Hola!*' yells Rafael. 'I thought I'd pop round for a chat and a beer.'

Tiny stars and a slice of silvery moon enliven a charcoal sky, and yet the hills remain dark and impenetrable, resembling a mysterious, ridged creature lurking beneath a black cloak. The old wooden table is littered with debris, used cutlery and dessert dishes, empty wine bottles and abandoned serviettes. A fat and flickering candle drips tears of white wax which gather in a small puddle at its glass base. Ollie digs a burnt match into the melted goo, pours it on to his hand and watches, mesmerised, as it instantly sets. George, replete after three gigantic portions of home-made paella followed by caramel flan, is leaning back in his chair nursing a cognac in one massive paw, and a Cuban cigar in the other. Marta and Paco, Catalina's parents, sit on either side of him, basking in the reflected glory of their daughter whose culinary efforts have been lavishly praised by one and all.

'You know what, guv?' yells George, cutting through the momentary calm. 'You're the luckiest woman in the world to have a chum like Catalina.'

'You're right,' I admit.

Catalina views us both with a quizzical smile. Her husband, Ramon, gives a little grunt.

'I mean, how long have you two known each other?' asks George.

Catalina scratches her head. 'Too long! I was an au pair for her sister in England fifteen years ago and that's how we met. Now I see her every week.'

'Yes, but she hardly ever cooks me paella,' I complain.

'It's true. I'm too busy working and I don't want her to get lazy! I only have time to do a little housework for her these days.'

Aside from helping me out around the house, Catalina is the custodian of the keys to many holiday homes in the Sóller Valley.

She maintains and keeps a beady eye on these properties for their owners and is the nucleus for news gathering and dispersal across the valley.

Alan blows out a plume of smoke. 'You see, George, we're all flat out with work. Life's no picnic over here.'

George roars with laughter. 'Give me a break! You lot are having a ball.'

'*Què diu?*' asks Catalina's mother.

'He says we have an easy life here,' I translate.

'Tell him to try being married to Catalina!' cuts in Ramon.

Marta looks thoughtful. 'I think we're lucky. Who wants to work in a city like Madrid or London? All that traffic and stress.'

Catalina translates her mother's words for George.

'Yes, poor old me,' he says. 'It's hell in London. All those five star hotels and restaurants, Fortnum & Mason and Harrods. Marta's right, I have a horrible, stressful life.'

'It's OK if you have money, I suppose,' retorts Ramon.

'True,' says George. 'I wouldn't want to be poor. Then I'd end up doing something ridiculous like building a cattery.' He leans across and prods me on the arm.

'Leave my cattery out of it. I'm doing it because I love cats.'

'Quick, give me a hankie someone, I'm going to cry!' guffaws George.

Catalina tuts while Paco and Ramon exchange amused glances. They can follow English fairly well.

'She'll go to heaven before you will,' Paco chuckles.

'I do hope so,' says George. 'I want to have a lot more fun before I depart this world.'

Ollie joins in. 'Lucky you don't have to go to school. At school there's never any fun, just work and more work.'

'Don't worry,' says George. 'I got expelled at sixteen and never looked back. You come and work for me in a few years' time and homework will be a thing of the past.'

'Cool,' Ollie enthuses, then he leaps up and runs to the far end of the patio and garden, past the inky pool and towards the telescope which Alan has set up by the olive tree.

Paco takes a large sip from his glass of *herbes*, the local Mallorcan liqueur.

'How are your tomatoes coming on?'

Alan frowns. 'Not good at all. I was going to ask for your advice. Some sort of blight.'

Paco nods in sympathy. 'The whole valley's affected. I was hoping it hadn't reached yours.'

'What's wrong with M&S?' asks George.

'Nothing beats growing your own veg,' says Alan, robustly.

'Sounds like too much hard work to me,' grumbles George. 'I hate digging, and worms give me the collywobbles.'

Alan decides to change tack. 'So were you happy with the shoot, George?'

'Jubilant that it's over! I mean, that Smirnoff woman was a pain in the backside. I nearly danced when I saw her off at the airport.'

'At least she was good looking.'

'You didn't see her without her teeth.'

'What?' cries Alan.

'Only kidding!'

Catalina pours herself a glass of red wine while her builder husband sticks to cola. 'So what were these leather products you were filming?'

George squeezes the life out of his cigar butt and stubs it in the ashtray.

'I've produced a range of leather beach and pool accessories. All made out of the best hide.'

'Really? But doesn't leather go bad in water?' she asks.

George relishes the question. 'Aha! That's what you'd imagine but a smart arse like me thinks of everything. I use BBG.' He smiles triumphantly, assured of our wholesale confusion.

'BBG? What's that?' I ask. 'You told me it was goat hide.'

'It is. Black Bengal goat.'

'What's so special about a Bengal goat?' the Scotsman says, hotly.

George lights up another cigar and waggles it at Alan. 'I'll tell you why it's special. It's very soft hide which I get treated in a way that makes it impervious to water.'

Catalina translates this for her parents, who coo in wonderment.

'Where do you get your supplies from?' asks Catalina.

George leans back in his chair, and exhales a plume of smoke. 'I've got a mate in Bangladesh.'

Greedy George has a mate in every part of the globe. It wouldn't surprise me if he had a string of intergalactic alien contacts across the entire universe.

'Did you know,' he continues, 'that there are over thirty million goats in Bangladesh?'

'Fascinating!' I cry in mock amazement.

He gives me a dark look. 'So, Miss Sarcastic, do you know what vellum is?'

'A kind of parchment paper. Used to be made from calves' skin.'

'Goat's skin, mostly. Poor old Charles the First had his death warrant written on goat vellum.'

'Is this leading anywhere, George?' I sigh.

Catalina momentarily slides a hand across her mouth to stifle a grin before translating the sorry tale about Charles I to her parents. Marta shakes her head at this news, as if the royal's demise were a recent occurrence.

'What I'm trying to say, guv, is that there's nothing I don't know about goats.'

We all get the giggles and Catalina and I start bleating just to put a stop to any more goat nonsense.

Paco scrutinises his watch in the half light. 'It's one in the morning. We must leave.'

Everyone rises and Marta attempts to clear the table but I shoo her away. 'We'll do it later, won't we?'

'Absolutely,' says Alan, yawning heavily. '*Mañana, mañana...*'

Ollie trips over to us. 'I think I've just seen a falling star.'

'Did you catch it?' laughs Marta.

'Not this time,' he replies, using Mallorcan dialect. He smiles and says good night to everyone. George grabs him in a bear hug.

'Take my word for it, young man. Give up all this school crap and join the firm.'

Ollie hangs his head on one side. 'How much would you pay me? A million pounds a year?'

'In your dreams, sonny Jim. You'd have to work your way up.'

'Hmm,' he replies coolly, turning back towards the telescope. 'I'll think about it.'

We wend our way through the house to the front courtyard to say our final goodbyes.

'Ollie's a sharp little bugger, isn't he?' says George.

'I like to think so,' the Scotsman grins.

The telephone is ringing incessantly. I glare at it across the desk, wondering why our erratic answerphone fails to connect. Rather crossly I whip up the receiver and give a curt greeting. It's my managing director, Rachel, calling from the office in London.

'Snappy!' she yells provocatively. 'What's got your goat?'

'Don't remind me...'

'About what?'

'Nothing really, just a silly conversation I had with George the other night.'

'I take it he's left your sunny shores now?'

'Mercifully, yes, but I've got a mound of work to do thanks to taking time out for his wretched film shoot.'

There's a gale of laughter. 'I can just picture what Dannie's supermodel friend was like!'

'Yes, well just add on some horns, a tail and have her waving a pitch fork.'

'How did George get on with her?'

'Badly, Rachel. Mind you, he spent two nights partying once she left so I don't think he was too traumatised by the experience.'

'Whatever did your friend Catalina make of him?'

'Believe it or not, she adored him. They even danced together at Sa Mostra, our folk dancing fiesta.'

'I'd love to have been a fly on the wall.'

I chuckle at the memory. 'He was pretty nimble, given his bulk.'

She explodes with laughter. 'Look, I know you've got to get on but I wondered when you'd next be over in London. I want to set up a meeting with the Peterson-Matlocks, those furniture designers.'

'Are they normal?'

'How do I know? They seem nice and they want to hire us.'

'OK, but remember I've got enough on my plate already with George and Dannie, not to mention mad Manuel.'

Somehow, since handing over the reins of the company to Rachel, I've ended up with all the misfit overseas clients. Manuel Ramirez, the owner of H Hotels in Panama, is another fruitcake. I'd even go as far as saying that he's more deranged than Dannie and George put together. He is soon to open a hotel in Maryland where he has a new investor, an ex-vice admiral from the US Naval Academy. I've got a bad feeling about him.

'Is Manuel giving you angst?'

'Not really, but I'm worried about this admiral guy he's linked up with. Sounds a bit of a nut.'

'I shouldn't worry, birds of a feather and all that,' she chortles. 'So, when are you back?'

'I'll be over at the beginning of September.'

'Cool. The Peterson-Matlocks are in Jakarta visiting the owner of Wild Woods, the franchise they're taking on. They won't be back until the end of August.'

'Good-oh.'

She's silent for a moment. 'Just one other thing.'

'Yes?'

'Can we have a private word some time? Nothing too heavy.'

I'm intrigued. 'About what?'

'The future,' she says.

'Of course.'

'No hurry.'

She rings off. A discussion about the future. How timely is that?

# TWO

# SITTING DUCKS

I set off at a gentle running pace along our stony old track, hoping that I might just avoid bumping into Rafael when I reach his house. Should our paths cross he will inevitably preach the dangers of running in the midday heat, a subject I would rather avoid. The pretty *finca* closest to ours is owned by Helge and Wolfgang, who pop back and forth to Sóller from their home in Berlin several times a year. Rafael, however, is a permanent fixture and has lived in his old stone house since the day he was born. His property lies midway between ours and that of our furthest neighbours, Pedro and Silvia, at the mouth of the track. They too have resided here for many years and historically both families have had the odd skirmish over land and access rights, and other neighbourly grumbles, but these days they get along well enough.

More than a year ago, Margalida, the elderly mother of Silvia, died, and I felt bereft. She used to occupy a smart white chalet opposite her daughter's house on the corner of the track, in full view of the lane. An alert concierge, albeit with appalling sight, she relished being able to sit on her veranda and watch the world go by. There would be small clusters of German hikers, the occasional car or *moto* rumbling by, a neighbour returning with shopping and gossip from Sóller town, and the biggest prize of all – random delivery vans. As soon as one of these vehicles turned into our narrow track, Margalida would hobble out onto her porch, wave her wooden stick and demand to know what was being delivered and to whom. With some trepidation the driver would draw to a halt and hand over a piece of official paper, perhaps some crumpled delivery note, for her to scrutinise with her unseeing eyes. When fully satisfied that the poor fellow wasn't some opportunist *ladró,* thief, she would sniff heavily and permit him to continue on his way. The postman, Jorge, was a regular visitor to her home as was my friend Gaspar, the paper delivery man. In a short while Margalida and I became firm friends, even though she could only converse in Mallorcan and I in poor Castilian Spanish.

Since then, my grasp of the Mallorcan dialect has improved but is still rudimentary. Luckily, I don't need to practise it on Rafael – he has a fairly good knowledge of English, having picked up vocabulary from British tourists who pop by his cake shop in the town. Similarly to me, he enjoys running, although at a greatly enhanced pace, which means that I try to avoid chummy runs with him at all costs. As I pass the muddy enclosure of Alberto, his Dalmatian, I can hear sizzling coming from the kitchen and a delicious smell of chorizo sausage wafts over. Rafael appears like a genie at the open door with a frying pan in his hand.

'You want something to eat?' he says with a sly grin, observing my running shorts and trainers.

'Very funny.'

'How far you go?'

'To the Port.'

He sucks his teeth. 'You'd be better going up to Fornalutx. There's more shade on the back road.'

Rafael always knows best when it comes to running.

'Yes, but I don't feel like it.'

He casts his eye over his watch. *'Hombre!* It's nearly noon. You'll fry!'

Alberto starts barking excitedly from his run.

'See, even Alberto agrees with me!'

I laugh. 'I had to finish a lot of work in the office this morning.'

'If you want to train for another marathon, you must go earlier, when it is cool.'

*'Si, si...'* I mutter. I'm certainly not going to tell him that I've already signed up for the Athens marathon next November. It shall remain a secret for now.

*'Bon profit!'* I say, Enjoy your lunch.

*'Gracias*! *Vagi bé!'* he cries. Go well.

I carry on jogging, already uncomfortable as sweat trickles down my face and back. The thought of undertaking another gruelling marathon fills me with dread but it's a great way of fundraising for the small Sri Lankan orphanage that Alan and I support, and it's also a fantastic discipline. In the past two years I've taken part in both the New York and London marathons and have derived a certain masochistic pleasure from the training and the bittersweet agony of running the actual course. Around me a wave of hissing cicadas grows louder across the *bancales*, the old stone terraces and the orchards. Perhaps the cicadas, like an ancient Greek chorus, are warning me of the perils of venturing out in such temperatures – and they'd be right.

At the end of the track where it intersects with a narrow country lane, I stretch my legs against one of the stone walls, surprising a small gecko, which gapes up at me and then disappears into a tiny hole. There isn't a sound save for the loquacious cicadas and a fretful dog barking in the distance. A film of ochre dust envelopes the vast Tramuntanas and, through the haze, they rise up before me like a herd of wild elephants, grey and parched in the harsh light and covered in dry scrub. A lone eagle soars high in a bright but colourless sky and across the valley comes the low and distant rumbling of thunder. Waddling along the road and quacking loudly, two ducks suddenly appear. In deep and earnest conversation, they scarcely acknowledge my presence as they patter by, heading who knows where. I imagine they've made a heroic escape from a neighbour's garden but I fear their freedom may be short lived. If a speeding car doesn't end their days, then a wily neighbour will have them in a pot before they have time to squawk, *Socorro!* Help!

I finish my stretching and am about to set off along the road when I hear the agitated whining of a *moto*, the pop-pop bike used by every Tomás, Diego and Horacio up here in the mountains. It's Gaspar, the paper delivery man, dribbling along and straining to keep both his buttocks firmly wedged on the narrow seat. He slows down, beads of sweat pouring from his plump face, and gives a half-hearted little toot toot. I wave and walk over to him. He cuts the engine.

'I've decided I want to come running with you,' he says breathlessly in Mallorcan.

'*Què?*'

'*Si, si*, I know I'm overweight, but I think it'll help me to exercise.'

I digest this news slowly. 'My pace might be a bit too quick for you, Gaspar. Maybe you should begin with fast walking. You know, *poc a poc.*'

He pulls a face. 'No, I'd like to run with you. We can have a nice chat, stop in the port for *un cafè...*'

He trails off when he sees the look of disapproval on my face.

'We don't stop for *un cafè*, do we?'

'No, we don't.'

'*D'acord.* When can we go?'

I wince. Maybe I could take him for a quick jog some time, but I'm worried about the stress to his huge bulk, especially in this heat.

'How about next week?'

He proffers a sunny smile, revs up his motor and gives me the thumbs up. Then he points to the sky.

'Don't run too far. A storm's coming. *Fins aviat!*'

See you soon, he says. He sure will, but in the interim, I'll take some advice from Rafael about how to train my gentle Hulk.

Finally, I start running at a good pace, turning left along the winding road which leads down towards the port. I feel a kiss of rain on my cheek and then a deep growl of thunder rips through the clouds. In a few minutes, violent streaks of lightning flash from above and soon the whole sky resembles a throbbing disco. Hardly able to see for the water running into my eyes, I hurtle along, refreshed by the cool air and pleased to have the place to myself. As it happens, I don't. Rather incongruously, splashing about in an enormous puddle at the side of the road, are the two escapee ducks. I observe them for a few seconds, wondering whether they really do have a death wish, but then who can put a price on freedom, however brief? For now my feathered friends quack happily in the rain, making the most of their fleeting flight of fancy.

The town of Ca'n Picafort, which spreads its suburban tentacles to Alcudia in the north and Arta in the east, was once a modest little fishing village, home to just 200 inhabitants only fifty years ago. It sits plum in the middle of the vast Bay of Alcudia, where swarms of tourists arrive during the summer to fry on the beach that unfurls seductively. Ca'n Picafort today is little more than an anonymous holiday resort with the predictable palm-lined promenade of cafes and bars, and grey, unprepossessing hotels crowding its coastline. It does have a few redeeming features, though; the untouched wetlands of Parc Natural de S'Albufera lie to the west, a twitcher's paradise, and the ancient burial ground of Son Real Necropolis, known as the Cemetery of the Phoenicians, are a stone's throw from Son Baulo beach. As far as I'm concerned, Ca'n Picafort has one saving grace and that is its annual event of Amollada d'Anneres, otherwise known as the duck-catching competition. This memorable but bizarre celebration, held annually on 15 August, allows Ca'n Picafort to hold its head up proudly and claim at least a small degree of Spanish eccentricity.

We have spent the best part of two hours crammed inside a hot and sticky car travelling to this unassuming resort and now spill out of our cramped jail like four wretched prisoners on release. Ollie and his good chum Angel stretch out their limbs and strain to see the craggy rocks of the harbour from where the ducks will be released. Hundreds of people are milling about the streets like hyperactive sand flies, anticipating the big event. Flanking the bay is a clutter of hotels and apartment blocks and beyond, in the far distance, a seemingly never-ending golden beach. Within a minute or two of our arrival, our friends Pep and Juana roll up and park nearby. They have travelled in relative luxury in their roomy, air-conditioned silver estate car. A door is flung open and Pep hauls himself onto the pavement. Angel and Ollie run up to him.

'So, you survived the journey in that old jalopy?' he says, threading his hands through his unruly grey locks.

The Scotsman plods over to him with stiff legs. 'It wasn't fun, I can tell you.'

Pep breaks into a sadistic smile, revealing a row of nicotine-stained teeth. 'Anyway, it's your own fault. I can't believe you're using that same old hire car after all these years.'

'Needs must,' sniffs Alan.

'*Què broma!* You're just an old Scottish... what do you say... skinflint.'

Pep has a point. It is a bit of a joke among our friends that we're still using a hire car but there is a good reason for this. We pay a tiny amount for extended use of the old banger and we don't have to worry about insurance, car servicing or breakdowns. The hire company takes care of all that. The other major perk is that hire companies remove hubcaps from their cars' wheels which means that the local *policia* never pull their drivers over to check documentation. Assuming that it's just a tourist at the wheel, the police leave the driver in blissful peace. The downside is that we have air conditioning that exudes gusts of fiery heat akin to a dragon's breath and the seats appear to have been embedded with small knives and knuckledusters. I try to convince myself that I'm getting a free shiatsu massage every time I get in the car.

Juana, elegant as always in a linen jacket and tailored cotton shorts, joins us on the pavement.

'You poor things, all squeezed in together. The boys should have come with us.'

Angel protests. 'I like it better in their car. It feels more like we're going on an adventure.'

Pep begins wheezing with laughter. He claps Angel on the shoulder with a heavy brown hand. 'You, my son, are an *idiota*.'

Angel breaks away, muttering *jolines* under his breath, a perky little untranslatable expletive used by Mallorcan children as soon as they can open their mouths.

'Come on, the race will begin any time,' shouts Ollie, scrutinising his watch.

'No it won't,' yawns Pep. 'It starts at noon, so we've still got fifteen minutes to wait. We'll have to walk down to those rocks and then, my *chicos*, you can get ready.'

The two boys listen attentively and then run ahead. Alan bustles over to the boot and pulls out a straw pannier full of towels. He tucks a leather loop under his arm while Pep observes him with a furrowed brow.

'And what, my friend, is that monstrosity?'

'It's a leather loop, an upmarket rubber ring. One of George Myers' mad inventions.'

Pep's face fills with pleasure. 'Ah, my new friend, George! You're lucky to have such an entertaining client. He proved to be a good dancer at Sa Mostra, too.'

'Give me a break!' I snort.

He examines the leather loop. 'In fairness, it's rather elegant. Not vulgar like the rubber ones.'

Alan raises his eyebrows and strides off with it towards the beach. We follow in his wake. It is difficult to fight our way through the excited throng clambering among the slimy rock pools and clumps of seaweed. Most of those picking their way through the pebbles to the water's edge are local Mallorcans. The pack of spectators in shorts and T-shirts standing high up on the road are no doubt expectant tourists keen to see whatever pageant is about to unfold. Pep finds a small area of unoccupied sand and plonks down his bag and a *sombrilla,* a large cream parasol. Then, with difficulty, he stabs the parasol into the sand and grinds it in. He is sporting a wide-brimmed Panama hat, linen shirt and beige shorts and puffs vigorously on a slim *puro.*

'Want one?' he enquires, thrusting a packet towards Alan.

The Scotsman extracts one of the cellophane-wrapped cigars.

'Now, boys,' says Pep, gesturing to Angel and Ollie to follow his gaze. 'See those five boats anchoring outside that hotel?'

They nod.

'That is Hotel Sol y Mar. Soon they will release the ducks.'

'They're not real, are they?' asks Ollie.

Pep gives a cynical shrug. 'They used to be but health and safety or some interfering anti-duck-throwing group has stopped that. Now they dole out plastic ones.'

Ollie hunches his shoulders. 'I'm glad they're not real. Poor things.'

'Come on, Ollie!' yelps Pep dramatically. 'Be a *macho!* In the old days we'd have had a nice free duck for supper.'

'What's *macho* about catching a duck?'

With a grunt, Pep waves the remark away with his cigar. Juana and I settle ourselves on towels under the parasol and watch as the boys strip down to their swimming trunks and rush towards the shoreline carrying George's leather loop between them. No sooner have they waded in to the sea, along with countless others, than there's the sound of a horn and a bright yellow flash as the boats unleash hundreds of plastic ducks into the brine. Angel and Ollie swim off in the direction of a few bobbling birds while a mass of adults and children struggle to capture the scattered booty in the frisky waves. In the midst of the mayhem a police patrol boat churns up the water as it heads briskly towards the throng. An officer stands unsteadily at the helm, loudly blowing a whistle, and agitatedly waving his arms in the air. Those gathered on the beach are jostling to see what's happening. Zooming into view across the waves appears a flotilla of small boats, crowded with masked men armed with snowy white, live ducks. The spectators begin slow clapping as the flapping, quacking birds are launched into the sea. Some try to catch them as they splash down indignantly alongside their yellow plastic imitators. It's hard to tell what's going on or indeed what role the police boat has in all this.

'What's happening?' I ask Pep.

He removes the *puro* from his mouth. 'They are the saboteurs, the fiesta traditionalists who make a stand every year. They want to bring back real ducks. The local police show up but really they just turn a blind eye.'

'But who are the saboteurs?' I persist.

He seems coy. 'Who knows? Locals, I imagine. It's just a bit of fun.'

The boys now appear, dripping wet and triumphantly carrying three small plastic ducks between them. Ollie wrestles the leather loop to the ground. I notice, begrudgingly, that it's still as dry as a whistle. People run from the sea in all directions, some boasting armfuls of plastic ducks while others carry live birds or simply go empty handed.

'Where are people taking those live ducks?' asks Ollie suspiciously.

'To the *torrent de son Bauló*, where they'll be released,' soothes Pep.

Juana looks up from her towel. 'You know that this whole event is illegal?'

'How come?' asks Alan.

'The agriculture and fisheries department tried to ban it but the local council wants to preserve the tradition and is prepared to pay a big fine each year for the privilege.'

'That could only happen in Mallorca,' Alan chuckles.

Pep claps his hands together. 'So that's it, my friends. End of the show. Now what?'

'How about heading off to the S'Albufeira wetlands?' suggests the Scotsman.

'Aren't we going to the museum?' clamour the boys.

I have promised Angel and Ollie that later we'll drive up to the Fundación Jakober in Alcudia which houses a collection of Old Master portraits of children and has a stunning sculpture park.

'*Si si*, later,' tuts Pep. 'But food comes first.'

He taps a finger against the side of his nose. 'I know just the place for lunch. Owned by a friend of mine.'

'Oh, what a surprise! The man with a friend in every port,' I tease.

'As it happens, he does a perfect *duck à l'orange…*'

'You're joking?' exclaims Ollie in some horror.

Pep tousles his hair. 'Naturally! I'm always joking. My friend does the best seafood paella in town and so rest assured, *mon amic petit*, there won't be a feather, webbed foot or beak in sight.'

The sky is louring as Catalina hangs washing on the line. She finishes her task and then, with hands on hips, contemplates the towering mountains beyond. She plods past the pool with the empty washing basket at her side and a tea towel over one shoulder. I am sitting at the wooden table under a parasol, correcting a press release on my computer for Sarah, one of my staff in London. Catalina clumps the basket down and leans over my shoulder.

'What you writing?'

'Something intensely dull. It's about a new range of porcelain animals that my client, Dannie, is launching in the States.'

'You don't like them?'

'Not really, they're very kitsch. I'd rather have the real thing.'

She sighs deeply. 'At the end of the day it's a job. Wait till you have the cattery up and running, then you'll be happy.'

'I wish we could just get on with it.'

'*Paciencia,*' she says. 'In September the men will finish clearing the land and then we can start building.'

Much as I like the holiday feel of August, I have to curb my impatience when things are put on hold. Everyone downs tools in Mallorca during this sizzling month because it's so oppressively hot. Projects are shelved, repairs go unfinished and the island melts into *mañana* mode. A delight for visiting tourists but a frustration at times for residents.

'Will you cut down on your workload when the cattery opens?' Catalina suddenly asks.

'Maybe, but between us we'll manage.'

She shrugs. 'Yes, but you won't be able to do so much.'

It's something that's been worrying me. Although Rachel knows about my plans, she won't admit to the cattery being a reality until it's finally built. Somehow my workload has been increasing, which isn't what was supposed to happen when I stepped back from the day-to-day running of the company. The problem is that Rachel is almost too good at her job and has brought in a lot of new business. I need to have a serious talk with her about the future, something which she seems eager to do, too. I wonder what's on her mind.

'Don't worry.' Catalina is smiling. 'It'll all work out.'

'No doubt.'

She taps me on the shoulder. 'Shall I make some tea?'

'Wonderful.'

'The mountains are not well today,' she remarks. 'They are sad.'

I like the way she personifies our ancient Tramuntanas. It makes me regard them more as a group of old pensioners who have good and bad days than mere mountains.

'It won't be long before the sirocco is here,' she muses.

This hot and dusty maelstrom blows in from the Sahara early in September, covering everything it touches with a fine, sandy grit. It creates a great deal of extra housework for Catalina as windows become grimy and a thin layer of yellow dust smothers floors, walls and tables. It even invades the pages of books and wriggles its way into clothes drawers.

Alan appears at the top of the stone steps leading up from the orchard. He is holding two terracotta pots with sprouting seeds.

'Where are you putting those?' Catalina demands imperiously.

'On the planting table,' he answers, wiping sweat from his face.

She marches over and peers into the pots. 'There's no more room there for these seedlings.'

He looks deflated. 'Of course there is! I'll just move up the others.'

She drags him by the arm over to the battered, old planting table which sits in a shady alcove outside, beyond the kitchen. I throw back my chair so that I can enjoy the spectacle from afar.

'This is no good. You have hundreds of plants and every day more. What you trying to do, open a nursery?'

He gives her a quizzical look before dumping the pots down on the ground. 'It's because I never have enough space! Gardeners need plenty of room to nurture their seeds.'

Catalina throws up her hands. 'You have a big garden. Find another place.'

He frowns. 'But this is the shadiest spot and I've no more room on the front porch.'

'Then put your wormery down in the field. It's taking up so much space.'

I try to hide my mirth behind the computer screen. The poor Scotsman has to endure a serious nagging session on a Monday when Catalina arrives at the house. Meanwhile I get to have a morning off from office drudgery, instead offering a helping hand to Catalina when she needs it and listening to their endlessly entertaining repartee.

'My worms are staying put,' he says firmly. 'They're already suffering in the heat, poor little devils.'

'I thought Mallorcan worms were more sturdy?' I goad.

'That's true, but they still like the shade.'

Catalina whips him on the shoulder with her tea towel. 'All I'm saying is that you suddenly have pots everywhere. It's becoming crazy!'

She leaves him to ponder the problem, and hurries off into the kitchen to fill the kettle.

He shuffles over to me. 'Just look up at the vines. Aren't those grapes spectacular?'

I turn to face the pergola, which is heavy with bunches of ruby red fruit.

'They're fantastic, but it's impossible to eat them all. We'll have to freeze the juice.'

'You're right. I'll make a start on it this afternoon.'

'Don't forget I've got my first English class later so I'll need the kitchen to myself.'

He groans. 'In that case I shall hide myself away upstairs in the office.'

'It's only for an hour.'

'I'd rather hide, just the same,' he says and plods into the house.

Some months ago my friend Fransisca begged me to teach her young daughter English. At first I resisted. I was busy enough as it was and also wasn't sure how I'd fare teaching a six-year-old Mallorcan child the English language from scratch. After some gentle persuasion, I finally agreed – at which point Fransisca cheerfully told me that there were five other children from her daughter's class who all wanted to learn, too. This news filled me with some panic but it was too late to turn back on a promise. The class of six children would go ahead. It is a few weeks since we agreed the date of the first lesson and in that time I have invested in some sturdy books, folders, pencils and colouring crayons.

Catalina emerges from the kitchen carrying two mugs of black tea and a plate of home-made muffins.

'That's good for the waistline,' I remark.

She smirks. 'You've made so many. I thought we'd better eat some.'

'That's because I made a big batch for the children.'

She gives me an old-fashioned look. 'Don't spoil them. They're coming to learn English, not to eat cakes.'

We sit munching, looking out over the garden and hills. The sky is a smudgy grey and yet perspiration drips off us.

'You don't think he's up to something?' asks Catalina.

'Who?'

'Alan, of course. Why is he growing so many plants?'

I hadn't stopped to think about it. All I hope is that it's not another of his loopy business schemes. Many moons ago he and Pep had a crackpot idea to open a whisky shop in Palma but fortunately tired of the notion. Since then, the Scotsman has amused himself helping Pep with bookings for his holiday apartment in Port of Sóller but Pep has just sold the flat. In some ways it came as a relief because what was supposed to be a bit of fun became a full time job for the Scotsman. Now he is occasionally wooed by Focus, a Palma-based film company, to appear in TV and print adverts. It keeps him off the street.

'I wouldn't worry, Catalina. You know what he's like about his plants.'

'Let's hope you're right,' she warns. 'It was better when he was out of our hair, doing those rentals. Why did Pep sell up?'

'He just wanted to cash in on his investment.'

'I suppose you can't blame him,' she says.

There is the sound of a powerful engine and tyres crunching across the gravel courtyard. We look at each other.

'Who can that be?' I ask.

Catalina gets up and together we walk through the kitchen into the wide marble *entrada*. A small, plump man is standing in the porch. He smiles as Catalina wafts through the open front door and they exchange greetings in Mallorcan. She listens to him for a few moments and then narrows her eyes.

'Did you hear that?' she calls to me from the doorway.

'Something about a delivery,' I say.

'Seedlings!' she says with exasperation. 'This man is from the nursery in Santa Maria. Apparently Alan has ordered a whole load of plants. They were on discount.'

The driver strides back to his van whistling merrily as he pulls out tray upon tray of plants.

Catalina regards them fiercely. 'Where is he?' she growls.

'I think he went up to the office,' I say, before sloping back through the kitchen to the table outside. I sit cowering in front of my computer as Catalina's voice rolls up the stairs: 'Alaaaaaaaaaan!'

Six little faces stare back at me from the big oak table in the kitchen. In truth, only five faces are in evidence because Iván has done a disappearing act under his chair. I try to unearth him by pulling gently on his arm. It's like trying to extract a reluctant mole from its hole.

'I don't want to come out!' he yells in Mallorcan.

'That's too bad. Sit up!'

He ignores me. The other children enjoy the show. It's a test of wills. Tofol begins making aeroplane noises while Sara jumps up and down pretending to be a frog. It has taken some effort to herd them indoors. Once the parents had deposited their offspring in the front courtyard and departed, I watched in some dismay as the children ran wildly about the lawn, before gathering at the pond edge to count the fish and frogs. With what authority I could muster, I clapped my hands and bellowed for them to come inside. They stopped and stared, understanding my tone but not the English. I tried in Spanish. This time they grudgingly tripped after me into the house and sat at the kitchen table. I had created folders and worksheets for them all and had also pilfered puppets and plastic animals from Ollie's room. There would be hell to pay should he ever find out.

Tina and Mateo start giggling while dreamy Marga begins drawing on her hand. Enough is enough. I clap loudly.

'Do you all like chocolate biscuits?' I ask in their native tongue.

They all shout out *SI*, even Iván under the table. I show them my watch.

'Now, we have one hour. If you work hard, at half time we will have chocolate biscuits and orangeade and then a fun DVD. If you're naughty we will stay here until your parents return.'

They exchange dismayed glances.

'So, what's it going to be?'

Somewhat reluctantly they take their places at the table again. Iván bobs his head up and is soon sitting on his chair. I hand out colouring pads and ask them to draw pictures of their favourite animals. Iván's mother has told me that her son has a mental block about English and is doing poorly in the subject at school. He and his friends have only been learning the language for one year so it's still very new to them. I wait until they've completed their works of art.

'What a fantastic dog,' I say to Iván. He is coy. I write 'dog' under his drawing and give him a tick and a gold star. While I'm examining the other children's work, he beavers away. I potter over to him.

'Cat,' he says, pushing his next oeuvre towards me.

'Super, Iván!' I exclaim, giving him another star. He can hardly contain his excitement. The others work diligently, keen to amass their own small constellation. Before I know it, half an hour has glided by and my busy bees are toiling away at their worksheets. We stop for biscuits and juice and then spend the rest of the time watching a DVD and singing along to a tape of nursery rhymes. The parents arrive to the sound of 'The Grand Old Duke of York' and find their children marching about the *entrada* like soldiers and showing little sign of wanting to leave. After several entreaties my charges join their parents and depart down the track on foot. 'Bye, bye!' they shout in unison, waving their hands wildly in the air.

I potter into the kitchen and find it relatively unscathed. A puddle of water collects at one end of the table where a plastic cup has been carelessly knocked on its side, crayons and bits of paper are strewn on the floor and biscuit crumbs are scattered across cushion covers of chairs, but nothing more. I find myself happily humming, 'Oranges and Lemons'. Despite my initial misgivings it's been great fun playing teacher for the afternoon. After all, when else would I have a legitimate excuse to skip around the kitchen as Little Miss Muffet, let alone a poor little piggy squealing 'wee wee wee' all the way home?

I'm lolling in a chair upstairs in the office with all the windows thrown wide open. The dry and musky smell of rosemary rushes in on the warm breeze as I close my eyes to listen to the sounds of the night. The room is dark but for my desk light. At this time of the year my beloved frogs and one fat toad whom I've christened Johnnie are in full throttle, calling to one another and splashing about in the pond beneath my window like a group of teenagers at a fun park. There's a deep sigh and I open my eyes. Inko sits curled on my desk, her paws twitching, her eyes darting behind closed lids. She emits another big sigh and then begins murmuring. I wonder what sort of dream she is having. The events of the day unwind before me. I am relieved that my first language class has been a relative success, and that I've started tackling the stack of paperwork listing precariously like a small tower of Pisa against the side of my desk. Soon I will need to return to London to meet up with clients and discuss the future of the PR consultancy with Rachel. Would she let me bow out and run it herself or maybe take on a partner? Could we merge it with a larger concern or just give up the ghost and close it down? The door creaks open and Ollie is standing there yawning in his pyjamas.

'I was looking for Inko. She needs to go to bed.'

I give him a hug. 'OK, you take her.'

He lifts her gently in his arms and wraps her round his neck so that she resembles a beige stole. She doesn't resist. He stops at the door.

'What are you thinking about?'

'Work.'

'What's the point of that?'

'I don't know.'

He gives me a bright look. 'Well then, come and read me a story instead.'

I laugh. 'You're too grown up for that now.'

'Who says?'

'Are you serious?'

'Of course,' he protests. 'Who doesn't like a bedtime story?'

He's right. What could be better than ending the day with a bedtime story? I turn off the light and together we slip off to his room.

# THREE

# OLD GOATS

**Tuesday 7.30 a.m., the club, Mayfair**

The alarm is bleating. I fling out an arm and bang it on the head. Bull's eye. It stops. The room is suffused with light and I am momentarily disorientated, feeling the coolness in the air, the weight of a heavy eiderdown bearing down on me and seeing a pale luminous sky filling the small square window beyond. I remind myself that I am staying at my home from home in London, a rather modest but endearingly eccentric club in Mayfair. Yawning, I get out of bed, stiff limbed, and head for the shower. This represents the first challenge of the day because there is only one shared shower on each floor of the club. I unlock my door and tiptoe along the corridor. Silence. With victory within my grasp, I lunge at the shower door. It's locked. Some lucky bugger has beaten me to it. I creep back to my room and regard the clock. Five minutes later I begin the whole sequence again. This time the shower door is ajar and when I push it, warm steamy air wriggles out into the corridor.

Behind me, a woman who sounds as though she's pinching her nose very hard is speaking to me in affronted nasal tones. 'Excuse me! I had just put my towel in there.'

I smile politely. 'I'm so sorry, I thought it was unoccupied.'

My opponent is kitted out in a pink candlewick dressing gown and what appear to be Turkish slippers. I am mesmerised.

'Do you work?' she asks abruptly.

'Yes, I do.'

She seems troubled. 'What sort of work?'

'Journalism, PR consultancy work, that sort of thing.'

The bejewelled and boney hand which has been reaching for the door handle stops in its tracks.

'I suppose you'd better have the shower before me then. I don't want you to be late.'

She runs a fretful hand through her thatch of snowy locks and steps back.

'Are you sure?' I ask. 'That's very good of you.'

'Not at all. Members should be considerate to one another.'

'Indeed,' I say, duly chastened.

She darts forward, removing her towel from the rail and swishes off to her room. Twenty minutes later I slam my bedroom door and am on the point of running down the staircase when Bernadette, the Irish housekeeper, spots me.

'Ah, she's back then? Now girl, how long are you here for?'

'Just a few days, Bernadette. How are things with you?'

She places a hand on her hip and lifts the feather duster on to her shoulder as if mimicking a rather camp army recruit.

'I've just had a whale of a time at the annual Puck Fair in Killorglin.'

'What's the Puck Fair?'

She drops the feather duster to her side and views me with incredulity. 'You're kidding me! Never heard of the oldest fair in Ireland?'

'Evidently not,' I say with ill-disguised impatience.

'Gosh, you'd love it. They catch a wild goat, right? Then it's crowned King Puck and everyone parties for three days.'

I'm intrigued. 'So what's the story with the goat?

'Apparently, a goat was supposed to have warned Killorglin villagers about the advancing army of that murderer Cromwell – may he rot in hell – and so to this day they honour it. They put a live goat on show in the town with a crown on its head.'

I laugh. 'I'd love to visit one year.'

'And why not? Your wee man, Ollie, would love it!'

I look at my watch. 'I've got to run, Bernadette.'

'Always running. Don't knock over any of the old ladies.'

I jog down the spiralling staircase, bemused that Bernadette always seems to think I'm a one-woman potential catastrophe for my fellow members. Then, hastily turning the corner on to the library floor I nearly crash head first into a frail elderly lady clutching a wooden stick. On second thoughts, I concede, maybe Bernadette is right.

## 1.30 p.m., the office, Mayfair

Our office is situated just off Berkeley Square, home to a raft of exclusive private clubs and a rather pretty garden which is transformed at intervals throughout the year into a revellers' den when fashionistas take it over for annual dress shows and award dinners. We are ensconced in a tall grey building with multiple floors that many years ago served as a hotel. Jim, the porter, tells me that there are the remains of a large tiled pool in the basement but I have never ventured down that far. It looks distinctly dark and creepy. Our own modest rooms occupy a section of the fifth floor which consists of an incredibly long, straight corridor flanked by endless doors on either side. These rooms are home to other companies but it is rare that any of us come face to face during the working day. At one time this floor must have been nothing but hotel bedrooms and I am constantly reminded of the horror film, *The Shining*, half expecting to see a manic toddler trundling up and down the empty hallway on a tricycle, yelling 'Red Rum'. Our offices spill to the right and left at the very top of the long corridor, close to the lifts and stairwell, and sport a big, polished brass name plaque which means that any visitor, unless severely optically challenged, cannot fail to find us. We have four interlinked rooms, perhaps once a lavish hotel suite, comprising a central office, two smaller bolt holes for Rachel and me and a boardroom. This afternoon we are meeting with our new clients, the Peterson-Matlocks, but we've already got off to a rocky start. They are apparently chain smokers and Rachel has caved in and allowed them to light up in the boardroom against my wishes. The windows are open but the room is thick with nicotine fug. She kicks me under the table when I begin coughing loudly.

'So Serena, you've just acquired the English franchise of Wild Wood?'

The woman opposite Rachel is thin and gaunt with huge grey eyes and an Angelina Jolie pout. She cocks her head and slides her mouth to one side as if she's about to make some wisecrack but she's merely exhaling smoke.

'Yes, that's right. Mr Vandenbosch has awarded us the exclusive franchise.'

'That's great!' chirrups Rachel. 'And the furniture you'll be designing and selling is made from sustainable hard wood?'

Sitting next to Serena and agitatedly gnawing the inside of his mouth is her husband, Marcus. He grabs centre stage. 'Look, we wouldn't be doing this if the whole project wasn't sustainable, right? Mr Vandenbosch is a god in Jakarta. I mean, those guys worship him.'

'Which guys?' I ask grumpily.

He breaks into a feverish laugh and runs an impatient hand through his gelled hair. 'The workers! Who do you think? Mr Vandenbosch employs thousands of Indonesians. They even have an altar for him. Seriously, this guy is a major job provider. He's a god. A phenomenon.'

'Presumably he pays them handsomely?'

He rounds on me aggressively. 'Look, Mr Vandenbosch more than meets their expectations. All he asks for in return is their unstinting loyalty.'

He hasn't answered my question. I'm beginning to think this pair have been utterly brainwashed on their Indonesian fact-finding tour of the Wild Woods factory.

'He's got an interesting name,' I muse.

'He's Belgian,' Serena cuts in. 'You know his name's very spiritual. It means "from the wood", and there he is, like a father, providing the poor with timber work.'

Pass the sick bucket. Rachel has a strained smile on her face.

'That's lovely,' she says rather stiltedly. 'First of all we'll study the range in depth and come up with some ideas for your London shop launch.'

Marcus draws irritably on his cigarette, and turns on his wife with some venom. 'It means "OF THE FORESTS" not "from the wood". Dozy cow, can't you get anything right?'

She crosses her arms and pulls a face. 'Same thing.'

'No, it isn't! And he's of Dutch origin.'

'No, he isn't!' she snaps.

I'm really not in the mood for a Punch and Judy show and wish I was many miles away back on my beloved island, sipping a strong espresso out on the warm patio, the sun caressing my face. I jolt back to the present. The Peterson-Matlocks are both quiet and glum and Rachel is busily writing notes. I decide that it's time to escape. Rising slowly, I extend a hand.

'Great to meet you both. Unfortunately, I've got another appointment so I'll leave you in Rachel's capable hands.'

She nods and turns to the two designers. 'Shall we just agree a quick action plan before you go?'

I close the door behind me with some relief. Sarah looks up from behind a computer in the main office.

'What do you think?' she whispers.

I cross the room to her desk. 'Completely barking.'

She shrugs. 'They've only visited here twice and both times they've been bickering constantly.'

'Rachel seems to like them.'

'She likes the idea of the product. You know what she's like about sustainability and all that stuff. One of her crusades.'

I groan and plod off to my office. Fifteen minutes later Rachel appears in the doorway.

'Thanks for the support.'

'What did you want me to do? Call 999?'

'They're not that bad.'

'I thought he was about to slug her.'

Rachel sighs. 'He's stressed out. They've invested all their money in this franchise, even re-mortgaged their home, so I hope it works out for them.'

It appals me that these people are risking so much for something which I feel instinctively is a bit of a sham. I want to get to the bottom of this heroic Belgian's business.

'You know, Rachel, as soon as I saw Marcus...'

Rachel frowns. 'What did you just do?'

'What?'

'You put your finger to your eye when you said, "I saw Marcus."'

I laugh. A lot of us foreign residents in Mallorca have picked up the local custom of pointing at an ear or eye when relating seeing or hearing something. It looks very silly out of context.

'It's a habit I've picked up from the locals. I don't even know I'm doing it.'

She taps me on the head. 'I'm not sure who's madder, you or our clients.'

'I'm uneasy about that pair, Rachel.'

She sits down heavily in a chair. 'Give them a chance. Like you, they're trying to live their dream.'

'I think theirs might be the stuff of nightmares. Don't say I didn't warn you.'

She smiles. 'Talking of new clients, I've taken on Yuri Drakova, the Bulgarian couturier.'

'Another of Dannie's eastern European chums?'

'Afraid so. In fairness, he's very charming. I hope you'll meet him when you see Dannie tomorrow morning.'

I'd momentarily forgotten I had that little treat in store. This time, Dannie is staying at the Mayfair residence of an old US senator friend rather than holing up at the Berkeley Hotel. The entire staff must be dancing in the streets.

'By the way, you said you wanted to have a chat about the future,' I say, trying to make it sound casual. 'We should.'

She nods. 'Yes, let's go out for a drink some time and have a chat. Next time you're over.'

'Fine by me.'

Traffic noise seeps through the open windows even though we are five floors up. I push the chair back and throw my pen and diary into my handbag. I notice that it's getting very old and worn but I have no interest in shopping for a new one. How times change.

'Are you off somewhere?' Rachel enquires.

'The Natural History Museum. I'm seeing my friend, Adrian Lister.'

'Ah, yes, I remember now – the good professor. He's the guy who'll be leading your next expedition.'

'Correct.'

'So what are you meeting him about?'

I shrug. 'He sent me a curious email saying he had something special to show me at the museum. Apparently it's relevant to Mallorca.'

'Intriguing,' she smiles.

I head towards the door. 'I'll see you tomorrow.'

She hesitates a second. 'Oh, just one small thing you might like to know before meeting Yuri Drakova.'

I'm fumbling absentmindedly in my handbag for Judas, the name I give to my traitorous mobile. 'And what might that be?'

She gives a mischievous smile. 'He's a cross-dresser.'

## 2.45 p.m., The Natural History Museum, Kensington

There's a bottleneck of visitors at the vast and elegant entrance to the Natural History Museum but Adrian deftly whisks me through the crowds and up a grand flight of stairs. Away from the public areas the old wooden doors have number panels, presumably installed to ensure privacy and security for the resident scientists beavering away behind the scenes. Adrian taps in a special code and a pair of grand double doors click open, unleashing a rich aroma of polished wood. We glide effortlessly down corridors and up winding staircases, and tiptoe past labs. It is like entering a Tardis and I am stunned by the sheer scale of the building. In one echoing hall, scores of metal cabinets groaning with fossil artefacts run with military precision in rows from floor to ceiling. According to Adrian, there are similar treasure troves of fossil specimens on each and every floor.

Adrian is a palaeontologist and an expert on mammoths and elephants. We have been on various scientific expeditions together in our capacity as trustees of a national charity concerned with scientific exploration. Our first, in Nepal, involved tracking the world's largest Asian elephant, Raj Gaj, but Adrian and I were also given the task of collecting specimens of small moths in the Nepalese forests. This was no mean feat. By night, we would suspend fishnet tights filled with chicken feathers, and other detritus, from the trees, and by day we would examine them for moth larvae. It was an absorbing and edifying experience, made more rewarding when we returned to the UK and had our valuable specimens analysed at the very museum I'm visiting today. For me, combining science and travel is an addictive pastime, but for Adrian, it's a lifetime's work. Today he has generously invited me to inspect his scientific lair in advance of our next expedition to Borneo and to show me something which he thinks will capture my imagination. What, I wonder, can it be?

'So, what do you want to see first?' he asks breezily.

'The odd mammoth or Tyrannosaurus rex would be nice,' I jest.

'No problem.' He smiles and off we go, rattling along more corridors and into rooms bristling with history.

It is a few hours later that we emerge into the hall we first entered. I have seen so much, plundering a universe that existed thousands and in some cases millions of years ago. I have examined the enormous tusks, horns, vertebrae, bones, fins, gills and teeth of creatures that were once kings of our earthly and watery kingdom. In truth, I am in awe.

Adrian claps his hands together. 'I've saved the best until last. As I said in my email, a little surprise.'

I pucker my brow. 'What sort of surprise?'

He beckons me to follow as he rushes like the white rabbit down a long, narrow corridor to an enormous oak cabinet. Slowly, he pulls out a wooden drawer. I can hardly contain myself.

'What is it?' I gasp.

'You can't guess?'

I haven't a clue. 'A pygmy elephant?'

'No!'

'A prehistoric toad... you know I love amphibians.'

'No,' he says impatiently. 'It's Myotragus!'

'What?'

'Surely you know about Myotragus Balearicus, the dwarf goat that roamed Mallorca as far back as five million years ago?'

A distant bell is ringing but not enough to convince Adrian that I know my prehistoric Mallorcan history.

'Have you never heard of the scientist, Dorothea Bate?'

'I'm afraid not.'

He shakes his head in some disappointment. 'Back in the early nineteen-hundreds she began working for this museum.

It was she who discovered Myotragus on Mallorca. She was an amazing woman. You should read up about her.'

I scribble her name down in my diary and peer at the fragile bones of the little fossilised goat before me. It is indeed very small, with straight little horns and an enormous pair of sharp incisors jutting out from its lower jaw.

'"μυς τράγος." If my Greek doesn't fail me, that means "mouse-goat".'

'It most certainly does. It was rather rodent like.'

I'm pleased to have redeemed myself slightly. Learning ancient Greek in my salad days has at last proved of some use. I inspect the creature more closely. It has a delicate skull and deep hollows at the front where once its eyes must have been.

'Were its eyes at the front of its skull?' I ask. 'Wasn't that unusual for a goat-like creature?'

'Very good,' says Adrian. 'Most bovids have eyes at the side of the head. This feature made it quite distinct because it gave it three dimensional vision.'

'When did Myotragus die out?'

He puffs his cheeks. 'More than four thousand years ago. There's still debate about how it met its demise. Interestingly, it was quite unique to Mallorca and Menorca.'

Adrian inspects his watch and apologises, explaining he has to leave for a meeting. He attempts to close the drawer.

'Wait a moment,' I hear myself say.

A small grin plays on his lips. 'Take your time.'

I hesitate for a moment. There is something mesmerising and utterly beguiling about this small, extinct creature with its straight little horns and thrusting lower incisors. Without understanding why, I feel an inexplicable desire to learn more about it, to understand an aspect of Mallorcan pre-history which to my shame I've never really given a thought to before. Perhaps this tiny specimen might hold the key to the island's heart, its magic and soul. Adrian touches my sleeve.

'Be careful or you'll get bitten by the bug.'

'What bug?'

He laughs. 'The Myotragus bug, of course.'

We say our farewells at the entrance to the museum on the Cromwell Road.

'Don't forget Dorothea!' he calls after me.

I most certainly won't. Dorothea Bate. This is one woman I simply have to become acquainted with.

### 6 p.m., Curzon Street, Mayfair

My friend Ed is wearing a worried frown. He sits hunched over a cup of black coffee in Caffè Nero, and fiddles constantly with a paper napkin. Ed is one of my oldest university friends, and possibly the most neurotic individual on the planet. He works as a producer at the BBC and spends much of his leisure time either composing jazz music or looking for a soulmate in cyberspace. He has fraternised with various women through Internet dating sites, mostly American, but none have proven to be the girl of his dreams, and I'm fast wondering if any of these babes ever will be. I've heard of opposites attracting but Ed seems to go out of his way to meet women who have absolutely zero in common with him. Most are looking for a cross between a punch ball, life coach and meal ticket and Ed fits the bill perfectly. I've got to the stage where I dread hearing about the next potential dalliance.

'This losing weight business is such a bore,' he whines, 'but Eric gets so angry if I break the rules.'

'And who is Eric?'

'I told you. He's the guy assigned to me at my Internet weight-loss club. He emails me every day to check up on my dieting.'

'And you pay for the pleasure?'

'It only costs about fifty quid a month and he keeps me on track.'

I find it extraordinary how Ed's whole life revolves around his computer. If he could marry it, that might prove the answer to his girlfriend problems. He stares mournfully at the row of cakes by the counter and opens the black holdall, to which I fondly refer to as his 'MEK' – mobile emergency kit. Inside this essential piece of urban survival gear for the hypochondriac can be found medicinal curatives, refreshments and other random items of no use whatsoever. Like his silent shadow, MEK goes wherever Ed goes. He gulps down two small white pills.

'I could kill for a slice of carrot cake.'

'So have one.'

'No, Eric would be furious. He says I should lose two stone.'

'You know, Ed, you've really got to get a life.'

He suddenly brightens up. 'Now, don't sneer, but I've been in touch with an interesting-sounding woman.'

I throw out my arm and close my eyes. 'I'm already getting a psychic impression: American, needy, physical deformity, penniless…'

'Oh, shut up. Her name is Veronica and she is a priest from Yorkshire.'

I'm too stunned to respond.

'Yes, it's surprising, but we have a lot in common. Classical and organ music. And travel.'

'Travel?' I blurt. 'You have to be anaesthetised to get on a bus!'

'OK, but I enjoy the concept of travel. I'm going to give this relationship a go.'

I take a sip of coffee. 'Good for you, but don't go all pious on me.'

He guffaws. 'Not much chance of that. Now, before I forget, how is this awful cattery scheme of yours coming on?'

'Sorry to disappoint but we're making headway. The land is being cleared and then we'll be putting up the wooden structure.'

He taps his hand irritably on the table. 'With my cat allergy I'll never be able to stay with you again in Mallorca.'

'We can always get you a face mask.'

He sniffs heavily. 'Very droll.'

'So, tell me more about Veronica.'

'I think you'll like her. She was an archaeologist before she got her calling to God.'

'Really? How bizarre.'

'She seems to know an awful lot about the prehistory of the Balearics. You'd be impressed.'

'I wonder if she knows anything about Myotragus.'

'What's that?'

'A goat that used to roam our islands up until about four or five thousand years ago.'

He leans back in his seat and shrugs. 'I can ask her. Anyway, why on earth are you suddenly interested in goats?'

'No real reason although it's odd how they keep cropping up in conversation. It could just be a series of coincidences but I do feel drawn to them of late.'

He eyes me with suspicion. 'I hope to God you're not considering breeding the damned things?'

'I hadn't thought about it, Ed, but now that you come to mention it...'

**Wednesday 8 a.m., Hill Street, Mayfair**

It's eight in the morning and I have been given strict instructions not to arrive a minute before the agreed hour for my meeting with Dannie. The immaculate terraced house in Hill Street has a miniscule patio that, rather like a pampered poodle, has been manicured to within an inch of its life. A trio of small box trees stand to attention in terracotta tubs at the side of the path that delivers the caller to the front door in a few bounds. In a neat and regimented window box, a shock of unnaturally bred oxblood-hued tulips stare up at the blue sky, their young green leaves clipped at the tips for symmetrical perfection. How different they are from my own wild and profuse assortment of Mediterranean blooms back home. I ring the bell, clocking that there's a spy hole in the door. A minute or so elapses and then a woman's muffled voice strains to reach me through the dense wood. Someone is releasing several bolts, and then battling with multiple locks. What is this, a twenty-first-century Fort Knox? Eventually, a frazzled face looks out from behind a sturdy door chain.

'Yes?'

'I have an appointment with Miss Popescu-Miller.'

The door slams shut. I wait. A postman's van stops a few yards from me on the road, its engine throbbing. The driver steals a glance in my direction and then observes himself in the vehicle's mirror and yawns. Finally he gets out of the vehicle, with two medium sized packages and heads towards me.

'Can you sign for these?' he grunts.

'I don't live here.'

'No matter.'

He proffers a pen. Obediently I scrawl my signature on a piece of paper and watch as he slouches out of the gate, gets in his van and drives hastily away. No pleasantries, no conversation. It's all a far cry from life in our valley with Jorge the postman popping by to see me for a chat and a glass of water. I could murder a coffee. Suddenly, the door flies open and there in front of me is Dannie, shrouded in a turquoise silk kimono. Well, I think it's Dannie but something's happened to her. God knows, but she looks terrifying, pallid, as if she's donned some horrific skeletal mask and her hair is... gone. All that remains are small wisps that rise up like cobwebs. I give an involuntary gasp.

'Dannie, whatever's happened?'

She bats away a wizened little woman wearing a black and white maid's outfit, confirming that at least in this part of London 'Upstairs, Downstairs' is still alive and well.

'Didn't your mother ever tell you it was rude to stare?' she drawls.

'I'm so sorry, Dannie. I just got a bit of a shock.'

'You didn't know I wore a wig?'

'A wig? No, I didn't.'

She gives me a crisp little smile. 'The rest is nature's joke.'

I regard her with some bewilderment. She rolls her eyes.

'I'm just not wearing any make-up.'

I try to give my cheeriest Girl Guide grimace. 'Let's face it, we all have bad hair days. I mean...'

It's too late to eat my words and in truth I'm too weary to care. Tetchily, she ushers me inside and rustles down the corridor to an enormous kitchen. I follow in her wake with the two bulky packages. The nervous, diminutive maid is standing by the polished Aga with her hands behind her back.

'This is Sacha,' says Dannie. 'She's from Romania.'

'Hello Sacha.'

Dannie lights up a cigarette. 'Don't bother. She doesn't understand a word of English.'

I stand awkwardly in the centre of the room, taking in the rather predictable lavish surroundings; the Smallbone and Conran furniture, the Oggetti gizmos...

'Do take a seat,' she cries. 'Yuri has been staying here while his flat's being decorated. He'll be down anytime.'

I deposit the two packages on the table. 'Wonderful. And is your senator friend here?'

Dannie gives a little snort. 'God, no. Now that would be a nightmare. He's a ghastly little man, a friend of my ex-husband. He rarely stays here, just offers open house to all his American buddies and clients.'

'That's very generous.'

'You wouldn't say that if you knew him. He's odious. Let me get you a coffee.'

'Fantastic.'

She issues instructions in what I assume is Romanian, and Sacha rushes over to the coffee machine.

'She's getting us both a vodka too.'

I protest.

'Come on,' she gives a girlish titter. 'It'll put hair on your chest.'

Maybe it would be better if it put hair on her own head.

'So, how are things in Mallorca?' She is going through the motions.

'Much the same. It's very hot and humid at the moment.'

'As you know, I'm a fan of Robert Graves's works. He describes your part of Mallorca in such glowing terms.'

'Yes, but of course Deià was his home.'

'I particularly loved his *Greek Myths*. I imagine with your classical background you'll have read them.'

Thankfully, I have, but not for some time. It fascinates me that Dannie is so well read. Our conversation is interrupted. The door clangs open and in walks a vision of some splendour. It is profoundly feminine in most respects but the auburn wig is somewhat unsubtle and the make-up is thickly caked on. The teetering heels scrape against the granite floor, and the brocade frock flounces about the knees in a froth of lace.

'At last, we meet!' he yelps in a deep and husky Slovak voice. 'It is I, Yuri!'

Sacha scurries over to me with an espresso and a shot of iced vodka.

I down it in one, wondering whether I've landed on the set of some exotic panto or perhaps I'm hallucinating badly. I stumble to my feet.

'Yuri! I've heard so much about you from Rachel. What a pleasure.'

'I hope my appearance doesn't disturb you,' he gushes, 'but not as bad as seeing Daniella without make-up, eh?'

I pump his hand and twitter about the weather, hoping to draw him on to neutral topics. He's having none of it.

He tweaks my curls. 'Your hair's nice and wavy. Is it a wig?'

'Certainly not.'

He sniffs deeply. 'Some of us aren't so lucky, are we Dannie?'

She sits silently like a sphinx, giving him black looks.

'All that dye, perming and backcombing catches up with you one day.'

I battle on, ignoring the comment. 'Rachel's shown me some of your exquisite couture designs and some pieces from the new collection. She's so excited about working with you.'

'And you?'

In truth, I'd rather hide out in the hills with a pack of mangy goats for company but that won't pay the bills.

'Of course. Any friend of Dannie's is a friend of mine.'

She sits opposite me, blowing smoke to the ceiling. 'That's so sweet. Anyhow, shall we get down to some work?'

'Absolutely,' I say, relieved to draw my notepad out of my handbag.

Sacha places a large cup of coffee into Yuri's hands.

'We have work to do, Yuri,' Dannie says pointedly. 'Can you amuse yourself for a while?'

He minces towards the door with his cup. 'Hey, don't worry about me, girls. I haven't even got round to plucking my eyebrows this morning.'

## FOUR

# A STING IN THE TAIL

The frogs bask on a carpet of lily pads in the pond, their silky skin turning an iridescent green in the rays of the early morning sun. These days my croaking, nightly revellers barely stir when I appear barefoot and unannounced at the pond to sit with them. They merely log my arrival with big glassy eyes and continue to puff out their chests like sopranos. I can only imagine they're still feeling groggy from their all-night partying beneath my bedroom window. Johnny, my toad, is only just visible in the dark water. He hovers near the rocky wall over which a steady stream of water trickles, and keeps his back legs outstretched and floating behind him like a pair of dead twigs. He occasionally gives a small thrust with his webbed front legs and rises enough to peer out through the bulrushes, and then sinks back again like a submarine. I draw my legs up under me on the warm dry wall and watch the tiny red fishes darting about. They flicker like small flames, gobbling up tiny insects that fall haplessly in their path. So absorbed am I in pool life that Jorge, our Adonis of a postman, startles me when he crunches across the gravel. He is holding out a packet.

'Looks like a book,' he says with a smile.

'Thanks for ruining the surprise.'

'But it says Amazon on the packet.'

'I know... I'm only teasing,' I say.

He throws down his yellow postbag and sits next to me on the wall. His long mane of hair is tied back with a small black ribbon and his sleeves are rolled up, exposing golden skin. 'It's so hot already and the sun's barely up. I've still got several more deliveries to make before I'm back at the depot.'

Jorge speaks to me in Spanish rather than the local dialect, in part because he is from Argentina, but mostly, I suspect, in deference to my dismal level of Catalan.

'Can I get you some cold water?'

He hesitates and runs a hand over his perspiring forehead. '*Vale,* maybe a small one. *Gracias.*'

I potter off to the kitchen and, when I return, find him leaning low over the pond.

'Be careful or you might fall in.'

'Is that a toad you've got in there?'

'Yes, I call him Johnny.'

Jorge seems fascinated. 'You know, it's hard to see but he looks very similar to the *ferreret,* the famous midwife toad they have up here in the mountains. Same sort of markings.'

I hand him the glass and shake my head. 'I promise he's just a common old toad. I've read quite a bit about *ferrerets* and apparently they're only found in deep canyon streams high in the Tramuntanas. There's no way one would have found his way down here.'

He laughs. 'Maybe he just got fed up having to carry his kids and did a runner.'

The *ferreret*, as it is known in Mallorcan, is unusual in that the male carries a string of fertilised eggs on its back, then protects and wraps them around his hind legs until they are ready to hatch out into tadpoles. This is why it is known as the midwife toad. I find it very endearing. Midwife toads are very rare and are now a highly protected species in Mallorca.

'You know the *ferreret* can carry up to a hundred and fifty eggs on its back.'

Jorge's blue eyes bulge. 'Poor guy! Anyway, when did you get so interested in toads?'

'It's just a small interest – actually more of a preoccupation.'

He puts his glass down on the wall and gets up. I notice that on his left hand he has a tattoo of the letter B enclosed in a tiny red heart.

'That's new.'

He waggles a finger. 'You never miss a trick. Her name's Beatriz. I met her at Sa Mostra.'

'But that was only a month or so ago. A tattoo so soon?'

'I'm in love.'

It wasn't so long ago that he had to remove a small letter R on his right wrist when he split with his Argentinean fiancée.

'Well, let's hope this one lasts,' I say dryly.

'*Seguro*, just wait and see.'

We walk to the gate together.

'By the way, I pushed the rest of your mail in the postbox here. I didn't expect to see you in the garden.'

'Don't worry, I'll collect it now.'

I pull open the tiny door to the postbox. There are four or five letters crammed inside which I take out and examine one by one. I am just studying an envelope when a scorpion scampers across its front. I scream and drop everything to the ground. Jorge jumps back in fright, exclaiming, 'Susto!', and squats down on his haunches.

'What is it?'

'A scorpion,' I yelp.

He kicks at a rock and then picks up the letters and shakes them. 'It was a small one. I wonder how it got in there.'

'You saw it?'

'Sure. You're lucky it didn't sting you.'

Jorge peers inside the box.

'It's empty. I wonder how it got inside?'

I wonder too, but I'll think twice about fumbling inside the postbox in the future without a furtive peek first.

It is Saturday and Sóller's *plaça*, the main square, is bristling with people because on market day the world and his *burro* arrives in force to soak up local life and colour. Even though September has arrived tourists still mill about the town in wonderment, capturing images of cobbled streets, quaint shopfronts, market stalls and our historic train and tram on digital cameras. Ollie heads for his favourite stall, which sells a massive array of olives, pickles, salted cod and *boquerones*, the exquisite and addictive little white anchovies that are prepared in olive oil. Salted cod, known as *bacallà*, is purchased in large slabs, and it took me some time to summon up the courage to ask Marga, the market stall holder, how to cook it. With delight, she and several regulars buzzing around the counter took me in hand, explaining how to prepare and serve this wonderful fish. In the past, salted *bacallà*

was popular with the poor because it was cheap and could be stored indefinitely. Now it has developed a reputation for being delicious and versatile. The fish does need to be soaked in multiple changes of water but once the flesh is soft, it can be used in all sorts of ways. *Bacallà* cooked in the oven with sundried tomatoes, black olives and a drizzle of olive oil is a treat indeed.

Marga greets me and without a thought begins filling a huge plastic tub with anchovy-flavoured green olives. Ollie stands on his tiptoes to point at the *boquerones* but she has already anticipated this. She half fills the container but he asks in Mallorcan for her to top it up. If my son had his way he would live on a diet of olives and anchovies. Before we leave, she clasps some anchovies with her tongs and passes them to him. He smiles and gobbles them down, dripping olive oil all over his T-shirt.

I pull a face. 'Yuk. Fish for breakfast!'

He licks his lips. 'Delicious, and now it's time for chocolate cake.'

Our weekly ritual is to have breakfast at Café Paris, just off the *plaça*, and so, with bulging bags, we squeeze past a throng of people at its entrance and by luck manage to bag a table that is just being vacated. Mateo, one of the cafe's long serving waiters, arrives.

'The usual?' he shouts above the din.

We nod. José, the owner, gives us a wave from the bar, and in a few minutes, Mateo returns with a gigantic slice of *pastís de xocolata* and Bitter Kas – similar to Campari but without alcohol – for Ollie, and a croissant and espresso for me.

'That's enough for two people,' I exclaim, eyeing Ollie's chocolate cake.

'Exactly, he's a growing boy, aren't you Ollie? Why have one slice when you can have two?'

He pats Ollie's face fondly and darts off to another table.

Elderly Senyor Bisbal, a frequent visitor to Café Paris, catches my eye and approaches the table.

'Is everything alright?' he enquires. 'How is the cattery going?'

I stand up and plant a kiss on his cheek. 'The men are clearing the land for the next few weeks and then we'll get cracking.'

He smiles. 'So it will become a reality?'

'I certainly hope so.'

He laughs. 'I never thought I'd live to see the day when a cat hotel opened in Sóller.'

He wanders back to his table to share this news with one of his old companions who rolls his head back and hoots with laughter. It's always gratifying to know that I provide endless amusement to the locals with my mad ideas. They both look across at me with broad smiles.

'They think you're a *loca*,' grins Ollie. 'And so do I!'

Our next port of call is HiBit, where Antonia is battling with a queue of customers who all seem to have complicated requests. We amble about until the shop has emptied. She leans heavily on the counter.

'What a day! It's never-ending. I wonder why Albert and I run this business. It's crazy and the phone never stops.'

'It's nice to be popular though,' I reply.

She gives a hoarse laugh. 'Sure, that must be what it is!'

We have ordered a new printer which she unearths from the *almacén*, the store, at the back of the shop. I tell her about the scorpion incident which surprises her no end.

'That's very rare. I haven't seen a scorpion in years.'

Ever since living in the Sóller Valley we seem to have broken the precedent when it comes to rare small creatures and creepy crawlies lurking about the *finca*. We have regular visitations from Horatio, our resident hedgehog, a genet we call George, and nightly sightings of civet cats and pine martens. During the summer months, snakes slither into our *entrada* for shade or hide in the rocks by the pond and we have a colony of frogs, Johnny the toad, and many fish and insects, particularly dragonflies, and cicadas. Whenever we mention this to local friends they regard us with amazement. Until now, scorpions haven't joined the happy throng, for which we've been grateful. It seems that might be about to change.

'You should be careful,' Antonia says thoughtfully. 'They may have a nest.'

I leave the shop in some angst. 'Surely we can't have more scorpions?' I ask Ollie.

'It'd be cool to see one. I wish you'd called me this morning,' he chides.

We pop by Colmado sa Lluna, Sóller's famed deli known by British residents as 'little Fortnum & Mason' because of its impressive selection of beloved British food brands. Here I have impromptu Catalan lessons courtesy of owner Xavier and his girlfriend, Teresa, who are determined to make a Sólleric of me, even if it takes them a lifetime to achieve their goal. They are always complicit with Ollie, joking with him in local dialect when I falter or make an almighty blunder. In return I provide much merriment for those waiting in the queue as I ask for my *tallades de dindia,* slices of cold turkey, *formatge,* cheese, and *panets*, rolls. While I toil away at Catalan, I realise that my Castilian Spanish is becoming worse by the day but *què fer,* what should I do? 'When in Sóller, do as the Sóllerics do' is my new motto, and when in the Peninsula I will just have to brush up rapidly on my Castilian Spanish and hope for the best.

Some time later, and carrying an achingly heavy amount of shopping, Ollie and I arrive at the vet's surgery. Our feline twins have been stripped of their manhood today, so they are bleary-eyed and disorientated from the anaesthetic when we collect them. Ollie doesn't look happy.

'You know, I think Pep's right. It's cruel to cut off the cats' *cojones*.'

'They had to be neutered or we'd just be adding to the feral cat problem here.'

'But Minky and Orlando will now never be able to father kittens.'

I wasn't expecting a philosophical discussion about cat castration but now is probably as good a time as any.

'The point is that if we don't stop the cats breeding, people will poison the kittens to keep their numbers down. We're doing the right thing.'

Ollie is glum in the front seat of the car. 'Hopefully they won't be too depressed when they wake up.'

I stifle a smile. Somehow I think the twins won't conjecture too much on their loss. We wrestle the bags and two cat baskets into the car and trundle off home.

Alan greets us at the porch with a furrowed brow.

'You'll never believe it. A scorpion has just scuttled across the desk in my *abajo!*'

'You're having me on?'

He isn't laughing. 'Absolutely not. I wonder where they're suddenly coming from.'

At least Alan's *abajo*, his stone built hideaway, is situated in the garden. I'd be far more concerned if a scorpion had found its way into the house, although that might just be a question of time.

'Perhaps it's sheer coincidence that we've seen two in one day.'
I try to be upbeat.

'Maybe,' says Alan doubtfully.

Ollie gives us a dazzling smile. 'Hopefully it'll be me that sees
one next time. You're both so lucky!'

Alan and I exchange looks. It's not quite the sort of luck we
may have had in mind.

The sleepy village of Biniaraix lies in the hills between Sóller
town and a larger and loftier village, Fornalutx. From Sóller it is
reached by a quiet, winding stretch of road, flanked on one side
by a wide and open *torrente* which during the summer produces
little more than a murmur of trickling water. When the dry season
passes, and the hills once again echo with rolling thunder while
blinding rains hit our little valley, the *torrente* gurgles joyously
and water gushes and skips headlong over broad flat stones and
craggy rocks, zigzagging down to the town where it races neck and
neck with adjoining *torrentes* to reach the open sea first. A mass
of towering, wild bamboo canes and thick, unruly papyrus grow
by the banks of this river and ducks potter contentedly among
the rocks while goats and unfettered sheep with clanking bells
roam around the nearby pastures. It could be a scene straight out
of a Wordsworth poem, a picture of bucolic bliss. This morning I
shall be spending some hours with Catalina and her aunt Maria,
culinary queen of Fornalutx, picking olives at the family olive
grove. I have agreed that I shall jog up to Biniaraix from my
house and meet them near the village's old communal washing
stands at 7.30 a.m. It's one of my favourite runs, and I like to
catch my breath by the *torrente*, exchanging baa-ing noises with

the sheep and goats before ploughing on up the steep hill to the Biniaraix turn off. Francesca Marti, a notable Mallorcan artist, lives in a rambling and idyllic *finca* at the intersection and from time to time we share *hola*'s as she whizzes by on her bike on her way into town. It's a rare thing to meet anyone on the road early morning although Carmen, a sturdy, ample-bosomed lady whose elderly father lives near us, is often sweeping dust from her porch. She lives a stone's throw from the *torrente*, and likes to beckon me over for a quick word when I pass by. Every day she gets on her *moto* and pops down the hill to check on her widower father, make his meals and clean the home. In rural Mallorca it is the norm for the family to take care of their elderly relatives, and the extended family all share the duties.

I run, panting, into the quiet village and arrive at the allotted time just as a large blue estate car swerves round the bend and clumsily mounts the curb. It stops and a horn blasts. If the inhabitants of Biniaraix aren't already awake, they will be now. Catalina is yelling to me from the driver's open window.

'Come on, lazy woman! We've been waiting hours. What sort of runner are you?'

I amble over to the car and pull open the door to the back seat. Her diminutive aunt Maria is chuckling from the front. 'Had a good run?' she booms.

'Wonderful. I could do with a coffee and croissant though,' I reply.

Catalina revs the engine. 'Later! Now we work.'

The car roars off, out of the village, past the *rentadores*, the old stone sinks once used by locals for clothes washing, and follow a very steep and curvy road which leads high into the Tramuntanas. The sky is peacock blue and a squat orange sun peers over the hilltops as we climb ever higher, negotiating perilously sharp bends and shaving the grass on the sides of the road. My hair dances madly in the breeze as I lean out giddily and peer down at the vertiginous drop below. The air grows cooler as we ascend and soon a feathery mist coils around the tips of the mountains, descending steadily until it caresses the jagged rocks below and blanches the dark trees. It moves fluidly in soft white swirls, seeping inland, and gathering up trees, orchards and terraces in its ghostly fingers.

With her foot hard on the accelerator, Catalina rattles on, past lush, verdant orchards, brittle woodland and small homesteads. From the road, dusty, narrow tracks dart off right and left dropping so precipitously that I doubt whether they would lead a hapless driver to a promised olive grove but rather to certain oblivion. For some miles we hurtle on, the car protesting on dicey hairpin bends, forcing Catalina to reverse and take the turn more keenly. After a while I realise that, to avoid palpitations, it's wiser not to survey the fast fading tapestry of pasture and forestland far, far below. At the next uphill turn Catalina wrestles the vehicle into first gear, grimly gripping the wheel as though it might suddenly take flight. Maria, who has been serenely observing the land rising and falling around us, sits up perkily for a mile or so more before nonchalantly instructing Catalina to take a sharp left. The car heaves itself over boulders and huge ruts in the soil until it is able to practically freefall down a long winding track bordered by wild scrub and enormous bushes of rosemary and thyme. At last we come to rest in sandy earth by a stone hut. Catalina breathes heavily and kills the engine.

'That was fun!'

'Rather you than me,' I say with some relief as we push open the doors and stumble, stiff-limbed, into sudden sunshine. 'Maybe we can walk back?'

Catalina thumps me on the back. 'You get used to it! Anyway, we made it.'

'So you want to try picking olives?' says Maria with a mischievous hint to her voice. 'The family will be picking all week so we can make a gentle start today.'

She strides off and begins scanning the terraces.

'Best if you start on the lower branches over here,' she calls to me. 'Here's a shoulder bag. Put all the olives in there.'

I notice that she has donned an apron which has an inbuilt cloth bag, a handy looking item. She stalks off up the terraces and is lost from sight. Catalina approaches a stocky and characteristically gnarled olive tree and taps the trunk. 'Start here and see how you get on. I'll work on the next one.'

I have taken the precaution of bringing gardening gloves with me but I soon realise that they are more of a hindrance, and end up hurling them to the ground. Picking olives is nimble work. The green fruit is secreted between clumps of strong bushy dark leaves and it is better to pull off each individual olive in a gentle drawing motion, rather like milking a cow, than by simply tugging. When we first came to the valley I remember nibbling a green olive from one of our trees and spitting it out in disgust at its acidity. Of course I soon discovered that you can't eat olives straight from the tree. Ignorantly, I knew little about olive oil production, having been a typical Londoner, buying my olives in a designer bottle from a bland supermarket and rarely stopping to think about the process involved. Today I'm learning first hand.

The sun gradually begins to split the clouds and soon I find myself sweating profusely. Shaded as we are in among the shadows of the trees, the heat is still penetrating. I pluck the fruit carefully from the branches and pop it into the bag swinging over my shoulder. It's not filling fast. There must be a tear in it. I

85

stick my hand inside and feel about, acknowledging with a tinge of disappointment that it's completely hole-free. Obscured but not far away I can hear Maria loudly singing a *glosa* of some kind, one of the Mallorcan ballads which are performed at local fiestas and traditionally were also sung during harvesting and fruit picking. The words to these songs were always relevant to the task in hand and so too are those of this cheery reaping song which now wafts over to me.

*'Si es segar, s'hagués posat,*
*A davall d'una porxada,*
*Segaria una escarada*
*Com es terme de Ciutat…'*

I listen for a few minutes. The reaper in the song proclaims that if she were able to work under a shelter, her harvest would be bigger than a city. Under a shelter or not, my harvest would still probably be very thin. I pluck away at the trees, hoping that Maria won't appear at any moment to mock my paltry offerings. We toil on for another few hours and with relief I see that my bag is filling up.

'Shall we stop for a drink?' Maria asks. She is standing under my tree. I have by this time risen into the upper branches on a small ladder.

'What a nice idea.'

We sit on an old blanket and eat chunks of fresh bread and olives with *manchego* cheese, all washed down with some delicious earthy red wine.

'So will these olives be used for oil too?'

Maria finishes her mouthful of bread. 'We'll of course use some for oil. It all comes down to the maturity of the olives.'

Catalina cuts herself a piece of cheese. 'The riper olives have a sweeter taste and make delicious oil. The green olives have a slightly bitter and spicy flavour.'

'That's the type they serve at Es Turo restaurant. They're delicious,' I add.

'Some visitors complain that the green ones are too bitter but I don't agree,' tuts Maria. 'We often use brine to preserve them, as well as olive oil. It's just a matter of taste.'

'Are there still a lot of people making olive oil on the island?'

Catalina pushes back a tendril of dark hair. 'Not so many now. In the nineteen hundreds, olive oil used to be Mallorca's main export. These days, it's less important.'

'So how much does gets exported?' I ask.

Maria shakes her head. 'Not very much. About one hundred thousand litres were produced this year but most of it's used for home consumption.'

We sip our wine slowly.

'How much oil do you reckon you can you get from one tree?'

They both shrug.

'About eight litres, but it depends on its size and how healthy it is,' says Maria. 'I mean a huge tree can produce hundreds of kilos of olives while another, maybe only fifty.'

I look down at my hands. They're red raw and scratched. Maybe the gloves weren't such a bad idea.

'So when do you lay nets under the trees?'

Maria pours herself another *copa* of wine and sits back against a sturdy trunk.

'Only in December when we pick the ripe black olives. We shake the trees with *cañas*, and the olives fall into the nets. You should try your hand at that too.'

She smiles impishly, probably conjuring up an image of me flailing around with the long stick and doing myself untold harm. Maria has for the last few years been initiating me into the ways of traditional rural life. We have picked *cargols*, snails, and wild *seta* mushrooms together, and she has shown me how to use a traditional *ximbomba* instrument which accompanies the singing of *gloses* at fiestas.

Reaching into her apron pocket, Maria examines a handful of olives approvingly.

'These will be good to use in the restaurant once they've been treated in brine.'

I briefly contemplate the delicious, salty green and black olives that are served at Canantuna, the restaurant she owns with her husband in Fornalutx.

She drains her cup and, rising to her feet, claps her hands together.

'*Vale*. Another hour or so and then we finish for the morning.'

I begin work on another tree, this time a larger specimen. Pushing the wooden ladder against the bottom, I gingerly climb up to the middle branches. Catalina and her aunt are thrashing about close by among the trees. The sky is now a fierce blue and cicadas surround me, hissing and hopping about the branches in the searing heat. My bag is heavy and wearily I descend and mop my brow. The others soon join me and together we dump our booty in the car and head back on to the road. The journey back is less daunting because I feel nicely mellow after the wine and happy that we are now in descent mode.

We arrive back in Biniaraix village just before lunchtime and park by the old stone church. Nothing stirs but voices can be heard from the lone bar. Slamming the car doors behind us we walk across the tiny square, more of a postage stamp, to an empty table outside a cafe. We flop into chairs, relishing the sun on our stiff backs. The door of the bar opens and the owner smiles over at us, pad in hand.

'So,' says Maria. 'What will it be?'

Sitting at the kitchen table I rip open the little package that Jorge delivered to me yesterday. I had absentmindedly misplaced it by the pond and was therefore overjoyed to rediscover it early morning on the stone steps damp with dew. Inside is a gleaming new book, a sight that always fills me with pleasure. It is entitled *Discovering Dorothea*, and is the biography of the scientist Dorothea Bate written by an author named Karolyn Schindler. I had found the title on the Internet and ordered a copy shortly after meeting my friend Adrian in London. The photo on the book cover shows a rather shy young woman wearing a long skirt and a broad-rimmed sun hat. I try to imagine her scrabbling about in Mallorca's rugged caves in search of fossilised goat remains. It must have been fairly avant garde in the early twentieth century for a woman to embark on such a curious Mediterranean adventure. I take a sip of tea and soon become immersed in the early life of the enterprising Dorothea. I find it remarkable that in 1898 a young woman of only nineteen years of age should have had the temerity to march into the austere Natural History Museum demanding a job. Happily, having proven to be an able scientist – although wholly unqualified – Dorothea was given work in fossil analysis and cataloguing. The museum was to become her home from home for fifty years. I am about to commence chapter three when the telephone rings. Knowing that the Scotsman is busy with his vegetable patch and Ollie is off playing tennis with a friend, I have no choice but to answer it. To my chagrin, it is my Panamanian client, Manuel.

'I am Manuel,' he announces.

'How lovely to hear from you – and how are things?'

We have recently announced a series of new H Hotel openings across the globe and the media has shown great interest.

'All is well and I am delighted with the press coverage we are receiving.'

Thank heavens for that.

'But...'

My heart sinks.

'There is a little matter I wish to discuss with you about the opening of the Maryland Hotel. One of my chief investors there is Vice Admiral Mason.'

'You mentioned.'

'*Muy bien*. Now as it happens he is coming to London in December and he would like to meet you.'

I shrug to myself. 'That's fine, Manuel.'

'I'm afraid he is a suspicious man like me. He needs to know that you and your colleagues are trustworthy, that you are not working on behalf of rivals.'

Rachel was right. Birds of a feather. Manuel has found an investor as bafflingly paranoiac as he.

'Manuel, how often do I have to explain to you that we are not working for any rival hotel company?'

'*Si, si*, I know all this but Vice Admiral Mason insists on meeting you and Rachel. It will be OK but I must warn you that he was in intelligence. He was an interrogator during the war.'

'How old is he?'

'He retired some time ago.'

I'm now picturing a paranoiac old goat. Maybe he doesn't know that the war's ended, and exactly which war are we talking about anyway?

'Whatever makes him happy, Manuel. We have a few months to think about it.'

Before he hangs up he gives a scratchy, embarrassed laugh. 'We are all friends, no? Mason is just a cautious man. With time will come trust.'

He hangs up. I worry about Manuel. The way things are going, he and his new American buddy might end up in a psychiatric wing long before we ever get the chance to meet.

Ollie is bristling with excitement. Our builder, Stefan, Catalina's brother, has been up to the house to oversee the workmen and has made a grim discovery: two scorpion hideouts, one under a pile of logs next to the *abajo* in the field and the other in the stone wall by the postbox. Having poked around in both places, he found a sleepy scorpion and some young in evidence in each one. He has suggested using a strong insect repellent recommended by the local *ferretería*. I watch as he reverses his van and turns out of the drive. We wave after him.

'What a nightmare,' I say.

Ollie is beaming. 'Isn't it great? I've never seen a scorpion before. I might borrow your camera.'

'You do realise that they have a highly unpleasant sting in the tail?'

He skips back up the steps to the porch. 'Most people survive scorpion stings and anyway the ones in Europe aren't dangerous.'

'Who says?' I call after him.

He ignores me and runs into the house, no doubt to share the joyous tidings with the Scotsman. I can see Rafael on the track playing with his dog, Alberto. I amble towards them, watching Alberto twist in the air as he tries to reach the stick in his owner's hand. Rafael greets me warmly.

'How are things?'

I shrug. 'We've got some scorpions in the garden.'

He looks unfazed. 'How many?'

'About four and some babies.'

'*Hombre*!' A fit of laughter. 'That's nothing.'

'Nothing? One would be bad enough.'

He places his hand on my shoulder. 'Look, if you want to get rid of them, just stick a few cloves of raw garlic and fresh rosemary into each lair and they will be gone in a few days.'

'Really?'

'*Segur*!' he yells.

I thank him heartily and potter back to the house where I vigorously begin peeling garlic cloves. Then, marching out into the garden and with the help of a long wooden spoon, I very carefully place them, together with a copious amount of rosemary, in the places where the scorpions have been spotted. With any luck, it might just do the trick.

Alan has ditched his gardening clobber in favour of a pair of chinos, shirt and linen jacket and I too have swapped old shorts for a dress, for tonight we are present at the annual La Vermada supper in Binissalem. Once a year this little town in the centre of the island holds a Grape Harvest Festival, Verbena de la Vermada, and one of the key events is a splendid supper served by residents to their families and invited guests at long trestle tables set up for the purpose in every street by the local council. Famous for its wine production from as far back as the Romans, and arguably the Moors, who were practised in the art of wine fermentation, Binissalem is today regarded as the heart of the Mallorca wine industry. On the night of the Vermada a traditional soup of *fideus*, fine noodles with either fish or meat, is served. The town is completely closed to cars for the occasion and invitees arrive on foot to their respective host's home in the town centre.

I have eaten more than my fair share of delicious fare and yet our generous host, Rosalia, the elderly mother of our friend, Jaume, insists I refill my plate.

'Have some more dessert,' urges Inès, Jaume's wife.

I drain my wine glass. 'Do you know, I couldn't eat another thing.'

It's nearly two o'clock in the morning, time to go. Alan is deep in conversation with Jaume so it's difficult to catch his eye across the table. My ears prick up when I hear the word 'scorpion'. I interrupt.

'Are you discussing our scorpions?'

Jaume laughs. 'Now you know why we live in Palma. We don't want snakes and scorpions in the house.'

'Absolutely not!' cries Inès.

Alan finishes his wine. 'Anyway, they seem to have gone. Their hideouts are completely empty.'

'*Gràcies a Déu* for that!' Jaume replies. 'Here, Alan, have another glass of *vi negre*.'

Alan holds up a hand and shakes his head.

'That red wine is superb but I think we really should be heading off. It's been a wonderful evening but we've quite a drive home.'

Jaume slaps the table. 'Well, it's nice to return a little hospitality for the lovely lunch we had with you in Sóller.'

I smile, remembering back to the day when Jaume turned up for lunch not only with his wife and family, but with his elderly parents and niece and nephew in tow. That had proven quite a culinary challenge. We rise from the table.

'So will you be back for the battle of the grapes?' Jaume quizzes.

'I think we might just miss that one,' Alan yawns. 'We did come last year, remember. I've never got those stains out of my shirt.'

'You're supposed to wear old clothes,' he rebukes.

'But all his clothes are old,' I say with a wink.

The enormous battle of the *uvas*, held in a field near the town's Plaça de l'Eglèsia, is great fun if you enjoy being smothered in grape juice by complete strangers, but on balance I think I prefer just to be a spectator.

We bid farewell to our fellow diners, mostly local Binissalem residents, and head off home. The town is buzzing with life and large groups of revellers stroll through the streets under a starfilled sky. Alan rests his jacket over one shoulder and slowly rolls up his shirt sleeves.

'Gosh, the heat's palpable, even at this late hour.'

We find our car, a few minutes' walk out of the town centre, and prepare to leave.

'What a great night,' I say sleepily.

'Fantastic,' he agrees. 'By the way, it's true what I said to Jaume. I think those wretched scorpions have finally gone.'

'I know!' I say, pleased as punch that he has brought up the subject.

'You do?' he asks.

'They've completely vanished; but what you don't know is that it's all thanks to the power of garlic and rosemary.'

'What?' he says with a mystified expression.

'Rafael taught me a little trick. Apparently you put garlic and rosemary into their dens to drive them off.'

He stares at me for a second and then hoots with laughter.

'You silly sausage,' he says. 'Rafael was just pulling your leg.'

'But the scorpions have gone,' I reason.

'Indeed, thanks to the poison Stefan put down from the *ferreteria*.'

'I don't believe it!'

'It's true. Rafael mentioned giving you some cock-and-bull story about a magic potion but I didn't think you'd have believed him.'

We drive off home, Alan chuckling most of the way about the scorpion ruse. I have been well and truly duped. Still, if Rafael enjoys practical jokes so much I'm sure I can dream up a special little prank just for him. One day soon, when he's least expecting it, I shall pay my chum Rafael back big time.

# FIVE

# HOPPING MAD

I awake after a terrific rainstorm to hear a rhythmic croaking emanating from the garden but something is wrong. The frog anthem appears to be coming not from the pond, but the swimming pool. The open shutters have been lashed with rain and small puddles of water have collected on the wooden floors. I should have risen and fastened them shut during the night, but in the haziness of sleep I had merely acknowledged the sound of hissing rain and returned to the land of Nod. The chances of the Scotsman rousing in the small hours would be near impossible unless perchance a random elephant padded into the bedroom and sat on his head, but that's not very likely here in the Sóller Valley. Ollie dashes into the room. He is sporting his bottle green school uniform and his hair is askew.

'Come quickly! The pool is full of frogs,' he says breathlessly, his face overcome with excitement.

Glancing at Alan's blissfully slumbering form, I jet propel myself out of bed and follow Ollie barefoot down the stairs and out into the back garden. We arrive at the pool just as about twenty glistening frogs dive in perfect synchronisation from the side into the azure depths. This is by no means the end of the display. In nearby puddles left by the night's rains, tiny frogs puff out their chests and hop about as if they own the place. On the water's surface I notice a large gathering of baby frogs splashing about. All they need is a beach ball and some rubber rings. How in heaven's name had this web-footed invasion occurred overnight? It's an accepted myth up here in the hills that in springtime frogs arrive en masse at precisely the same time across the valley and depart without a croak in early October. I ponder whether some new frogs on the block have got their time clocks muddled. They should be packing their bags, not arriving. We watch, mesmerised.

'They can't stay here,' I say.

'Well where else can they go?' asks Ollie.

'The pond would be the best bet. Stefan's up today with his men so I'll ask his opinion.'

Ollie shrugs. 'OK, but don't move them till I get home from school.'

'I have no intention of frog catching at this time of the morning or at any other time for that matter,' I tut.

We enter the kitchen where the three cats are waiting anxiously for their breakfast. They swish against our legs, their tails rising in the air like charmed snakes. I put on the kettle and prepare Ollie a breakfast of mini blinis and olives, one of his latest fads. He likes to wash this down with a mug of sweetened gunpowder tea. Sitting cross-legged on the floor with his bony knees bent up like a little cricket, he sifts through his books for school.

'It's going to be a terrible day,' he groans. 'A science exam and double maths.'

'That does sound pretty grim,' I admit. 'Mind you, worse things happen at sea.'

He rounds on me. 'What a ridiculous thing to say. I bet they don't.'

I place hot tea in front of him and begin preparing his *merienda* for school. In the Spanish system, most parents prepare a substantial mid-morning snack for their children because school lunches are often served later than in British schools.

'Maybe I should become an entrepreneur like Richard Branson or Greedy George; then I wouldn't have to worry about exams and boring homework,' he sighs.

'Even Richard Branson and Greedy George couldn't avoid school I'm afraid.'

He shakes his head. 'You're wrong. They both got expelled and look where they are now.'

'True, in their respective ways they've done rather well, but for all you know they may secretly regret leaving school early.'

'Yeah, right,' he scoffs. 'And what about Rafa Nadal?'

'What about him?'

'I doubt he bothered much about school and he's the world's number one tennis player.'

'You might be a world tennis player one day.'

'How can I be when I have to go to school? I never have enough time to practise!'

'You have to make time,' I say wearily.

Alan breezes into the kitchen, his hair wet from the shower. 'Is there a coffee going?'

'Maybe,' I reply. 'but you really ought to have a go yourself at using this new Nespresso machine. It's so simple.'

He peers over my shoulder as I press the button.

'I'm not good with these damned fangled machines, as you know.'

'Look, a blindfolded baboon could work this,' I say impatiently.

Ollie bursts into giggles. 'Poor old daddy. Maybe we should hire a baboon to make you coffee every day.'

Alan mumbles darkly under his breath and knocks his espresso back quickly.

'Right, let's hit the road, Jack.'

Ollie gets up and flings his rucksack of school books over one shoulder. 'What is it with you adults? Greedy George called me sonny Jim and you call me Jack. Is my name that difficult to remember?'

The Scotsman gives him a playful tap on the head, and the two set off for school, Ollie clutching his tennis racket in the passenger seat as if it's a lifesaver. I watch as the car slowly pulls out of the courtyard. It's time to have a quick shower before Stefan and his builders arrive. Hopefully they'll have sage advice to dish out on the subject of frog inundations.

Stefan is squatting by the side of the pool, deep in thought.

'So what do you think?'

He raises his eyebrow quizzically. 'First scorpions, now frogs… it's like the ten plagues of Egypt.'

'Very comforting,' I say.

'It's interesting that they're immune to the chlorine,' he muses.

'Maybe they're some new super breed.'

'I think you'll have to drain out the water, catch the frogs and relocate them to the pond.'

'But won't they just come back?'

He shrugs. 'If you keep the pool cover on, that'll see them off.'

'We'd better do it soon.'

Stefan smirks. 'Ollie will enjoy catching the frogs in his net.'

'Yes, that will prove another welcome distraction after his tennis lesson tonight.'

We stroll from the pool down the stone steps into the field where his workers battle with the wild briars, massive weeds and old, dead trees. Salvador, our disdainful and nosy cockerel, struts about the grass, watching their progress through the fence of his corral. His harem, led by Minny and Della, cluck loudly behind him, evidently discussing today's local gossip.

Stefan looks up into the sky. 'They're forecasting a lot of rain next month, and then we'll be into the Christmas holiday season. I don't think we'll be able to build the cattery for some months.'

I take this news on the chin. 'Fine, well let's just plough on while the sun's still shining.'

He beams. 'Of course.'

Raking up the gravel, a car skids noisily into the courtyard and comes to a shuddering halt. It can only be Catalina. I share a smile with Stefan, who acknowledges that it must be his irrepressible older sister. In the time it takes me to exchange morning greetings with Stefan's men and make my way back to the kitchen, Catalina has already put on the kettle and a CD of Abba, and is busy ironing. The woman's a whirlwind.

'When is this man arriving?' she yells by way of greeting above the music.

'What man?' I say.

She thumps down the iron and bustles over to the CD player to turn down the volume.

'You said a friend of Ed's was coming to stay for a few days?'

'Gosh, I'd nearly forgotten. Yes, he's coming next week.'

'Who is he?'

'Some biologist who's studying frogs. He's called Bill Spears. I've never met him.'

Steam billows from the iron as Catalina rests it back on the ironing board and wanders off to make the tea. She thrusts a mug in my direction.

'You want me to make up the spare room?'

'Seems like a good idea. I do hope he's normal.'

She resumes her ironing. 'Why shouldn't he be?'

'Well, he's a friend of Ed's, so he might have a screw loose.'

'Like you, you mean?'

'Touché! Anyway, he shouldn't get under our feet. He's at some conference organised by GOB, the environmental lobby group here, and then he's doing some field work in the Tramuntanas.'

She sniffs. 'Good. What you doing now?'

'I'm off for a run.'

She laughs. 'Training for the Athens marathon?'

'Yes, but there's no pressure because it's not for another year. I'm just going to build up gradually. Anyway, this one is special. We'll be following the original route.'

'You must be crazy. It will be boiling hot.'

'Not in November.'

'You told me the man who originally ran it dropped down dead.'

'That was about 2,500 years ago! Besides, what a lot of people don't know is that Pheidippides, the Greek soldier who ran the original course from Marathon to Athens, had already been running for two days solidly all the way from Sparta.'

'For fun?'

'No of course not! He was on his way to Athens to announce the Greeks' victory over the Persians.'

Catalina takes a sip of tea. 'And it's forty-two kilometres from Marathon to Athens?'

'Apparently so. It's supposed to be a tricky course.'

She puts her hands on her hips. 'Well let's hope you don't suffer the same fate as Pheidippides.'

I'm just panting into the courtyard after a brisk forty-minute run up to the village of Biniaraix and back, when there's the sound of an engine and then tooting behind me. I jog over to the side as Llorenç, the woodman, draws up in his white van. He is grinning at me through the open window.

'Got your running gear on! Perfect, you can help me unload the wood.'

I narrow my eyes at him. 'In your dreams.'

He gets out of the car and gives me a smacker on each cheek. 'I could do with a small coffee if you're feeling kind. I've just been giving blood to the Red Cross.'

'Are you feeling weak at the knees?'

'What do you expect? One woman in Lycra and another...' he eyes Catalina, now standing at the front door, '... holding a mop. How much more can the heart take?'

I give him a push. 'You look pretty robust to me.'

He saunters round to the boot of the van and begins unloading logs.

'You're a bit early with the wood, aren't you?'

He shrugs. 'Senyor Alan asked me to deliver it this week. He wants it to be bone dry for the winter.'

'Fair enough.'

I leave him to his work and potter into the kitchen to make him a coffee. 'It's like a hotel here.'

Catalina follows me. 'More like a bus station. Hey, what happened to Gaspar? I thought he was running with you now?'

I use the back of my hand to wipe the sweat from my forehead. 'Poor old Gaspar. We only managed two short runs and then he wrenched his back carrying some heavy mower. Dr Vidal has forbidden him to do any violent exercise for some time.'

She gives a snort of laughter. 'So much for his new exercise regime!'

'Don't be mean. He'll be back on his feet again soon.'

She pauses for a second. 'If Dr Vidal says he shouldn't exercise, Gaspar must listen to him.'

Dr Vidal is the most revered and liked private practitioner in Sóller and what he says always goes.

She begins mopping away at the *entrada* floor. 'It's so dirty. Alan is always bringing mud in from the garden. He should keep his gardening boots outside.'

'I've asked but he never remembers.'

She tuts. 'I'll speak with him.'

Woe betide him when he returns. As Llorenç trudges in to claim his coffee, the telephone begins ringing. I thrust the cup and saucer in his hands and grab the phone.

'Hello, it's Fiona here.'

This is a good chum from London who works for Condé Nast Publishing. We exchange pleasantries.

'Anyway, the reason I'm calling is to find out if you're interested in merging the company.'

'What?'

'Last time we spoke, you mentioned wanting to cut loose.'

I give a wary 'maybe'.

'It just so happens I know of a fashion PR company looking to acquire a luxury goods agency like yours. I mentioned your name and they seemed dead keen to meet up.'

'Oh.'

'I know this is a bit sudden, but it could be your Monopoly get-out-of-jail card.'

Much as I have contemplated packing up the PR business to concentrate on other projects, I haven't really given it serious thought. 'No, the timing's perfect,' I hear myself say. 'Thank you so much. I'd love to take it further.'

'Good,' she says decisively, 'because I've given Marilyn Hughes, one of the joint MDs, your numbers and she'll be in touch. Discreetly, of course.'

'What's her company name?'

She pauses. 'It's a bit hip but don't let that bias you. It's called Red Hot PR.'

'Euch!'

'It's Soho-based, so what do you expect? Her partner's a lovely queen called Jay Finch.'

A bird twitters from the patio. Chaffinch. Jay Finch. I mask a smile.

'Look, I've got to go. Keep me posted.'

She's gone. I put the telephone back on its cradle. Llorenç clatters his empty cup and saucer on the table and smacks his lips before plodding off to his van to carry on unloading.

'Who was that?' asks Catalina warily.

'A friend who's trying to help me merge the business.'

She nods slowly. 'Just be sure that's what you want.'

Llorenç reappears. 'I've nearly finished but I wanted to give you these.'

He is carrying an enormous crate of fat, juicy red tomatoes.

'Now it's my turn to go weak at the knees!' I yelp. 'That's one sure way to a woman's heart.'

He gives a wink. 'I heard Alan's tomatoes had taken a turn for the worse. So far the blight hasn't reached us.'

Llorenç and his family live high in the mountains in a veritable garden of Eden. I thank him and bite into a fat tomato. Juice spurts everywhere. It is pure, unadulterated heaven. Catalina views me with some frustration. 'You're as bad as your husband. Just look at my nice clean floor!'

It's 6 p.m. and Ollie, Alan and I have donned green wellies, ready to commence the task in hand – frog catching. It took two days to drain the swimming pool, a task we normally only perform every few years given that we keep the water clean and cover the pool over in the winter. Now we are faced with a sea of tiny frogs hopping about on the slimy, wet tiles, while the more timorous ones hide in clumps of wet leaves that have collected in the depths.

'It's a shame we have to turf them out,' I say.

'We couldn't let them stay. I mean, it's hardly got the cachet of swimming with dolphins, has it?' says the Scotsman crisply.

Ollie bites his lip. 'I hope they'll be OK moving. I mean, it's like a New Yorker going to deepest Africa.'

'What?' Alan regards him with utter confusion.

'Just think. They're in a nice, clean blue pool and suddenly they find themselves in a dark, murky pond full of strange creatures.'

'Don't worry,' I soothe. 'They'll be thrilled to meet all the other frogs there.'.

'Yes, but these frogs are shiny green and the ones in the pond are mottled grey. Perhaps they're two rival gangs?'

'This is what reading *Harry Potter* does to you,' grumbles the Scotsman. 'Over-developed imagination.'

'Do be quiet.' I give him a tap on the arm.

'Don't worry, Ollie,' says the Scotsman. 'I'm sure they'll get trauma counselling once they're ensconced in their new watery abode.'

Ollie shakes his head with impatience and gives his father a dark look.

Alan ventures into the shallow end first with his net, slides helplessly down the tiles which graduate sharply to the deep end, and lands on his backside. Ollie doubles up with laughter. Never has home entertainment been so good! Alan, ruffled, tries to rise but falls back down again, slithering in the slime and silt. His net, suspended on a thin pole, clatters down onto the tiles. He curses loudly and crawls onto his knees. In an attempt to lend a helping hand I enter gingerly and immediately find myself sliding out of control. Gripping on to the side of the pool, I manage to use my pole and net to steady myself and slowly reach the Scotsman. He is now laboriously pawing his way up the glistening tiled slope like an inebriated mountaineer. The frogs are watching us silently with startled expressions on their faces, while Ollie flops by the steps, overcome with mirth.

'Instead of acting like a clown, why don't you come in and help!' barks Alan.

'I can only see one clown,' counters Ollie, 'and he's in the pool already!'

With a smirk on his face he steps down into the shallow end and, to our joint irritation, walks effortlessly towards us even though he's weighed down with a bucket of water in one hand and a fishnet on a pole in the other.

'Just look at that,' I wonder.

'He'll be over in a minute,' grunts the Scotsman.

There's a loud '*Hola!*' from one of the *bancales,* the terraces above our garden, and to our dismay we see Emilio, the farmer whose land joins our garden.

'Are you having fun?' he yells down good-naturedly.

'No,' cries the Scotsman. 'We're trying to catch the *ranas.*'

Emilio stands high above us with arms crossed, a sadistic little smile playing on his lips, or so it seems. 'It could take you some time.'

'*Sí!*' I say, in an attempt at cheerful insouciance.

Ollie sweeps past us and with a swing of his net manages to scoop up several baby frogs. He plops them in his bucket. The farmer cheers.

'*Bravo*, Ollie! Show your parents how it's done!'

Alan mutters an expletive and rises unsteadily to his feet. I pass him his net. Shuffling like a geriatric to the side, he holds the rail with one hand and attempts to swish his net towards a group of frogs. They hop off.

'Damn them!' he shouts.

There's guffawing from above. The farmer is shaking with laughter.

'*Molt divertit!*' he calls. Very funny. Not.

Ollie watches as I catch two tiny frogs.

'Well done, mother. At this rate we'll be here till midnight. Try and get a bunch at a time.'

'I'm doing my best,' I snap.

Fifteen minutes later, Emilio, wiping his eyes, waves and plods off, no doubt to the neighbourhood bar where he'll regale the locals with our absurd antics. Alan waits till he's gone and then huffs and puffs his way to the pool's steps and clumsily plods out.

'Are you giving up?' I ask.

'I've had enough. I shall leave the task to the experts.'

'Great,' I moan.

Two hours later, wet, cold and exhausted, I collapse onto a kitchen chair and take a well earned swig of red wine. Ollie is upstairs doing his homework, having triumphantly caught more than fifty frogs. Between us we managed to transfer all our chirruping lads and ladettes to their new lily pad laden home, carefully covering the pool over once it was cleared of our tiny friends.

'Let's hope they don't try to return,' says Alan.

'No chance of that,' I reply. 'Come and take a look.'

He follows me out onto the patio and gives a broad smile. Erected by the side of the pool, and ballasted by rocks, is a crude cardboard sign written in felt pen which reads: 'NO FROGS ALLOWED.'

I laugh. 'As you can see, Ollie's firmly put paid to that.'

Bill Spears – Dr Bill Spears, if you please – is wearing a concerned expression. We stand by his bed in the guest quarters, the basement which was once home to bottled and dried fruits, strings of garlic and onions and wild herbs preserved by the *finca*'s previous elderly owners.

'I'm afraid I have a terrible allergy to feather pillows,' he says in a flat voice.

'No problem. I can find some synthetic ones in the airing cupboard.'

He grips his chin between the thumb and fingers of his left hand as if his head might drop off at any moment, and clicks his teeth.

'Is it a feather duvet?'

I try not to show irritation. 'Yes.'

'Ah. No good I'm afraid. Have you a sleeping bag, maybe?'

I shuffle towards the bedroom door. 'I'll find something.'

It's late. Bill's plane was delayed by two hours and then he called from a taxi to say he hadn't had time to change any money, and could we meet the fare when he arrived. Finally, the car rolled up at 11.30 p.m. Alan paid the taxi driver somewhat grudgingly and carried Bill's case and rucksack into the house.

'No chance of a quick bite, is there?' he asks plaintively.

'Of course, come up now and I'll fix you something.'

Somewhat morosely he follows me up the stairs to the kitchen. Hurriedly I make him a salad with some cold meats and a hunk of fresh bread. Alan pulls a bottle of red wine from a shelf. 'Fancy a quick glass?'

He raises his hand in horror. 'Good Lord, no. I don't drink alcohol. A Fanta would be nice.'

'Fresh out of Fanta,' the Scotsman replies stiffly, offering him a Coke instead.

Bill Spears chomps through his salad with great gusto, telling us in between mouthfuls that he is doing advanced studies on the biological systems of frogs and toads at Aberystwyth University. In fact, he tells us proudly, it was the subject of his PhD.

'So why Mallorca?' asks Alan.

'I heard about a fascinating conference being held on the ecosystem of the Tramuntanas and I am also keen to study the midwife toad if I get the chance.'

Alan guffaws. 'Ah the *ferreret*. Well, you've come to the right house. We've got a resident toad and hundreds of frogs at the moment.'

His face becomes animated.

'A toad?'

'His name's Johnny,' I say. 'You can meet him tomorrow.'

'I'm not sure if I approve of naming non-domestic animals,' he honks. 'What breed is he?'

'God knows,' I say, put out by his snide remark. 'Just a common old toad.'

'Let me be the judge of that,' he says parsimoniously.

Alan winces. 'So how do you know Ed?'

'I met him when I was doing an interview for a BBC wildlife programme about amphibians. I remembered he mentioned a friend living in the Sóller Valley so I asked whether you might be kind enough to put me up for a few days.'

I'm not very pleased to discover that Bill is just a very passing acquaintance of Ed's. I shall have words with him.

'So this is just a flying visit?' Alan attempts nonchalance.

'Just two days this time.'

I pray there won't be another.

He rises from the table. 'Thanks for the snack. I think I'll be off to bed.'

I follow him to the stairwell. 'I've put new pillows and a synthetic duvet down there for you.'

'Marvellous. Thanks.'

'Would you like some water for the night?'

'Yes, please, and a mug of chamomile tea and a hot-water bottle would be nice.'

I manage to maintain a rictus smile. 'No problem, but it's very warm.'

'Creature of habit, I'm afraid,' he replies, giving me a goofy grin.

There's the sound of feet crunching on gravel and a thread of light, possibly from a torch, fleetingly hits the bedroom window. I sit up in the darkness and feel my heart racing. The Scotsman is snoring lightly. I grapple for my alarm clock. The luminous hands tell me it's 3 a.m. I jump out of my bed and scuttle over to the window. The courtyard is swathed in silky obscurity but to the right, hovering near the pond, is a moving trickle of light. I sit heavily down on the bed and shake Alan awake.

'Quick!' I hiss. 'We've got an intruder.'

He wakes up with a start. 'What?'

'In the front garden; someone's walking around with a torch.'

Leaping out of bed half asleep, he opens the bedroom door and stumbles on to the small landing. I follow him down the stairs to the *entrada* whereupon he floods the front garden with light. The front door is unlocked.

'Great security,' I chide.

He frowns. 'But I'm sure I locked it.'

'Hm, I don't think so,' I grunt.

In the cool, early morning air, the eerie, insistent hoot of a scops owl can be heard, and a small bat flies under the arch of the porch. There's a cough.

'Who's there?' bellows the Scotsman.

A lumpy shadow appears from behind the olive tree. I gasp. Then in the bright light, he emerges. It's none other than the good Dr Spears.

'What on earth do you think you're doing?' says Alan crossly.

'I… I'm so sorry,' he stutters, lamely. 'I was just observing your amphibian life in the pond. I firmly believe, on initial investigation, that your "Johnny" is a midwife toad.'

'I don't give a damn what he is! You frightened the life out of us.'

'My sincere apologies, but this is the best time to study nocturnal creatures.'

Alan gives a snort and turns tail. 'We're off to bed.'

Bill Spears follows us into the house like a scolded child.

'Goodnight. I'll lock up.'

On the bottom stair I turn to him. 'And you're wrong about Johnny. He is not a midwife toad.'

He gives an arrogant shrug. 'We'll see.'

Rachel's on the blower.

'We desperately need an account executive to help with the extra workload. We can afford it.'

I exhale deeply. 'If you're sure, Rachel. Just go ahead and place an ad in *PR Week*.'

'Great. I'll run it by you first. You sound tired.'

I run a hand through my hair and yawn. 'I am. We have a painful biologist staying, a friend of Ed's. He was up half the night studying our frogs.'

She laughs. 'At least you have something in common.'

'I'm not so sure. Anyway, he's gone out for the day, thank heavens. Left a note saying he was off to the mountains.'

'Obviously a nut.'

'Most definitely. Anyway, how are things?'

'All OK. The shop launch for Wild Woods is on course for May. I've had a brainwave and got Yuri Drakova together with the Peterson-Matlocks.'

'How will that work?'

'Well, Wild Woods sell luxury furniture and beds and Yuri Drakova sells luxury couture.'

'So?'

She laughs. 'So I thought we could marry the two for the launch with the theme of the Princess and the Pea.'

'Mm… a marriage made in heaven. Go on, tell me more.'

'The idea is that we have a photocall with a supermodel wearing a sensational dress created by Yuri, the stuff of dreams, lying on a Wild Wood bed piled high with different mattresses.'

'Oh, and let me guess: we ask Dannie's chum, Anastasia Smirnoff…'

'Mirnov…'

'… to model it?'

'Spot on.'

I rub my eyes, wishing I was back in bed myself. 'God help you.'

'It's a dream come true.'

'All I can say, Rachel, is be careful of what you wish for…'

Catalina is flicking through a copy of *Grazia* at the kitchen table.

'I like this magazine but everyone is so thin,' she clucks.

'That's why women buy it, so that they can feel more inadequate.'

'Really? You think so?'

I take a sip of tea. 'Oh, I don't know. Anyway, it's a good light read and helps one focus on the trivia of life.'

She looks up. 'So Bill goes today?'

'Yes, the taxi's due any time. It's possibly been the longest three days of my life.'

She grins. 'He seems OK. Boring but not so bad. He has a very big nose.'

'Yes, he could easily double as the child catcher in *Chitty Chitty Bang Bang*.'

She gives me a scornful glance. 'You're cruel.'

'But honest,' I smile.

The front door bangs open. Bill Spears appears, his rosy hooter more pronounced than ever, and gives an unctuous smile.

'I'm just back from an invigorating walk. I must say, this has been an enlightening sojourn.'

'I'm so pleased,' I say. 'All packed up?'

'Yes, ready to go.'

He saunters over to us and sucks his teeth. 'I've a little confession.'

Catalina eyes him keenly. He appears shifty.

'Which is?' I prompt.

'It's about your toad, er, Johnny.'

I freeze. 'What about him?'

'Seen him about today?' He is a touch supercilious.

Funnily enough, Johnny has been absent for the last day or so. I imagined he was hiding from Bill Spears.

'I've released him up in one of the ravines to be with the other midwife toads.'

I stare at him in disbelief. 'You've done WHAT?'

Catalina furrows her brow as he ploughs on.

'Now, don't be alarmed. I just felt it was kinder to return him to his natural environment.'

'He isn't a *ferreret*, you daft buffoon!' I exclaim.

He is offended. 'Now, steady on...'

'How dare you kidnap Johnny! I cannot believe your deviousness.'

Catalina stands up. 'You've made a big mistake. Johnny is not a midwife toad. *Ferrerets* are very different. They are much smaller and they have a very distinct cry. A bit like a scops owl.'

'Are you a biologist?' he asks rudely.

'No, I am a Mallorcan,' she snaps.

He bites on his thumb and lowers his eyes. 'Well, I'm sure he'll be happier in the mountains.'

'He was happy here,' I say bitterly.

There's a loud tooting from the courtyard. The taxi has evidently arrived.

Too angry for words, I follow him to the front door where he has neatly piled up his belongings and his orange anorak. Catalina walks on to the porch and waves to the driver. Stiffly, Bill thanks me for his stay.

'Sorry I've missed Alan,' he says rather awkwardly. 'Do send him my best.'

Luckily for the Scotsman, he is on the school run.

'Have a good flight,' says Catalina woodenly.

He settles himself in the taxi and then leans out of the window as the car pulls out of the courtyard. 'I look forward to staying again!'

For once, I really am speechless.

Ollie and I are studying a multitude of fungi specimens on trestle tables in front of the town hall in Sóller's *plaça*. People are swarming around, peering at the labelled exhibits and nodding sagely at each written explanation. It is mushroom advisory day, an important bi-annual event at which seasoned experts from the valley explain which varieties are safe to pick from the woods. They are known as *setas* or, in Mallorcan, *bolets*.

'I like the *peu de rata*,' comments Ollie.

'But they're poisonous.'

'I know, but I like the name. Rat's feet sounds so sweet and they look beautiful, like coral.'

Senyor Bisbal appears at my elbow. 'Do you know your mushrooms?'

'Not at all, I'm afraid. I've been mushroom picking with Maria from Canantuna but I proved a hopeless student.'

He pats my shoulder. 'Take heart. There are hundreds of *bolets*. It would take several lifetimes to know them all.'

He takes Ollie's arm and leads him to a clump of yellowy, globe-shaped fungi.

'These are *bolet de pi*. Very toxic. And over here are *Pota de Cavall*.'

Ollie peers at the big round heads, brown and mottled. 'Urgh, I don't like the look of those.'

'A good thing!' laughs Senyor Bisbal. He picks up a strange black mushroom, shaped like a little fir tree. This is a *Murgola* – it's quite rare. These are my favourites; red *esclata-sangs*.'

I tap his arm. 'You certainly know your stuff.'

A few representatives from our local museum, the Museu Balear de Ciències Naturals, are here. I am a huge fan of this jewel of a museum, which sits on the edge of the splendid botanical gardens on the main road to Port of Sóller, although I haven't visited for some time. It is a mine of information about the fauna, flora, animal and amphibian life of the Baleares. In fact, if my memory recalls, it has a fine exhibit of Myotragus. I make a mental note to revisit.

Lluc Garcia, a biologist and editor of the local newspaper, *Sóller*, waves across the table at me. 'I'm glad to see you're mugging up on your fungi.'

'*Poc a poc*,' I reply. 'Do you know what this is?'

'That's a *pixacà*,' he replies.

I congratulate him. 'You know your subject.'

'To be honest, I'm better informed about woodlice. That was the focus of my biological studies.'

The more I get to know people in Sóller, the more I'm fascinated by their often bizarre areas of knowledge.

We say our goodbyes and head off for a coffee at Café Paris which, as it's Saturday, is mobbed.

'That was fun. I hope it took your mind off Johnny,' says Ollie.

'A little, but I'm still angry with that mollusc of a man Bill Spears and I shan't rest until I find Johnny.'

He pulls a face. 'Mm... you might have to search every mountain.'

'Well, if that's what it takes, I shall do it. I intend to leave no stone unturned until we're reunited and that's a promise.'

The night sky is clear and bejewelled with tiny white stars. We have just returned from a cheering supper up at Es Turo in Fornalutx, a restaurant which, with its cosy interior and welcoming staff, is guaranteed to liven the spirits. I sit with my feet up on the desk, relieved to have completed a pile of work and edited and sent off the advertising recruitment copy to *PR Week* for Rachel. Hopefully we'll get some good graduates applying for the new job. I have spent the day visiting frog-friendly sites in the Tramuntanas in search of Johnny. Even nauseating Bill Spears demonstrated a twinge of guilt or pity when he emailed me details of the exact place where he had dumped Johnny, but it has all been to no avail. Apart from one tiny frog peeping out from a rock, I failed to see any amphibian life up in the Tramuntanas. The biography of Dorothea Bate is sitting on the top of my in-tray. I reach for it and open the page at chapter eight. It has been an enthralling read up until now, and I haven't even reached the pages about Dorothea's discovery of Myotragus yet. So far, this pioneering and feisty fossil hunter has discovered pygmy hippos in Cyprus and elephants on Crete. How victorious she must have felt returning to the Natural History Museum with her extraordinary finds! The office door creaks open and Alan potters over to my desk.

He smiles. 'Reading your Dorothea book?'

'I'd have loved to have met Dorothea Bate,' I sigh. 'She must have been such an interesting woman. She coped with hellish conditions on her overseas expeditions, exploring dangerous caves and wild terrains in search of fossils, and never gave up.'

The Scotsman shakes his head and laughs. 'It's not just Myotragus that fascinates you. It's the whole thrill of scientific endeavour and adventure experienced by one dogged Edwardian woman more than a hundred years ago.'

I shrug. 'I suppose that's part of it.'

'Come on! Why do you think you have such a passion for going on remote scientific expeditions yourself? You're a scientist manquée!'

'I've left it a little late.'

'Nonsense. Where there's a will...'

'Yes, I'd rather like to turn amateur scientist one day,' I say with a smile.

'Not just any scientist,' he says with a wink. 'What you'd really like to be is a modern day Dorothea Bate!'

It's a bright and sunny morning. Rafael is rapping on the front door.

'*Hola, com va?*' I greet him.

'I'm fine. I came to see if your frogs had gone.'

'Our frogs? Well Johnny the toad isn't here, but that's another story.'

He grabs my arm. '*Venga*!'

We walk over to the pond. Silence. There isn't a plop, a croak, even the tremble of a leaf.

'All the frogs across the valley have gone, just like that,' he says.

I trace my finger in the cool water, thinking of the time we took to transfer the baby frogs from the swimming pool into the pond, seemingly all for nought.

He laughs. 'You move your frogs and they go anyway. Perhaps they were playing a joke on you all the time.'

Maybe so, but when the little devils return from their amphibian-only holiday resort, we'll have the pool cover at the ready. In fact, we'll re-erect Ollie's 'NO FROGS ALLOWED' sign, which should stop our amphibian jokers in their tracks.

# SIX

# TRICK OR TREAT

Gusts of warm, fragrant air waft across the fields as the sleepy Sóller Valley awakens from its deep slumber. Our neighbour, Emilio, is up at his customary hour of 6 a.m., feeding his horses in the half light and playing with his sheepdog in the field. I watch him from the bedroom window, marvelling at his energy at such an early hour.

Pottering downstairs, I find Minky and Orlando standing to attention by their food bowls. I wonder if they've been waiting there all night long in the misguided hope that one of us will stir in the dark hours and replenish their food bowls. I feed them and open the door for Inko, who is standing imperiously on the other side. She pads into the kitchen, flashing me a look of utter contempt as if I am the reason that she has been left out in the cold, when clearly it should be the Scotsman she points her accusing paw at. It is he who pads around the house last thing at night shooing the cats from their secret, cosy bunkers. Wily

Inko usually escapes his clutches by lying low in Ollie's bed. She must have been caught out last night.

Through the glass panes in the kitchen door, I rest my eyes on the profusion of juicy grapes covering the pergola beyond the patio. They hang in clusters, a feast for ants and insects until we manage to haul them down and distribute them among friends and locals. The front door bangs open and Pau, one of Stefan's builders, shouts *hola* at the top of his voice. He's totally unfazed to see me barefoot and sporting a baggy old white T-shirt that serves as a nightdress.

'I saw the light on, so I guessed you were awake.'

'Good thinking,' I say. 'I woke early.'

He nods. 'I was wondering whether you had a spare extension lead we could use in the field for the electric saw. Ours is kaput.'

I jog down the steps to the cellar and fumble around in the walk-in cupboard, home to the freezer and a jumble of domestic appliances, wine bottles, spare bulbs, candles and tools. The vacuum cleaner tube has somehow wound its way around the tool box like an intractable grey and rubbery snake. When I pull on it, it merely elongates like a piece of elastic and springs back on itself. I give it a hefty kick which causes it to topple over, unleashing a pile of candles, tennis balls and, hurrah, an extension lead. Triumphantly I pick it up and run up the stairs.

'I heard a crash. Are you OK?' ask Pau.

'*Si, no problema*!' I hand the long white lead to him. 'Everything else OK?'

'Fine,' he says, then pauses. 'Have you met the new English neighbours?'

'I didn't know we had any.'

He gives a sniff. 'They're renting the house just beyond the bottom of your track, a few doors from where Carmen's father lives. You know Carmen?'

'You mean Carmen who lives up near Biniaraix.'

'The same.'

'Well, I've not met these people yet.'

He shakes his head. 'They're trouble.'

'Why's that?'

He puffs out his bottom lip. 'They've only been here a few days and the son's playing loud pop music, and the woman's been rude to the neighbours. I parked my van outside her house yesterday and she went mad.'

'Maybe you'd blocked her drive.'

'She hasn't got one.'

I digest this information carefully. When residing in a foreign domain, it's always embarrassing to find one of your own countrymen acting churlishly towards the locals. I try to avoid such people at all costs.

Pau heads for the kitchen door.

'I'm sorry about these English neighbours,' I say.

He laughs. 'Why? It's not your fault! I just wanted to warn you about them.'

He walks briskly past the patio and down the steps to the field. I step out in to the balmy air and stare up at the saucer of the sun as it emerges from behind a puff of cloud. In between the tinkling bells of distant sheep and the neighing of Emilio's horses, I listen as Pau breaks into song. It's a poignant folk song that seems to reverberate across the whole valley. I translate the words, *'If only you would love me, if only you could...'*

Rafael is sucking on a pomegranate that he has pulled off a nearby tree. He spits the seeds out on to the path in front of his *finca* and flashes me a seductive smile.

'That's very good of you. I love your chocolate muffins!'

Placing the fruit onto a stone bench, he takes the plastic container from me. He taps the lid.

'I'll return this, when they're finished.'

'*Segur,*' I say sweetly from the open window of the car. '*Hasta luego!*'

He waves as I drive slowly along the track. I watch his cheery face in the front mirror. It's Halloween, a time for fun, and Rafael is going to get a taste of silly British humour very soon. I set off for the town. This morning I'm meeting with Jackie Waldren, a long-time resident of Deià village, whose artist husband became a well-known archaeologist locally. During the sixties he discovered a remarkable stash of Myotragus Balearicus specimens quite by chance, deep in a cave between Deià and Sóller. It was one of the largest Myotragus finds in the Baleares and, on the strength of that, what began as a hobby developed into a serious lifetime's work. In his latter years he completed a doctorate at the University of Oxford, where Jackie herself has lectured in Social Anthropology for some time. I have already visited the Waldrens' cosy little archaeological museum in Deià, a tribute to the man who gathered many historic artefacts of archaeological significance during his life in Mallorca. On his death, Jackie decided to carry the baton and, with her daughter's help, has been running the museum herself. Today we will be having a coffee with Professor Jelle Reumer, a palaeontologist and director of the Rotterdam Natural History Museum, who took part in many of Bill Waldren's digs for Myotragus remains during the seventies. He too seems to have the Myotragus bug, sending specialist students to Sóller's Natural

Science Museum each year to catalogue thousands of Myotragus bones still unclassified. What better way to pass the morning than to talk about Mallorcan old goats and their massive impact on the world of science?

Rachel is very cross. I hold the phone away from my ear and settle myself under the parasol at the patio table. I give a little cough.

'Hang on, Rachel. I understand that *PR Week* didn't like the wording but so what?'

'So what? When I asked you to add your thoughts to the job advert I didn't expect you to be so puerile.'

'All I wrote was "no PR flopsies or mopsies need apply". What's wrong with that?'

'*PR Week*'s ad manager says it's sexist and implies some PR girls are dimwits.'

'Precisely.'

She growls. 'You are a nightmare. They are refusing to print it, so now what do we do?'

'I'll think about it and call you back.'

The line clicks off. Honestly, how ridiculous. Has this precious trade organ got zero sense of humour? Apparently so. Why is the world becoming so damned politically correct? The telephone rings. Who now? It's a chum from the *Evening Standard*. I tell him about *PR Week*. He roars with laughter.

'That's so funny. We must use it in the diary.'

'For heaven's sake don't. Rachel's mad enough with me already.'

'Don't be a silly old thing. See it as a free ad. I'll do a little story and you'll be flooded with brainy applicants for no cost.'

I rap my fingers on the table. Now that's not a bad idea and Rachel will surely congratulate me on my financial prowess.

'You're on.'

Sometime later Alan wanders out. He shields his eyes from the sun.

'How did you get on with Jackie Waldren and Jelle from Rotterdam?'

'Brilliant. They were both a mine of information. I've agreed to visit the local museum with Jelle when he's next in Sóller. He's promised to introduce me to the director and to see the Myotragus bones behind the scenes.'

'These goats really are a fixation, aren't they? You'll be crawling around caves next in search of the Mallorcan Big Foot.'

I give him a poke in the ribs. 'Gosh, you're a wit!'

'Yes, well, your own wit has just got you in big trouble.'

'What have I done now?'

'I've just seen Rafael, and he says he's going to kill you over some little prank.'

'Ah. Excellent.'

He frowns and sits heavily in a chair next to me. 'Is it?'

'You remember the little trick he played on me with the scorpion remedy?'

'I certainly do.'

'As it's Halloween I thought I'd play a little joke on him. I gave him some chocolate muffins with a plastic scorpion hidden in the box and plastic beetles embedded in two of the cakes.'

The Scotsman tries to look disapproving. 'That was very naughty.'

'I know, but great fun. Unfortunately, my little jokes aren't going down too well today. Rachel's fuming because I added some slightly controversial words to that job advert.'

He holds his head in his hands when I tell him about the debacle. 'You really are the limit. God knows what she'll say when the story appears in the *Evening Standard.*'

I take a sip of water. 'I don't think they'll run the story. It's hardly that newsworthy.'

'Let's hope you're right,' he says doubtfully, and plods off to do some weeding.

The children are seated in a circle inside the tent on the front lawn. All are donning masks and costumes of witches, goblins, devils and elves in celebration of Halloween. Ollie has just celebrated his birthday and was thrilled when he discovered that all his classmates had clubbed together to buy him his first tent. He immediately insisted on rigging it up in the garden, and here I am, a week later, cheekily commandeering it for my English class. We have been playing a game of trick or treat, and each child has amassed a little pile of chocolates and sweets. I clap my hands together.

'OK. Now who can tell me what Sara is?'

Sara's pointy black hat is fastened with a piece of elastic under the chin. She draws the black cape around her and fiddles with her plastic warty nose. Six little arms shoot into the air.

'Pig!' says Iván.

'No, that's an animal, isn't it? A pig goes oink oink.'

Lots of 'oink oink's fill the tent.

'Any ideas, Tofol?'

'She is teacher.'

'Oh dear, Tofol! I don't think your teacher has a long, warty nose.'

'*Si, si,*' he insists.

They all hoot with laughter.

'I know, I know!' Tina is jumping hysterically up and down in her elf outfit. I fear she may burst.

'What do you think, Tina?'

'She is BITCH!' Except she pronounces it as *beach*.

My eyes nearly pop out.

'Beach, beach, beach!' they all yell. I manage to hush them.

'Very good, Tina, but I think you mean WITCH!'

'Witch!' they all ape happily.

I look at my watch. Time for orange juice and biscuits and then fifteen minutes of their favourite *Muzzy the Monster* DVD.

'Break time. Let's go to the kitchen now.'

Obediently they rise to their feet and follow me out of the tent and across the lawn to the house. I feel like the Pied Piper with my six little recruits striding purposefully behind me, dressed in their colourful costumes. I never imagined Halloween could be such fun. Whoever said life's a witch was wrong. It's a beach.

From high above the port, we can see a myriad of tiny lights glinting from the cluster of yachts in the treacly black sea far below. We have climbed up the broad stone steps that wind up from Santa Catalina district in the port to a wide viewing platform known as La Miranda de Santa Catalina. The views across Sóller's bay are spectacular. The old lighthouse, El Far del Cap Gros, winks at us from on high across the water, and a tram rattles by on its way to Sóller town. A warm breeze tugs at my pashmina as we carry on our ascent to the beautiful floodlit Oratory of Santa Catalina. This golden limestone gem was built in 1280 and now no longer serves as a monastery but as a seafaring museum, known as Museu de la Mar, and its accompanying chapel as a concert and events hall. Tonight is the start of the popular Festival de Música Clásica, organised by hotelier Jos Kuiper on behalf of his fellow hoteliers in the port. We arrive at the splendid archway that leads into the cobbled courtyard. Amber light floods through the grounds and the wind whips our hair. There's a whiff of jasmine and wild thyme in the air and a shower of soft rose petals spirals down from the heavens, although no rose bush is in evidence. A gift from the gods. We take our seats in the crowded chapel, delighted that we shall be treated to a performance by a trio from The Berlin Philharmonic Orchestra. The artistic director strides on to the short stage, shortly followed by the violinist and cellist. Ollie fidgets next to me.

'Some of the paint on the wall is peeling.'

'Don't worry about it.'

I look down at my silk top and see that it is sprinkled with little white deposits. I shake them off.

'Told you,' he whispers.

'Just flick it away and concentrate on the music.'

Alan gives him a stern look. Ollie averts his eyes and studies the programme a tad moodily. I hope bringing him along was the right decision. The trio begin and I am transported away from office cares, catteries and old goat bones. This is, after all, what moving to Mallorca was all about: having time out just to enjoy local events and culture. Before long, it's the interval. I glance at Ollie, who is sitting transfixed, his mouth slightly ajar. I smile to myself. There's applause and we squeeze our way out into the fresh air, where glasses of sparkling cava are being served. Several friends come over to chat and we all agree how lucky we are to have this jewel of a festival in our very midst. Soon it is time to take our seats once more. An hour later, after repeated encores, the three men take their final bow. Ollie is animated.

'That was incredible. So cool.'

The Scotsman has a faint tear in his eye. 'Gosh, that was beautiful. We must come again.'

We set off down the steps towards the port. The streets are full of families out for a Friday night supper. I look across the bay towards the beach of Can Repic and at the dark mysterious craggy cliffs beyond.

'You know there are loads of caves tucked inside those cliffs?'

Alan eyes me curiously. 'Don't tell me that's where Dorothea Bate found her Myotragus bones?'

I shake my head and clasp the pashmina around my shoulders. 'No, she found a fossilised limb bone and skull on the east of the island in the Cueva de la Baix near Capdepera.'

Ollie follows my gaze. 'And where did the archaeologist guy in Deià find his Myotragus bones?'

'William Waldren? Ah, now that was closer to home. He discovered about three and a half thousand bones in Cova de son Muleta about halfway between here and Deià.'

'Can we go and look around some caves now?' he asks.

'Yes, we're in just the right gear for a late night expedition to some perilous sea caves,' says Alan with irony.

'Maybe we could come down tomorrow and take a look around?' suggests Ollie.

I put my arm around his shoulder. 'Most of the caves are sea-facing and precarious. I think we'd be better leaving cave excavation to the experts.'

'That's boring. So now what are we going to do?'

'How about dinner at Agapanto instead?' says Alan.

This idyllic restaurant, owned by our German friend, Maria, is one of the culinary treasures of the Port. It sits alone on a rocky outcrop at the far end of the bay with its terrace spilling out on to the beach.

'I suppose so.' says Ollie. 'At least we can go hunting for crabs in the rocks.'

'Who knows, we might come across something mysterious in the dark crevices,' says Alan. 'An old fossil perhaps.'

'As if!' scoffs Ollie.

'Well if we don't, we can always plant your father in the rocks and pretend we've just found him. A rare old Scottish fossil if ever there was.'

'Old fossil indeed,' protests Alan loudly. 'What cheek!'

We make our way briskly down the hill, Ollie and I giggling madly while the Scotsman follows in our wake in mock indignation.

Rachel is attempting to keep her voice level. 'You heard, three hundred enquiries!'

'To be honest, I didn't think the *Evening Standard* would print it,' I fib.

'Yes, well you were wrong.'

'Think how much money we've saved on the advert, Rachel.'

She breathes heavily down the line.

'Look I don't want to sound churlish but I'm up to my neck in work for the Wild Woods shop launch, have loads to do on Manuel's Maryland hotel and that's without all the other client stuff. Receiving three hundred calls out of the blue wasn't that helpful.'

'By the way, did you get the draft press pack I wrote for the Maryland Hotel? I just needed a couple more facts.'

She gives a brittle laugh. 'Yes thanks, but Manuel isn't prepared to give us the extra information until his new buddy Vice Admiral Mason gives him clearance.'

'That's absurd!'

'Tell me about it. Anyway, good news on the Greedy George front. He's getting a fantastic response to the ad you all shot in Mallorca. It went down a storm in the States. Well done.'

'It's Nick, the film director, who deserves a medal.'

'Yes, but you wrote the script.'

'I suppose. Anyway, tell me the worst. What did the *Evening Standard* write?'

'I'll scan it for you. It appeared in *The Londoner's Diary* and I have to admit was very witty... along the lines of the PR business no longer being the last bastion for dim-witted flopsy mopsy girls, thanks to our company.'

I giggle.

'You may well laugh. I've had to grovel to *PR Week*. I told them you were a complete loose canon and that we've banished you to a cell in the Mallorcan mountains.'

'Although occasionally I escape.'

'Exactly.'

I apologise.

'It's OK. At least we've got some excellent applicants. Sifting through all the CV's will be tough though.'

'Send them to me, and I'll do a shortlist.'

She sounds relieved. 'Are you sure?'

'Well, it is all my fault.'

'Don't choke on that humble pie, will you?' she taunts. 'Seriously, thanks. I'll let the girls know and they'll send the best to you by email.'

I'm about to hang up when she gives a cough. 'Where did you dream up flopsies and mopsies anyway?'

'I didn't. It was Beatrix Potter in *The Tales of Peter Rabbit.*'

'Give me a break!'

'They were rabbits who liked bread, milk and blackberries for their supper.'

Her voice ripples with laughter. 'Well this rabbit's going off for a long glass of Chardonnay and I suggest you go and see a good shrink. Better still, why not curl up in bed with a copy of *Peter Rabbit*?'

Never has a proposition sounded so good.

It's a hot, sticky day as we arrive in the centre of Palma and find ourselves stuck in heavy traffic on Calle Jaume III. Ollie sits in the back seat, frantically biting his nails and staring at his watch.

'We've got plenty of time,' I soothe.

'The race is going to begin in less than an hour and there's nowhere to park.'

This afternoon the Procession of the Blessed will take place, otherwise known as the Colcada de la Beata, and already massive floats have arrived, proudly sporting the livery of different villages across the island. The occasion celebrates the beatification of Saint Catalina Tomàs and is an annual event. I'm rather hoping that after Ollie's charity race, in which a few hundred children are competing, I can take a peek at some of the floats. Aside from his obsession with tennis, Ollie also loves sprinting and is always keen to participate in local races. On occasion we have tried to run together, somewhat unsuccessfully given that I'm a plodder and he's a whippet. Rather like a Duracell bunny I can keep going for miles whereas he runs out of steam after a sharp and speedy sprint. As I peer out of the car window, I see groups of young women clad in traditional Mallorcan costume making their way towards the starting point for the procession.

'Blimey, they're early.'

Alan shoots a glance out of the driver's window. 'I suppose they have a good gossip before the event kicks off.'

'Where are we going to park?' asks Ollie fretfully, drumming his fists on his bony knees.

'Patience,' says the Scotsman. 'Just wait and see.'

A phenomenon that exists in Mallorca that I've never been aware of in the UK is the parking pitch system. Driving into Palma on a busy day when parking is near impossible in any of the underground car parks or on the street, we head for the small *plaça* by Es Baluard museum in the hope that Miguel the *toro* will be there.

Our *toro* is a parking pitcher, one of a posse of scruffily clad men and women whom the more cynical might tag 'down and outs', who leap gamely in front of drivers to indicate vacated parking slots. With hysterical Spaniards hooting impatiently at one's rear end this can prove an annoying distraction. When we first arrived in Mallorca, the Scotsman would curse when one of these sozzled pariahs would roll up in front of us demanding money for finding a parking slot which we'd already found for ourselves. Sometimes the parking pitcher would grow abusive if we didn't relinquish a handful of *centimos*, and we vowed to avoid them at all costs. Then one day, as we mournfully circled Es Baluard's *plaça*, seemingly without a hope of finding anywhere to leave the car, Miguel hopped out from behind a tree like a little goblin and beckoned us over.

'Listen, senyor, that Renault Clio driver will be back in one minute. I know his timetable. Wait here, and I shall call you over.'

Too weary to argue, we did as instructed, wondering if this was some tourist trick or scam. About sixty seconds later, a burly Mallorcan jumped into the Clio and was off. Miguel waved us over, rebuking other hopefuls who'd circled like a pool of sharks around the spot, and the slot was ours. We were horribly late for a meeting, so felt jubilant and hugely grateful to Miguel.

He became our chum and told us that he was known as Miguel the *toro* because he protected the cars in his zone like a proud bull. That's dedication for you. So, for two years we have only parked on Miguel's pitch. He may at times have more than the odd snifter so his coherence level is slightly questionable, but he guards our car like a Rottweiler – or rather a small bull – and treats the Scotsman like his best friend. Even when we lag behind other vehicles, Miguel will fend them off with a sharp word or an impatient wave of the hand when he spies us. Then he will stand stubbornly in the midst of the only available parking place until we reach him. One day when a group of teenagers were fiddling with the windscreen wipers and aerials of parked cars, he chased them away, perching like a protective mother hen on a bench next to our old jalopy. Now when expat friends complain about the parking pitchers we tell them cooingly about Miguel the *toro* and they smile indulgently, no doubt thinking the Mallorcan sun has finally addled our brains.

We pull into the *plaça* at Es Baluard and see that it is bursting with parked cars.

Ollie groans. 'Tell me you're not hoping that Miguel will find you a place? He'll be in Bar Español by now. He likes to go there on Sunday afternoon.'

'How do you know?' I quiz.

'He told me once.'

We drive around the square several times with no sign of Miguel. Then, just as we are giving up hope, we see him darting across the formal little garden, past the central monument and towards us. Alan rolls down the window.

'*Miguel, como estás?*'

'*Bien, bien, senyor. Mucha gente hoy! Pero, espera...*'

Indeed there are a lot of people today, what with the children's charity race and the procession. He tells us to wait. Suddenly a car pulls out and Miguel begins running like a madman towards it. He beckons us over. Other desperate drivers honk angrily, furious that this diminutive man is reserving the space for us.

'He's going to get a big *propina* today,' whistles the Scotsman.

'Yes, a *really* big tip,' whoops Ollie, relieved that he'll be in time for his race.

We dash out of the car. Miguel doffs an imaginary cap at Alan and winks.

'I'll keep an eye on it while you're away.' He taps Ollie on the arm. 'In sports gear? Are you doing the big kids' race?'

'*Si,*' says Ollie quietly.

'Well, win a medal for me, *campeón.*'

'I'll do my best,' my little champion replies.

Loud pop music can be heard from the broad street by the marina, the Passeig Maritim. The annual children's charity race is about to begin.

It is dusk by the time we arrive back on our track. Ollie has come fourth in the race and sports a shiny medal. We have celebrated with a hearty meal at Pizzeria del Puerto in the Port of Sóller, owned by our friends Jaime and Sara. Their son, Jamie, is a cat lover and animal expert who feeds our cats whenever we go on holiday. I'm hoping he might be able to get involved with the cattery when it's up and running. Rafael's house is ablaze with light and at the sound of our car he comes rushing out like a raging *toro* and jams his hand against my window. Alan grinds to a halt.

'Ah, so you play a little Halloween trick on me?' Rafael growls, waggling his finger.

'Well, I thought you might find it funny,' I say disingenuously.

'Very funny. My girlfriend, Isabella, put her hand in box of muffins and scream her head off. You could have given her heart attack!'

I chortle. 'I was only trying to get you back for that scorpion joke you played on me. Poor Isabella, is she alright?'

'After some medication,' he laughs. 'I'm kidding. Next time, you wait!'

'Come on, can't we have a truce?' I implore.

'Maybe.' He peers in at Ollie.

'*Campeón*! You win medal?'

Ollie is flushed with pride. 'I came fourth out of a few hundred participants.'

'*Fantástico*! Soon we run together and then we'll show your *madre* a thing or two.'

They slap palms and we drive on.

'I hope that's the end of the pranks,' I sigh.

The Scotsman chuckles. 'Don't depend on it.

'Well, I guess I've only got myself to blame!'

# SEVEN

# SAINTS OR SINNERS

The rain pours down. Ollie and I stand at his bedroom window, our breath forming ghostly white streaks on the icy panes. It is hard to see beyond the blur of fast-falling pellets of water that hit the ground running and flow in frothy rivulets to the gullies. The water makes a rude slurping noise as it gushes down the drain pipes into the belly of the earth. There's one enormous watery burp after the other.

'Pardon me!' I say.

Ollie gives me a scathing look. 'You're so silly.'

'I know. That's how I keep you endlessly amused.'

He groans. 'What can we do? The computers are all down, the electricity's died so we can't even watch a DVD and we've got no heating or phones working.'

'We can dance,' I proffer an arm.

'Can you try to be serious?' he sighs.

'To be honest, I'm feeling horribly serious. I've got a mountain of work to get through for Rachel, and Greedy George has asked me to check the copy for his new print adverts, but I need the computer. On top of all that mad Manuel Ramirez is refusing to let us write any press releases about his new Maryland Hotel because he says the information's classified.'

'What sort of secret information might the hotel have?' he asks.

I laugh. 'None whatsoever, he's just completely barking. All we're trying to do is help him to get publicity.'

'You don't know many normal adults, do you?'

'No, not really,' I sigh.

The rain patters down monotonously.

'OK, what about a game of I Spy?' I say.

He rolls his eyes. 'Wow, that's exciting.'

Then he bangs the window. 'Poor Inko! She's drenched. Quick! Let her in!'

Between us we pull open the window in the driving rain and a bedraggled Inko jumps up on to the sill and down into the room. We are soaked in an instant.

'Thanks a lot, old girl,' I say.

Inko shakes herself down and gives us a low growl as if we are jointly to blame for her dismally wet state. Ollie walks gingerly across the dark room. Although it is only eleven in the morning, the sky is black and moody.

'Hopefully it will be better tomorrow when we camp.'

I was rather hoping that my son might have forgotten the limp promise I made about camping out in his new tent in the field. Notably, the Scotsman didn't volunteer to join us.

'It might be too damp.'

'Are you trying to bottle out of it?' he asks suspiciously.

'No! Of course not. I'm very excited at the thought. After all, I am a jungle girl.'

'Exactly,' he says. 'So you keep telling us.'

Alan walks in, dangling a paraffin lamp.

'If this keeps up the builders won't be able to work on the cattery come Monday.'

I'm beginning to feel thwarted at every turn. 'A spot of rain isn't a reason for complete meltdown.'

He settles the lamp on Ollie's desk. 'Yes, but this isn't just a spot of rain, is it?'

I click my teeth. '*Paciencia, paciencia*!'

'True,' he smiles. 'Never fear, we'll get there in the end.'

There's a sudden flash of light and the electricity comes on.

'At last!' says Ollie.

'Good, I can get on with a bit of work. Rachel's piled it on this week. Poor thing's under terrible pressure at the moment.'

'She's got the new girl starting next week, hasn't she?'

'Yep, Siobhan, and she sounds a real star. Irish, beautiful and intelligent.'

He grins. 'I'll be on the next plane.'

I give him a playful knock and ascend the stairs to my office, keen to make headway with some PR work before the electricity goes off again. The phone suddenly springs to life. I rush into the office and grab the receiver.

'Hello, it's Marilyn Hughes here... Sorry to call on a Saturday but I'm off to New York on Monday and run off my feet.'

'No problem, Fiona told me to expect your call.'

'I just wanted to touch base. My partner Jay and I are very keen to meet you. Any chance on your next trip back?'

'Sure. I can email you some possible dates.'

She gives me her contact details. 'Let's catch up then. I've got to fly. Be in touch. *Ciao*.'

She's gone. Just like that. Cool, confident and businesslike. Surely a good sign, and yet something in the brittleness of the voice makes me uncomfortable – or am I, like my mad client Manuel, becoming inexplicably paranoid?

The cemetery is buzzing with locals, for today is Tots Sants, All Saints Day. Some people refer to 1 November as All Souls Day, but the purists would argue that this is incorrect and that All Souls is actually held on 2 November, the day after Tots Sants. Given that there are more saints than days in the year, the Catholic Church hit on the idea of All Saints Day as a means of venerating those saints who would otherwise quite simply have missed out. Nowadays the two days are rolled into one and Spaniards across the Baleares and the Peninsula pour into the cemeteries to honour departed friends and loved ones. There are more flowers sold on 1 November in Spain than on any other day of the year so flower vendors come out in force. Business is business. In the days leading up to Tots Sants, Las Ramblas in Palma, famed for its street florists, is awash with lavish bouquets and gigantic floral wreaths.

In the late Middle Ages and even into the early part of the twentieth century, bread was traditionally placed on the tombs of the dead and distributed to the poor and disabled. Sweet breads and candies such as *panetets mort*, little bread biscuits, are still sold in the more traditional *panaderias*, as are the ghoulishly named *ossos de sants*, saints' bones, which are small cylindrical pieces of marzipan filled with crushed chestnuts and sugar. Unlike in British graveyards, the Spanish place images of their loved ones on headstones, which somehow makes viewing them all the more personal and poignant. The wealthier Spanish families favour grand mausoleums and crypts, most in creamy white marble with towering, somber crosses and religious sculptures and icons on their facades. Entering one of these can be a spine tingling experience for the uninitiated and best avoided by those lacking morbid curiosity. Absence of space in urban areas has led to cemeteries using the vertical stacking system which sees coffins imbedded in shelves in large walled edifices. These multi-storey coffin parks can often be seen in the environs of motorways and in glum, downbeat zones of no natural beauty.

Today, in our town's main cemetery, we are visiting the grave of Tyler, younger son of our friends Antonia and Albert from HiBit, who was senselessly killed a year ago by a tourist performing an illegal U-turn on the main Port of Sóller road. Riding his motorbike without a care in the world, nineteen year-old Tyler didn't stand a chance when the car collided with his bike, propelling him over a wall.

Sóller's graveyard is set on a steep hill and enclosed by sturdy stone walls. At first glance, the visitor might be forgiven for thinking it a serene and beautiful park or secret garden, and if a body had to finish up anywhere it would be hard to think of a more tranquil resting place. Ancient cypress trees and wild flowers line the stone paths, and a gentle breeze kisses the dignified tombstones. Lining the wall on the far side is a cluster of serious-looking family mausoleums in heavy marble. Some are so ornate and vast that they could be mistaken for small chapels. For the main part the graves run informally throughout the cemetery, some beneath trees, others shielded by bushes and tall flowers.

Tyler's coy smile greets us as we arrive at his simple and unostentatious gravestone. His handsome face carries a dreamy expression, his eyes full of light. Many people have already laid flowers and tokens of love, perhaps the most touching being packets of sweets and a can of Coca-Cola, presumably left by friends of his own age. There are little poems and words of affection written in Catalan. I feel guilty for reading them because they are so heart-breakingly tender and moving, but somehow I want to be complicit, to have been a very tiny part of this boy's life. I remember Tyler's visits to our house when he came to help me set up a printer, bought at HiBit, his father's shop. Painfully shy and endearingly unworldly, he worked away diligently, saying little, until I asked him to help me with some technical problems. He came and sat with me at the computer, obviously hugely amused at my incompetence but far too polite to laugh. After much persuasion he caved in and accepted a cold can of Coke and then we shared some jokes. The next time he visited, he was less guarded, effortlessly setting up a programme for me on the computer and chatting through the process. He reddened with pride when I told him he was a veritable genius. We sat and talked about his future dreams and he told me how he was taking an advanced computer course so that he could be of greater assistance to his father in the store. As he left I tucked a twenty-euro note in his hand. He blushed. 'There's no need.'

'Please,' I insisted.

He gave me a broad smile. 'OK, then. If you insist.'

He drove off with a wave. It was the last time I saw him alive.

Alan touches my arm. 'Such a terrible waste.'

I nod, lost in my thoughts. Ollie has wedged a message between two rocks. I've no idea what he has written. He leaves a small bunch of roses. The traditional flowers on All Saints Day are chrysanthemums and asters but we buy lilies and roses, our favourite blooms.

'Tyler must have had lots of friends,' says Ollie. 'Look at all the flowers.'

The funeral, held at Sóller's main church in the *plaça*, had been full to bursting. The whole community, it seemed, had felt Antonia and Albert's insufferable pain that day, and had come to pay their respects to a boy whose rosy future was cruelly cut short through no fault of his own. We walk arm in arm along the pebbly paths, the cold sun caressing the tombstones and dispersing glinting light throughout the skeletal branches of the trees. Families stroll around the grounds, on the grass, on the paths, some sobbing, some with heads bent in prayer by the graves of the cherished. I think about my elderly neighbour, Margalida, who died the year before. Foolishly, I forgot to ask her daughter where she had been buried. Now I will not be able to pay my respects. As if reading my thoughts, Alan gives my hand a squeeze. 'We must find out where Margalida is buried. We'll visit her soon.'

We walk out through the main entrance. The old, wrought iron gates have been pulled open to allow for the large influx of visitors on this special day. A little girl with dark ringlets is playing with a tiny bouncy ball on the broad pavement beyond the gates while her parents, armed with chrysanthemums, try to cajole her inside the grounds. She pauses as we walk by and, with a big smile, says, 'Don't be sad. It's the weekend.'

Then she skips, with a tinkle of laughter, behind her parents, into the cemetery grounds.

The Scotsman is furious. It appears that a cat has been digging up his new seedlings and he is keen to find the guilty party. Catalina has told him it was his own fault for having his seedling boxes so exposed to the elements, and she has a point.

'I'm sure it's Orlando,' seethes the Scotsman. 'He's always very furtive.'

'All cats are furtive, that's why they're cats,' I say.

He furrows his brow. 'What on earth is that twaddle supposed to mean?'

'Cats, by their very nature, are cool customers, slinking around the joint like undercover cops.'

'Give me strength!' he sighs. 'Well, I shall be on the lookout for whoever it is and when I find him, by Jove...'

'By Jove what?'

He puts his hands on his hips in a manner which is supposed to imply resolve.

'I shall have strong words.'

'That'll really frighten the paws off the culprit,' I taunt.

He gives a dismissive grunt and plods off down a gravel path towards his vegetable patch. I glimpse my watch face and dash to the car, realising that in fifteen minutes I am due to meet Carolina Constantino, director of Museu Balear de Ciencies Naturals, and Lluc Garcia, who, aside from editing the Sóller newspaper, is on the museum's steering committee. Jelle Reumer has flown in from Rotterdam and is also joining us directly at the museum. As promised, he is going to show me the thousands of 'mouse-goat' bones discovered by the archaeologist, William Waldren, and also the fine Myotragus Balearicus specimen on show.

The rain is pounding down as I park in front of the museum. Clutching an umbrella, I make a dash for the wrought-iron gates and run up the stone path to the glass-panelled doors. The elegant building, beautifully restored, looks out on to lush vegetation and mature trees, for it sits right on the edge of the botanical gardens. A staff member welcomes me into the warm *entrada*, commenting on how atrocious the weather is. She takes my dripping umbrella and rings through to the director. Apparently Lluc is on his way. I make use of the few minutes' waiting time to browse through the many titles on fauna, flora, amphibians and animals of the

Baleares, sold in the little shop. Some are written in English but the majority are in Catalan, which reminds me that I have my first lesson of Catalan at Ollie's school the following evening. I had previously attended a beginner's Catalan course in Sóller but that finished and now Ollie's school is offering free lessons for non-Catalan parents.

The old wooden door crashes open and a slice of icy wind whips my legs as a bedraggled Lluc dives into the entrance, shaking the rain from his jacket.

'*Què día!*' he says.

Indeed, what a day.

A smiling and serene Carolina Constantino appears from a large room of exhibits ahead of us, together with Jelle Reumer, and we all exchange kisses on both cheeks. The protocol for Mallorcan greetings is so much more relaxed than in the UK. The female director of a local regional museum in England would probably be horribly embarrassed if, at first meeting, a perfect stranger leant forward to kiss her on both cheeks. In Mallorca it is totally normal, and gives a feeling of sorority and immediate trust which I find rather touching. Protocol between men and women at first meetings is a little different depending on circumstances. If introduced by a mutual female friend, it's quite normal to exchange pecks on both cheeks. If there is no female conduit, a handshake is the usual form at a first meeting.

Carolina leads us through into the main exhibition area on the ground floor, where we rest our eyes on the raised glass cabinet containing a fragile, delicate little skeleton of Myotragus. It sports the characteristic short, pointed horns and pronounced lower incisors of the one I viewed in London with my friend, Adrian Lister.

'Why did it develop those jutting lower incisors?' I ask.

'No one can be entirely sure,' says Jelle. 'They were possibly for clipping branches or chewing tough vegetation. It had no front teeth in its upper jaw but a horny pad like all sheep and cattle do.'

'What did it eat?'

Jelle shrugs and turns to face me. 'That's the weird thing. About two or three million years ago it seemed to have had a penchant for *Buxus balearica*. Box, to you and me. It's a toxic plant that is harmful to many animals so it's intriguing that, over time, Myotragus was able to digest it and suffer no ill effects.'

Carolina peers more closely at the cabinet. 'The horns were probably to ward off predators such as large birds of prey. You'll notice its legs became short and stocky to adapt to its environment.'

'It certainly was a weird looking creature, what with those big eyes at the front and the rodent-like teeth,' I comment. 'What was it, about fifty centimetres in height?'

Carolina nods. 'About that. You'll notice from these artists' impressions that it had a little hump high on its back.'

I study the drawings by the cabinet.

'During your visit to the Natural History Museum, did Adrian explain why Myotragus ended up in Mallorca?' asks Jelle.

When Jelle and I first met in Sóller, he explained that Adrian Lister and he were old scientific buddies. Small world.

'From what I understood, about five million years ago Myotragus was happily roaming about the Mediterranean basin when the land became flooded with waters from the Atlantic, which made the Mediterranean rise. Poor old Myotragus became isolated on the Mediterranean peaks which formed the Balearics.'

'That's the theory,' says Jelle. 'About a million years before that, the Straits of Gibraltar closed and the Mediterranean basin dried up, causing the highest parts – such as the Balearic highlands – to become land. These parts could then link up with the European mainland, so many creatures at the time could roam freely about. In ecological terms, the Mediterranean Sea went through what is known as the Messinian Crisis. For some reason, the Gibraltar threshold gave way about a million years later, flooding the Mediterranean and leaving many species isolated on islands. Myotragus, the ancestral shrew and the dormouse, for example, ended up in Menorca and Mallorca.'

Carolina nods. 'It explains why they found hippopotami on Cyprus and elephants and hippos on Crete.'

'What's interesting is that these island creatures, including Myotragus, evolved into dwarf species because of the environment they found themselves in,' says Lluc.

'So why did Myotragus become extinct?' I ask.

Jelle smiles. 'The scientific community is still debating that one. The big question is when did the first human settlers arrive on Mallorca and how long did they interact before the creature became extinct?'

'And what's the general view?' I ask.

'Present thinking is that humans came here about five thousand years ago and Myotragus, being a vulnerable island species, disappeared shortly afterwards.'

'The poor chap must have got quite a shock,' I say.

'Absolutely. Think about it. The little mouse-goat was roaming the Balearics for about five million years, from the Pliocene age through to the Pleistocene and half the Holocene ages. Then Neolithic man shows up.'

'There was probably intensive hunting,' says Lluc. 'The human settlers might have had dogs and introduced other animals such as cows and pigs, all competing for food.'

'It's likely that the first settlers ate Myotragus,' says Carolina. 'They may have even tried to domesticate it.'

'So to conclude,' says Jelle, 'little Myotragus, having been so isolated, didn't know how to defend itself against these newcomers and probably its whole ecosystem was disturbed.'

I follow my three guides into a small private room away from the main exhibits. Here, behind secure metal shutters, in a climate-controlled environment, are the 3,500 bones discovered by William Waldren, which are being catalogued by Jelle Reumer's scientific students from Rotterdam. As Carolina pulls out drawer after drawer of neatly catalogued and bagged remains, I wonder how on earth anyone was ever able to reconstruct such a creature. It would be like attempting an enormous and baffling anatomical puzzle.

'We have so much to identify and catalogue. There are thousands of fragments of bone, horns, teeth and skull parts,' sighs Carolina.

'A lifetime's work,' I reply.

She laughs. '*Més o manco.*' More or less.

When my eyes are weary with the sight of little white horns and incisors, Carolina locks up. Lluc has another meeting to attend to and says his goodbyes at the front door while Carolina hurries off to make me some photocopies. I collect my umbrella, staring out at the dark sky with Jelle at my side until she returns with a sheaf of paper.

'A little bedtime reading about Myotragus for you,' she grins. 'Thank you for coming. I must rush to a meeting now. *Fins aviat!*'

I take the big bundle of paper and stuff it in my rucksack. Jelle grins at me.

'So tell me, why are you really so interested in Myotragus?'

I'm lost for words. 'I don't know, Jelle. Perhaps it's because I'm fascinated by Dorothea Bate or because of the scientific expeditions I do. Maybe I'm just intrigued by the idea that Mallorca was such a wholly different place before man got his hands on it.'

He laughs. 'Or perhaps you just have a natural curiosity for the more meaningful things in life?'

'Yes, perhaps that's what it is.'

We raise our umbrellas to the wind and walk together out in to the tumbling rain.

I am returning from a run in Port of Sóller when someone calls to me in a quavering voice just as I am about to jog up my track. Heading towards me, with a hint of a limp, is a small, rounded woman of some eighty years or more.

'Thank you for waiting, senyora. I just wanted to say *hola*. I am Neus Adrillon. I was a friend of Margalida's.'

I regard her closely. There's a flash of recognition. '*Si, si,* I remember seeing you walking back with her from church a few times.'

'That's because I live close by, just along this road.' She points into the distance. 'I was very sad to lose an old friend.'

'I'm sure. I was very fond of her too.'

She nods. 'Yes, she talked about her little English friend on the track.'

I laugh. 'We got on very well despite a few linguistic problems.'

She sighs. 'If only everyone tried to be a good neighbour.'

I'm not sure how to reply. She touches my sleeve.

'I wanted to have a quiet word with you. As Margalida's friend I thought you might help me.'

'Of course. In what way?'

She has a wheezy chest, I notice, and leans against the wall to catch her breath.

'An English woman has rented the house next to mine and she is being very difficult. Every evening she plays loud music, or rather her teenage boy does, and she keeps bright lights on in the garden all night long. I don't sleep a wink.'

I chew thoughtfully on her words.

'Have you spoken with her?'

She shakes her head. 'Another close neighbour and I went round to see her but she didn't seem to speak Spanish and practically slammed the door in our faces.'

'Can't you contact the council? You could denounce her?'

It's great sport to denounce your neighbours in Spain, and indeed the Baleares. Mallorcan friends claim it's a throwback to the chilling Franco days of *denunciació* when Franco zealots spied and informed on neighbours. These days it's not quite so sinister but can be used for small misdemeanours such as owning noisy dogs, playing loud music or burning bonfires during the summer, or for more serious matters – illegal building extensions or trespassing on a neighbour's land. It's the epitome of snitching and no one frowns on it.

'That is the last resort. I just wanted to see if we could resolve things peacefully.'

'Good idea,' I say. 'Do you want me to speak with her?'

She gives me a hopeful smile. 'If it isn't too much trouble. Just to reason with her.'

She fumbles in her old shopping bag and, with a tremulous hand, holds out a scrap of paper. 'She is called Senyora Walton and the *finca* is Can Cabra.'

My ears prick up. The house of the goat? I can't get away from them.

She pats my arm. '*Moltes gràcies.*'

'*De res,*' I reply; in other words, don't mention it.

She sets off laboriously along the road, pulling her worn woollen coat around her. It must be the same troublesome English neighbour that Pau, one of our builders, mentioned to me. I don't like the sound of her one bit but perhaps there's been a huge misunderstanding brought on by her lack of the *lingo*. I hope so, for her sake, because I have zero patience for those who intimidate nice old ladies, Mallorcan or otherwise.

Ollie's excitement is palpable. The flimsy two-person tent is erected in the field next to Alan's vegetable patch and a few yards from the orange trees. We have kitted it out with two waterproof sleep mats, sleeping bags, a torch, an alarm clock and a large bottle of water. Rafael is grinning from ear to ear.

'You are *loco*, Oliver! Why you want to sleep in field?'

Ollie shrugs. 'I thought it would be cool.'

Misinterpreting him, Rafael stretches out his hands. '*Claro!* It's November. It will be very cool.'

'I mean, *divertit*, you know, fun,' says Ollie.

Rafael throws his head back and laughs loudly. 'Fun? I bet it will rain and you will be running like little chickens into the house.'

'I'll have you know that I've slept in far worse conditions in the jungle,' I reply.

'We'll see,' he goads. 'Anyway, where are the tent pegs?'

'Alan doesn't think we need any.'

He gives me a sadistic smile. 'Let's hope not, eh?'

I pull down the tent flap and zip it up. We walk slowly up to the front garden.

'I nearly forgot,' says Rafael. 'The reason I came round was to ask about your toad.'

Immediately I feel deflated. I have tried to put Johnny's abduction by mad Bill Spears to the back of my head having spent fruitless days searching for him in the hills. Ed had quivered with fear when I had telephoned him in some fury about his biologist chum. Much as he had apologised profusely, I was still grudging in my forgiveness.

'What about him?' I ask.

'He hasn't returned?'

I sigh. 'No, and I doubt he ever will now.'

Rafael tries to stifle a grin but puts a steely arm round my shoulder. 'I was telling an old farmer about your toad yesterday and he said it would return. He said it would sense its way back to you, just like a dog.'

I wonder if this is another of Rafael's little leg-pulls.

'Really?'

'*Si,* this is what he said. He believes the toad will return in the spring. Frankly I think he's as mad as a *cabron*, but I thought I should tell you.'

'Thank you, Rafael. That's very cheering news.'

When we reach the courtyard he slaps Ollie on the arm and strolls off up the track.

'Enjoy your nighttime adventure!' he calls back to us.

There's an enormous crash. I sit bolt upright in the pitch black wondering where the hell I am. I can hear steady, rhythmic breathing next to me and something is flapping madly. The wings of a killer bat, or a gargantuan hornet, perhaps? Throwing out an arm from my stuffy and cramped swaddling I hit a cold wall of canvas and remember that I'm in a tent. Sssssssssssssssssssssss ssssssss. What's that? A persistent hissing, and now so deafening, I wonder if we're under attack from some enormous basilisk. In some alarm I gently feel the inert body of my son. Surely to God, he can't still be asleep? The tent suddenly wobbles and then yields to the thunderous rain that now slams down. I am stiff and aching all over and my head feels as though it's been clamped between two clashing cymbals. Mummified in my cold nylon sleeping bag, it takes me some minutes to crawl out on to the floor which is very wet. I stumble to the net doorway and feel stinging rain on my face. With difficulty I manage to unzip it in order to close the external plastic flap. I get soaked in the process and sit dripping and shivering in the dark as lightening cracks and thunder stomps across the sky like a stroppy toddler. Still Ollie doesn't stir.

There's a sudden gust of wind and the tent begins to levitate on one side. I throw myself at it in reclining position and moan loudly. Why on earth didn't the Scotsman use the tent pegs? An absurd but scary thought enters my head. Could we really take off, up into the sky, imprisoned in our canvas cell only to land from a great height in someone's swimming pool, or worse, on the spire of the church in Sóller's *plaça*? Imagine the locals' surprise to find us there, suspended in Gothic splendour aloft their local church? I can hear footsteps outside in the whistling wind. Am I imagining it? No. Definitely something or someone is out there, slowly circling the tent. My heart is beating so hard it almost blocks out the moaning of the wind. What if this is some freak tornado? Just our luck! There's the sound of breathing and a rustling on the other side of the tent. There's only one thing for it. I will have to face my adversary, not remain here wretchedly like a sitting duck. I claw at the netting and manage to unzip the front flap. Rain rushes in, drenching my face and hair so that I am completely blinded. I place a foot out of the tent into about four inches of freezing and muddy water. Placing down a heel, I squelch through the mud, at the same time sweeping strands of sopping hair behind my ears. As my eyes battle to open in the deluge, I see before me in the blinding rain the ghostly blur of a white face. Uttering a scream, I slip over in the mud, at which point a little voice calls out from within the tent. 'WHAT IS IT?!'

I clamber onto my knees in a fearful state, only to focus on a pair of horns. It can't be. Is this one of Rafael's sick jokes? It's a white goat! I duck my head into the tent and crawl inside.

'It's alright. Sorry I screamed but a goat just came right up to the tent door. It frightened the life out of me.'

Ollie scrambles over with a torch and shines it on my face. 'Where? Let me see?'

He pokes his head out of the tent and shines the light right and left. 'There's nothing.'

'What?'

He returns, soaked to the skin. 'There's no goat.'

'It must have hidden,' I stammer, the chill making my teeth chatter.

'Sure,' says Ollie sarcastically.

We zip up the tent securely and watch the strange shadows cast by the light of the torch.

'As they say, I think we'll just have to ride the storm,' I mumble.

Ollie regards me sternly. 'Are you sure you're OK?'

I give a grunt. 'Yes, pneumonia will be a new experience.'

'Oh for heaven's sake, maybe we should just return to the house,' he says impatiently.

'Now you're talking! Do you have the key?'

Ollie eyes me critically. 'No.'

'Nor do I.'

'You're joking?' he scoffs.

'What about waking Alan?' I suggest.

'Are you mad? He sleeps like a hog.'

'Log,' I correct. Given his father's snoring habit, maybe hog is more fitting.

We crawl back into our sleeping bags, wet and shivering. 'Let's put them as close together as possible. It might prove more insulating.'

'Whatever makes you happy,' Ollie sighs.

We shimmy up together and lie there like stones, the howling wind and rain battering down on our little tent, until daylight.

It's early morning. Ollie is gnawing on a cheese roll and drinking a cup of hot gunpowder tea with far too much sugar piled into it.

'Anyway, so she screamed and said she'd seen a white goat!'

There's a huge burst of laughter from Alan. 'A goat? She's obsessed with the damned things.'

He nudges me. 'You're a constant source of amusement. Anyway, how's the back now?'

Having risen at 7 a.m., I had finally managed to battle my way out of the tent and walk slowly in my slippers, with aching back, through the quagmire to the house. The Scotsman had failed to hear the thundering on the front door so I had resorted to hurling gravel at the upstairs window. Eventually, he had woken up.

'It's still agony despite the hot shower. I think that's the end of my camping days.'

He grins. 'Well, camping out on one of the coldest nights of the year on rock-like soil wasn't the best idea.'

I steal a glance at Ollie. 'Remember it was his idea.'

'I thought it was cool! The storm was the best thing.'

'You little liar!'

He slurps at his tea. 'I could do it again tonight.'

'Ha! You'll be on your own,' I growl.

'Suits me. Anyway, it's far more fun than playing with a Wii.'

Alan pounds his fist on the table. 'Good lad! You see, you enjoyed being in the fresh air...'

'It's more to do with seeing my mad mother hallucinating about goats and wallowing in muddy water.'

'You are a wit,' I say grumpily.

Alan begins doing the washing up. We still haven't got a dishwasher because we are yet to find a home for one in the kitchen. First we must find a place to house the washing machine. It's complicated. The telephone rings. It's Ed, calling from London.

'Are you still speaking to me?'

'Maybe, but I haven't forgiven you for inflicting that wretched Bill Spears on us.'

He gives a loud sniff. 'I can't blame you. Poor Johnny, let's hope he finds his way home soon.'

I laugh. 'Don't pretend to care about my toad. You hate amphibians!'

'I'm not mad about them but I feel somewhat responsible...'

'Good. I want you to feel stricken with guilt. Anyway, what's your news?'

He has a soppy sound to his voice. 'I was ringing to see if we could fix a date for dinner when you're next over in London. I'd like you to meet Veronica.'

'Your high priestess?'

'Yes, we're getting on famously.'

'That's a turn up for the books. Fine by me, but don't expect me to be a saint.'

He lets out a guffaw. 'You wouldn't know how, Scatters.'

I sneeze violently.

'Oh no, I hope you're not catching a cold.'

'It's nothing,' I say and, before I can stop myself, add, 'Ollie and I camped out last night and got drenched.'

He gives a screech. 'Camped? In November? Are you stark raving mad?'

'Of course we are.'

'You could have caught pneumonia or hypothermia. How irresponsible!'

'We weren't on Everest base camp, Ed. Get a grip.'

He tuts loudly. 'Listen, I'm at work so I'd better go. Email me some possible dates.'

'Of course... and in the meantime you can say a prayer for poor lost Johnny.'

I expect him to giggle but instead he gives a deep sigh.

'The truth is that Veronica and I have included him in our prayers every night.'

I resist the urge to giggle myself. After all, they really are a pair of saints.

# EIGHT

# DOG IN THE MANGER

**Monday 7 a.m., Piccadilly**

A streak of light falls on the bed. I am swaddled in layers of clothes and blankets and submerged beneath a thick eiderdown. I twiddle my toes and feel the matted cashmere socks, bought for me by my sister last Christmas. Either Catalina or I accidentally put them on a hot machine wash and they shrank to about Barbie's foot size. Not one to give in, I had squeezed my toes into them and wriggled them about until the socks had just stretched enough to cover my feet – uncomfortably. What of it? They were warm.

I poke my head out and see that a thick trace of ice has formed on the far window. My club does have radiators but I've rarely been fortunate enough to find them in working order. In some of the single bedrooms there are small convector fires which spew out lukewarm air and rattle and click with such ferocity that I think they are about to explode at any given moment. I spring out of bed, dash over to the heater and turn it on, hoping that I will immediately be cocooned in warmth. Instead, an icy blast, akin to an Atlantic gale, engulfs me and with chattering teeth I begin doing a mini war dance on the spot and curse loudly. Throwing back the stripy cotton curtains, I stare out at a bleak, grey day. Beyond the window is a small, trellised garden in which two naked, grey lime trees vie for attention with a few scrawny bushes, their leaves yellowed and drooping. I wonder who owns it and why it has been so badly neglected. The old, white house that it partners is shuttered up and the window boxes have long lost their inhabitants, whose shrivelled remains can just be seen dangling over the edges. I reflect on how easily the building could fall victim to squatters and, in a moment of bolshiness, think it would serve the negligent owners jolly well right.

Hanging on a chair in my oversized fridge is a pair of lycra running tights, a T-shirt and a warm fleece. I must have been feeling optimistic some time in the small hours when I finally arrived after a two hour delay at Palma airport. The window panes are icy to touch and I am on the point of dismissing all thoughts of an early morning run, when a good fairy impulse hits the brain. A forty-minute run will clear the head, aid fitness levels and get me in the right mindset for the Athens marathon next year. However, there's also a little devil in my head prodding me with a sharp fork and urging me to stay in bed. What should I do? I step into the freezing corridor and try the door of the shower room. It doesn't budge. Damn.

'Someone's in there and I'm next!'

A shrill voice rips through the chill and a woman with big hair and wearing a winceyette nightdress glares furiously at me from the far end of the corridor. Bother. I make my decision. Time for a run. I turn tail and return to the bedroom, throw on my running kit and head down the corridor and out into the breach. As I pass by, the same woman calls out, a tad less menacingly.

'Lord! Are you going for a run?'

She is leaning against the corridor wall, a towel draped over one arm and, I notice, wearing pompom slippers.

'It's such a glorious day,' I smile, scrunching up my nose cheesily. 'How could I possibly resist?'

### 9.30 a.m., Hackney

Havana Leather HQ is tucked away, quite anonymously, in a grubby, run down, four storey block in Hackney. It's hard to say when this monstrosity was spawned but the astute visitor would probably surmise the mid seventies. The walled entrance is a brisk ten minute walk from Hackney Central station through busy, traffic-jammed streets and past a multitude of drab housing estates and heckling hoodies. Above Havana Leather, which occupies the ground floor and basement of the building, are a multitude of rag trade sweat shops, each in its own cramped labyrinth of small, dingy rooms, where a jumble of women of all nationalities toil away for an undignified wage. They arrive early morning and the stutter of sewing machines and whir of machinery can be heard quite clearly from Havana Leather's bald and bleak front reception. Late afternoon, small cuts of brightly coloured fabric in cottons and polyester can be found by the bins in the tarmac yard outside, fugitives that have somehow escaped sloppily fastened refuse sacks. Some break rank and float around the yard, even wriggling their way through half open doors and windows downstairs, much to Greedy George's consternation.

Trudy White is the life and soul of Greedy George's empire, an East End girl with a loud Cockney twang and tough exterior, but a marshmallow heart. She answers the telephone perkily with a flirty, girlish giggle which inevitably sends the pulses of male buyers, retailers and customers racing wildly. I pull open the scuffed, old front door and stand before her in the reception. A small three bar electric heater glowers from a corner of the room close to a low glass table and grimy blue sofa, moulting with age. She finishes a call and observes me cheerfully as I remove leather gloves, scarf and camel coat.

'Nice and warm here, innit?' A huge peal of laughter.

'Heavenly, Trudy. The walk from the station was particularly enjoyable in sub-zero temperatures.'

'You didn't have any hassle?'

Recently several employees have been mugged on their way to and from work by local hoodlums so there's now a strict dressing down rule at the company. I have worn jeans but the camel coat and gloves are probably a red rag to a bull.

'Nope. I mean what does a girl have to do to get mugged around here?'

'Well your accent might help. Open your gob on Hackney High Street and you'd probably find your wallet gone in a jiffy.'

She gets up and takes my pile of damp outerwear and locks it away in a cupboard.

'Just in case it gets nicked,' she says without a jot of irony. 'Fancy a coffee? I can do you a swanky espresso if you like?'

I express mock shock. 'What? Real coffee?'

'Yeh, George came back from Mallorca and got one of them Nespresso machines. Costs a bloody fortune though, somefink like fifty pence a throw.'

'Worth it though'.

She gives a snort of dissent. 'Mind you, I like them adverts with George Clooney, but I don't reckon he drinks the stuff, do you?'

'Who knows, but I haven't seen him at the local Nespresso store in Palma.'

She tosses back her head. 'Exactly!'

I watch as she bustles off down a corridor to the galley kitchen. No sooner has she disappeared than a door to my left bangs open and a disgruntled looking Fred, the production manager, walks in.

'Bloody marvellous! Some bastard's taken my chair!'

'Hi Fred.'

He observes me with bloodshot eyes and a heavy, bulldog jowl.

'What you doing here? Don't think of parking your arse anywhere, 'cause all the chairs have gone. Bastards.'

Greedy George operates the 'last in, no chair' philosophy. How this works is that every morning, of the forty-six full-time staff, only forty-five will find a chair to sit on. The person who arrives at the company last will be chair-less all day unless he or she steals another's chair when vacated. It's an adult version of musical chairs except there are no prizes awarded to the winners. This is one of Greedy George's little jokes, a way of intimidating and controlling his staff and brutally encouraging them to get to work early. Desperate staff members have even taken to engraving their names with pen knives on the back of chairs and the part time elderly accountant keeps a shooting stick with portable leather seat in his lockable cupboard.

'Don't worry, Fred, I won't be here long enough for it to bother me.'

'Lucky you. Bloody awful hole. We've got no heating on the factory floor and I've already got two girls off sick with flu. He doesn't care. Just swans around in his big, black, bloody four-wheel drive...'

'Anyone I know?' yells George, barging through the same door and cuffing him on the head.

'Ow. What's that for?'

'Nothing, just felt like it.' George is beaming, full of bonhomie. 'Where's Trudy?'

'Gone to get the coffee.'

'Great. Come on guv. Gotta crack on. I bought some fab almond croissants from Maison Blanc on the way here.'

'Yum.' I lick my lips.

Fred curses under his breath. 'Got no ruddy chair.'

George pushes me through the door and turns to stare at him. 'Shouldn't be so chair-less, geddit?' A quick cackle of laughter, then, 'Well fatso, you'll just have to sit on your hands.'

He walks jauntily through the factory, winking at the girls and making risqué asides to the pretty ones. We arrive at his shambolic office where, thankfully. there are two chairs.

'Ah, thought I'd be sitting on the floor.'

'No worries, guv. I just nicked Fred's chair when he was in the depot.'

'That's a bit below the belt. Poor guy. You never give him a break.'

He yawns heavily and rustles the bag containing three whopping iced croissants. 'He's a lazy bastard so having to stand all day might chivvy him up a bit.'

The door opens and Trudy walks in with a tray.

'Two coffees and a bottle of Evian.'

'Good girl, and what about those letters for signing?'

'Cheeky sod! You've only just given them to us. I'll type them up now.'

She waltzes out.

'She's a good egg,' I say.

'Yeah. Wish I could clone her.'

He shares out the croissants – two for him, one for me. We sip on the hot coffee.

'So how's the Christmas stock coming along?'

He sits back and, with a big paw, wipes some crumbs from his cashmere jumper.

'All in place. We've ordered extra Santa stockings after that piece you got us in the *Telegraph* shopping supplement. The girls in sales have had three hundred enquiries already.'

'You can't be serious?'

'Goat power, you see.'

I grimace. George's Santa stockings have been made out of black Bengali goat hide which I have to admit, somewhat begrudgingly, have proved a good gimmick. Shopping editors can't have enough of them and we've had endless PR about their coolness factor.

'What else is selling well?'

'The dog's leather range is doing great guns. The leather toy bones have been walking out of the door.'

He stuffs half a croissant in his mouth so that his cheeks bulge.

'You're like an anaconda.'

He chews thoughtfully and finally swallows. 'A what?'

'You know how anaconda snakes bung their victims in whole and digest them slowly.'

'Cheers, guv. I'll take that as a compliment.'

'So has the new Christmas window gone into the shop yet?'

His face lights up. Bounding over to a battered wooden cupboard, he pulls some sheaves of paper from a drawer and spreads them out on his desk.

'The window dresser's over there now. What d'you think?'

In coloured pencil, the sketches depict Havana Leather's pristine shop in St James's. It is in marked contrast to the squalid office and factory here in Hackney. I wonder what his obscenely rich customers would think of the dump he works in away from glitzy St James's. One of the drawings gives a detailed layout of the new display in the huge front windows of the store. In the background there are Christmas gift boxes piled high and leather items dangling from festive ribbon with mistletoe intertwined. A tall, bushy Christmas tree crammed with small leather products sporting red bows is positioned to the left of the front window while on the right, goat hide Santa stockings are suspended from the ceiling by invisible threads, all bursting with Havana Leather products. With some incredulity my eyes rest on what can only be the pièce de résistance. Centred on a big, gaudy gold plinth, plum in the middle of the window display, is a colossal wooden manger. I shake my head. 'Is this for real?'

He heaves with laughter. 'A nice twist on the Christmas story, eh?'

'The traditionalists won't like it.'

'Who cares?'

At the corners of the manger hang little leather dog toys and, sitting amidst yellow straw, with its paws flopping over the side, is an enormous toy Dalmatian dressed in a black leather jacket. An inscription in shiny silver studs reads: DOG IN THE MANGER.

'What can I say?'

George grins at me. 'Only one thing to say, guv. I'm a phenomenon, a bleeding retail genius.'

### 12 noon, the office, Mayfair

Rachel is sipping at a cappuccino while I knock back a double espresso with sugar. She eyes me critically.

'All that sugar is going to ruin your teeth.'

'I know, but I'll probably die first.'

She tuts loudly. 'What sort of attitude is that?'

'A realist's? Anyway, what was it you wanted to speak with me about?'

She places her cup on the desk and looks up. 'It's just really to talk about where the company's heading. I know you're becoming pretty immersed in Mallorcan life and finding it a bit of a schlep to come back to London each month.'

I shrug. 'It's not so bad. I'm OK about the flying now it's not so frequent. I suppose I'm just trying to weigh up how much longer I want to be in the PR game.'

She gives a nod. 'Well, I'm at a crossroads too. Max is fed up with London and wants to return to his northern roots.' She raises her eyebrows a little.

'What's wrong with that, Rachel? I loved my time at Leeds University. I can hardly blame Max for wanting to return up North.'

'Funnily enough, the idea appeals to me too when I'm not fretting about kissing goodbye to Topshop and window shopping in Bond Street.'

'You can always buy *Grazia* and dream of the good old days. Anyway, what would you both do if you moved?'

'Max has already been offered a computer programming contract with a large company in York, and I suppose I'd just look for a PR job of some kind.'

I drain my coffee cup. 'Where would you think of basing yourselves?'

'In my parents' village outside York. There are still a few reasonably priced properties on the market in need of renovation.'

We sit in silence for a minute. 'If we can find a buyer or someone to merge with, that would solve both our problems,' I say. 'Mind you, you're free to move on whenever you want, of course.'

She shakes her head vehemently. 'No way. I'm staying to the end. I want to see the company pass into new hands and help with the transition. Max and I don't have a particular time frame and he has an open invitation to start the new job whenever.'

'That's unusual.'

She sits back in her chair. 'Not really. He's a damned good programmer and they're desperate to lure people like him up North. They're happy to wait.'

'It'll be the end of an era,' I say, a little morosely.

Rachel jumps up and crosses the room. Opening the door to her office, she pops out and asks Sarah to make us some more coffee.

'Don't be daft,' she laughs. 'It's not the end of an era. It's the beginning of a whole new one!'

### 1 p.m., Wimpole Street

Dr Barney Zimmermann is an ozone pioneer. According to Dannie Popescu-Miller, this man injects ozone into the rumps of European royals and half the presidents of the Latin-American world, not to mention the Congo and the Baltic. Numbered among his clients are some of the globe's wealthiest players – shipping and property tycoons, Russian oligarchs, bankers, legal eagles, Hollywood luvvies and a host of millionaire playboy entrepreneurs. And Dannie. Now why Dannie needs ozone pumped into her backside is anybody's guess, but today I'm about to find out. She has invited me to meet the famed Dr Zimmermann in his Wimpole Street rooms because, it transpires, he is keen to increase his media profile. I expressed horror at getting involved with one of Dannie's bizarre alternative medical practitioners but Rachel begged me to pop by just in case he turned out to be a good potential client. Dannie's other guru is her psychic tea leaf reader with an obscure name, whom I've nicknamed Tetley. It is she who first got Dannie involved with Dr Zimmermann.

The black front door of the imposing terraced house in Wimpole Street has three copper name plates by the bell. There's a Dr Moss, a Professor Sweeting and my man, Zimmermann. A husky voice greets me when I press the bell and the door catch is released as if by magic. Ahead of me is a winding marble staircase with gleaming mahogany rails. I ignore it and, as instructed by Miss Husky, slip along a dark, fusty corridor with ornate tiled floor to a vintage glass fronted door. Barely have I touched the handle than the door springs open and an Amazonian tree of a woman stoops to greet me. She indicates to follow her into a wide library-cum-reception area where she settles herself behind an oak desk, her dark, glossy hair swishing over one shoulder.

'You are here to see doctor? Please, take seat.'

I wander across the room and sink heavily into an old, velvety armchair. Never a good move. One of the first lessons I ever learnt when attending job interviews was to sit in an upright seat. Sprawling like a beetle on your back in a deep armchair with your skirt riding up rarely creates a favourable impression with interviewers, I discovered. Anyway, this isn't an interview and I don't even want to be here. I look irritably at my watch and then around at the walls. Bookshelves on all sides stretch up to the ceiling, full of dusty tomes, their spines cracked with age. I squint at the shelf nearest to me and see to my disappointment that most titles are concerned with anatomical issues, which is hardly surprising. What was I expecting to find, the complete works of Shakespeare or D. H. Lawrence?

'You want drink?' The dark eyed Miss Husky is staring at me challengingly.

'A glass of water would be great.'

She gets up and stalks over to a fridge just beyond her desk and pours me some water from a bottle, giving a little wink as she does so.

'Liquid ozone. It's very good.'

I lower the glass.

There's a flash of a pearly white smile. 'Just joking.'

A door flies open a few yards behind her desk and a small, hunched and bearded creature hurtles towards me, one hand fiddling impatiently with the bifocals perched on his nose. He juts out a hand which I take in mine. It is cold and clammy, rather like shaking a dead fish.

The accent is guttural, the tone curt. 'Come this way. Miss Popescu-Miller has just had her treatment.'

We enter his office, a high ceilinged room with swag curtains in dark green velvet and a pea green carpet. Dannie is reclining on a chaise longue in the centre of the room.

'Darling! How marvellous to see you. I've just been ozoned.'

I give her a peck on the cheek, wincing at the overpowering smell of Coco Chanel. She has a weird spaced out look but I suppose she can be forgiven for being an airhead this afternoon having just been blasted with the stuff. Without an invitation, I sit on a pert chair by the good doctor's desk. He ignores his leather throne on the other side, and, grabbing a stool, draws it up close to me.

'You want to talk about ozone, yuh?'

Dannie appears to be all ears, leaning her cheek coyly on one upturned palm with her head cocked towards us.

'Well I know a little about the ozone layer. What's different about your sort of ozone?'

'Ozone is ozone,' he says impatiently. 'What do you think ozone is?'

I squirm a little in my chair. 'Isn't it a toxic gas?'

Rather impertinently he slaps my knee. Steady on.

'Predictable and negative foolishness! It's so much more,' he says excitedly. 'It is colourless, unstable with a pungent odour ...'

For a fleeting moment I think he's describing Dannie.

He pauses. '... and without it, what would become of our fragile society?'

'Tell me.'

'The world would be a more damaged place. Ozone absorbs ultraviolet radiation which at ground level contributes to global warming – but of course you must know all this.'

I nod sagely.

'You will know that ozone is three atoms of oxygen, what we call $O_3$...'

'To be honest, Dr Zimmerman, I have a very basic understanding of ozone verging on total ignorance.'

He rubs his hands together and pushes the frail glasses hard against his nose. 'Well, there are three ways to produce ozone – hot spark, cold plasma or ultraviolet light.'

I wince. 'The hot spark method doesn't sound so attractive.'

He waves a hand impatiently through the air. 'That is mainly an industrial method. I use the other two for patient therapies.'

'So how do you ingest ozone exactly?'

'There are many ways. You know in Germany they've used autohemotherapy for more than sixty years. You extract a pint of the patient's blood, ozonate it and return it to the body.'

I begin feeling queasy. Why isn't Rachel conducting this meeting instead? The chicken.

'Ozone injected or ingested can cure a number of ills... arthritis, herpes, and serious conditions such as cancer.'

I jot down some notes. 'But if it's such a cure-all, why isn't the NHS using it?'

He seems to find this very funny. I'm glad to have cheered him up.

'Pharmaceutical companies and organised medicine like your NHS want to suppress it, and why?'

'Because they're spoilsports?' I hazard.

'Look, a cured patient equals lost revenue, right? An ill patient equals long-term financial investment.'

'That's a bit cynical, Dr Zimmerman.'

'The world is cynical, young lady.' Young lady. What's he trying to prove?

'So what do the majority of your patients come here for?'

He stands up, a ball of fractious energy, and paces around the hideous oriental rug that swallows up the centre of the room.

'Most of my clients want to be rejuvenated.'

'And does it work?'

'Sure, it works. Look at Dannie.'

I give her a weak smile. She's hardly a walking advertisement for the good doctor, rather more for a zealous plastic surgeon.

'So Dannie says you want to represent me?' he suddenly blurts.

She gives me an encouraging smile. 'Dr Zimmermann wants to be a part of your PR family.'

Did she really utter those words? I think murderous thoughts about Rachel. Yet another fine mess she's got me into. Somehow Rachel always lands me with complete fruitcakes posing as potential clients while she bags the relatively normal ones. I turn to Dr Zimmerman.

'First I need to know a great deal more about your services.'

He nods and throws me a manic smile. 'I'm all yours.'

'Right, Dr Zimmermann' I say wearily. 'Let's start at the very beginning…'

**3 p.m., the office, Mayfair**

Rachel is eating a prawn sandwich while she shuffles paper around her desk. I observe her for a few seconds.

'So next time, you can go and pay Mr Ozone a visit.'

She takes a glug of coffee from a Starbucks paper cup. 'Look, it wouldn't be that hard to do his promotion.'

'Rachel, you didn't meet him. He's like a character from *The Addams Family*. And as for the Brazilian receptionist, she's terrifying. God knows what she put in my water. It tasted weird.'

'Don't complain. It's knocked ten years off you.'

'Very droll. Anyway, I've told him you'll be in touch. Good luck.'

'Cheers. Well, I'm getting used to nutters working with you.'

I drum my fingers on her desk. 'Look, I'm off to see this couple who own Red Hot PR soon. Want to come?'

'I think it's better you see them first. I'll come for the second round if it gets that far,' she replies.

'Fine by me.'

She scans her emails and then her watch. 'Anyway, it would be too tight. I've got to see the Peterson-Matlocks and Yuri Drakova this afternoon.'

I groan. 'How's the shop launch coming along?'

She taps her desk. 'Touch wood, swimmingly well.'

'Was that a deliberate pun? As in Wild Wood, touch wood?'

Her nose crinkles. 'Oh God… didn't even cross my mind! Anyway, the dream dress is almost finished. It's fabulous, covered in thousands of Swarovski crystals. Anastasia Mirnov will look stunning in it.'

'Are Marcus and lovely Serena still at each other's throats?'

'They're trying to behave in front of Yuri but I think the truce won't last.'

Tonight, after my meeting with Red Hot PR, Rachel and I have a reception to attend at the Spanish Embassy. A few clients will be there including mad Manuel Ramirez from H Hotels and, heaven help us, his new investor in the Maryland hotel, Vice Admiral Mason.

'Listen, I'd better be going. Are you all set for the reception tonight?'

She yawns. 'I'll meet you in the bar at the Berkeley Hotel at 7 p.m. It'll only take us five minutes to walk to Belgrave Square.'

'Let's hope we don't bang in to Dannie at the Berkeley.'

Rachel frowns. 'I thought she was staying at that Senator's house again in Hill Street?'

'She is but, being Dannie, she's also booked her favourite suite at the Berkeley to stop anyone else using it. She said she'd like to know it's always available.'

'Must be costing her a fortune, too,' cries Rachel. 'What a dog in the manger.'

I shake my head and laugh. 'That reminds me, I haven't told you about Greedy George's Christmas window display.'

She looks up. 'Go on, tell me the worst.'


**4.30 p.m., Golden Square, Soho**

The offices of Red Hot PR are situated in an elegantly refurbished terraced house in Golden Square. I imagine the rents in this part of town must be crippling. Every other building is home to film production agencies and photographic studios and there's a hip, slick feel to the area. The company occupies three floors, the top one having been turned into a minimalist studio for shoots and for storing clothes and accessory samples belonging to its fashion label clients. It is in here that Marilyn Hughes, Jay Finch and I are sitting at a long glass table surrounded by heavy duty clothes rails. Crammed on each metal rod is a mix of fashion items – mini skirts, clingy evening dresses, trousers and flimsy silk camisoles. A gold and scarlet bustier with yellow lace catches my eye. Who in God's name would wear that?

'Nice piece, isn't it?' says Jay Finch, admiringly.

'Yes, it has a certain *je ne sais quoi*.'

'I'd wear it myself if I could squeeze into it!' He gives me a playful wink and slips me a suggestive grin.

'So, the bottom line is, do you really want to merge?' booms Marilyn, with an Essex twang.

'It makes sense,' I say quietly, 'providing I can hand over the reins fairly quickly and smoothly, and my clients are happy.'

Jay Finch begins rubbing his palms together in a fast friction motion that makes a sound rather like an excitable cicada or perhaps a flock of finches in flight.

'You know, darling, it's all about letting go. We'd need you to help out during the transition period, and then you'd be free as a bird.'

He illustrates the point by flapping his arms up and down. Marilyn eyes him impatiently while I gather up the dossiers of information that she has prepared for me about Red Hot's client base and finances. The logo is of a smouldering red chilli, more the sort of image you'd see above a Mexican restaurant chain.

'OK,' I hear myself say. 'Once I've read through all this, I'll discuss it with our accountants and lawyers and get back to you both. Thanks for your time.'

Jay Finch gives me a blinding smile. 'Our pleasure entirely!'

Marilyn appears steelier. 'We're obviously talking to several like-minded agencies during our expansion period, but we really like your client portfolio.'

I step out into the icy street. Lights twinkle from the lofty, terraced buildings that flank the square. There's a spit of rain in the air. Pulling up my collar, I glance at my watch. Time to meet Rachel. Now where's that cab?

### 7.20 p.m., Belgrave Square, SW1

The sky is in an ugly mood. Rain slams down onto the dark pavements licking our shoes and pricking our skin. Hazy street lamps emit a sickly yellow light which neither brightens nor adds cheer to the gathering gloom. Rachel is hollering at me above the din of the wind as she attempts to totter behind me in her four inch heels towards the Spanish Embassy. Gripping a stack of designer bags in both hands, she valiantly tries to prevent them from floating off heavenwards as they lift on the wind. Ahead of her I do battle with my black telescopic umbrella which has turned inside out so that it resembles a floppy satellite dish, drawing me by the metal handle towards certain death on the busy road. I brace myself on the edge of the pavement and turn to Rachel.

'Come on! We're late. The Embassy's just over there, isn't it?'

She squints over my shoulder, long strands of hair sending dribbles of water down her red coat.

'Yes. Look, I think a guest's just gone in.'

We run across the road, narrowly missing a fast-moving taxi which flashes us angrily. Dashing into the elegant, curved drive, we hurtle up the wide stone stairs to the front door. A maid immediately ushers us inside the warm and brightly lit hallway. Rachel pushes the wet hair from her face and begins unbuttoning her coat.

'Please to leave your belongings, madam,' the maid says.

'Thanks. Can you take all my bags too?' Rachel hands over the spoils of her forays into various boutiques over a lunchtime spent hunting for Christmas gifts. The maid waits until we have smoothed our hair and smartened up our makeup before handing

175

us over to a butler. He nods courteously and leads us off through the grand entrance with its candelabras and ornate decor.

'I don't remember him, do you?' I whisper.

She gives a little shrug. 'It's some months since we were last here. The whole place seems very quiet. Maybe we really are very late.'

I look around me. I don't seem to recognise a thing. Perhaps this is the onset of old age, an inability to remember venues after only a matter of months. We reach a beautifully polished and imposing wooden door. The butler halts. What's he waiting for? I give Rachel a look. She returns a frown of confusion. Surely he can just discreetly show us into the back of the reception room even if speeches are in progress? With two hundred or more guests attending, they won't pay us any attention. He leans forward.

'And you are?'

Something is definitely not right. We mutter our names and watch helplessly as he throws open the door with aplomb and announces us both in a booming voice. We step inside. Silence. Rachel gives a sharp intake of breath; almost imperceptible, but I can hear it. My heart is thumping. There in front of us is the Ambassador, what appears to be his wife and a small gathering of guests, all in formal evening gowns. However, it isn't the *Spanish* Ambassador – no, this is some other Ambassador. He is perfectly groomed, grand, and wearing a curious expression on his face, and rightly so. No doubt he is wondering what on earth a pair of rain-swept women in work attire are doing on his turf, at his exclusive, private bash. Rachel smiles graciously and shakes his hand. I follow suit and then step back towards the butler who by now is scowling at us as if we are treacherous imposters.

'I think there's been a mistake,' I say in an offstage whisper to him. 'We wanted the Spanish Embassy.'

He puts his hand to his head and gasps. While the Ambassador and guests continue to observe us in the sticky stillness, we walk slowly back through the door and into the corridor. The butler closes the doors behind us.

'This is the Portuguese Embassy!' he announces. 'How in heaven's name could you not have known?'

'It was dark and raining,' says Rachel. 'We just dashed in and assumed...'

The man gives a small groan and wearily takes us back to the maid, who quickly hands over all our sopping possessions in swift, bird-like movements. At the door, the butler fixes us both with a grimace.

'I think you will find that the Spanish Embassy is next door.'

We stand on the drive in the rain as the door slams behind us. Then, before we make it onto the street, we burst into hysterical laughter.

'You fool!' I shout.

'Me? That's rich coming from you. You told me that was the Embassy.'

'No, I asked you for confirmation...'

Rachel shoves me forward. 'Give me a break!'

'The maid said *obregada,* which means thank you in Portuguese. I thought that was a bit odd.'

'Well you could have said something!' she says.

On the next corner, we wobble up the drive, relieved to hear loud conversation and laughter pouring out of the front doors. A Spanish friend who works at the Embassy approaches us.

'What's so hilarious?'

He breaks into a chuckle when he hears of our mishap. 'My God, how could you make such a ridiculous mistake?'

We have no real answer, save incompetence. He tuts and leads us into the main reception room where Manuel Ramirez espies us across the heaving room and begins riding the wave of people between us. To my dismay I see he has an elderly man in tow, dressed in a dark double-breasted jacket with gold sleeve stripes.

'Oh no, it must be his investor, the Maryland vice admiral.'

Rachel bobs her head above the crowds. 'Let's not be intimidated. We're doing a good job for H Hotels and if this old walrus has a problem, I'd like to hear it.'

Manuel finally reaches us. He is perspiring heavily and mopping his brow with an immaculate white embossed handkerchief. I notice he is wearing one of his favourite suits from Norton's on Savile Row. He leans over to kiss me on both cheeks.

'Not wearing your bullet-proof jacket today?' I tease.

Manuel has on several occasions shown me bullet-proof wear made by his favourite Colombian tailor, Mr Caballero, who lives in Bogota. I have never got to the bottom of why Manuel needs such protection but the fact that he has a golden Kalashnikov hanging above the desk in his Panama office might hold the key.

'I don't need to wear bullet proof garments in London. Only in New York and Latin America,' he says sombrely. 'Anyway, allow me to introduce you to Vice Admiral Mason.'

I fleetingly take in the gold buttoned jacket which on the left side boasts several rows of assorted, brightly coloured ribbons. The watery blue eyes are uncompromising.

'Mr Mason! I've heard so much about you. What a pleasure,' I trill.

Rachel shakes his hand. 'Yes, a delight. Manuel has spoken so warmly about you.'

He regards us warily. 'Hey, nice to meet you girls too. I'll be honest though, now that I'm investing in H Hotel Maryland, I need to be sure of your commitment to my pal, Ramirez, here.'

I give a concerned nod. 'Is there any reason why you might doubt that commitment?'

He clicks his teeth and briefly brushes one of the ribbons on his lapel. 'Ever heard of industrial espionage?'

Am I really hearing this? 'Indeed, but hopefully Manuel knows from our track record that spying isn't really our game.'

Rachel gives a little splutter as she tries to swallow a giggle. A waiter saves the day by passing us glasses of cava. I watch as she takes a deep sip and manages to recover the situation.

'We are devoted to H Hotels,' she says robustly. 'Quite frankly there are many hotel chains out there, but there's only one for us.'

Manuel gives a crocodile smile. 'You see *mi amigo*, they are trustworthy.'

'We bring him luck,' chirrups Rachel. 'It's true. Manuel always seems to pull off a hotel deal after meeting up with us in London.'

Manuel rolls his head back and laughs. 'Is that you bringing me luck or my own genius?'

The vice admiral offers a half-hearted smile and pats his thinning silver locks.

'The only lucky mascot I know about is Bill the Goat.'

My ears prick up.

'Who's Bill the Goat? I'm very interested in goats.'

'You are? Old Bill the Goat was our lucky mascot at the US Naval Academy in Maryland. We won every damned football game when that goat showed up.'

'How intriguing,' I reply. 'Was he an official mascot?'

'Sure, there have been Bill the goats at the Naval school for many generations. The first one was inaugurated way back in 1893, I reckon.'

'That's fascinating.'

He frowns. 'Poor old Bill's been kidnapped a fair few times over the years. There was a nasty incident back in 1953 when those chumps from West Point Army Academy stole off with him before a football game. There was hell to pay. Even Eisenhower got involved and forced those cowardly cadets to hand him back.'

Rachel is incapable of raising her head from her glass. She mumbles something incoherently and sniffs deeply. I am buffeted by a large group of Spanish revellers, and move closer to the vice admiral.

'You know, we used to have an interesting type of goat living on Mallorca. It was called Myotragus.'

He takes a sip of his drink and narrows his eyes. 'What do you know, I think I've heard of it. Some kind of ancient creature. Means mouse-goat if my Greek serves me right.'

'I'm impressed.'

He beams. 'Always been into palaeontology. It's a bit of a passion really. I've been heavily involved with the Natural History Society of Maryland which took off in 1929...'

Probably about the time he was born.

'Of course, that was way before my time but it's still very active today and then there's the Maryland Dairy Goat Association. My younger sister's very proactive in that.'

Rachel is having convulsions and, suddenly excusing herself, rushes off through the crowd, a hankie clamped to her nose.

'Is she OK?' asks Manuel, with a concerned expression.

'She's just got a very nasty cold.'

Vice Admiral Mason exhales deeply. 'Ozone cures that, you know. Builds the immune system.'

I pat the gold brocade of his sleeve. 'You won't believe it, but just this morning I was with one of the world's greatest ozone practitioners.'

'You're kidding?'

'No, absolutely not. His name is Dr Zimmermann.'

He stands back, aghast. 'Barney Zimmerman? I haven't seen that old devil in years! Why, he gave me one of my first ozone shots in Germany back in the eighties. My God, this is swell. Can you put me in touch with him?'

I nod enthusiastically. 'Of course.'

He gives Manuel a slap on the back and breaks into laughter. 'Any girl that likes old goats and knows about ozone is good enough for me.'

Manuel raises his arms in the air and gives a nervous little chuckle, maybe finally realizing that his new investor – and his PR – are both genuinely unhinged.

'So we are all friends?' says Manuel with a manic grin.

'*Si mi amigo*, we sure are,' honks Vice Admiral Mason.

My eyes wander across the sea of faces in the reception room until they alight on Rachel. She is giggling helplessly next to one of our Spanish clients, who is obviously in on the joke. He cocks his head in my direction and, shaking with laughter himself, gives me a thumbs up sign and an enormous wink.

# NINE

# A CHRISTMAS CAROL

The air is as crisp and aromatic as a newly picked apple. Puddles of water have turned to ice and a crusty layer of frost has spread like crystallised sugar across the front lawn. High above, a blue sky casts a benevolent eye over the Sóller Valley and a sun the colour of lemon sherbet limbers up, extending soft rays of light across the fields and orchards brimming with oranges, heralding a gloriously bright day. On the porch Scraggy, the pathetic, abandoned tabby with a lazy eye and stunted legs who now haunts our gardens, is mewing weakly at me. I can almost hear the muted words: *adopt me, adopt me.* Stretching against a pillar, I stop to admire a clump of wild clematis in flower before flexing my toes and gently moving my joints. It is 8 a.m. and any minute now Gaspar will be joining me for another run. He called the previous evening to say that, following a long convalescence, his back was feeling much better and that he really wanted to shed some weight. Even though Dr Vidal has apparently given him the OK to do a little light jogging I have severe reservations about his current fitness level. There's the telltale sound of a *moto* struggling up the track and a glint of metal as a sudden needle of sunlight catches at the rider's helmet. A moment later, Gaspar dribbles his bike into the courtyard and parks it against a stone wall. It seems to sigh in relief as he dismounts. Removing his helmet and voluminous windproof jacket, he reveals a bobby dazzler of an orange T-shirt, on which are scrawled the words *T'ESTIM!*, which means 'I love you' in Catalan, and a pair of baggy red running shorts. He beams at me and does a thumbs up sign.

'Nice colour scheme, Gaspar.'

He walks over to me. 'You like it? I thought it would be safer to wear on the roads.'

A driver would have to be blind to miss seeing Gaspar plodding along the road, with or without his incongruous apparel.

'Let's warm up,' I say.

He stands beside me and begins copying my movements. After a few minutes he's puffing.

'This is hard work.'

'We haven't even started the run yet, so take it easy.'

He yawns and turns to Scraggy.

'Your cat looks hungry.'

Scraggy is whining pitifully, his lazy eye searching the sky while the other rests on Gaspar's chubby face.

'Trust me, he's a fraud. I fed him a massive bowl of cat food this morning and he's not even my pet.'

Gaspar tuts. 'You can't trust a cat. Dogs are more reliable.'

I clap my hands together. 'Come on then, let's hit the road.'

We start off at a slow pace down the track. Rafael is in Alberto's pen cleaning out his bowl. Grinning inanely, he calls out, '*Venga,*

*venga!*' as we pass by. My bulky running companion pokes his tongue out at him.

'Hey, Gaspar, come by my shop for an *ensaimada* later,' taunts Rafael as Alberto leaps against the fence, barking loudly.

We reach the end of the track and head off in the direction of the port. The wind is cold against our faces and soon Gaspar is sweating and exhaling heavily. I tell him to slacken his pace.

'OK, let's do fast walking for a bit like we did before, and then slow running. *Poc a poc*, Gaspar.'

He concedes and begins walking.

'This is very hard. Maybe we just go round the block today.'

I smother a grin. We've barely done a kilometre. '*No problema*. Let's run to the *Monumento* roundabout and do a loop back to the house.'

He nods enthusiastically and then seems struck by a bright idea.

'That's good. Now we'll have time for a coffee before I start my afternoon round.'

I raise my eyes heavenward. So much for the zeal of my new running recruit.

As I walk up the short and stony path to Can Cabra, I can hear a dull, methodical beat coming from somewhere deep in the bowels of the building. It isn't exactly what I'd term music although my hip nephew, Alexander, might care to differ. I ring the doorbell. After a while I can hear the sound of footsteps and a persistent cough. A middle aged woman with bleached, coiffed hair and hoop earrings observes me with some suspicion.

'Hello?'

'Ah, Mrs Walton?'

'I am, and who are you?'

Hearing that I'm a neighbour, she opens the door further and somewhat reluctantly ushers me inside. I follow her along a wide, tiled corridor to a cosy kitchen at the rear of the *finca*. The ceiling is low and the walls whitewashed and strung with old copper pans and traditional Mallorcan artifacts.

'What a lovely room.'

She directs me to a seat at the kitchen table while she lights up a cigarette and stands with her back against a tiled work surface.

'It's not really my style to be honest. We're just renting for a while.'

'Ah, I see. Have you just moved here?'

She exhales a plume of smoke. 'I'm here with my son. He's in between schools in the UK and I've just got divorced so Sóller just happened.'

'Why Sóller?'

She shrugs. 'One of my friends has lived in Mallorca for years and suggested I take a six month break here. She thought it would be nice and quiet.'

The music in the basement is turned up a level. She seems a tad embarrassed, the irony not being lost on her.

'That's my son, Ben. He's going through a tricky period, what with the divorce and being expelled from his school for drug-taking.'

I give a limp smile. 'It sounds as if you've got a lot on your plate.'

She coughs deeply. 'You could say that. Anyway, is this just a social visit?'

'Not entirely. One of your close neighbours...'

She holds up a hand. 'Don't tell me! That old Spanish busybody next door sent you?'

'Are you talking about Neus Adrillon? If so, yes, she did ask me to pop round.'

With some irritation she wanders over to the window and looks out at the small garden. It is forlorn and clumps of weeds sit in a neglected and overgrown lawn surrounded by skeleton trees and patches of bald earth.

'I didn't have a clue what she was on about, babbling in Spanish, and some other old geezer came here, rabbiting on. I suppose it's about Ben's music.'

'It's the loud music and the bright lights you leave on at night.'

She gives a bitter little laugh. 'Bloody neighbours. It doesn't matter where you are. They're always complaining about something. Anyway, this place is a dump. I'd rather be somewhere with a bit of life.'

I nod sympathetically. 'Are you tied in on a long contract?'

'A month's notice. My friend found it through a local guy, not an agency.'

'Perhaps you could find something in the town or in Palma.'

'Not Palma. It's too big. Somewhere in Sóller, near the bars would be good. Ben would like that. We're both night birds.'

'How old is Ben?'

'Seventeen. He wants to be a DJ. My old man's trying to get him into another boarding school but it isn't easy with his track record. The boy's a free spirit.'

Heavy footsteps trudge along the corridor and Ben, the free spirit, appears. Small diamond studs wink at me from his chin and left nostril, and a kohl-rimmed eye hazily searches my face. The dark hair is long and lank and the attire screams punk-meets-gothic.

'You one of mum's friends?'

'A neighbour,' she says warily.

'At least you speak bloody English. Everyone around here just jabbers on in Spanish or something.'

'Yes, the Spanish have the strange habit of wanting to speak their own language in their own country.'

'Whatever,' he grunts.

'Do you want a tea?' his mother asks.

I get up to leave. 'No thanks. I've taken up quite enough of your time. I just wonder if you might do something about the lights in the evening?'

She stubs out her cigarette. 'If it keeps them off our backs.'

'Can you turn down the music too?'

Ben looks up at me and shrugs. 'Whatever.'

At the front door, I turn to her. 'Maybe I can help find you another place?'

She pulls a Marlboro Light from its packet and dangles it, unlit, from her lip. 'Really?'

'I know a few estate agents who do rentals locally. Can I give them your phone number?'

She darts back to the kitchen and emerges with a small scrap of paper, her cigarette now lit. She hacks loudly.

'Here, this is my mobile. Thanks a lot. The name's Liz, by the way.'

I potter off down the path. A call to one of my local estate agent friends should do the trick. Perhaps one of them can suggest a pad situated over a disco or an all night bar, something that might be conducive to the Waltons' nocturnal activities.

Sóller is heaving with shoppers and once again I find myself leaving Christmas shopping to *el moment ultim*! Struggling with a mountain of shopping bags, I pop by my last port of call, Colmada Sa Lluna, for my usual trough of Christmas culinary goodies. Luckily, I arrive just as there is a lull. Xavier gives me a broad grin.

'Have you got your turkey?'

'Of course I have,' I chide. 'I ordered it from San Matarino's weeks ago.

'What about tickets for El Gordo? You know the draw is tonight?'

'We've shared a row of numbers with Pep and Juana,' I reply, 'so we'll get rich together.'

The *El Gordo Lotería* is Spain's biggest lottery, and is purported to be the richest in the world with more than one billion tickets sold, equivalent to two billion euros in sales. The grand draw is held on 22 December on a television show which is so kitsch and excruciatingly dull that it makes the Eurovision Song Contest seem positively enthralling. There are two enormous golden bowls, one containing the winning ticket numbers and the other a set of balls with prizes. The protracted results are announced during a three hour show which includes performances from a choir of orphan boys from a school in Madrid and all sorts of other variety acts.

One might ask why this event has such significance in Spain but the concept of *loterías* has been around since the first was inaugurated by Carlos III in 1763. One of its aims was to help good causes and it abides by the same principles today. The Christmas lottery was conceived in 1812 roughly at the time that the Duke of Wellington had entered Madrid and was fighting off Napoleon's troops. It took him two more years to claim victory against the

French by which time the good old Christmas lottery was up and running. There are a multitude of lotteries taking place in Spain throughout the year and they are loyally supported by the local community. In fact, it is common to see blind or disabled lottery ticket vendors standing on street corners and in supermarket car parks attracting queues in local towns and villages. The key to *El Gordo's* success is that it is a social, rather than financial event. The winnings are relatively modest and whole communities club together to buy a string of tickets, meaning that some villages become moderately well off overnight. The lucky winners may not be able to afford Ferraris with their prize money but they have enough cash to splash out on new domestic appliances, a good holiday or to spruce up their homes.

Xavier is observing me over the counter.

'So what are you going to buy if you win *El Gordo*?'

I have a long think. 'Maybe a dishwasher.'

'*Per favor.* That's not very exciting.'

'No it isn't, but if I've learnt one thing living here, Xavier, it's that simple pleasures really are the best.'

It is Christmas Eve – Vigilia de Nadal in Catalan, or *nochebuena* in Castilian Spanish – and the house is brimming with light. A tall and bushy spruce sits to one side of the log fire in the *entrada*, its branches weighed down with tiny white lights and decorations. A few days ago, Ollie and I spent a good hour or more unravelling the fiddly, entwined strings of lights, then winding them around the tree and hanging the decorations. Somehow we gobbled down more of the chocolate lanterns and snowmen than we managed to hang. Empty foil wrappers lay all about us like silent witnesses until, guiltily, I cleared up the evidence before the Scotsman arrived home. Despite only having been in the house for a short while, the tree has already begun to shed its needles, which lie scattered in small clumps around its base, a sturdy terracotta pot. I'm thankful that the *entrada* has a stone floor which makes removing them so much easier. In London we were forever finding pine needles embedded in the weave of our thick living room carpet, long after Christmas had passed.

We have spent the earlier part of this evening enjoying a delicious Christmas family meal at Catalina and Ramon's house in Fornalutx and, after a heavenly pasta soup, followed by suckling pig, tucked into all manner of popular and festive sweetmeats – *turrón*, marzipan, *polvorones,* and *ensaimadas* filled with custard. Having returned to the *finca* with groaning stomachs, we are now gearing ourselves up to face the frosty night once more by heading off to the cathedral in Palma for the Christmas Eve service, otherwise known as La Misa de Gallo, the cockerel's mass. The origin of the name of this service, which commemorates the birth of Christ, is attributed to the good old rooster that supposedly first announced the Messiah's birth. Our friends Pep, Juana and Angel have agreed to meet us directly there. Alan looks at his watch.

'Come on chaps. It's ten past ten. We'd better hit the road.'

Ollie pulls on his jacket, woollen scarf and gloves. 'Should I bring anything to read?'

I pull a face. 'You're supposed to be listening to the service, not reading a book.'

He mumbles something and stomps off to the car. The sky is raven in hue and filled with luminous stars, and for a moment I'm severely tempted to call off the drive and persuade the boys to huddle round the log fire for the night. Alan turns off the house lights and gives Scraggy a menacing look as he attempts to sneak through the front door.

'That cat's a damned menace! It's bad enough having him bleating outside night and day without him trying to worm his way into the house.'

'It's Christmas, have a heart,' I plead.

We lock up and head towards Palma. There's a fair amount of traffic on the roads despite the late hour. We arrive just before eleven o'clock, miraculously finding a parking space close to the cathedral.

'Miguel the *toro* will be sad not to see us,' I grin.

'I imagine he'll be in Bar Español by now, having a few beers,' the Scotsman replies.

We step inside. The vast, gothic cathedral is awash with people and warm amber light sweeps the wooden pews and high alabaster altar. Most of the seats have been taken and still more visitors are arriving behind us. We walk down the central aisle, stopping to admire the enormous vaulted roof and the elegant rows of pillars in the central nave.

'The stained-glass windows are pretty cool,' mutters Ollie. 'What's that enormous wrought iron thing hanging down over the altar?'

Alan studies it for a few moments. 'Ah, now that's a baldachin, a sort of canopy, which the famous Catalan artist, Gaudí, designed. It's a bit oppressive.'

'I like it,' says Ollie. 'The hanging lanterns look awesome all lit up.'

I am suddenly aware of someone waving from one of the front rows. It is Juana. We head for her pew where she and Pep have saved us some seating space. Angel grins at Ollie and beckons him over.

'What a disgrace arriving so late,' says Pep. 'You accuse us Spanish of being *mañana* but you British just turn up when you feel like it. Pah!'

I give him a smack on the head.

'That's not a very Christian greeting,' he complains.

'Will you behave?' chides Juana. 'We're not in Café Paris now.'

Alan gives a furtive wink to Pep and they begin chuckling. Within a short while the bishop, priest, altar boys and choir arrive and the service begins. I am impressed by the size of the congregation. Aside from the locals there appear to be many overseas visitors. A group of vivacious Scandinavian girls sitting behind us prove very distracting to Pep who is constantly turning to give them the glad eye. Juana shoots him a warning frown. *'Hombre!'*

'What?' he says, palms upturned in innocent gesture. 'I've done nothing. Just looking.'

I peer around me, once again overawed by the majestic grandeur of this colossal golden limestone edifice which has presumably mesmerised congregations from the time of its construction in the thirteenth century. Pep taps my shoulder and whispers hoarsely.

'You know why the cathedral is called *La Seu*?'

'It means "the seat" in Catalan; in other words, it sat plum in the heart of Palma.'

He pushes out his bottom lip. 'Correct, Miss Clever Clogs, but do you know why it was built?'

I sigh wearily. 'Something to do with Jaume I winning a battle.'

He gives a sneer. 'Pathetic. The correct story is that Jaume I of Aragón promised to build a church to the Virgin Mary if he gained a victory over the Moors. When he won, he rather sadistically placed it right over the Great Mosque in the old Moorish citadel.'

'Yes, I knew all that,' I say impatiently.

'No you didn't. OK, do you know how Gaudí died?'

'Painfully.'

'As it happens, he was run over by a tram in Barcelona.'

'You don't consider that a painful death?'

'I give up with you,' he says sulkily.

'Anyway, you're wrong. Gaudí died ignominiously a few days after the incident, in a pauper's hospital. That's how you Spanish reward your great artists,' I goad.

'That's not true. He was offered a better hospital but he refused to leave…'

'Sure.'

Juana tuts. 'Sh! Stop bickering both of you! The Cant de la Sibilla is coming up.'

Alan raises an eyebrow. Pep and I, duly admonished, sit upright and study the robed youth gliding slowly, with sword held high, towards the pulpit steps. There's the slightest ruffle of silk as the angelic form reaches the platform and turns to face us all.

If there's only one reason for coming to the Christmas Eve service, it is to hear the spine-tingling song of the Sibyl. Before the mass, and directly after the matins, a young boy or girl of twelve years old garbed in flowing silk robes will ascend the pulpit, clutching a glinting sword in both hands. The sword symbolises many things, not least the massacre of the innocents and the wrath of God. He or she represents the Sibyl, the pagan prophetess, and is chosen for the purity and pitch of voice. The haunting delivery in high, treble voice leaves audiences spellbound. The song of the Sibyl isn't a cheerful Christmas ditty, more an apocalyptic message foretelling Christ's second coming, and the disasters and signs preceding judgement day and the end of the world. Each doom-laden stanza is separated by thunderous musical interludes played by pipe organ, and one half expects Vincent Price, with trademark fangs, to drop down on the altar, *deus ex machina* style. It is a seriously thespian performance, and some scholars maintain that the Sibyl's song is the oldest Catalan theatre piece. The musical version dates as far back as the tenth century, when a boy would take on the role, dressing as a woman for the part, although in convents many sisters would have a go, eating raw eggs, sweets, figs, sweet wine to smooth their voices before the performance. Combining any of these ingredients before performing the piece would surely induce queasiness in most normal mortals but the nuns were evidently made of sterner stuff. I listen to the half-tone cadences of the Sibyl now resounding through the cathedral. There is total concentration on the faces around me. Even Pep is speechless. As the final note is struck, people emerge from their stupor, nodding their heads in wonderment, exchanging hushed whispers, some even bending their heads, overcome with emotion and tears. The Catalan service continues, thankfully with a little more levity, full of happy carols and hymns led by the choir. The bishop and priest deliver the final prayers and blessings and we all begin to leave our pews as the organ once again strikes up.

The wind whips our hair as we leave by the north door and walk along the road. At the steps leading down towards the lake and waterfront, we pause to take in the beauty of the Bay of Palma and the twinkling lights from ships in the harbour. The cathedral clears quickly and soon we are alone, huddled by the dark and solid rock walls, staring out at the sea. Juana gives a little shudder.

'Come on! It'll be one in the morning before we know it and what will happen if you collide with Father Christmas at your house?' asks Juana.

Ollie and Angel exchange little grins.

'He'll wait till we're in bed,' says Ollie.

'All the same, we should make a move,' yawns Alan.

We say our goodbyes and set off, relieved to have parked the car nearby, while the others have to walk some distance to an underground car park. The street is deserted and our footsteps sound eerie in the silence. We reach the car but Ollie stands for a moment in the still of the night, his ear cocked.

'What is it?' I say.

'Can't you hear it?'

'What?' asks Alan, puzzled.

'It's a cockerel crowing.'

We stand, gripping our coats in the icy breeze. Suddenly there's the sharp cry of a cockerel, distant but distinct.

'There!' says Ollie. 'It must have known that it was the cockerel's mass.'

Alan laughs. 'I'm not sure a cockerel would be bright enough to work that one out.'

'Maybe it's competing with the Sibyl and delivering a *cant de gallo*,' I add.

Ollie gives a big yawn and tugs his father's coat sleeve. 'Come on then, let's hurry home in case Santa really does beat us to it.'

Rachel is full of good cheer on Boxing Day night. I hold the phone away because her laughter is drilling into my ever-so-slightly hung-over, delicate head.

'So this year's Christmas Day was a success?' she asks mischievously.

Our previous year's festivities were fraught with problems, not least the cooker blowing up on Christmas Eve.

'Thankfully, this time nothing went wrong. My sister and nephew came over and we had a very relaxing day. Mind you, today my head feels as though a pack of frenzied bell ringers have taken it hostage so perhaps we sank a few too many bottles late last night.'

She gives a snort. 'Serves you right! Anyway, I wanted to let you know that Manuel Ramirez and his chum Vice Admiral Mason couriered a massive hamper of Fortnum & Mason goodies over to the office on Christmas Eve. They made some hammy pun about the name Mason. Oh, and Dannie and Greedy George have left you rather nice bottles of champagne.'

'Excellent. The rest of you can keep your mitts off them.'

'We had a discussion about it and decided to share out the hamper and leave you the bottles.'

'You're all heart.'

She gives a cough. 'Have you given any more thought to Red Hot PR?'

'I've read through all their bumph. I'm a bit worried that they're so fashion led.'

'A bit of fashion could complement some of our luxury lifestyle brands.'

'Maybe. I'll email you across my thoughts and those of our lawyer and accountant later this week. In the meantime, stop thinking about work and have a break,' I say.

'As it happens I'm just off to a carol concert. What about you?'

'Pep and Alan have gone off on the razzle so Ollie and I are about to curl up on the sofa and watch an old film.'

'Don't tell me, *Oliver Twist*?'

'No, *A Christmas Carol*.'

'Enjoy. Toodlepip!'

I pop the phone back on its perch, unaware that Ollie has crept up behind me.

'Did you know that Dickens only took six weeks to write *A Christmas Carol*?' he asks.

'I do now,' I say, as I search on the shelf of DVD's for the film.

He sits on the sofa observing me. 'Apparently he needed to pay off a debt.'

'Don't we all?' I reply distractedly. 'I can't seem to find the film.'

He dangles a DVD case in front of me. 'What's this?'

'An elephant?' I grab it and tap him on the head. 'Perhaps, Mr Bright Spark, you should try reading the book sometime.'

'I have,' he replies.

'I meant in Catalan.'

'Bah humbug!' he says and pokes out his tongue.

Angel is proudly showing Ollie his *Belén*, the miniature Nativity scene that adorns a low table in the *entrada* of Juana and Pep's house. The *Belén* is a common sight in Catholic homes in Mallorca and includes all the traditional elements of this celebratory biblical event, as well as additional bits of local colour. In Angel's *belén* there is a tiny replica of the Sóller train running through a green plastic mound representing the Tramuntana mountain range. He's even recreated Sóller's *plaça,* a stone's throw from where Mary and Joseph are leaning over a miniscule papier mâché cot with hay. Pep is smoking a *puro* and waiting impatiently for Ollie to alight on a small character squatting in a corner of a field.

On cue, Ollie pipes up. 'What is that?!'

Angel begins giggling while Pep smiles impishly. 'It's *el Caganer*.'

'That's gross!' says Ollie, picking it up and shoving it under my nose.

With undisguised disdain, I observe the little peasant figure with its trousers rolled down to its knees. I take a sip of my cava. 'I imagine it's some puerile joke?'

'Of course, you British are far too proper to appreciate it,' says Pep, putting on a toffee-nosed English accent. 'You call it toilet humour in English, no?'

Alan and Juana wander over with their drinks.

'You know, this disgusting little man is a beloved figure in Cataluña,' says Juana.

Alan laughs. 'Where on earth did the idea come from?'

'No one really knows, but it's a little bit of fun that's become an institution.'

Pep nods. 'Some years ago, Barcelona City Council banned *El Caganer* from its *belén* because it had just introduced some by-law making peeing and crapping in public illegal, but there was a national outcry. The next year they had to reinstate him.'

'It's all very distasteful,' I say in exaggerated tones.

Pep inhales deeply and puts the figure back in the field. 'You think that's bad? When I was a kid we used to stay with my cousins during Christmas in Barcelona and they had a *Caga tió*.'

'I dread to think what that is,' Alan says.

'A crapping uncle?' asks Ollie.

'It doesn't translate very well,' Pep concedes. 'It was a little log dressed up as a character in a traditional Catalan *barretina*, a red stockinged hat with black band. Anyway, the children would bring food to the little log-man every day in the lead up to Christmas Eve and then thrash him with a stick.'

'The idea,' says Juana, 'was to extract the Christmas gifts from his backside.'

'A charming concept.' I say.

Pep heaves with laughter. 'Let's all sit down for dinner before you faint from shock at our vulgarity.'

We follow Juana through to the dining room where a heavy wooden table is laid with a white linen cloth, matching napkins and a sea of crystal glasses. She lights three cream candles in an elegant silver candelabra and shows us to our places. Ollie hops over and whispers urgently in my ear. I give him a wink and he sits down opposite. Reaching down into my handbag, I find exactly what I'm searching for. Pep returns with an enormous roast pork joint while Juana follows with tureens of vegetables and rice. Pep sits down heavily next to me and places the pork in front of him. A bowl of steaming rice is placed on my right by Juana.

'You know my cousins used to have a little rhyme about *Caga tió…*' begins Pep.

'Not at dinner,' remonstrates Juana.

He ignores her. '*Cago tió. Ameltes i turró, si no vols cagar, garrotada va!*'

I flick my serviette open and place it on my lap. 'I think we can all work out what that means.'

Alan looks mystified. 'Which is?'

Ollie shakes his head impatiently. 'It's saying that if the log-man doesn't give the children nice things to eat, then he can go and hang himself.'

'Not bad, Ollie,' says Pep, as he walks round the table filling glasses. He places the bottle down and heads off to the kitchen again with Juana.

Ollie gives me an urgent nod. I delve into a small plastic bag hidden on my lap and, while he is distracting Angel, I sprinkle some black plastic ants on the rice and then pat them down with a serving spoon so they can't be seen. When Pep returns he begins carving the pork and attempts to serve everyone rice. I pretend not to see when his face crumples in horror. He peers into the rice tureen, pushing the spoon in and out in some confusion.

'Hurry up!' says Ollie. 'We're hungry.'

Pep gives an awkward smile and, picking up the tureen, says he has forgotten to add something to it. Juana and Angel exchange confused looks. A few minutes later he returns and puts the tureen back on the table. Ollie can hardly suppress his glee and begins giggling at which point Pep rushes round the table and begins putting the plastic ants down the back of his neck. Ollie squeals with laughter.

'What are you doing?' demands Juana in exasperation. 'It's like living in a kindergarten.'

Alan, who has been in on the joke, shouts out, *'Inocente! Inocente!'*

Pep sits back down and shakes a fist at Alan. 'I see you are playing a little Spanish joke on us.' He claps slowly.

On 28 December, or el Día de los Santos Inocentes, the Spanish play practical jokes on one another, similarly to the British on April Fool's Day. It is rather gallows humour though, given that this was supposedly the time when Herod ordered the death of the *inocentes,* babies under two years old, in Bethlehem in his quest to destroy the future Messiah. Of course the joke was on Herod because Mary and Joseph had supposedly already been tipped off and had fled with the baby Jesus to Egypt.

Pep points a finger at me. 'Was this little practical joke your idea?'

'More Ollie's,' I say.

Pep throws his hands in the air dramatically. 'They looked so real.'

'It was your attempt at normality that was really funny,' I say. 'I loved it when you disappeared to the kitchen, presumably to flick the ants out?'

'He raps the table and gives a warning growl. 'Just wait until, what do you say, April Fool's Day? I'll get you back.'

'A brave boast.'

He waggles the carving knife at me. 'If you've no more jokes up your sleeve, can we eat now?'

'Of course,' I say. 'Whatever have you been waiting for?'

# TEN

# A LOST CAUSE

The rain pitter-patters down on the roof of the Scotsman's *abajo*, his secret lair in the field. He stands in the doorway with a *puro* in one hand and a rake in the other. Wearing his tweed cap and a green Barbour, he occasionally sticks his head out and then ducks it back in again like an indecisive jack-in-the-box. I watch him from the upstairs bedroom window, wondering whether he's going to venture forth and begin work on his vegetable patch or continue moping under the overhanging roof tiles. Beyond Alan's *abajo,* a vivid amber streak across the orchard bears testimony to a new bumper crop of oranges. The leafy branches sag with the sheer volume of fruit, which hangs in abundance from every tree. High above, the tips of the Tramuntanas peep out from behind a fluffy duvet of white cloud and the valley is all but lost behind. Inko jumps on to the bed behind me and hisses furiously at Orlando, our grey, fluffy puffball of a feline, who has foolishly dared to enter the room at the same time. With one wary eye trained on him, she begins elaborately licking her paws and wiping her wet, mud-stained fur against the white duvet cover.

'Thanks a lot, old girl,' I say, as she rolls over on to her back and begins purring. Orlando darts out of the bedroom and disappears down the staircase in a cowardly retreat. The builders were supposed to pop by today to continue clearing the land for the cattery, but in this abysmal weather it is impossible. Realistically, it will be March before it is dry enough for them to resume work. Pushing on my trainers, I set off down the stairs. Today I have a meeting with Tolo, the deputy manager at Banca March, and then am due to have a coffee with my friend Cristina at Café Paris.

On my way to the car, I pop down to the *abajo* to see the Scotsman. He doesn't seem to have budged from the doorway.

'If you stand there for much longer I might buy you a Busby and a rifle and you can pretend your *abajo*'s Buckingham Palace.'

'Very funny. I'm waiting for the rain to stop.'

'You might be here for some time. Look at the sky.'

He sighs. 'Who knows, it may clear up in the next few minutes. I'll hang on here for a bit.'

I shake my head impatiently and set off.

'Send my best to Tolo,' he calls after me.

In Banca March, there is a sizeable queue but Tolo catches my eye and beckons me over.

'It's OK, they're all waiting for the cashier. How are things?'

'Pretty good.'

'Still raining out there?'

Despite having an umbrella I am rain splattered.

'Sure is. I think it's in for the month.'

He bobs up from his desk and, peering over the partition that separates his desk from the bank's wide front windows, looks out at the grey day. He shudders. 'How depressing. Let's hope it improves. By the way, are you still thinking of merging your business?'

I nod. 'I'm putting out a few feelers.'

He smiles. 'I think it's a good idea providing that's what you really want.'

I shrug. 'It feels the right thing to do. I'd like to spend more time in the valley, develop my cattery and spend more time writing.'

Tolo places one hand on top of the other. 'So then it must be. Just think, you can stay in the hills and live a relaxed existence instead of all this flying about.'

'Nice idea.'

'Talking of flying about, we've set up your Sri Lankan orphanage account. We can complete the paperwork now.'

'That's good. We'll be off there again next Christmas, so hopefully we can raise more funds before then.'

He leans back in his chair. 'So this orphanage that you support, what do they really need?'

'Last year we took them money for the children's upkeep and a whole lot of clothes. There are about seventy little girls.'

He taps the desk. 'We have some promotional T-shirts, would they be useful?'

'Absolutely. Anything would be a help. A lot of local Sóller mums are now bringing me clothes which is fantastic.'

'Leave it with me. Are you doing another marathon?'

'You bet. Athens next year. I raise a lot of money that way.'

As a keen runner, Tolo shares my enthusiasm for competitive races but is having severe problems with his back. He shakes his head wistfully. 'I wish my back was up to running again. Maybe I'll do the Palma half-marathon this year if it improves. *Nos veremos*!' We'll see.

He pulls out a file and places a pile of official papers in front of me.

'Now, I need your autograph here please.'

We wade through multiple forms, signing triplicates of each.

'So many copies to sign,' I puff.

'*Si*, in fact we only need one signature, the rest we sell on eBay.'

'You do that with all your customers?'

'*Segur*!' he laughs. 'How else can we banks make money these days?'

We exchange kisses on both cheeks and I amble down the cobbled street to the main *plaça* and Café Paris. On the way, I collide with our German friend, Frederika, from the estate agency, Kuhn & Partner. I tell her about Mrs Walton and the urgent need to relocate her to a less residential area of Sóller, preferably close to a cemetery.

She grins. 'Working on the principle that you can't wake the dead? I'll do my best. Let me look at our books and see what we can come up with. She doesn't want to buy something?'

'I do hope not,' I laugh. 'Just a six-month rental will do.'

'Is she a bit difficult?'

'More of a lost cause. Anyway, here's her phone number. Good luck.'

The rain is now torrential and the gangly branches of the planes sway wildly, their few remaining leaves fluttering then plummeting helplessly like wingless birds, to the ground. I walk gingerly, the paving stones being slippery and strewn with slimy leaves. Despite the weather I find myself smiling at a recurring image in my head: that of the optimistic and patient Scotsman, clad in his Barbour and tweed cap, waiting in vain on the porch of his *abajo* for the relentless rain to stop.

Ollie is sitting downstairs reading a *Horrible Histories* paperback while sipping on a mug of green tea, heavily sweetened no doubt. He now has every book the enterprising children's author, Terry Deary, has ever written and we are frequently treated to a diet of seriously gruesome historical facts. He looks up as I walk in to the room.

'Did you know that the Vikings ate polar bears?'

'Nothing would surprise me,' I mutter absentmindedly.

'You know the song "London Bridge is Falling Down"?'

'Mmm,' I say, filling the kettle.

'Well, it's about the time when the Viking King Olaf attacked Britain and used ropes to try and pull down London Bridge.'

'Fascinating. Now, can I give you a fact? Did you know that we're off for a *torrada* in the mountains today?'

He groans. 'Do we have to walk in the rain?'

I look out of the kitchen window, wondering if the planned school excursion to the top of the Ofre, one of the 1,000-m peaks of the Tramuntanas, is such a good idea if the weather worsens. Having a *torrada*, a barbecue, in blustery conditions doesn't seem too appealing either.

'It's a bit drizzly but we can bring some waterproofs just in case.'

'Will any of my friends be there?'

I shrug. 'I've no idea, but I think we should support your school.'

He gets up and gives Inko a cuddle. 'I've just had to dry her down. She was soaked in the rain.'

I notice one of his white school shirts lying next to her basket, streaked with mud.

'You didn't use that to dry the cat?'

He gives a sheepish smile. 'It was all I could find hanging on the clothes dryer.'

'You are the limit.'

Alan strides into the *entrada* from the front courtyard. 'Maybe we should set off fairly soon. I've packed a rucksack with waterproofs and something to drink.'

'I need to rustle up some sandwiches.' I yawn. 'Let's hope the weather improves.'

He gives a cheerful smile. 'Ah, I've faced far worse than this in the Highlands. A drop of rain never hurt anyone.'

Famous last words.

The picturesque little white *refugio*, a hikers' stone hut, tucked between a rocky outcrop and a mass of scrub, squats on the far side of the reservoir at Cuber on the scenic mountain route to Pollença. According to the school's instructions, this is where we will be having the *torrada* after a bracing walk up to the Ofre peak. We park our car in a muddy lay-by as close to the reservoir as we can, and stare across the rippling water at the little house on the opposite bank. It looks incredibly welcoming in the mounting gale. We reach a metal gate and, after a battle with the wind, Alan manages to raise the catch and usher us through on to a rough track.

'Are you sure this is such a good idea?' I whine.

The Scotsman pulls the collar up on his cagoule and adjusts his rucksack. 'It's a bit blustery, but it should settle down.'

Ollie grimaces and, gripping the handles of his rucksack, plods off down the wide, muddy path which forms a long semi-circle around the reservoir.

'Have you seen how far away we are?' he grumbles.

He has a point. We walk on in spitting rain and some twenty minutes later arrive at the hut's front garden. A gaggle of Spanish parents are standing under the porch in sturdy rainwear. Small children scream and run around the rocks on the edge of the reservoir, throwing tiny stones into the water. There's no sign of any older children.

'Great,' mumbles Ollie. 'A whole load of screaming brats and no one from my class. This just gets better and better.'

We introduce ourselves to the other parents and exchange pleasantries.

'We'll be going to the Ofre very soon. Some parents have gone on ahead. You're welcome to join us.'

Ollie digs me in the ribs. 'I'm not walking with all those five year olds.'

I politely decline their offer and say that to beat the inclement weather, we'll set off immediately. They urge us to return afterwards for the cheery barbecue. So, gathering our belongings, we wave goodbye to the assembled throng and head off confidently along the track. Some thirty minutes later we see a battered wooden sign veiled in mist. Under closer inspection, we read the magical word, OFRE.

'There we are!' says the Scotsman, wiping the rain from his face. 'It can't be far now.'

We turn off as directed and find ourselves in a deep wood.

'Surely we should be heading uphill by now?' shouts Ollie above the wind.

My bargain basement rainproof is soaked through. I wonder why I didn't just wear a sieve. Rain dribbles down the back of my neck and my walking boots feel like mashed potato.

'Look! There's another sign.'

Both of them give me the thumbs up and, breaking free of the wood, we follow a narrow track on to a wide open, blustery plain. There are paths running in all directions. We scratch our heads and shrug. Two bedraggled and incongruous specimens now appear out of the mist like Tweedledum and Tweedledee. One, as tall and lean as a runner bean, is furiously wiping his rain-splattered spectacles.

'Excuse me,' he calls out in some desperation, the broad Yorkshire accent cutting through the wind like a harpoon. 'We're a bit lost, experienced hikers though we be. Any chance you'd know the path for Fornalutx?'

Alan gapes at him. He is wearing tiny red polyester shorts, a white running vest and blue rainproof loosely wrapped around his waist. His compatriot, a small rubber band ball of a man, is attired in voluminous yellow shorts and a red fleece.

'It'll be quite a walk from here,' Alan shouts back. He waves an arm vaguely towards the right. 'I think you should find a path in that direction. We're a bit lost ourselves. Do you happen to know the route to the Ofre?'

The little one shakes his head in the negative. 'Haven't a clue, mate. We've been walking round in circles.'

Alan shows the tall one our map, on which a small black thread seems to indicate where the Fornalutx path is.

'Cheers, mate. That helps a bit,' he says. 'If I were you, I'd go up that there hill.'

We thank him for his advice and watch as they stride off towards a craggy path.

'They haven't got a clue where they are,' says Ollie gleefully.

'Nope,' I say, 'neither have we. Let's just plough on up the hill. It feels right.'

The rain grows heavier and is soon falling in white sheets. We are a quarter way up a steep and rocky path on a vertical hill. Ollie and I clamber on in the mud and grime, occasionally slipping and grazing our legs and hands. Alan stands still, breathing heavily, exhaustion sketched on his face.

'Do you want to turn back?' I yell.

'No way, we're going up!' he shouts back.

Another few metres and the path disappears completely. We are now rock climbing, using our bare hands to project us as we trudge over sharp rocks and up precarious inclines. Alan slips down one of the slopes and is covered in mud. Ollie and I have a fit of uncontrollable giggles and have to sprawl on a rock to catch our breath. We too are saturated and specked with mud and grime.

'There's supposed to be a proper path,' grumbles the Scotsman. 'Where the hell did it go?'

'I think we've taken the mountain goat route,' Ollie announces, enjoying the sense of drama. I pull myself up, grabbing fearfully at a clump of sodden weeds and find myself face to face with a ghostly form. I let out a scream and nearly topple backwards.

'What is it?' Ollie and Alan yell behind me in unison.

A goat is observing me coolly. It is chewing thoughtfully on some grass and tossing its head in the air. In the low cloud it takes on a strange form. Its legs appear stunted, its jaw pronounced and its horns short and straight. Could it be, just possibly, a Myotragus, a throwback caught in a strange time warp, in another dimension of time and space?

Ollie has heaved himself up on a rock and is staring into the goat's eyes. 'It's just a damned goat, for crying out loud! What's the matter with you, mother?'

'Don't you think it looks odd?' I whisper excitedly.

He pats my arm. 'No, I don't. It's a normal, boring old goat, a bit like you. Now come on!'

Alan is chuckling behind him. 'For a moment there, you really thought it was your prehistoric goat, didn't you? You really are a hoot!'

'More importantly, do you think this is leading to the Ofre?' I say trying to recover my dignity.

'God knows!' Alan replies. 'Let's just hope so.'

I stomp on, oblivious now to the pain, cold, sopping wet clothes and mushy boots. All I damn well care about is reaching the top. Another forty minutes pass and suddenly in the fog I see a rocky platform. We've arrived at the top of a peak.

'I think we've reached the summit!'

'We've done it!' trills Ollie.

Both he and Alan crawl up on to the platform and we lie gasping on the rocks. Alan battles with a map which is flapping in the strong gale.

'This is definitely the Ofre,' he says peering round.

'We may have got here but heaven knows what path we took,' I say.

I fumble in my pocket and dig out the digital camera.

'Come on, we've got to have some photos for prosperity.'

The boys yell *manchego* and the shutter clicks.

Alan looks at his watch. 'Heavens, we've been gone ages and the sky's getting darker. I think we should head back down.'

'The same way?' asks Ollie.

'Better the path we know, however precarious,' I mumble.

We chew on a few sodden sandwiches, gulp down some water and set off. It is getting on for two hours before we find ourselves back outside the *refugio*. There's a tinkle of laughter coming from within, cheerful conversation, and the delicious smell of roast meat.

'What do you think?' asks Alan.

I sneeze loudly. 'To be honest, I really think I'd just like to get home to a hot bath.'

'Me too,' says Ollie.

'It seems a bit rude, and yet...' Alan faces us both. 'OK, let's give it a miss, but for heaven's sake creep by. We don't want them to think we're being odd and antisocial.'

'That's exactly what we are being, though,' titters Ollie.

Everyone is apparently having such a good time at the *torrada* that they fail to notice three drenched, pathetic figures staggering by. We reach the car and collapse inside.

'That was fun!' says the Scotsman.

'Yes, must do it again some time,' replies Ollie with heavy irony.

Alan looks at his watch. 'Bugger it, let's get cleaned up at home and go to Es Turo for supper. I don't know about you two, but I need a huge plate of *croquetas,* and some *arroz brut* washed down with some good red wine.'

*Arroz brut*, literally dry rice, is a delicious soupy stew and one of Ollie's favourite local dishes. 'Yay!' he says happily.

I start the engine. 'I'll drink to that.'

We pull out on to the road.

'I don't believe it,' exclaims Ollie.

There in front of us is an ambling old white goat.

Tofol and Mateo are sitting together on the sofa while Sara, Tina and Marga sit side by side on the rug. On the rocking chair Ivan is squeezed up next to Inko and is stroking her fur. We are all watching a *Muzzy the Monster* DVD and repeating together the colours, numbers and basic grammatical pointers that are being spoken.

'I'm big, you're small,' says little Marga, playing the part of Muzzy.

'I'm Bob. I'm brave,' repeats Ivan.

'One, two, three,' shouts Tofol.

The others sit totally engrossed in the story. We have spent nearly an hour doing word games, bingo, drawings and singing songs. I really enjoy my time with the children each week. They are endlessly entertaining and so full of enthusiasm.

'We went to the big bonfire in the *plaça* last night,' pipes up Mateo in Catalan. 'I didn't see you.'

The Sant Antoni fiesta is a popular event and one which we never miss in January. It is shortly followed by another established *fiesta*, that of Sant Sebastià, and both involve the construction of huge bonfires which are lit in villages across the island. Barbecued meat and free wine is enjoyed by all.

'I went up to Fornalutx,' I say. 'We've got lots of friends there.'

'Did they play the *ximbomba*?' Mateo says.

The *ximbomba* is a curious, locally made instrument with a terracotta base and a surface covered in taut goat hide. A vertical bamboo cane is inserted through the centre so that when rubbed it makes a noise similar to someone blowing a loud raspberry or the splutterings of a constipated cow. Traditional Mallorcan *gloses* are sung along to the rhythm of this crude contraption.

'Our friend Maria from Canantuna restaurant is an expert so she played for all of us.'

'I know Maria!' says Ivan.

I laugh. 'I think just about everyone knows Maria. Now let's stop talking and watch.'

'Did you eat sausages?' asks Sara.

'*Si*, now watch the end of the story.'

'I like *costelles de xot*,' she says.

213

'In English we say lamb chops.'

They all repeat the words. Lamb chops, lamb chops, lamb chops. The DVD ends and I lead them downstairs to the *entrada* where their parents have collected politely by the door until the allotted time. We discuss the children's homework and, in a boisterous group, step out into the blustery courtyard. The sky is dark and a spit of rain hits our faces.

'More rain,' tuts one of the mothers as her daughter, Marga, run around her legs.

'*Sempre pleura,*' another replies. It's always raining.

Oblivious to the black clouds and drizzle, the children cheerily wave goodbye and skip along the gloomy track. I stand in the darkness listening to their receding footsteps, the sound of childish and infectious laughter and then, carried on the breeze, the unmistakable words, Lamb chops, lamb chops, lamb chops!'

I am about to turn up our track when a small, excited figure begins flagging me down. I stop the car and wind down the window. It is Neus, her shock of snowy hair standing as stiff as beaten egg whites atop her head.

'Senyora! I wanted to thank you.'

I frown in puzzlement. 'Really? What for?'

She comes up to the driver's window, and rests a quivering, translucent hand on the ledge. Her wheezy chest rises and falls like a great wave. I wait for her to catch her breath. 'Senyora Walton is going! *Si,* she came round to my house, very friendly and said you found her a nice flat in central Sóller.'

I give her a smile. 'That's fantastic! You should really thank my friend, Frederika at Kuhn & Partner, not me.'

She suddenly looks thoughtful. 'In truth, after you spoke with her, she stopped shining those lights and her boy cut down on the noise. In some ways it's sad she's leaving.'

I can't believe my ears. 'Of course, I can always persuade her to stay,' I say mischievously.

She gives me a wink and stretches her back. 'No, I think it's best she goes. She'll be happier in the town with all the nightlife.'

I start the engine and wave goodbye. I can hardly drive for laughing. The nightlife of Sóller? What planet, I ponder, is Neus on?

## ELEVEN

# MAD DOGS AND MALLORCAN MEN

Caught on the wind, two empty plant pots spiral through the air and fall giddily and with a clatter on to the lawn. Like old winos, they roll around on the damp grass as if trying to find the strength to rise and then, with the next gust, are up and hurtling along once more. I watch from my office window, wondering whether the Scotsman might mourn them should they fly away forever over a neighbouring wall. I could, of course, jog downstairs and rescue them, but I have a mountain of work to finish on the computer and I am shoeless. Lazily I contemplate donning some old mules or flip-flops and nipping down into the garden, but is it really worth it? I mean, what value have a pair of fairly hideous brown plastic pots? None, that's what. I turn back to the computer to find an incoming email from Rachel. Apparently a rock-climbing expert named Charlie Wheeler, with a camping and trekking retail business, has expressed interest in hiring us. As it happens I am familiar with Trek & Track, his chain of London stores, having purchased items at its Regent Street outlet in the past. Rachel further informs me that Charlie is thrilled to learn of my passion for remote scientific expeditions and has asked that I attend the first meeting. For many years now I have fulfilled my love of adventurous travel by taking part in various expeditions with the scientific charity of which I am a patron. Despite pressures of work and family life, I try to squeeze in a trip to a remote corner of the world every few years. With some chagrin I think back to my recent, not-so-successful camping expedition with Ollie to the bottom of our field and wonder if I'm the best woman for the job. A moment later, the Scotsman drives into the courtyard. He emerges from the driver's seat with a pile of mail. Perhaps Jorge the postman can't face walking up our drive in the chill.

With his nose in the air, the Scotsman runs a sharp eye over the lawn and, glimpsing the jumping pots, rushes over to retrieve them. He grasps them by the scruff of their necks and strides back to the house. The front door slams and a minute later he appears in the office.

'Two of my plant pots were about to disappear!' he announces.

'Ah, yes, I did see them hopping about but I didn't think they were that important.'

He rears back. 'Do you know how much they cost from the local *ferretería*?'

The ironmonger's is one of the Scotsman's favourite haunts, usually because he regularly gets healthy discounts and bargains.

'Fifty *centimos*?'

'No. Two euros each! We would have lost four euros just like that.'

'Wow! Thank heavens you braved the elements to reach them.'

He gives a long sniff. 'Pray, do not mock me: I am a very foolish fond old man.'

He plops some envelopes down on my desk. One of the letters has been forwarded unopened from the London office. I slide my finger under the glued flap and give it a tug. Inside is a typed and formal letter signed by a rather pompous sounding Lord. I scrutinise the wayward signature, which is scrawled by hand, and then begin to read the contents. By the end I am seething. I toss it on to the desk.

'What's up?' quizzes the Scotsman.

'You won't believe this letter. It's from some Lord Hack-in-the-Bush asking me to pitch for his business. I can hardly make out the signature, his writing's so bad. He's apparently setting up a human rights charity that will press for the release of so-called 'victims' such as Ian Brady, the moors murderer, and other undesirables.'

I pass the letter to the Scotsman. He reads it quickly, a look of bewilderment and disgust on his face. 'I've never heard of a Lord named Delamore. Throw it away!'

I waver. 'No. I'm going to give him a piece of my mind. Lord or no Lord.'

In some rage, I type a humdinger of a letter, ending it with a flourish of a signature. I go on to Google but can't find a name similar to the one in the letter. Neither can I find it in my copy of Debrett's Peerage.

'I can't find him listed anywhere.'

The Scotsman looks up from his desk.

'I reckon he's one of those new Blairite peers you've never heard of. They're two a penny nowadays.'

'Maybe you're right.'

I seal the letter and pop it in my handbag ready to post. Ollie suddenly emerges. He has been in bed for three days with a dose of the *gripe*, flu, and seems to be deteriorating.

'Can I watch a film?'

I look at his flushed cheeks, his hair glistening with perspiration.

'I really think we should take you to see Dr Vidal.'

He sneezes heavily. 'I'd rather stay here.'

'Too bad, we're going.'

I pick up my handbag and car keys and head for the door. Ollie puts his hands on his hips and coughs deeply.

'Any chance that I can get dressed first?'

The small surgery is practically empty. An old man with a crooked black beret perched on his head is reading a copy of *Ultima Hora* in the corner of the room and hacking deeply. He gives us a cursory look when we enter and manages a crusty, '*Bon día*!' We wait in silence. The white walls are devoid of distractions. There are no pictures, promotional material or information posters on any surface and two rows of modest, grey plastic chairs face each other on either side of the room. A few dog-eared and heavily out of date women's magazines sprawl on a small wooden table by the exit. Suddenly the door springs open and Dr Vidal, portly and wearing an enormous smile, bounces into the waiting room.

'*Venga*!' he cries and ushers us through his door.

I turn to the old man. 'But this gentleman has been waiting for a while.'

Dr Vidal gives a snort. 'That's Luis. He just pops by to read his newspaper.'

We enter and take a seat in front of his large wooden desk. A massive and teetering pile of hardbacks is lined up on one side while a stethoscope, coiled like a silent white snake, sits in the centre atop a simple prescription order book. A biro and a child's Chupa Chups lollipop lie next to it. My eye rests on the weighty Spanish tome which tops the mountain of other books. Dr Vidal leaps up with enthusiasm and whips it off the pile.

'Have you read this?'

I shake my head.

'This is one of the most outstanding accounts of the Spanish Civil War and the Franco period. You simply must read it.'

'I have several other fascinating books about that period.'

'This is different,' he insists.

Tapping the spine, his bushy moustache quivering with excitement, he gives me a blow by blow account of the arguments expounded in the book.

'We have to ask ourselves, senyora, what is fact and what is fiction.'

I nod slowly. 'I suppose that's true of any epoch. One has to furnish oneself with as much impartial information as possible in order to evaluate what is true and what is hypothetical or deliberate distortion.'

He rushes over to an old bookcase. 'Now, see here, there are other books about this period that counter everything that is said in here. *Mira!* Look!'

I pull out my chair and join him at the bookcase. He gets to his knees and hands me over several titles, a few of which I have already read in English. I notice he has a copy of *The Spanish Civil War* by Hugh Thomas.

'That book is excellent. Did you read it in English?'

'*Si, si*,' he shrugs impatiently. 'Of course, that's because Professor Thomas asked the right questions. Why, for example, did the British and US governments not intervene in the war? And why did the Republican cause crumble so utterly?'

There's a sharp cough. We both look round at Ollie who is sitting forlornly in his chair.

Dr Vidal rises to his feet and strides back to the desk, grabs the Chupa Chups lollipop and passes it to him.

'So, *guapo*, what is the problem?'

'I've got the *gripe*.'

'The problem of our age. Everyone has the *gripe*! We must ask ourselves why?'

I'm waiting for a long hypothesis on the subject but he halts, takes Ollie by the hand and leads him into his examining room. He checks his temperature, throat, ears, eyes, listens to his chest with his stethoscope, asks him to cough, examines his back and then gives a sigh.

'You are your own doctor, Ollie. You have the *gripe* but it will pass.'

He scrawls a prescription and hands it to him. 'Aside from ibuprofen to keep your temperature down, I would personally recommend drinking lots of water, having plenty of fresh air, honey, fruit, laughter...' He hesitates. '... and mischief.'

He gives Ollie a wink and a pat on the cheek. The door opens and an elderly woman appears.

'*Si*, Senyora Flaquer?'

'Will you be much longer, doctor?'

He gives a frown. 'What pressing things have you to do today?'

She thinks about it. 'None really.'

221

'Are you in pain?'

'No.'

He leads her back to the waiting room. 'Then you can wait a bit longer.'

She smiles genially. 'Thank you, doctor.'

He closes the door.

'Is she alright?' I ask.

'Of course,' he says with a dismissive wave of the hand. 'She just likes to visit the surgery every day. She enjoys having a chat with me.'

I try to imagine this episode unfolding in an NHS surgery and grin at the thought.

'You are a writer?' he says, and without waiting for a response, 'I would like you to read a copy of my novel. It isn't published yet but I have a photocopy.'

I'm slightly taken aback. 'I didn't know that you were an author.'

He bounds to the door. 'I am just an amateur but I enjoy words. Now, if you will excuse me I will collect you a copy at the *estanco*.'

I wonder why he would have photocopies of his book at the newspaper shop.

'It will take about fifteen minutes to get hold of a copy. Can you go for a coffee and come back?'

Ollie nods. 'We can go to Café Paris.'

'*Molt bé.* I will see you in a short while.'

He kisses my hand, tousles Ollie's hair and disappears out of the surgery and into the street. The elderly woman and man are now in deep conversation in the waiting room. They look up and smile sweetly as we pass.

'He won't be long,' I say uncertainly.

They shrug. '*No hi ha problema.*' It's not a problem.

We leave them chatting away.

'He's not like any doctor I've met before,' says Ollie sucking on the lollipop.

'No you're right about that. It's fair to say our lovely Dr Vidal really is one in a million.'

I am jogging back up the track after an energetic run when Rafael jumps out onto the path in front of me. At his side is Alberto, his Dalmatian, and also his retainer Paulo, who helps him to tend his lemon and orange trees.

'Quick! *Venga.*'

He grabs my arm and draws me over to his *dipòsit*, the outdoor cemented water tank, which sits at the entrance to his orchard. I peer into it.

'*Non, non, non!*' He tuts irritably. 'Look over there!'

He points down into his orchard and across into his small pasture. My eyes land on three still white forms. They are sheep.

'Dead,' he says. 'All of them.'

Paolo sucks his teeth and rubs his grizzled hair. 'It came from nowhere. A huge, black creature running across the fields.'

I give an involuntary shudder. 'What do you mean?'

'An enormous dog,' yells Rafael emotionally. 'It appeared from nowhere and ripped the throats out of my sheep. We must find him!'

I feel very sad for the poor animals and vow to be vigilant. If the beast appears on our land I promise to report back immediately.

'Once a dog has tasted blood, it is a danger to us all,' says Paolo ominously.

'I've just called the *Guardia Civil*. They are on their way,' says Rafael.

It never ceases to amaze me how quickly the police react to any minor incident in our valley. If this had happened in the UK I imagine Rafael might have got a very different response from our bobbies. I create the scenario in my mind.

*'Sorry, Sir, is this a wind up? Three dead sheep?'*

*'Si, an unidentified black dog is culprit. Can you come immediately?'*

*'You're having a laugh, right?'*

*'No, I not laughing. I want police line up with all local dogs.'*

*'If you don't get off the line, Sir, I'll have to report you for wasting police time.'*

*'But what about my dead sheep?'*

*'I suggest you invite your friends round for a barbecue, Sir.'*

I offer Rafael my sympathy and return, shivering, to the house. It is still icy cold and a strong wind ripples across the orchards, violently shaking the trees and ruffling the feathers of the robins and sparrows huddling in our bird bath. The thought of a killer dog roaming about our land makes me uneasy and I begin fretting about the cats, and more so our hens. Much as they are penned in, I worry that this dog may find a way to attack them. I notice Catalina's car is in the drive, parked at a crazy angle as usual. In the kitchen, the Scotsman is making coffee while Catalina pounds away with an iron, the steam rising in great puffs above her head. I tell them about Rafael's sheep.

'Killer dog?' says the Scotsman with a grin. 'Look, it's unlikely it would attack a human and the cats are far too swift of foot to be caught by a dog. It'll be miles away by now.'

'I hope you're right.'

Catalina places the iron down and slowly stirs some sugar into her cup of coffee. 'The problem is that once a dog has killed, it gets a taste for blood. It must be found or it will surely strike again.' She gives me a smile. 'More importantly, what time are we coming for pancakes?'

Tomorrow is Shrove Tuesday and I have offered to make pancakes for Catalina and her family. I intend to make good use of our lemons in the field. My childhood memories are always of hot crispy pancakes smothered in crystallised sugar and lemon juice.

'Seven o'clock?'

'Perfect, then we can get the kids to bed early.'

Ollie wafts into the kitchen, sneezing heavily and reading a book. With some agitation I see that it's my biography of Dorothea Bate. The spine is bent back and it no longer appears to have a bookmark.

'Hey, that's my book! You've lost my page.'

He looks up absentmindedly and flops into a chair. 'It's quite interesting. Apart from Myotragus, Dorothea Bate discovered pygmy hippos in Cyprus and elephants in Crete.'

'I know that,' I say grumpily. 'Look, it's my one little bit of respite at the end of the day so please put it back where you found it.'

Catalina lets out a sigh. 'You know your mother's books are sacred to her.'

'OK. It's not a big deal. I was just looking.'

I take a sip of coffee. 'Anyway, why don't you read one of your own books?'

He shrugs. 'I am. I just thought I'd take a quick peek at yours too.'

'I'll test you later,' I give him a poke in the ribs.

'I'll be waiting,' he grins and jumps up. 'Is there really a killer dog on the loose?'

Alan laughs. 'No, of course not, just a local dog trying its luck.'

Ollie walks slowly over to the window. 'Yes, but just in case I'm going to fill my water gun. It'd better not try its luck with me.'

There we are, George Clooney and I, expertly performing the tango to a wildly appreciative audience on TV's *Strictly Come Dancing*, when suddenly there's a tremendous thud followed by the sound of shattering china. My dream evaporates as I sit bolt upright in bed at the same time as my bleary eyed Scotsman. It is pitch black save for the luminous hands of my alarm clock which indicate that it's 4 a.m.

'What was THAT?' I hiss.

Without a word he bounds to the door, switches on the light and hotly descends the stairs with me scampering behind. The kitchen floor bears witness to a struggle. Broken crockery is strewn across the tiles but there's no sign of the culprit. We step gingerly around the mess in our bare feet and exchange shrugs. We rarely close our doors at night, and the only real risk is that some stray bat absentmindedly flies in and has to be released the next morning. The way we've always rationalised it is that the things we consider to be of great worth are purely of sentimental value and would be of no interest to an intruder. The idea of owning some priceless masterpiece or a metal safe bursting with baubles and gaudy Rolexes would fill both of us with dread. I often wonder how the seriously rich sleep at night knowing that their homes are a magnet for thieves. Now I'm wondering if we've been foolishly naïve. Perhaps some oafish would-be robber hasn't done his homework and thinks we are a bone fide target. What great disappointment lies in store for him! Then another thought hits me like a mallet. What if the killer dog has somehow broken in, tearing its way like the Incredible Hulk through the house in search of fresh blood? Alan taps my arm.

'What's the matter?' he whispers.

'You don't think it's the killer dog?'

He almost laughs. 'For heaven's sake!'

We search the premises. Ollie is still blissfully asleep in his bunk bed, Inko curled up by his side. I slip cautiously downstairs to the basement, the guest bedroom, and pull the creaky wooden door back. Peering into the void, I hear myself let out a scream when a wild, screeching ball of fur crashes out of the darkness, hurtling past me and up the steps into the *entrada*. It is Scraggy, the pathetic feral cat that hangs around our front porch. Alan gives chase and, after a struggle, manages to shoo it out of the kitchen door. He examines the scratches on his arm.

'Damned creature must have got in through the kitchen window, knocked over the mug tree then panicked and gone on the rampage downstairs,' he grumbles. 'Are you OK?'

'Yes, but he gave me a near cardiac arrest.'

We start laughing.

'Killer dog, my eye!' chortles the Scotsman.

We pull out the dustpan and brush, clear up the mess and return to our bed.

'Sweet dreams,' I yawn.

Before turning off the bedside light, he gives me a mischievous smile. 'By the way, did you ever read Sir Arthur Conan Doyle's *Hound of the Baskervilles*?'

I grab a pillow and hit him squarely on the head.

The sky is an effervescent blue and there isn't a whisper of a breeze. I return to our golden valley from dropping the Scotsman off at Palma airport where he's en route for meetings in London. Having spent a fair amount of time last year accepting 'walk on' parts in various adverts for a Palma based film company, and then managing our friend Pep's flat, he has found more lucrative freelance work with a large corporate company in London. Although, as a newly retired, he's quite happy pottering about our land and has no desire to take up gainful employment again, he is happy to consider one-off assignments as long as they are fun and interesting. This current project entails putting a company annual report together and he has agreed to fly over for a few nights to complete it with the chairman and PR chief. While he's away, I decide to get down to some serious office work. Rachel has asked me to put together some ideas for our first meeting with the rock climbing retailer next month and I'm up to my neck in legal documents relating to the potential sale of the business to Jay Finch and Marilyn Hughes. Whether I should merge the company with theirs is anybody's guess but the only other random offers on the table have come from large PR companies wanting to tie me into a board position for several years.

I drive up our track, waving at my neighbour Pedro on the way. He and his wife Sylvia live on the corner and are always especially kind and friendly on account of the warm friendship I enjoyed with Sylvia's elderly mother, Margalida. I pass Rafael's house, clocking that it is shuttered up. Maybe he's in Palma. Our nearest neighbours, Helge and Wolfgang, have not visited the valley for some months and their *finca* is still and forlorn. Tomas, their son,

lives in Sóller, and pops up on his bike every day to feed the cats.
In a brief conversation with him last night he assured me that his
parents would be back again next month, much to Ollie's delight.
No sooner have they arrived and unpacked than Ollie becomes
an evening fixture, playing football with Helge in the garden and
cards with Wolfgang on the terrace.

I park the car and head off up to my office, opening all the
windows on the way. A slash of amber sunlight cuts across my
path on the staircase and for a moment I bask in its warmth. In
the office, Inko is curled up on my chair and protests loudly when
I turf her on to the rug. She sashays out of the room, knotted tail
held indignantly in the air. There are ninety emails awaiting my
attention, most of which are junk mail and the rest a mixture of
work, joke circular mail, and promotional newsletters. I throw
open the office windows and stare out at the Tramuntanas which
are bathed in honeyed light. What a heavenly day, and here I am
holed up in my office. The house seems so quiet now that Ollie is
back at school and the Scotsman on his way to London. I sit down
at my desk and begin sifting through my emails. The hours flash
by and I am just on the verge of setting off to pick Ollie up from
school when all of a sudden I hear a great commotion outside.
Rushing to the open window, I see Minky climbing frantically up
a rock wall while a massive and alien black tail sends a terracotta
pot tumbling by the pond.

Tremulously, my eyes move from the tail to the body. A large
and aggressive looking canine with lolling tongue is staring
up at me. He barks fiercely, and then, with teeth bared, begins
growling menacingly. The Hound of the Baskervilles has found
me and, to my horror, I realise that I have left doors and windows
open throughout the house. I rush downstairs and, grabbing the
kitchen broom, run out into the courtyard. The big dog is still

there, now barking wildly. How he has managed to get into our garden is baffling. I shake the broom at him. He doesn't budge. I try shouting. He looks away, then ambles down into the orchard as if he has nothing to fear, and of course he's absolutely right. A shoeless woman clutching a broom is hardly likely to instil terror in a sheep throat-slashing beast. I give chase, and find him swaggering along our concrete-covered water channel. He heads off in the direction of the wild piece of terrain we intend to use for the cattery.

As he disappears among the trees, I realise that he must have found access to our field via the stream that lies beyond our land. A white house backs on to the stream and it is from here that I am forever hearing the sound of barking dogs. I return to the courtyard, lock up and set off for Ollie's school. At least I can now identify the culprit and I'm fairly sure in a police line up I'd be able to recognise that swagger and lolling tongue. Rafael will be my friend for life.

The next night is stormy and with the Scotsman away in London I decide to batten down the hatches. It is just before dawn that I awake with a start. Despite the howling gale, I can distinctly hear the low whirr of a car engine and then the sound of tyres crunching on the gravel in our drive. The engine is killed. Silence. I cannot believe that, for the second night running, we have intruders. Our normally tranquil mountain eyrie is fast becoming the set for a horror movie. I tiptoe over to the window in my voluminous white nightshirt, only to glimpse two swarthy figures sitting in the front of a white van. They peer out of their open windows, probably casing the joint. What should I do? My immediate instinct is to dial Catalina's number, but from my watch face I see that it's barely 6 a.m. I exercise some logic. The house is locked up and in an emergency surely I can quickly telephone a close neighbour or the local *policía*? I wonder whether I should wake Ollie and bundle him away in a wardrobe for safety. Then I dismiss the idea and decide that, instead, I should fearlessly face my foes. Therefore, with what *macho* spirit I can muster, I turn on all the house lights and defiantly throw open the bedroom windows. In a commanding voice I call out in Spanish, 'Who are you?'

Two heads poke out of the windows and then the driver slowly steps out. To my consternation I see he's holding what looks suspiciously like a cup of steaming coffee. Some cocky burglar to be sipping at a coffee on the job! Then, strolling casually across the gravel, he looks up at me, concern etched on his face.

'Senyora! I am Pepe! We're here to fix your husband's irrigation system in the orchard. He asked us to come by today.'

'Why so early?' I say suspiciously.

'We always start around now but we thought we'd have a quick coffee and a sandwich in the car first. I tried to keep the engine low so as not to disturb anyone.'

In the half light and to my embarrassment I can now see that it is indeed Pepe, the irrigation expert.

'Not to worry,' I say in mock cheer. 'I woke early myself.'

He smiles up at me. 'That's good. So we didn't wake you?'

'No, not at all!' I chirrup.

I make a mental note to strangle the Scotsman when he returns from London. He did mumble something about a problem with the lemon trees but nothing about a visit from Pepe.

Rafael is sitting on the stone bench outside his *finca*, gorging on an apple.

'So now that the police have talked to the owner of the black dog, what will happen?'

He licks his lips and hurls the core into his orchard. 'Another free apple tree!'

'Well?'

'The owner must either put the dog to sleep or keep it safely secured in her garden. As Paolo said, once a dog has tasted blood, it can never be trusted again.'

'Will you be compensated for the three sheep?'

He nods vigorously. 'Yes, the owner must pay for my new ones.'

'That's not so bad.'

He slaps me on the arm and grins. 'Not so bad? Why, it's fantastic! One of my *amics* has just given me three sheep he can no longer keep. I can pretend I've had to buy them. So now I will make some good money too!'

'You're incorrigible.'

He lets out a gale of laughter. '*Si*, I am bad Mallorcan man. Now when is Senyor Alan home?'

'He's away just one more night.'

'*Molt bé*. Remember I'm here if you need anything at all.'

I get up to leave. 'Maybe just one thing.'

'*Si*?'

'You wouldn't have any spare lamb chops?'

It is a blustery night. I go to bed armed with a chamomile tea and a good novel. Ollie is fast asleep in his room with Inko at his side and the house is locked and secured. After an hour or so I find myself dozing and wearily switch off the bedside light. It is dark and raining heavily when I jolt awake. Did I hear a bump? Footfall? I can hardly believe this is happening all over again. The door slowly creaks open. I sit up in bed transfixed. A light glares at me from the landing. It's Ollie. He wanders, yawning, into the bedroom in his pyjamas.

'Sorry, can't sleep. Can I snuggle up with you?'

I sigh with relief. 'Of course.'

He shoots under the warm feather duvet and together, at last, we enjoy a blissfully peaceful night.

# TWELVE

# A LUCKY ESCAPE

**Friday 4 p.m., the office, Mayfair**
Rachel and I are sitting in the boardroom waiting for Charlie Wheeler of Trek & Track to arrive. I have put together an initial PR proposal for his chain of camping and hiking stores, which Rachel seems quite excited about. She flips over a page.

'It's obvious from this that you get a real kick out of all this trekking stuff.'

I get up and stare out at the grey and drizzly London sky. My eyes wander the tops of the buildings, the skeleton trees and the litter-strewn, grubby pavement far below in the hope of seeing a bird. Not one.

'Where are all the birds?'

'Come again?'

'I was just wondering where all the birds have gone. I mean, there's not a hint of wildlife around here at all.'

She sucks on a biro and gives me a quizzical look, the sort a psychiatrist might give to a particularly unstable patient.

'Could that be because we're in a major city, perhaps?'

'I suppose. It's just that you get used to the constant twittering of the birds in Mallorca. Mind you, the frogs are the noisiest, but they won't be back until next month.'

She nods slowly. 'Sorry Miss Mowgli, but you're in the big bad city now so you're just going to have to put up with it. By the way, what happened about your toad? Did he ever turn up?'

'No, but I've a gut feeling he'll find his way home.'

She lowers her head and behind a curtain of hair I can see she is trying to control an impish smile. She looks up. 'I'm sorry, it's just so insane. The idea of a toad sniffing his way home like a dog. But who knows? Stranger things have happened.'

'You wait and see. Anyway what's this Charlie Wheeler like?'

She slowly turns back to the brief in her hands. 'I met him at a networking breakfast a few months ago. He's a bit unctuous and sexist, one of those rather know-it-all Cambridge types. To his credit he's an experienced rock climber with a PhD in civil engineering who also speaks fluent French.'

'If you're trying to endear me to the guy, it's not working.'

She laughs. 'He's OK. It's just that I remember he kept breaking into French bon mots. We all found it a bit tedious.'

I sit down at the table. 'He sounds like a prize buffoon.'

'That's the least of my concerns. I'd like his business. Besides, I know you'll love his product range.'

'Believe it or not, I did visit his shop some years ago when I was off on a scientific expedition. I bought quite a nice fold up machete and some anti-leech socks.'

She taps a long, tapered nail on the table. 'You really are a sad case.'

The door opens, and a short man in a cravat and a beige safari jacket bursts in. Rachel and I jump to our feet.

'Ah, hello *chérie*! Long time...' He leaps forward and plants a kiss on Rachel's cheek. She rears back.

'Ah, Charlie, great to see you again. May I introduce you to...'

He leaves her words trailing in the air. Darting towards me, he grabs my right hand and brushes it with his whiskery moustache. It feels like the kiss of a particularly hairy tarantula.

'*Enchanté*! I think we've met before?'

Now that he mentions it, he does look very familiar. Perhaps he was serving the day I visited his Regent Street store.

'I did buy some gear in one of your shops some years ago.'

'Aha! I never forget a pretty face.'

Oh dear. This meeting is going to require a great deal of patience and strong coffee.

Sarah walks in. 'Can I get you guys some coffee?'

I give her a wink. 'A big espresso for me, please, and Charlie what would you like?'

He shows me his sharp little incisors and honks madly. 'A *café au lait, s'il vous plaît.*'

'A poet and you didn't know it,' says Sarah sweetly.

Rachel smothers a grin. 'A workman's tea, thanks.'

Charlie pulls out a chair. 'What a lucky chap I am. Two *belles* all to myself.'

Rachel gives one of her watery laughs and then picks up the document I have prepared.

'So what did you think of our preliminary ideas?'

He dazzles us with a manic smile. 'I loved it all. You girls obviously understand the trekking and expedition business. I really liked the idea of monthly survival seminars with experts.'

'I think it would go down really well with your clients.' I say. 'You could cover everything from jungles, icecaps, insect and environmental problems, to serious survival techniques.'

Rachel fakes enthusiasm while Charlie animatedly throws his arms up in the air like an excitable conductor.

'Absolutely,' he cries. 'You would not believe the number of customers who haven't a clue about basics such as removing leeches. Child's play.'

Rachel gives a nervous cough. 'So how do you remove a leech?'

He gives a snort of laughter. 'You see, you glamorous young women would be lost in a jungle.'

'Oh I don't know. If I had my hairdryer and Chanel make-up kit, I'm sure I'd get by.'

Charlie enjoys the humour. 'Touché!'

I butt in. 'In fact, Rachel, there are several theories about leeches. Some people tell you to burn them off with a lighter or salt but in Sri Lanka they just cover their legs in Dettol or lathery soap and water before entering a jungle and the leeches keep away. In Borneo, they have this masterly way of just rolling them up in a ball, especially Tiger leeches, and flicking them off.'

Rachel stares at me in silent wonder while Charlie claps his hands. '*Bravo*! Do you know, I too hold with the soap and water theory. Mind you, it doesn't feel too pleasant on the skin when it dries.'

'I imagine not,' says Rachel wearily, quite obviously not enjoying the subject matter.

'Thanks for the tip about Dettol,' he smiles.

'Yes, a revelation,' says Rachel with an evil glimmer in her eye.

Charlie sits up straight. 'Look, let's cut to the chase, girls. I want to go with this programme starting from next week. I might need to shave the fees a touch.'

Rachel pulls her long, shiny hair back behind her ears. 'I'm sure we can reduce the programme to suit the budget.'

He grins. 'So if I want all of this,' he thumps his copy of my proposal down on the table, 'I have to stump up the suggested fee.'

She nods and throws him a radiant smile. 'Precisely.'

'You're a good business woman, Rachel. What the heck! Let's do it.'

'We need to visit a few of the shops together,' she suggests.

He hesitates and turns to me. 'Why don't you pop over one evening after work and I can show you the range without customers getting in the way? We can share a quick drink.'

I don't like the sound of that.

'Great idea,' Rachel replies. 'Probably better for you to go than me.'

I give her a stiff smile. 'Fine, I'll check my diary.'

'Excellent,' says Charlie.

Sarah walks in with a tray of coffees and homemade biscuits from the local deli. Charlie takes his coffee then his hand wavers over the plate.

'I'd love one, but we rock climbers need to be lean and mean. No love handles for us. Pure muscle.'

'I'm going to have one,' says Rachel.

He chuckles, 'Go on then. Let's live dangerously. I can see you girls are going to lead me astray.'

In your dreams, Charlie. In your dreams.

### Saturday 3 p.m., Birmingham Exhibition Centre

Greedy George is barging his way through the crowds. I follow behind, rather like a minnow trailing a shark in a choppy and savage sea. A few people tut as they find themselves knocked sideways but George is a man on a mission and isn't going to let niceties distract him from his goal.

'Look, guv,' he bellows over the heads of various people. 'I'll go ahead and bag us a couple of seats in the front row. Priscilla Burton is going to be a massive draw.'

I nod and watch as his huge frame disappears from view, leaving me to lurch and sway with the throng. I can't believe so many people have come all the way to Birmingham's Exhibition Centre to catch up on the latest vogues in cat and dog fashion accessories. I'm personally interested in visiting the section on catteries while George is keen to pick up some buyers and distributors for his pet clothing range. After what seems like an age, I finally make it to the auditorium of the exhibition hall where the famous American canine author, Priscilla Burton, will be making her address. She has personally invited George to attend her talk on account of his dogs' clothing range, and is a regular visitor to Havana Leather in New York, where she kits out her nine chihuahuas. Greedy George is waving to me from the row closest to the big stage. I make my way over to him.

'You know, guv, there's nothing that woman doesn't know about dogs.'

'What about cats?'

'Sod the bleeding cats. I want to know what big fashion trends she's predicting for dogs next year.'

'I thought your cat range was doing OK.'

He pulls a face. 'Nah, the dogs' kit beats it hands down. The real problem is that not enough cat owners are fetishists. Leather doesn't float their boat.'

'That's a relief. The whole thing's nonsense anyway.'

He gives me a shove. 'You're supposed to be my bloody PR adviser.'

'Then can I suggest you give up the canine S&M gear and do something less silly.'

He beams at me. 'Impossible. Silliness sells.'

'Anyway how's the goat hide stuff selling?'

'Brilliant. I'm going to send you some prototypes for a goat hide stationery range.'

'That sounds a bit more my cup of tea. I'm quite into goats these days. I've been doing some reading up about an ancient creature called Myotragus, a mouse-goat that roamed the Baleares five million years ago.'

His frown puckers. 'Haven't heard of it. Still around?'

'Of course not. It's extinct.'

'Shame, might've produced a Myo-what's-it goat hide range.'

'Don't be ridiculous.'

The seats around us have filled up fast and a blaze of light hits the stage. George looks about us. 'Must be about five hundred people here, guv. You know, this woman has earned more than thirty million dollars with her dog website and books. She's a phenomenon.'

'A sort of dog-eared Martha Stewart?'

'Nothing dog-eared about her. She's a stunner.'

I give a cynical little laugh. 'I wish some of the Sóller locals could witness all this. They wouldn't believe their eyes.'

George is about to reply when a massive screen displays the moving form of the author gliding elegantly, with coiffed hair and clingy silk dress, along an aisle towards the stage. She smiles continuously and waves cheerfully at her whistling, clapping fans. When she arrives in front of the mike, she begins blowing kisses to the audience, puckering her big glossy lips in much the same way Dannie does when she's being photographed.

'I wanna say first of all how much I love you all.'

Wild applause. Oh, give me a break.

'You know, England has to be one of my most favourite places in the whole, wide world. My special home from home.'

More clapping and hooting. I look at George who is grinning like a fool.

'Isn't she the biz?'

I decide to keep my mouth firmly shut.

'So today what I wanna share with all you wonderful, fellow canine lovers is my vision. Where are the hottest dog trends? Have we the courage to push the boundaries?'

Pause for effect. There's a frisson in the crowd.

'Ladies and Gentlemen, please look at the screen. Today, it's my immense pleasure and honour to present to you my very latest title.'

Another dramatic pause. Then in an excited voice Priscilla screams, 'DOG POWER!'

Pink and powder blue light splash onto the stage and the soundtrack, Who Let the Dogs Out, is blasted from speakers across the auditorium. On the screen is an image of a mincing pug in a white lacy ensemble and little pink booties. It sports what looks like a purple turban on its head at the centre of which is a pink jewel, possibly rose quartz. Who can say? George is overcome with mirth.

'Isn't this a hoot?'

'A riot,' I say curtly. 'Actually George, if it's OK with you, I might just creep off to visit the cattery section. All this saccharine is making me feel nauseous.'

He gives me a punch on the arm. 'Go on then Miss Sarky, this stuff is wasted on you.'

'Too right!'

'Let's meet up in the foyer in an hour or so. Keep your mobile on.'

I gather up my jacket and handbag and creep off to an exit during the tumultuous applause. One more minute in that place and I might just lose what tiny amount of sanity I still possess.

**Sunday, noon., the office, Mayfair**
It's a bright and cold Sunday morning. I am at the window of my office nursing a Starbucks coffee and staring down at the empty street far below. The building is silent and devoid of life. I recall how before moving to Mallorca I often popped into the office over the weekend. It was always blissfully quiet without phones jangling and the sound of human noise swamping me in all directions. Given that I've had to stay on in London for an extra few nights in order to meet up with Charlie, the Francophile rock climber, and to attend the Wild Wood launch, I decide to spend a few hours here catching up on work. It took me some effort to enter the building. The heavy double wooden doors opening on to the street have three different locks and once inside I had to re-lock them again. During the week Frances, the receptionist, or Jim, the porter, open up long before any of the occupants arrive but today there's no one on duty. Worrying that the lift might get stuck and I'd be all alone in the building until Monday morning, I took the precaution of using the staircase to the fifth floor and then carefully unlocked the door to the main office and to my own.

I walk to my desk and begin tapping away at the keys of my computer. It's about two hours later that I hear a tremendous crash from the floor above, followed immediately by the sound of tinkling glass. I sit up, startled and with heart pounding. A door creaks somewhere in the distance and then I hear the thud of heavy footsteps. Could it be a maintenance worker? I get up quickly, tiptoe into the main office via the internal door and grab my bunch of keys on the reception desk. I lock both the main office and internal doors after me and stand uncertainly in my room, wondering what to do next. My small office has the advantage of possessing two entrances, either via the central office where the reception area is, or straight from the main corridor. Cautiously peeping out of my own office door to the central corridor, I step out on to the soft grey carpet. All I can see before me is an endless stretch of closed doors flanking either side of the corridor. There isn't a sound but as I turn back, I hear the loud reverberating bang of a door. I stop in my tracks. As if in a nightmare I see, at the far end of the corridor, a big man walking purposefully towards me. Even at a distance I register that he isn't a maintenance worker. There is something menacing and determined about his demeanour and physical bulk. Ridiculously I hear myself yell out in a quavering voice, 'Who are you?'

The man has his eyes fixed on me. He doesn't flinch, doesn't say a word. He just keeps walking slowly, and steadily. I wonder if he can't hear so call out again, trying to sound authoritative but failing miserably. As he gets a little closer I can see the outline of an impertinent smirk on his face and some well honed, weight trained muscles. He is near enough now for me to hear the creak of his trainers. Without another thought I edge quickly back to my door at which point he begins pounding up the corridor. As if in slow motion I see myself slam the office door shut behind me, flick up the Yale lock and begin inserting the second key with shaking, useless hands. I turn it and stand back in horror. The man smashes against the door. It sounds as if he's square on, pushing with his powerfully built shoulder against the wood. Then silence. I pick up the office phone but there's a fuzzy sound on the line. In panic I grab Judas, grateful it's not out of battery, and dial 999. A voice answers. I am almost incapable of words, my head throbbing with spine tingling terror. Every hair on my body is rigid in a salute to fear.

'Can you just give me the address again, madam.'

I am whispering and hissing at the police operator. 'Please help me. He may get in at any moment…'

The man is hugely calm and collected. He tells me to wait in the locked room and to push any heavy item I can find against the door until help comes. He says he's sending a squad car immediately. I throw my mobile on to a chair and with some effort roll my heavy wooden desk forward. Easier said than done. I shout out to the intangible yet malevolent presence lurking outside my door. 'The police are on their way!'

There isn't a sound. I pace up and down the room, wondering how in heaven's name this can be happening. The windows are closed so now I throw them open and stretch out in the vain hope of catching the sound of a police siren. My mobile rings. I pounce on it.

'Hello?'

'Ah, hello darling, I hope this is a convenient moment… it's just that Veronica and I have hit a very bad patch. We're sort of in crisis mode.'

'Join the club. Look, Ed, I'm sorry but this really isn't a great time to talk.'

He gives a little cough. 'Oh dear, I'm sorry, Scatters. Anything I can do?'

'Not really, I'm all alone in the office with a psycho outside the door and I'm waiting for the police to arrive.'

Ed begins guffawing. 'I wish you'd be serious sometimes. Look, if you're tied up, perhaps we can chat later?'

'Fine,' I say breathlessly and end the call. I tiptoe over to the door and put my ear against it. Nothing. Judas begins whining again. Now what?

'Hello Scatters. It's me again. You haven't really got a psycho outside your door, have you?'

'Afraid so. Now look I'd better go because the police will be here in a minute.'

He sounds as though he's having palpitations. 'Oh my God, is he armed?'

'I'm not sure. He didn't look too friendly.'

'Now listen. Maybe you should try bonding with him. Can you maybe ask him what sort of music he likes or books?'

I have a fit of nervous laughter. 'You really are being serious, aren't you, Ed?'

'Look, I saw this marvellous film once in which this negotiator gets the murderer to talk about his hellish childhood and problems with women...'

I'm tempted to shout at him but decide this will only have him retreating to the innards of a brown paper bag to gulp air like a fish out of water. Totally distracted now, I lean out of the window and am massively relieved to hear the distant wail of a siren. It gets louder and louder and suddenly a large unmarked black van and a police car are rushing towards my street, lights flashing wildly. Hurrah! The troops have arrived. As in a movie I look down and see a small crowd of onlookers huddling at the side of the road. They point up at me and in a flash I realise they think I'm some deranged suicider. I find myself laughing uncontrollably at the sheer Monty Python absurdity of the situation.

'What the hell's that racket? Where are you?' shouts Ed, irritably.

'It's the police. Gotta go.'

'Wait!'

I kill the mobile and toss it on to the windowsill and lean out. Far below three policemen and a female officer are staring up at me.

'Throw down your keys!' instructs a young copper.

This is like a skit on Brothers Grimm. *Rapunzel, Rapunzel, let down your hair!* I pull the key fob of jangling keys from my pocket and hurl it out of the window, surprised to see the young officer catch it effortlessly midair. He disappears with his colleagues under the stone arch that juts out above the front entrance. A few minutes later I hear footsteps and a voice yelling, 'Police. Open up!'

I crawl on to the desk and shout, 'How do I know it's you?'

A woman's soothing voice replies. 'It's OK, love, we're the police.'

With difficulty I pull back the desk and open the door. I have never been so pleased to see a uniform in my life.

'Thank you so much for coming!' I cry dramatically.

The officers' radios are alive and making loud squeals. They look around them.

'Right, we're going to search the premises. You stay here,' a senior guy is saying.

'No way!' I reply.

He shrugs, indicating that I can stick with the female officer. Two men head upstairs while the other man and the female officer take my floor. I walk timorously behind them, waiting for my burly would-be assailant to leap out from somewhere any minute and say, 'Got yer!' We reach the far end of the corridor where a door leads to a public bathroom with three cubicles. The woman enters while the other officer rushes in and kicks back the doors to each stall. It's like being in a scene from *Starsky & Hutch*. How the hell do these guys do this for a living? I'd be a wreck. The female officer's radio crackles. She gabbles into it in some strange police speak.

'They've found the entry point. Come on.'

We race up the stairs to the sixth floor. Almost directly above my office is a door leading to a fire escape hatch which opens directly onto the roof. The timber hatch is smashed to pieces and swinging on one hinge. Glass from its window and splinters of wood lie scattered about.

The older, more senior policeman puffs out his cheeks. 'The guy's obviously escaped over the roofs now. You're very lucky, you know. Anything could have happened.'

'Do you think he was a random burglar?' I ask.

'Who knows? Could have been a thief trying his luck or, worse, a more sinister type who's been casing the joint for a while.'

I shudder at what might have happened had my door not been lockable and the police hadn't been quite so swift to arrive. Together we gather my belongings and lock up. Before they go, the sergeant offers me a word of advice.

'Don't go into the office alone at weekends. It's just not worth it. London isn't that safe anymore.'

Then he grins and, lightening the moment, says, 'See that crowd? I reckon they think you're a suicider who had a change of heart.'

'That's what I thought.'

We all laugh.

'How are you getting home?'

'I'll catch a cab, it's not far.'

'OK, but please ring a partner or friend and talk this through. You've had a shock.'

I nod, making a mental note not to ring the Scotsman yet. He'd be worried out of his wits, especially being at a distance. Never has my cosy and safe little idyll in the Sóller hills seemed so far away. The police toot. I wave them off, embarrassed to see the small, crowd of gormless onlookers still monitoring my every gesture. Judas begins ringing. I see from the screen that I've had three missed calls. It's Ed. He is hysterical.

'My God! What on earth is going on? I couldn't reach you. I've been fraaaaantic!'

## Monday 11 a.m., the office, Mayfair

Marilyn Hughes and Jay Finch rise from the table and shake our hands. We walk out to the main reception area and Sarah reaches for their coats.

'That was very productive,' I say.

Marilyn fixes me with her penetrating, emerald eyes. 'I think we're getting there, don't you?'

'Yes, I truly believe we could be a great team, and there's so much synergy between our clients,' gushes Jay.

Rachel is polite and rather formal. 'Naturally there's a lot more to discuss in terms of staffing issues, handover of clients and time frame.'

Marilyn nods vigorously. 'We've time to sort all of that out.'

'Good,' says Rachel a little crisply.

The door closes behind them.

'She's a bit scary, isn't she?' I say.

Rachel clicks her teeth. 'She is, but after what you went through on Sunday, I imagine an encounter with Marilyn Hughes is a walk in the park.'

## 6.30 p.m., Trek & Track, Regent Street

Trek & Track is tucked away in a small cut-through off Regent Street next to a bicycle parts shop and a Scottish woollens discount store. It has a fairly modest frontage displaying some rather frumpy women's linen safari wear, camping equipment and hiking gear. Various types of Swiss army knife, tin beakers and small outdoor accessories dangle from thick cord on either side of the wide bay window, while in the centre a selection of mountaineering literature is propped up against coils of thick rope and mounds of bright crampons. Charlie is wafting through the store in a blue blazer, spotted silk cravat and beige cords. As I walk through the door he grips my arm and draws me inside.

'It's marvellous to have you on board!' he twitters. 'We have so much in common.'

I'm not sure if a joint regard for anti-leech socks constitutes a match made in heaven. I place my bag and coat by the till, forcing him to relinquish his grasp, and begin scrutinising some of the products on the nearest rack. A rather robust blizzard cape catches my eye, as well as a state of the art anti-mosquito hood. Charlie rubs his chin.

'Do you know, my love, I wouldn't go to the Amazon without one of those hoods. They are literally flying out of the shop.'

'How much is the blizzard cape?' I ask, ignoring his familiar tone.

He sucks in his cheeks. 'It's pure gold. Made in France from a lightweight, breathable material that has a triple waterproof layer. It retails at eighty-eight pounds.'

I feel the rubbery outer layer. 'That's quite expensive.'

'Ah, but we only sell quality here, my dear.'

He walks nonchalantly over to the front door. 'I'd better lock this or we'll have no end of pesky customers dropping by thinking we're still open.'

I don't like the idea of being trapped in the store with Charlie, especially after my traumatic encounter of yesterday. Still, I reason that Rachel is but one mobile call away and has even threatened to pop by in an hour or so to take me for a drink. It will depend on how quickly she gets through her meeting at Wild Woods.

There are three months to go before the shop launch and there's still a lot to get done.

'Now why don't we go downstairs?' says Charlie with a wink. 'I've put some bubbly on ice and we can sit and relax in my private lounge.'

That doesn't appeal one little bit, although a glass of bubbly does.

'Perhaps, it may be better to conduct our meeting upstairs so that we can view the product range at the same time,' I say.

He gives me a slithery smile. 'That's not a problem. I've laid out all the new ranges downstairs for you to see. Come on, let's make ourselves comfortable. You first, *ma chérie!*'

I plod down the spiral staircase to the basement, Charlie's lair. It is a surprisingly large space with a dining room area and a small open plan kitchen. Charlie skips downs the stairs behind me and waltzes over to the fridge, where he pulls out a bottle. I hear a pop, followed by a tinkle of glasses. He is humming some schmaltzy sixties tune. It rings a bell but I can't quite recall the words. Then it dawns on me. Adam Faith's 'What Do You Want if You Don't Want Money?' I'm wondering whether, on some subliminal level, Charlie is sending me a message. He brings me a glass of champagne and, pottering over to a large wooden table piled with cellophane-wrapped products, raises his own glass and takes a sip. I reciprocate the gesture and say a business-like, 'cheers'. Charlie is studying various packages in the pile and fumbling with a bunch of papers in a red dossier.

'So, down to business. I've prepared a price list and some new product samples for you to see, as well as a descriptive sheet about each item.'

'Excellent,' I say. 'Perhaps you can talk me through the most newsworthy.'

He takes a sip of champagne. 'Isn't that marvellous? Can't beat Pol Roger, can you?'

'I guess not,' I reply, studying some of the samples intently.

'So, when you're in London without the family, where do you stay?'

'At my club or with Jane, a close friend from university days.'

'And what does Jane do? In the media business like you?'

I can't see of what interest this is to him.

'She's an insurance broker as it happens.'

He pulls out a cigarette. 'Mind if I have one?'

I'm about to protest but remind myself that we are in his premises. 'By all means.'

He blows a small ball of smoke into the air.

'So, I suppose you girls are out on the town every night, eh?' He gives a knowing laugh.

'No, Charlie, we sit and knit in the evening or read Enid Blyton together. Now, can we discuss these items because I don't have too much time.'

He looks wounded. 'I hope you're not going soon. The night is but young.'

I hold up a packet of small cooking pans. 'Are these made from titanium?'

He places his empty glass on the table. 'Er, yes, spot on. The best in titanium mountain cookware. Just launched.'

'Titanium ware's not so new.'

He nods. 'True, but this is particularly light and easily transported.' He gets up a tad restlessly. 'Would you like a little snoop around my pad?'

I frown. 'Why?'

'It's just that I'm rather proud of how my designer converted it. The bedroom's through there.'

'To be honest, Charlie, I think we should plough on.'

He hangs his head despondently.

'For heaven's sake. A very quick look then.'

He brightens up, and takes me into the kitchen zone to admire the cherry wood and granite work surfaces, the Smeg cooker and gigantic powder blue fridge. Then we examine the various wall hangings and minimalist art hung at intervals on the white walls. The bathroom is a shrine to Philippe Stark.

'No expense spared,' I say.

'Only the best,' he purrs. 'But come and see *la pièce de résistance*.'

He pushes an internal door in the bathroom to reveal a bedroom beyond. I peek through in stunned silence. There's a bed the size of a small football pitch covered in black satin sheets and hideous pink and purple cushions in a loud geometric design. The walls are deep vermillion, and, oh no, can it be? I peer upwards at a section of mirrored ceiling placed squarely over the bed. Charlie stares admiringly about him while I try to mask a smirk.

'A very iconic statement,' I mutter.

'You like it?'

I step back into the bathroom just as my mobile rings. It's Rachel.

'I'm on my way. The meeting went well. Gosh, I need a drink. Are you nearly through?'

'You bet. Charlie and I are nearly done. See you soon,' I say in exaggerated tones.

Charlie's face falls. 'Who was that?'

I stride through into the main corridor. 'Just Rachel. We have another meeting in half an hour. It's non stop for us career girls. So, let's get cracking. *Tout de suite*.'

He becomes a bit grumpy. 'Alright, let's go through this stock. Are you sure you need to go? I mean, I was hoping we could have dinner.'

'A wonderful idea, Charlie, but sadly I can't. Maybe when Alan's in town we can all meet up and you can bring your wife along.'

He coughs heartily. 'Yes, indeed.'

We work quickly through the new product range, and are just finishing a detailed tour of the shop when Rachel arrives and tries the door handle. Her brow furrows when she finds it locked. Charlie wearily walks over and lets her inside. I quickly pull on my coat.

'Well, must be off, Charlie. Thanks for the brief. We'll be in touch.'

I shove the dossier into my handbag, shake his hand and walk out into the frosty street. Rachel gives Charlie a wan smile and follows after me. We flag down a cab and collapse on the seat in the warm interior. I begin laughing.

'What happened in there?' she asks.

'Charlie showed me his mirrored bedroom.'

Her mouth falls open. 'OH. MY. GOD.'

'To be frank, I felt a bit sorry for him.'

'Are you mad?' she yells.

'He's a harmless little mollusc, really. I wouldn't be surprised if he's never stepped foot in that room. It's like a mausoleum to his fantasies.'

Rachel tries to control her mirth. 'All I know is that none of us are ever meeting that man alone in his shops or anywhere else for that matter.'

I lean back in my comfortable seat. 'Ah, London life, you can't beat it.'

She gives me a grin. 'Yes, it's been a thrill ride. In just two days you've been pursued by a psycho and a delusional, amorous dwarf. Can't think why you moved to Mallorca.'

'Me neither.'

She shakes her head. 'The truth is, you're just a magnet for nutters. The sooner you get back on that plane, the better for all of us!'

# THIRTEEN

# CRAZY CHICKS

Soft, white light steals under the shutters and plays in front of my eyes. I lie in bed listening to Salvador striking up in the field, crowing until his lungs might burst, while below my window the cats yowl discordantly, impatiently awaiting their breakfast. I can hear the fluttering feathers and animated twittering of the family of sparrows that have built a nest in the roof tiles directly over our bedroom. Another nest, built by robins, has become embedded at the top of a drainpipe, causing havoc when it rains, with water spurting over the top like a mad fountain and splashing on to the back patio below. I cock my head towards the window overlooking the courtyard, for I can hear a new sound, one that is veritable music to my ears. The frogs appear to have returned and are croaking and splashing about in the pond with gusto. I get up and pull back the shutters. Warm, golden sunlight envelopes me. Spring has arrived at last! The Scotsman is oblivious to the sounds beyond the window and sleeps deeply.

With a sudden rush of joy, I jog down stairs, pull open the heavy wooden front door and stand under a canopy of bright blue sky. By the porch, a wild froth of pure white jasmine kisses my hair, its intoxicating fragrance making me giddy. A few yards away, in one of the borders by the lawn, a sea of blue lavender vies for attention, its dry, musky aroma blurring with that of the sweet jasmine. I patter across the stone patio to the pond. A handful of tiny, emerald green frogs dive from the rocks into the bulrushes at the sound of my footsteps. I lean over the dark water, my eyes trying to penetrate the murky depths, but only a blurry face stares back at me, disappointed and a tad resigned. I study the rocks, the tiny dark crevices in the nearby wall, and then begin a thorough search of the bulrushes. There's a cough.

'Lost something?' Alan is standing a few feet away, yawning and squinting up at the sun.

'Maybe.'

He comes over and sits on the wall's craggy edge. 'Listen, it's unlikely Johnny will return but if he does, I'm sure we'll know about it.'

I slump down next to him. 'I suppose it's a crazy thought. I mean how the heck would he get off a mountain? He's hardly going to hop all the way down.'

The Scotsman laughs. 'I don't know, he might hitch a lift on the way. Come on, how about a cup of tea?'

We walk into the kitchen. Ollie has opened the back door and is feeding the cats.

'Are we going to the Fira del Fang today?'

Alan shrugs. 'Is that the pottery show?'

I nod. The week-long Fira del Fang, which literally means 'Mud fair' (and has nothing to do with vampire artefacts), is a much treasured local event which has been running for twenty-five years.

It was created by a bright spark in the village of Marratxi and has been supported by the local council ever since. It now welcomes more than 100,000 visitors through its portals, and has a hundred or more artisans exhibiting and selling everything from mugs and figurines to tiles and cookware. Ollie puts the kettle on.

'We could visit the birds in the port and then go.'

Our trips to feed the assortment of domestic and wild birds that gather by the beach of Can Repic have become a weekly ritual.

'OK, let's have breakfast and head off.'

Alan stands by the kitchen door. 'I think I'll stay here and get on with some gardening if that's alright with you two. I must pick some of the new crop of lemons.'

We smirk at one another. The Scotsman will use any excuse to tend his garden on a Sunday.

'Fine by us.'

'We'll buy you something at the fair,' says Ollie.

'Really? What kind of thing?' asks the Scotsman.

'An ashtray, perhaps.'

'Ashtray?' exclaims the Scotsman, indignantly. 'I hardly ever smoke! Besides, I have a fine one down in my *abajo*.'

'Did,' smirks Ollie. 'Last night I heard a clatter in your *abajo* and saw Scraggy running away. Your ashtray was in bits all over the floor. He must have jumped up on your desk and knocked it over.'

The Scotsman is apoplectic. 'That damned cat! Today I shall deal with him once and for all.'

At Can Repic beach, running parallel with the sea, is a pedestrianised walkway, flanked on the right by a clutter of modest hotels, bars and restaurants whose tables and chairs spill out onto the stretch of paving stone beyond. A modest stone footbridge crosses a broad channel of river water flowing directly into the sea and, depending on the time of the year, the water either gushes or dribbles its way out into the big, wide aquatic world. Ambling and flapping around on the big flat stones and concrete boulders lying on either side of it are a motley assortment of birds. There are ducks, a few hens, the odd goose or heron and occasionally a stray peacock or two. Armed with a bag of old bread, Ollie and I squat down on the stones and throw our offerings into the mêlée. Today, there are only ducks in evidence and, as soon as they sense a food drop, they dive under the cold water with a tremendous quacking and splashing and zoom towards the booty. Ollie bends down and traces his finger in the water just as several ducks come speeding past towards the mouth of the channel, and land with a plop into the sea.

'That must be such fun for a duck. It's like being on one of those water slides at Alton Towers.'

'You've never been.'

'That's true, but I've seen pictures of it.'

We get up and walk slowly over the bridge and down on to the other shallow bank. Ollie touches my arm. There in the reeds and long grass are two little chicks. They appear to be alone. Ollie crouches down and approaches them with crumbs of bread. At first they scurry away but, after conferring together in the reeds, return for a tiny nibble at the crumb deposits on the stones. After a few minutes they take tentative steps towards the channel, appear to lose their balance and go tumbling in, drawn into the fast flowing water towards the sea.

'Oh no!' squeaks Ollie and rushes off to the mouth of the channel just as they come shooting out into the waves. Both are submerged for a nerve-wracking second, and then bob up like a pair of corks, a look of bewilderment on their faces. A hefty mother duck views them with some disdain as they flap their wings and battle their way towards the edge of the water. Ollie leans down and scoops them up in his hands and delivers them back to the bank.

'Crazy chicks!' he exclaims. 'You could have got lost at sea'.

They give him a pathetic 'cheep, cheep' and run back to the bushes.

'You're a hero!' I yell. Then, pulling off my sandals, I shout, 'Beat you back!'

Together we run onto the beach, pounding along the soft yellow sand, splashing in the water and laughing and tumbling, all the way back to the car.

We are standing at a small table laden with pottery products. There are bowls and mugs, crudely shaped plates and oven dishes. The Fira del Fang is bursting with visitors. Ollie is bargaining hard with the elderly woman on the other side of the table. She holds the coarse, brown terracotta ashtray in her hand and swivels it around.

'*Fet a ma,*' she says sternly. It's made by hand.

Ollie shrugs and shows her his two euro coin. He stares at her with round eyes.

She breaks into a chuckle and nods. '*D'accord.*' OK.

Wrapping the item in newspaper, she passes it to him, patting his cheek at the same time. He hands over the coin and, with a smile, pushes the ashtray into his rucksack. We wave goodbye and walk down one of the crowded aisles.

'You got a euro off,' I protest.

'I know. You see, it's a test of nerves. It's a bit like buying Magic cards from your mates. You give them a price and stick with it.'

'Blimey, where did you learn all this?'

'In the *Horrible Histories* books...'

I groan. One day I'd like to have words with the author. He has single-handedly turned my son into a walking bible of historical trickery and trivia.

'The other day, I was negotiating for a mint condition farthing on the Internet and the guy...'

I prick up my ears. 'What did you say?'

'I was buying a coin by auction and managed to pressurise the guy into selling below market rate.'

'Sorry to be a bore, but what are you talking about?'

'You see, I buy and sell a few coins and Magic cards on the Internet. It's quite profitable. If I get ten euros pocket money a week, I can double it.'

'But how do you send them the money?'

'In the post.'

'WHAT?'

'It's easy. I just explain that I only have cash, and send them euro notes.'

It takes me some time to digest this nugget. 'But it could be stolen.'

'Yes, it's a risk, but worth it.'

'What else do you do on the Internet when we're not looking?'

'Nothing much. You really need a credit card to make bigger purchases.'

I shake my head. 'Thank heavens for that. You really are something.'

He pushes out his lower lip. 'You should be pleased. I don't watch TV or have any electronic games. I'm just a small-time entrepreneur.'

I decide to have a serious chat with the Scotsman about this later. We seem to be breeding an Arthur Daley of the mountains.

'Here, come and look at this.'

I follow Ollie over to a stand with the most beautiful hand made pottery animals. There are also Mallorcan *siurells*, small white folklore figures which have been delicately decorated with different colours. A tiny white goat catches my eye. I pick it up and twirl it in my hands.

'Isn't he exquisite?'

'*Quant costa això?*' asks Ollie.

'*Deu* euros,' comes the reply. Ten euros.

He delves into the pocket of his jeans and pulls out a crumpled note.

'Here,' he says. 'Have your goat.'

'Don't be silly,' I say. 'You can't afford that.'

He persists and hands the note to the male stallholder. The young man eyes him in wonderment.

'Buying your *mare* a present? Then you get a discount, young sir. Six euros.'

Ollie thanks him and passes me the small wrapped packet. I go to give him a hug but he winces.

'Try and act cool, mother. That's what the art of negotiation is all about.'

An hour later, we make our way to the car park with a carrier bag of new mugs and oven dishes.

'What a great event,' I say. 'Thank you for the little goat. I'm really touched.'

'Don't mention it. One day, when you're in an old people's home, I'll probably be doing this sort of thing all the time.'

With a cheeky grin he runs off with the car key before I have time to draw breath.

Alan holds an ice pack to his forehead while Pep sits at his side on the patio, puffing on a cigar and admiring the verdant hills.

'So let me get this straight. You chased after Scraggy with the garden hose, tripped over and cut your head?'

Pep can hardly contain his merriment. 'It's perfect. Listen, Alan rings me to say you're at the Fira del Fang and to pop by for a drink. I arrive to find my *amic* sitting on the porch soaked to the skin and with a bump on his head.'

Ollie taps his father's shoulder. 'That'll teach you for being mean to Scraggy.'

Alan curses. 'I thought I'd give the little devil a quick spray, but my foot got stuck in the hose and I fell over.'

'That's karma for you,' I say, dryly.

Pep raises his hands dramatically. 'Women are all the same! Take my wife. Juana will always take the side of the dog. Always.'

'Poor little Scraggy. He's homeless and unloved,' I say.

Pep bursts into laughter. 'Have you ever asked yourself why?'

'Exactly. He's a menace,' says the Scotsman. 'No one will tolerate him.'

Ollie gives the two men a look of disapproval and then pulls something from his rucksack.

'This might cheer you up.'

The Scotsman removes the newspaper wrapping and examines the little brown terracotta ashtray. 'Thank you, Ollie. This is fantastic. I shall keep it in a safe place in my *abajo*, away from Scraggy's claws.'

He gives Ollie a hug.

Pep slaps him on the back. 'Good lad. At least you buy your father a sensible gift. Ashtrays, whisky and *puros* are always acceptable.'

I give a cynical grunt. 'Sadly, I have some work to do, so if I can leave you gentlemen to your busy afternoon...'

'See how she mocks us?' sighs Pep, blowing a perfect circle of smoke into the still air.

'There's only one thing we can do,' says the Scotsman resignedly.

'What's that?' asks Pep.

'Have another drink, of course!'

They sprawl in their chairs, laughing like two old codgers. Never has there been a better time to escape to my upstairs den.

Rachel is in one of her business-like moods. I can tell she's having a tough morning in not-so-sunny London.

'I met up with Marilyn and Jay yesterday to talk through our client base and ongoing projects. They're very gung-ho about the merger, but I wonder how much expertise they really have.'

'What do you mean?'

She sighs. 'Sure they've got the flash offices with a small army of staff running about like crazy chickens, but I question how much they all know about luxury goods and travel.'

'They have some pretty convincing clients.'

'I suppose. Time will tell,' she says ominously.

'Was it something they said?'

'I don't know, just a gut feeling. We'll need to do a lot of training with their personnel. Also, I wonder how our girls will interact with them.'

Rachel and I have already confided in our staff about the possible merger and they all seemed fairly positive about the move. The idea of being in plush offices in Soho proved a winner.

'These things take time to evolve, Rachel. I'm not going to rush headfirst into this merger. Let's see how it goes.'

She brightens. 'OK, as long as we're cautious. By the way, a very contrite Charlie popped by the office today. He was on his best behaviour at the meeting. Not one French bon mot!'

'I would hope not, after his recent bad form.'

'Also, Greedy George rang to say he's found a potential site for a new Havana Leather store in Paris. He wants you to know.'

'That's good news. They'll love the dog gear in Paris. They're into their pooches.'

She titters. 'Oh, and Dannie called to say that Dr Zimmerman has apparently lost his licence to practise ozone in the UK.'

'I wondered why we hadn't heard back from him. Do you know why he lost it?'

She chuckles. 'No, but apparently it's just a glitch. Until he gets it sorted he's going to continue at his practice in Berlin. You won't believe this, but apparently Dannie got Vice Admiral Mason back in touch with Zimmerman and then persuaded Greedy George to meet him too, and now they've all become bosom pals.'

I laugh. 'A meeting of minds. As some might say, what a gas!'

'That's terrible,' she groans.

A van pulls into the courtyard. I stand at the window of my office and strain to see who it is.

'Must run, Rachel. I think the builders are here.'

'Are they working on the cattery?'

'Of course.'

She groans. 'You and your cats. One day you're going to be a mad old woman surrounded by moggies...'

'Ollie's threatening to put me in an old people's home when the time comes.'

'Don't worry, no one would have you!'

Downstairs, someone's calling my name. I cut loose from Rachel and open the window.

Ramon, Catalina's husband, is standing in the courtyard with her brother, Stefan. They are carrying some complicated looking electric motor and equipment between them. Now that the weather has improved greatly, the builders can get cracking. Stefan has now left Ramon to finish clearing the land in advance of the building work because this is one of his areas of expertise. He in turn has brought two friends along, Joaquin and Hugo who have specialist equipment to deal with wild terrain. I look at the trio, a rugged and rural version of Ghostbusters, as they stand surveying the heavy scrub with thick gloves, electric saws and scythes. Hugo is no youngster but he has a spring in his step that belies his years. Joaquin is powerfully built and gives the terrain before him a Dirty Harry scowl.

'We're going to be doing some heavy work with the electric saw so don't worry about the noise,' Ramon shouts.

I nod.

'Is Alan around?' asks Stefan.

'Look in his *abajo*.'

They grin. 'Where else?' says Stefan. 'We'll follow the *puro* fumes.'

They plod off to the field below. I walk through the kitchen and, pouring myself a glass of fresh orange juice, spend a few minutes dawdling over the *Majorca Daily Bulletin*. Hearing a loud clucking, I walk out on to the back patio, only to find Minny and Della, two of our hens, and a chick staring up at me. How they have got free from their coop I do not know. I shoo them all down the back steps to the field and, with a great deal of fuss and flapping, they finally re-enter the corral. The door has been left open. The Scotsman is some feet away in deep discussion with Ramon and Stefan but suddenly puts a hand to his mouth when he spies me by the chicken coop. He rushes over.

'Sorry, I got distracted and left the gate open!'

'Mm, so I see. Just as well the cats weren't prowling about or this little chick might have met a sad demise.'

He laughs. 'They're so fast on their feet, little rogues! Anyway, Ramon reckons he, Joaquin and Hugo will be finished clearing the land in the next week and then Stefan and his men can start on the building.'

'Great news.'

'They'll only take a few days off for Easter.'

'Easter? Of course. That reminds me, our charming Berliners are arriving tonight. We must have them over for a drink.'

The Scotsman laughs. 'Ah, their cleaner came up yesterday and was turning the house upside down. Now I know why.'

Helge and Wolfgang are visiting with their daughter, Luisa, a beautiful and leggy air hostess with a mischievous sense of humour. She is constantly notching up air miles around the globe so is rarely able to touch down in Mallorca unlike her brother Tomas who has made Sóller his home. I return to the kitchen and put a few bottles of cava in the fridge. Much as they may be tired after their journey, I'm taking no chances given that Luisa loves to spring surprises on Ollie when she visits.

The silvery green Tramuntanas, like an enormous, ridge-backed dinosaur, rise up into an unblemished sky the colour of bluebells.

Neither a feathery cloud nor whisper of wind can budge the sun from its glorious throne high in the heavens. In Rafael's field, newborn lambs with curly coats as white as snow gambol playfully about their mothers while, in our corral, Salvador and his belles stroll quietly, deep in thought. Farmer Emilio's horses frolic in the mud and grass, whinnying and shaking their glossy manes in cheerful abandonment.

On the concrete ramp that leads down into the field from the courtyard, Catalina, her twin girls, and Angel and Ollie are rolling painted eggs. We have spent the best part of the morning boiling, selecting and then decorating them, ready for the big contest. Some are covered in abstract patterns, others with Easter themes such as chickens and rabbits. The aim of the game is to roll the eggs as fast as possible, and the ultimate winner is he or she whose egg gains most wins without becoming an unidentifiable, squishy mess. The young girls give up when their eggs meet a sticky end on some rocks, and they run off to play hide and seek in the field. Ollie and Angel struggle on to the bitter end. Catalina acts as arbiter, having seen her own egg smash to pieces against a tree. Mine met its demise when it rolled into a drain. Even though both boys' eggs are battered and bruised, they are still whole. They kneel, faces etched with concentration, hunched over their eggs.

'On your marks, get set, GO!' yells Catalina.

The eggs go flying through the air, jumping along the rough camber of the ramp, until both burst and lie splattered in the caked mud far below.

'So who's the winner?' asks Angel.

'Difficult,' says Catalina.

Ollie bites his finger tip. 'It's a tie, surely?'

'*Si, si*, a tie. You are joint winners. Come on, prize time!'

The four children now gather round as we solemnly dish out the Easter eggs. The boys seem satisfied that theirs are marginally bigger than those of the girls. They sit gorging their spoils on the front lawn in the sun and then in a flash are back down into the field, running around in the tall grass, playing catch-catch and climbing the trees without a care in the world.

# FOURTEEN

# FOOD GLORIOUS FOOD

It is 9 a.m. and Stefan's men have downed tools for their *merienda*, a hearty snack consisting of a *bocadillo* jammed full of Serrano ham and ripe tomato slices and a bag of raven-black olives. For dessert, they will pull a few fat oranges from our trees, spitting the pips onto the soil and licking the sweet juice from their hands. They sit in the grass by the half-constructed shell of the cattery and swap jokes while the Scotsman prowls about the wooden edifice, inspecting the joints and admiring their handiwork. True to their word, Ramon, Hugo and Joaquin managed to clear our mini jungle in just a week so that Stefan and his men could commence building work. Without the six-foot-high brambles, sprawling palm trees, bushes and weeds, the field and orchard appear so much bigger. I have just returned from a run, and am gnawing on some toast and Marmite when I hear someone calling at the front gate. I jog out to the courtyard and see Neus waving to me. The workmen have wedged the gate open so she is able to come straight in. I notice she is gripping a bulging plastic carrier bag in one hand, which rustles as she walks.

'Neus! What a nice surprise.'

She is wheezing, as usual, and stops at the porch to catch her breath.

'The sun's up early. Look how I'm sweating!'

I take her by the arm and lead her inside. Once in the kitchen she sits down heavily in the first chair she sees and closes her eyes.

'Are you OK?'

She taps her chest. 'I have to take pills for my heart. My doctor says I have a quick pulse.'

'In that case you mustn't overdo it, Neus.'

She waves her hand in the air. 'Pah! As if I care what he says. I don't have a man around the house anymore so I have to do things for myself.'

'You have children?'

She rests her chin on her plump hand. 'Two boys. One lives in Santa Maria and the other in Bunyola. They live far away with their families but they visit at weekends.'

Both villages can be easily reached within thirty minutes by car, but to an elderly Mallorcan in the rural areas this represents a great distance.

'Can I get you a coffee?'

She looks uncertain and then acquiesces. 'Only if you have one. *Un espresso.*'

I walk over to the coffee machine and switch it on. Neus is studying the walls of the kitchen with interest.

'I like these artefacts you have hanging on that stone wall. I remember using old iron ladles like that as a youngster. Is that an old olive measure?'

'Yes, did you use those?'

She laughs. 'I haven't seen these things in years. It takes me back to my childhood.'

I carry a tray of coffee cups, sugar and biscuits to the table, and sit next to her.

'I love traditional cooking utensils. I've been collecting them from local fairs and junk shops in Palma.'

She nods. 'Good for you. It's nice to see your little culinary museum.'

She plops two sugars into her cup and stirs it slowly.

'I've brought you something – a little thank you for your help with that English woman.'

I protest but she just smiles and pats my hand.

'Here, I went out collecting *espàrrec* this morning. I got a full bag.'

I am a huge fan of the spindly, green, utterly scrumptious wild asparagus that grows in the hedgerows of Mallorca at this time of the year. Neus could not have brought me anything better. I open the plastic carrier bag and drink in the indescribably gorgeous aroma of young green shoots.

'Neus, I adore asparagus. Are you sure you don't want some of this?'

She gives me a wink. 'I know the best place for asparagus in Sóller. It's been my secret for years. My kitchen is full of it.'

I pull a thin stick from the bag and bite off the head.

'Wash and boil it first,' she chides.

It tastes delicious, cooked or uncooked.

She takes a long sip of coffee. 'I saw Senyora Walton in the town. She is happy in the new flat but she says her son Ben is returning to England to start at a new school.'

'That's good. He seemed a bit aimless here.'

She touches her hair. It is flattened down with some sort of unguent and pulled back with clips. 'I have a terrible mop. It sticks up on end as if I've just seen a ghost. The hairdresser says it's too thick and stiff to do anything with.'

I can't help smiling.

'Worst still, I've got my nephew's wedding coming up and I've bought a nice dress but my hair will let me down. Maybe I should just wear a scarf?'

I'm amused that she is so fixated with her appearance. 'I've got something you can use.'

She shakes her head. 'I'm too old to try new things. I just put olive oil on it and pin it down. Only thing I can do.'

I run upstairs and return with a tube of my leave-on hair conditioner.

'Neus, I have the maddest, curliest locks and this keeps them tame. Just leave it on after you've washed your hair.'

She makes a big fuss about accepting it but finally succumbs. She rises to her feet.

'I shall try this and let you know how I get on.'

'When is the wedding?'

'Next Saturday.'

I offer to wash and comb her tresses for the occasion, but she won't hear of it. She bustles out of the front door and, with a little peck on my cheek, walks slowly towards the gate, her right leg dragging slightly behind the other. Like a little girl triumphantly holding some small trophy from a party game, she grips the conditioner tightly in her hand and with a last coy smile in my direction, she wanders off along the track.

I am just leaving Calabruix bookshop in the town when my mobile rings.

'Hello, I am Marina. I am on my way to your house now with ten cats.'

I pause for a second, hoping that my Spanish has utterly failed me on this occasion.

'*Lo siento.*' Sorry, I say. 'Can you repeat that slowly?'

'*Si, si*, I have ten cats I would like to put in your cattery. I am already in Sóller. I will be with you in fifteen minutes.'

My mind goes blank. How can this have happened? I haven't gone public about the cattery and it is far from finished. Besides, who in heaven's name has ten cats to accommodate without any prior warning?

'That is impossible, senyora,' I say breathlessly. 'We are not open yet.'

The line is silent for a second. 'But I read that you were opening today. It was in *Ultima Hora.*' This is one of the island's leading newspapers.

By now I have more goose bumps than a plucked chicken. 'But that's impossible!' I squawk.

She sounds a little cross. 'Look, we can talk about it when I arrive. I have a little map to your house which I cut out of the newspaper.'

The line goes dead. In total panic mode, I call Alan and repeat the conversation.

'This is ridiculous! It must be a joke. If the woman comes, we'll just have to send her away. You'd better get hold of a copy of *Ultima Hora.*'

I rush to the *estanco* in the *plaça* and snatch a copy of the newspaper from the stand. Scanning the pages frantically in the street, I cannot see anything about the cattery. I call Alan back.

'Perhaps it was in an old edition?' he says unhelpfully. 'You'd better come home now.'

'I promised to pick up some new paints and brushes for Ollie in Art I Mans.'

'That can wait. I think this is a tad more urgent.'

I scurry to where the car is parked and head off to the house. Fifteen minutes later I explode through the front door.

'Any sign of her yet?'

Alan is sitting calmly reading the *Majorca Daily Bulletin*.

'You don't seem very worried.'

He looks up. 'Nothing we can do about it. We'll just have to send her away.'

The telephone rings. A ripple of fear runs through me. What if this is another potential customer who has seen this phantom article?

Alan answers the telephone, mirth etched on his face. He begins laughing so loudly that I find myself becoming incensed. This is no time for tomfoolery. He beckons me to the receiver. 'It's for you.'

'What?' I hiss.

'Hello Sweetie! April fool in England is today, no? Ha ha! I got my sister-in-law to call you with a crazy story about the cattery. She said you were panicking.'

I look at Alan, who is doubled up with mirth.

'Pep! When we meet, I am going to kill you very slowly with as much pain as I can possibly administer,' I growl.

He gives a loud snort. 'Promises, promises. I can't wait! I told you I'd get you back for those plastic ants. Happy April the First, *guapa*!'

I put the phone back on its perch and fix my gaze on the Scotsman.

'Now, before you suspect me of having anything to do with this...' he blusters insincerely, taking a wary step towards the open back door.

I whisk up a tea cloth and lunge at him but it's too late. He dives out into the patio, chuckling wildly, and makes his escape down into the field and to the safety of his smoke-ridden *abajo*.

A soft sun smiles down on the valley. We have all awoken early and are awaiting the arrival of our house guests. Alan is clipping the honeysuckle bush, while I am once again searching the rocks around the pond in the hope of surprising my corpulent toad, but of course he's nowhere to be seen. Suddenly there is the roar of an engine. We both look up and see our friends James and Sophie at the gate in their sleek motor. Both are hotshot lawyers from London who like nothing better than to chill out in the Sóller hills for a few days with us. Ollie stands on the porch eyeing the aquamarine-tinted bonnet with admiration. They drive regally into the courtyard and park up near our mud caked car. We wander over to greet them.

'We made it!' cries James. 'Wonderful journey, smooth as anything.'

'How was the ferry from Barcelona last night?' Alan asks.

'Fantastic. No problems. We had a good kip and drove off the boat this morning fresh as a daisy!'

That's the thing I like about James. He is one of life's enthusiasts, and meets every challenge with great gusto and cheerfulness. Sophie is crease-free despite an overnight trip on the ferry and an early start. We exchange kisses.

'As usual, you're disgracefully bright-eyed and bushy-tailed,' I say.

She laughs. 'Chanel and a good hairbrush can cure most ills.'

'How's London?' asks Alan.

'Cold, wet, bleak. Next?' James's voice rings out cheerily.

Ollie is studying the car's interior. 'What model is this, James?'

He tuts. 'You don't know your cars, young man, do you?'

'I don't have a lot of opportunity,' he says crisply, stealing a glimpse at our old rented banger.

James gives a grunt. 'Ah, good point. This is a Jaguar Coupé. It's not new, but it's all about how you look after your car that matters. Even old bangers can look good after a wash and brush up.'

'Maybe,' says Ollie doubtfully.

We walk inside, the men struggling with cases and bags of shopping. Although staying for less than a week, these two foodie fiends always arrive at our home with a serious selection of cookery books and have apparently already stopped at a supermarket en route.

'We just popped by your local Eroski supermarket on the way here. It was just opening. Thought we'd pick up some wine and nibbles,' says Sophie.

I laugh. 'Trust you. Anyway, the kitchen's on stand-by.'

'Great,' says James. 'You can put your feet up while we do most of the cooking.'

It is rare for me to let others crowd my kitchen but with these two London gourmet lawyers it's different. While I work away at the computer during the day, they pop off to the local market, delis, bread shops and *bodegas* and come home laden with the most delectable morsels for our supper. Effortlessly, they create mouth-watering concoctions accompanied by delicious wines, allowing me a well-earned break from the kitchen. This time we have a few gastronomic haunts we'd like them to visit.

'Is Catalina coming over?' asks James. 'I'm desperate to see how she does that marvellous pepper dish.'

'Try and stop her,' says Alan. 'She's popping by for lunch tomorrow.'

Catalina and I spend most of our time together discussing food and recipes, and she is always delighted when James and Sophie visit to share a few culinary secrets.

'Excellent,' says James. 'I've got a new Moroccan dish I think she'd like.'

'Do you fancy a potter in Sóller town – today is market day – or would you prefer to rest?' I ask.

'Rest? Heavens, no. Let's hit the town,' says Sophie. 'We'll dump the cases and be ready in a jiffy.'

Ollie perks up. 'Can we go for breakfast at Café Paris?'

James picks him up and twirls him round. 'A brilliant idea. Café Paris sounds just the ticket!'

'What I'm thinking,' says Marilyn, 'is that if we merge the two businesses by July, then we could be up to speed in time for the autumn.'

I stand in the porch, fiddling with some ivy tendrils on the wall. Inko is watching me haughtily from the cavernous hole half way up the olive tree.

'It seems a bit rushed,' I sigh. 'It will take some time for the handover, and I need to talk through the merger very carefully with my clients.'

She sounds startled. 'Jay told me you'd already spoken about the merger to your clients?'

'In broad terms, yes, but they need to know how it's all going to work in practice and how long I'll be involved in the newly merged company.'

She clicks her teeth. 'That's easy. We just say you'll be fully involved for the first year and that their accounts will be handled by your existing staff when they join us.'

'They'll want to know the long-term plan though.'

'Sure, well, we can cobble something together. Look, I've got to rush, got another merger meeting would you believe?'

'Really?'

'It's more of a takeover, really. We're absorbing New Look PR. They've got some nice alternative fashion brands from Latin-America and Russia.'

I can't think of anything to say but it's obvious that I'm bored rigid when I open my mouth. I am not a fashionista and have no interest in promoting clothes brands. It's all so ephemeral to me. 'Great, sounds exciting.'

'We'll catch up when you're in London. Ciao.'

In fact, what she shrieks into the receiver is 'ciaowww', as if she's just stubbed her toe and is hopping about in pain. I carry the telephone through to the kitchen. James is at the table, reading a book while taking long sips of lemon tea.

'Difficult call?'

'Just about the potential merger. I have some niggling doubts.'

He puts his book down. 'If you have any serious concerns, I'd advise you not to go ahead.'

I shrug. 'It's gone a bit too far for that.'

He shakes his head. 'Your choice, but as a lawyer, take it from me: it's never too late to pull out of a deal if it's a bad one.'

'I'll bear that in mind.' Of course, he's right. Why go ahead with something that instinctively I know isn't right?

He gives me a sunny smile. 'After all, there are plenty more pebbles on the beach.'

In Mallorca, lunchtime isn't bound by conventions and, rather like an elastic band, is a flexible affair. In other words, it can stretch to any hour, and so, at 3 p.m., we finally decide to wend our way to Calle Luna for lunch. James is lugging an enormous carrier bag in either hand while the rest of us carry slightly more modest packages. Ollie has invested in a stunning red pepper plant for his window box and hugs it to his chest, receiving admiring glances from passers-by, several of whom stop and ask him where he bought it.

'Only two euros?' they exclaim. 'What an *oferta*! In the market, you say?'

We have rifled the shelves of Benet Autentics, Sóller's luxurious patisserie-cum-deli, and emerged with fresh olive *chapata* bread, crusty rolls, jars of freshly roasted almonds crusted with grey marine salt, handmade plum jam and local olive oil. At the fish market, Sophie insisted on buying five plump *lubina*, seabass – which she and James said they would prepare for supper, pan-fried with garlic and olive oil – and also succumbed to *gerret*, a delicious (if bony) little Mallorcan fish which, at only two euros a kilo, had Sophie gasping, opening and closing her mouth like an excited little fish herself. After purchasing two pots of Sóller's special red-skinned prawns, she and James went on the rampage in the *carnisseria* zone, where they bought up chorizo sausage, salamis, pork belly and beef.

By the time we arrive at Can Gata, we are all in need of sustenance. The set menu, at ten euros, includes three courses, wine, mineral water, bread and olives.

'What a steal,' mumbles James.

We walk through to the back of the restaurant and into the pretty garden, where Florentina, who owns Can Gata with her husband, Guillem, comes out to greet us. It takes some time for us to order given that James wants to try just about every morsel on the menu. Florentina laughs.

'If you like cooking, you should come and meet Guillem.'

In a state of great excitement, Sophie and James traipse after her into the busy kitchen. Guillem, cook and thespian manqué, doubles up as a Catalan teacher in his spare time and has a raft of adoring students all over town. He pauses from his frying to shake their hands and to discuss the *menu del día*, speaking in clear Catalan for my benefit.

'Everything is produced locally, and what we serve are traditional Mallorcan dishes – recipes passed down from generation to generation.'

I give a general translation, seeing the glint in Guillem's eye when I falter over a phrase or two. He grins.

'She's one of my past students but she needs to do the next level of the course.'

James nudges me. 'Maybe opt for a Catalan cooking course instead?'

'Do you ever stop thinking of food?'

'Good God, no.'

Guillem lifts the lid on a pot of broth. We all drink in the delicious aroma.

'This is my homemade fish soup. I hope you'll all like it.'

A good moment for us to scuttle back to our table in preparation for the first dish. As we re-enter the restaurant, Florentina catches my arm.

'By the way, we were at the wedding of Neus's nephew last week. We couldn't believe how nice Neus's hair looked. She said you gave her a magic potion.'

I touch my nose. 'A trade secret.'

She smiles. 'Believe me, she was so proud. You may have to keep her in regular supplies.'

'I'll do my best!'

Lunch is a languid affair and after fish soup, fresh *albondigas* (meatballs), rice and salad, followed by *Crema Catalina*, coffee and *herbes* liqueur, we stagger out into the street at 5 p.m.

'I can't eat another thing,' mumbles Ollie.

'What?' says Sophie. 'We're going straight home to prepare the fish. This is the beginning of your gastronomic marathon.'

The Tramuntanas are tinged with soft, ruby light – it's that time of day when the valley hangs up its work apron and allows itself a moment of repose, basking in the last rays of warm sun. Catalina is sitting on the patio, nursing a glass of deep red wine.

'The thing is, James, you have to let the peppers rest in the oil and garlic for some time. This dish lasts for at least three days if you keep it in the fridge.'

James mops up some oil with a chunk of baguette. 'But your oil is so glorious here in Sóller. I think that makes a difference.'

She nods. 'Yes, you should take some bottles back with you.'

'We've bought a dozen already,' says Sophie.

Catalina laughs. 'That should keep you going. Did you buy the salted *bacallà* I told you about?'

'Ah, the cod? We'll get some before we leave.'

'Here, I also wrote out the recipe for *coca* for you.'

She hands him a piece of paper.

'This is the sponge cake we tried?' asks Sophie.

'*Si*. The secret is in the yoghurt.'

'So, it's five eggs, flour, sugar, plain yoghurt and lemon zest?'

Catalina looks at the paper again. 'I forgot to write something. You need a glass of oil and *levadura*. Baking powder, you say in English?'

Sophie pulls a pen from her handbag and scribbles on the missing ingredients.

The Scotsman plods up the stairs from the field, carrying a bag bulging with fresh lemons.

'Thought you might like to take these back with you too.'

James claps his hands together. 'Heavens, that'll keep us in *coca* for some months.'

Catalina fixes the Scotsman with a razor eye. 'Before I forget, where have you put all your pots of seedlings? I've noticed they've all vanished.'

He looks very pleased with himself. 'I've planted them all.'

She sits up. 'Where?'

'Now that the field has been cleared by your dear husband I've been able to find all sorts of places to plant my seeds and saplings.'

'At least they're not clogging up the patio anymore,' she says crisply.

'Mark my words,' says the Scotsman dreamily. 'In a few years' time, you'll be seeing almond, avocado, apricot, olive and cherry trees springing up in the orchard.'

'A few *years*?' I gasp. 'Couldn't we have bought them at a more advanced stage?'

He gives a frustrated sigh. 'You see, that's the typical remark of the armchair gardener. You've no appreciation of the nurturing and gradual blossoming of the harvest, which can take decades.'

Catalina gives a cackle and nudges me. 'Something to look forward to in your old age.'

'All I do know,' jibes James, 'is that your wife hasn't lost her impatient Londoner persona quite yet.'

'Too true,' sighs the Scotsman. 'Only when she's happy enough to wait five years to see a conifer grow will I know she's kicked the London habit for good.'

It is a dreary and drizzly April day in the Sóller Valley, but this does nothing to dampen the enthusiasm of the many olive oil *aficionados*, who, rippling with anticipation, have turned out on to the streets of the port and the town to celebrate the annual Fira de L'Oli. The olive oil fair is an annual bash, stretched out over a week, which celebrates the first oil produced from the new season's olive harvest. Festivities are held in different parts of the town and port, and restaurants create menus to accompany the theme. This year, in a break with tradition, the olive oil producers have joined forces with the fishermen to create Fira de L'Oli i del Gerret. In recent times, the *gerret* has become a much maligned and shunned little fish, partly due to its puny and bony nature but predominantly because other more fashionable fish have taken its place. In truth, the working woman of the *casa* today has found bigger and better fish to fry in the form of the chunky boys on her cutting block such as cod, tuna and hake. She can't be bothered with filleting and fussing and wants flaky, meaty flesh, fewer bones and a less fish-fragrant kitchen. Yet hark the lark! Suddenly, with the economic downturn, *gerrets* are back on the map, being dusted down with salted flour and given a revival. At just a few euros per kilo, *gerrets* might just hold the key to good nutrition at exceptional value. This, of course, is exceedingly bad news for the poor little *gerrets*, who previously had little to fear from the fishermen's nets. Now, on the eve of this *fiesta*, one can only imagine shoals of the quivering little *peix* hiding out in the murky waters beneath the harbour, playing tag with the descending nets.

To kick off proceedings, the local Association of the Third Age in the port has already organised a supper for the public at large. One hundred kilos of the little *gerret* were served up to more than four hundred diners by the sea and then, up in Fornalutx, there was a grand opening of the fair, with politicos and dignitaries arriving from Palma to make cheerleading speeches along with the town's Mayor Guillem Bernat. A large marquee has been erected on a piece of wasteland opposite the *Cooperativa*, the warehouse where one can purchase locally grown fruit, olive oil and vegetable in bulk. It is here that locals can pop by to learn more about the new olive oil and sample a few culinary dishes. Various restaurateurs have donated plates of canapés and snacks using *gerrets* and we are keen not to miss out on this gastronomic treat.

We park the car in Biniaraix village a short distance away and, with umbrellas to the wind, make our way along the country road to where the giant marquee has been secured. Scores of people are already making their way into the field and so it is some time before we find ourselves under dry canvass. Catalina is already at the front of one of the queues with her mother, Marta. She waves and a minute later approaches us with a plate of little *gerrets* sitting aloft miniature brioches. They are delicious, and within seconds the plate is empty.

'I rather fancy trying the *pa amb oli*,' says James.

'You remember the name. Very good,' enthuses Catalina.

*Pa amb oli*, literally bread and oil, is a stalwart of the Mallorcan diet, served in a multitude of ways. Today, slices of traditional brown bread are smeared with the new season's oil, fresh tomato pulp and rock salt. Marta and I manage to extract two plates from a trestle table and together we sit down and share the slices around. Llorenç, the wood man, enters with his wife and comes over to see us.

'Wait there,' he yells. 'I'll bring some plates of olives and salad.'

Catalina's father, Paco, arrives together with Stefan, Ramon and the twins, and soon our table is the largest and loudest in the room. Sophie and James scribble down recipes, delighting in some of the traditional methods of cooking passed on by Marta.

'What do you think of the cattery plans?' Ramon asks Sophie.

'You've done a terrific job clearing the land. We didn't recognise the place.'

Ramon smiles. 'It was a big job, but worth it.'

'We're more into dogs than cats but we think the cattery's a great idea. Might book in ourselves next time.'

'So, you leave for London tomorrow?' asks Ramon.

'Sadly,' sighs Sophie. 'Time seems to race by here.'

He laughs. 'For us it passes quite slowly. One season comes, another follows. Every *fiesta* has its turn.'

'Yes, but, for us, it has to be concentrated in one week,' she replies.

'Then there's only one thing for it, you'll have to pack up your jobs and move out here.'

James gives him a wistful look. 'You never know, Ramon, one day.'

Packed to the brim with bottles of wine, *herbes*, olive oil, bags of lemons and oranges and salted cod, the elegant Jaguar purrs out of our drive. We wave until the car reaches Rafael's house and disappears round the kink in the track by Silvia and Pedro's *finca*. We stand in the courtyard, surprised to see that the rain has ceased and a magnificent rainbow has been drawn crudely across the sky. A weak sun bobs up behind the Tramuntanas, dispersing the clouds, and soon the valley is flooded with creamy gold light.

'Ah, that was fun. Mind you, I don't think I shall ever eat again,' says the Scotsman.

'Neither will I,' agrees Ollie. 'That was some foodathon.'

My mobile phone trills. It's Pep.

'OK. Sounds good. What time?'

I click the phone shut.

Alan and Ollie look at me in some trepidation.

'That was Pep. How do you fancy supper in the port tonight? Apparently he and Juana have got us invited to some swanky five course dinner up at the lighthouse.'

'You have to be kidding?' says Ollie.

'Impossible!' shrieks Alan.

'OK, I'm just having you on. It's tomorrow night.'

'Fine, but let that be the last of it,' Alan says, firmly.

'Of course,' I say, judging it better not to remind him of the impending seafood *fiesta* in our immediate neighbourhood. Surely that can wait one more day?

# FIFTEEN

# A WILD SUCCESS

**Wednesday 8.30 a.m., Mayfair**

A slither of sun weaves its way through the clouds and glares down at me as I stand vacantly outside the entrance to my club. South Audley Street is unusually quiet. A lone road sweeper in a fierce orange PVC jacket wends his way slowly along the opposite pavement, tipping dust and sweet wrappers into his mobile bin while singing along to a disco track on his Walkman. A courier is perching on the concrete step of a nearby office block studying a road map and speaking curtly into a walkie-talkie. His eyes wander up and down the street irritably as if the numbers of the buildings have utterly confounded him. A white, mud splattered Mini Cooper drives by, its owner's head jerking out of the window when he sees the courier.

'Know where Curzon Street is, mate?'

The courier points impatiently into the distance without getting up or uttering a syllable.

'Cheers, mate!'

The Mini Cooper passes me, its red brake lights stopping at the top of Audley Street at the intersection with Curzon Street. It turns right. What's happened to all the cabs this morning? My hair feels icy against my neck, the after-effects of a shower following my early run around Hyde Park. My arm is still jutting out, hoping that a taxi with glowing amber light will appear on the road at any minute to whisk me away. Where to? That is the question. Someone bangs me rudely on the arm.

'Cooee! Penny for them!'

It's Bernadette, one-woman comedy store, en route to scrub and polish the club to within an inch of its mahogany life.

'Everything all right in your room? Did you see the biscuits I left by the kettle?'

A barrage of questions.

'Everything is fine, Bernadette, thanks.'

'On your way to work? How long you staying this time?'

'Just a few days,' I mumble.

A taxi acknowledges my flapping arm.

'Where you going, love?' the Cockney vowels sing out over a vibrating engine.

'Erm, I'm not sure. I'll get in and have a think.'

Bernadette tosses her head back and gives a howl of laughter. 'God love her! Nothing between the ears this morning. Too many brains. Ta-ra, love.'

I clamber into the warm belly of the cab as she bustles up the front steps to the club. The cabbie looks at me expectantly in his front mirror.

'Sorry, I've gone blank.' I give him my office address. What is the matter with me this morning? I've spent a sleepless night worrying about the merger, thinking about James's wise words of caution and wondering whether we're making the right move. I pull out my diary and realise that my first meeting is not at the office but with Greedy George at his showroom. I ask the driver to change direction. He smiles.

'Can't decide where you wanna go this morning, eh?'

'Something like that,' I reply.

'Know what you mean. Sometimes, I'd rather just dump the cab and spend the day in the park.'

'Why don't you?'

'Gotter earn the dosh, haven't I?'

'We should all play truant now and then.'

He laughs. 'Maybe you're right. Just try and tell the missus that!'

We arrive at Havana Leather's elegant showroom in St James's. I proffer a ten pound note. The driver fishes for some change in his pocket. He gestures with his eyes towards Havana's frontage.

'Met George Myers, the guy who owns this shop, once. Took him in me cab. A real laugh, he was. Told him it was my birthday and he invited me in to choose a gift.'

'Did you?'

'You bet. Got meself a lovely wallet. Here, this is it. Still use it.'

I examine the heavy tan wallet and put the change he offers into my own purse.

'That's so nice to hear,' I say.

'As I say, a real good egg, that Myers. I tell everyone about him. A diamond geezer with a heart of gold.'

He drives off. I stand on the pavement once again, lost in thought. Appearances can be deceptive but, then again, what was George doing? A genuine, spontaneous gesture of goodwill towards the taxi driver, or a cynical attempt at viral marketing? The door of the showroom springs open. Richard, the flamboyant store manager, hops out to greet me like an over-eager spring bunny.

'What ho! Back from Mallorca? George is upstairs. In a naughty mood this morning.'

'How so?'

'He's just told the window dresser to pull out the window and start again.'

'It looks OK.'

He lowers his voice. 'Fortnum & Mason had run out of his favourite almond croissants this morning so he took it out on poor Mel. He's had her in tears.'

I tut and stride into the showroom. So much for good eggs and goodwill.

Upstairs, George is sitting at his voluminous desk like a grumpy giant, slurping at a huge coffee cup.

'You're late,' he growls.

'I got lost.'

'Eh?' He stares at me darkly.

'Strange, but I thought I was at the shrine of George Myers, saintly bestower of leather wallets to random taxi drivers, but instead I've landed in the lair of moody Myers who bullies window dressers. I'm truly lost.' I put my coat down on a chair. 'What's got your goat?'

He leans back in his chair. 'I should have given you the push years ago.'

'Yes, well you missed your chance.'

I call down to Richard. 'Can you get me a double espresso, sweetie?'

'Coming!' he yells up.

George gives a little chuckle. 'Did you really meet that taxi driver?'

'I sure did. Thinks you're a saint but don't worry, I disabused him of the fact. Told him your goodwill gesture was a cynical attempt at viral marketing. *Boca a boca*, we say in Mallorca.'

'Doesn't that translate as mouth to mouth, guv?'

'Yes, but they mean word of mouth.'

He yawns. 'Yeah, well it wasn't a cynical gesture Miss Sarky. I liked him. Nice guy.'

I sit down opposite him. 'Have you got a tissue? I think I'm going to cry.'

He tries to swipe me across the desk, a broad grin on his chops. 'OK, very funny.'

Richard comes up the stairs with my cup and a plate of chocolate biscuits.

'These will put the twinkle back into your smile, George.' Richard gives a little wink and, wiggling his hips, disappears back down the stairs.

'I don't know how Richard puts up with you.'

He gives a snort. 'I'm a walking charity putting up with him and that half-witted Mel. The girl hasn't got a clue.'

'Stop being so irascible. Anyway, down to business. I've got the new press pack done and a draft marketing brief for the forthcoming goat hide stationery range.'

He perks up. 'Fabbo. By the way, still investigating those dodgy Myo-whats-it goats?'

'Believe it or not I've been reading a fascinating biography about the British scientist Dorothea Bate who found Myotragus on Mallorca.'

'I'd like to have a read of that.'

'Are you taking the mick?'

''Course not. I'm just thinking out loud. How about we link this old goat with our new goat hide ranges in the shops? You know, have an ancient Myotragus carcass in the window and some story boards about this Dorothea woman.'

'But Myotragus has nothing to do with the goat of today, or Bengali goats for that matter.'

'Who cares? The public is pretty dumb. We can say the Bengali goat is a direct descendant of Myotragus. Be a fun story.'

I laugh. Who would argue with him? And if a paleontological storm did blow up, George would just milk it for all the marketing it was worth.

'Where would you get the Myotragus carcass, as you put it?'

'Couldn't you nick one from your local Sóller museum?'

I stare at him for a second in disbelief.

He snickers. 'I love winding you up.'

I take a sip of coffee. 'I'll lend you the book when I've finished it. Just a few more chapters to go.'

'Don't forget, guv. I think this old mouse-goat has got a lot going for it. We could mount a little exhibition in the London and New York stores, even Paris when we get it sorted, and have a few old bones lying about... I can see it now.'

He gets up and wanders around his office. 'By the way, that Priscilla Burton, the dog writer, has just given us two hundred grand's worth of business in New York.'

'What? You're kidding.'

'Nope. She wants me to develop a Burton leather line in the stores using her canine fashion predictions for each season. If it goes well, she'll invest more.'

'That's all very well, but don't let her take over. She'll be like one of those unstoppable vines and soon it'll be Burton Leather stores before you can blink.'

'Don't worry, I'm restricting her to a small range in the downstairs accessories section. I've got her ticket.'

He snaps a biscuit in half. 'So how's the merger going?'

'OK, but there's still a lot to sort out. What do you think of Marilyn?'

Rachel had set up a meeting between the two last month and said it had gone well.

'She's got all her marbles but that Jay's a bit flaky. I don't think you should rush into anything.'

'She's keen to merge in August.'

He shakes his head. 'Too soon. Stall her. Anyway, you should be calling the shots, not her.'

I nibble on a biscuit. 'You're right. Besides, Rachel's in no rush. She'd rather wait until we get things totally straight.'

'Sensible girl, is Rachel. Trust your gut, and if I were you I'd hold out for a few more offers. I mean why take the first one that comes along?'

'Bird in the hand.'

'Not if it's a Jay.'

I laugh. George sits opposite me with a triumphant smile playing on his lips. For all his faults, he's not such a bad egg. In fact when the going gets tough he can be a diamond geezer. A diamond geezer with a heart of gold.

**11 a.m., the office, Mayfair**

I'm sitting in my office checking a press release about Charlie Wheeler's new mountain survival range, when the telephone rings. Sarah buzzes me.

'I've got a Mr Samuel Owen on the phone. He says he's a lawyer. Shall I put him through?'

I shrug to myself. 'Why not?'

The voice is very pukka and precise. 'I just wanted to congratulate you on the response you gave to that hoax letter. I found your number through Directory Enquiries.'

I'm mystified. 'Sorry, Mr Owen, what hoax letter?'

There's a pause. 'You haven't seen the latest issue of *Maxim*, the men's magazine?'

'I usually take the *Beano* and *Private Eye*.'

'What I mean is that they've printed excerpts from a letter you sent in reply to one they sent to you about taking on a new human rights charity... It was a hoax.'

A bell is clanging in my head. 'Hang on, it's coming back to me. I received a letter from a Lord something or other whose name I couldn't find in Debrett's or anywhere else.'

'That's because he didn't exist. It was a cruel hoax to see how many PR companies would agree to take on a client however odious and amoral the account. You sent in a corker of a reply. We've all been reading it in the office.'

I feel my face flush. I was well and truly duped and yet in my defence I had smelt a large rat.

'Did they print other replies?'

'Loads. You were the only PR company who turned down the business despite the supposed high fee.'

I'm stunned. Surely other PR companies wouldn't have been quite so shallow – or would they?

'Anyway, must be off, just wanted to say that my colleagues and I were impressed by your no nonsense stand. Well done.'

I'm flabbergasted. What have I started?

Rachel taps on my door. 'I've just taken two really weird calls from guys who wanted to speak to you about something to do with *Maxim* magazine.'

I bury my face in my hands. 'You sent me a privately addressed letter some months ago purporting to be from some Lord.'

'So what?'

'It offered us the chance to take on a human rights charity he was launching for a lot of money.'

'And?' she asks cautiously.

'In reality, it was a load of twaddle. In fact it infuriated me because it was talking about releasing child-killers so I wrote off a fairly savage reply.'

She breathes deeply. 'So what does this have to do with *Maxim*?'

'It appears it was all a hoax set up by the magazine to show that money-grabbing PR bosses have no moral integrity and will take on any account for dosh.'

She sits down in the chair opposite me. 'So what on earth did you write?'

'Just a bit of moral indignation about how we wouldn't touch the account with a barge pole.'

She relaxes. 'Thank heavens. I'd better ask Sarah to run out and get a copy.'

'It's quite funny, I suppose.'

She exhales deeply. 'Not if you were one of the PRs caught out. So, now you've got yourself a male fan club, Joan of Arc.'

She gets up and pauses at the door with an evil smile. 'I suppose at your age that really can't be all that bad.'


**4 p.m., the office, Mayfair**

Dannie is wafting a pristine, white linen handkerchief under Yuri Drakova's nose. Seemingly unaware of it, he sniffs deeply, mascara coursing in sooty rivulets down his cheeks.

'Is bitch! Sometimes with Anastasia, I want to kill her!'

Dannie gives an impatient cough. 'Take the goddam handkerchief, Yuri.'

Huffily, he runs it over his pale, moonlike visage, rubbing his blackened cheeks in circular movements.

Rachel is calm and practical. 'Look, Yuri, the show must go on. If Anastasia refuses to wear the dream dress, we'll just have to find another model. We've got until tomorrow to find someone.'

Yuri resumes his sobbing. 'It is a perfect fit for Anastasia. Do you not know the story of Cinderella? Only one foot fits the shoe. Only one girl fits the dress.'

'That's all very well, but if she's swanned off, we have no choice,' snaps Rachel, thoroughly bored with Yuri's histrionics.

'Maybe I could speak with her,' drawls Dannie, inhaling on her cigarette.

I eye the window, wondering whether I can hop up and open it while they're all deep in discussion.

'What do you think?' Dannie is observing me with dancing eyes.

'I think that Anastasia will come round. Look, Yuri, all she said was that she didn't like the feathers on the bodice. Can't you just remove them?'

'Are you mad? That is part of its magic,' he yelps.

'I'm aware of that, but the Wild Woods launch is tomorrow night. We have two hundred guests descending on us, including the Dutch Ambassador and a raft of press. You've also been paid a lot of money to make the dress. Think about it.'

He gives me a deep frown.

'What she's saying, darling, is cast aside your artistic integrity, take the money and keep Anastasia happy,' says Dannie. She slips me a cool smile.

Rachel is tapping her foot against the table and secretly eyeing her watch.

'OK, I'll do it, but I tell you this: I will never work with that cow again.'

'Fine,' says Dannie. 'I'll call Anastasia to tell her you're removing the feathers.'

'Do what you like. I won't speak with her on the night.'

We all rise.

'Great,' says Rachel impatiently. 'So, let's get on. I've a mountain of calls to make before the launch tomorrow, so if you'll excuse me.'

Dannie kisses her on the cheek. 'It'll all be fine on the night. These Wild Wood guys are going to have a blast. Wait till they see Anastasia in Yuri's spectacular creation. She'll knock 'em dead.'

'I'm sure,' coos Rachel.

Yuri wipes his eyes and snaps his diamante encrusted sun shades back on. We say our farewells at the front door, waving them into the lift.

'Anastasia will knock 'em dead,' I say, mimicking Dannie's laboured American tones. 'She and Yuri will have the press begging for mercy.'

'Yeah,' says Rachel flatly. 'That's what I'm worried about.'

### 7 p.m., Covent Garden

In a smart Italian eatery in Covent Garden – Ed's choice – we wait for the virtuous Veronica to arrive. Apparently she has been increasingly busy with her church duties in Yorkshire which has put a strain on the budding relationship. Ed is nursing a fizzy lemonade and looking morose.

'I can't keep getting on the train to visit her in Yorkshire at weekends. It's exhausting.'

'I thought you said you hadn't been to Yorkshire yet?'

He huffs and puffs. 'OK, fair enough, she's been the one coming down to London but she wants that to change. She thinks I should visit her sometimes.'

'That does seem fair.'

He glugs his lemonade. 'Yes, but I get palpitations on trains.'

'What about your Beta Blockers?'

He flicks a breadcrumb across the table. 'I'm not sure they'd be enough. Besides, I don't want to keep traipsing off to Yorkshire.'

I wonder why on earth Ed started this romance knowing that his paramour was running a church in the far north. He glances up at the door and shooting me a nervous look, stands up. 'She's arrived.'

A smart and composed forty-something woman is heading towards our table. I offer as welcoming a smile as I can. She gives Ed a peck on the cheek and shakes my hand.

'Lovely to meet you at last,' she enthuses.

'You too. Ed talks about you all the time.'

'Is that so?' she says, a tad icily.

A waiter ambles over.

'What would you like?' I ask. My glass of mineral water is nearly empty. Much as I'd love a glass of wine, I'm not sure whether this will meet with Veronica's approval. She holds the drinks menu in front of her and then fumbles for some gold rimmed specs.

'Ah, that's better.' She looks across at my glass. 'Is that all you're having? No wine?'

'Perhaps I could have a little red wine,' I mutter.

'Good idea. Can we have two large glasses of the Merlot,' she says commandingly. 'Best that you stick to the lemonade,' she instructs Ed.

He gives a little cough. 'Absolutely. No alcohol for me. After all, I'm interesting enough without it.'

We both eye him incredulously.

'Naturally, that was a stab at irony,' he says quietly.

'I hear you're an archaeology scholar,' I say.

She laughs. 'Hardly. I was always a bit of a jobbing archaeologist. I wrote a few papers and books but nothing of any real merit.'

Her confidence is overwhelming.

'So what made you change careers?'

She gives me a crisp smile. 'I don't see becoming a deaconess much of a career. More a calling.'

Ouch. First faux-pas of the evening. Ed pulls a face at me when she is fumbling in her handbag for a tissue.

'You know, Scatters is very interested in a strange mouse-goat called Myotragus that once lived in Mallorca.'

She regards him with some impatience. 'You've already told me about this.' She turns to me. 'So what's your fascination with Myotragus?'

'I can't really explain. I just find it exciting to think that, for millions of years, Mallorca had a unique creature roaming its hills. It somehow gives the island a sense of dignity and scientific worth.'

Veronica laughs. 'Goodness, you are hooked! I read about Dorothea Bate at university when I was doing my archaeology PhD. She discovered many things besides Myotragus.'

I nod enthusiastically. 'She had an extraordinary life.'

'I never wanted an extraordinary life. Science only interested me so far and at times sat uneasily with my faith.'

'So are you happy with the life you have now?'

'I'm content with my lot and much happier than I've been in years.'

The wine arrives.

'Shall we look at the menu?' asks Ed. 'I'm starving.'

'He's always hungry,' sighs Veronica, darting him with a motherly glare.

The waiter returns with menus. We study them in silence for a few minutes and then place our orders. As he saunters off, Veronica takes a large swig of wine and then faces both of us with a serene smile.

'Now, before we dine, I'd just like to clear the air.'

I sit up in my chair in some surprise.

'What do you mean?' stutters Ed in alarm.

'I've decided that I'd rather we were just good friends, Ed. It seems silly to pretend that we could be anything more. We simply don't have enough in common.'

His mouth falls open. 'This is a bit sudden and harsh. I mean, you could have told me in private.'

She pats his hand. 'Better to be honest, and why not in front of one of your very closest friends?'

I struggle to keep my composure, feeling horribly awkward in the midst of this romance-not-to-be.

'Now, that's an interesting thought,' I say. 'I suppose we could just have a nice meal together as a way of moving on.'

Veronica gives a little clap. 'Excellent. There we are, let's do just that. Why make a crisis out of a small drama?'

With that, she excuses herself and waltzes off to the Ladies room.

Poor Ed looks crestfallen and utterly confused. I lean across.

'Do you want me to disappear?'

'God no! Please stay.'

I tap the sleeve of his worn jacket. 'Sure you want to stick to lemonade?'

He gives a large sniff. 'On seconds thoughts, no. Bugger it, I'm going to have a double gin and tonic.'

I call the waiter over.

'Veronica won't be pleased,' he says huffily.

'That's the good news, it really won't matter what Veronica thinks anymore.'

'No,' he says with a lightness to his voice. 'You're absolutely right.'

### Thursday 9.20 a.m., Golden Square, Soho

I am sitting on the doorstep of the offices of Red Hot PR wondering whether any member of staff intends to turn up for work today. I have agreed with Marilyn and Jay that I will give a training session to three of their young account executives, partly to gauge their general aptitude but also to ascertain whether they have a clear understanding of how the world of luxury and travel public relations operates. Impatiently, I check my watch and tap out the number of Jay's mobile. He answers on three rings.

'Ooh! Naughty, naughty! Haven't they shown yet? The receptionist should be there by now. Sometimes staff have trouble on the tubes. You know how it is?'

'Not really, Jay. In my office we start at nine. The tubes are a problem for everyone. Your staff just need to get up earlier.'

He gives a nervous laugh. 'Yes, of course, you're right. Must be a hitch. I'm on my way to a meeting but I'll ring one of them and find out what's up. So sorry about this.'

I throw the mobile into my handbag and blow on my icy cold hands. It's a cool, grey day but at least there are birds tweeting in the square. Things can't be so bad. I hear fast footsteps.

'Hi there! So sorry. Had a bit of a late night!'

The young receptionist, in a frightening combination of violet and red, is fumbling with the door keys. She wears a tartan beret over her golden locks and seems to be having difficulty inserting the key. Maybe she's got the DT's.

'There we are,' she says eventually. 'Come on in. Gosh it's chilly out there, isn't it?'

'After the first twenty minutes, you don't feel it,' I say with a glacial smile.

'Right,' she replies sheepishly.

We trudge up two flights of stairs to the reception area where she unlocks another door and begins turning on lights and machines. The photocopier whirrs, the fan heater strikes up and the printer splutters. The sounds of morning in an average office in the city. How different from the crow of a cockerel or the braying of a donkey.

'How d'you take your coffee?' she asks.

'Espresso, please.'

She ambles off into the galley kitchen, while the switchboard begins buzzing. Little coloured lights flash on the display on her desk. I call to her.

'Do you want to take these calls?'

She returns with my cup. 'No, don't worry. The answer machine's on. I'll call them back.'

Heavy footsteps can be heard on the staircase. Two young women poke their heads round the door.

'Hello! Sorry I'm late. Got held up on the tube,' says the thin, petite one.

I size them both up. 'Perhaps I'm mistaken but did we agree to meet at nine?'

The taller one of them bites her lip. 'Yeah, that's right, sorry. I'm afraid I had a bit of a late night, you know how it is?'

I take a sip of my coffee. 'Right, we are now running half an hour late so we'll just have to work through your lunch hour. I have to be out of here by 1.30pm.'

They both stare at me but say nothing.

'I thought there were three of you?'

The taller one, who tells me her name is Bethany, gives a little grunt. 'Nick's always late. Let's just start without him.'

The petite girl extends her hand. 'I'm Sadie, by the way. I've only just started here.'

I follow them both up another flight of stairs to the studio on the third floor. Oh joy of joys, the scarlet and gold bustier is still there hanging on a rail. Bethany and Sadie hang up their coats and fuss around the open kitchen area.

'Can we make a quick coffee?'

'Very quick,' I say.

When they are seated at the big glass table, pen, paper and notes in front of them, the door bangs open and in walks Nick. He is in his early twenties, and sports a black cockatoo punk hairdo, black drainpipes and shirt, and a tan leather jacket. He pulls out a chair at the end of the table and sprawls his legs in front of him.

'I'm Nick. Bit late.'

'Thirty eight minutes late to be exact. That's very late in my books.'

He puffs out his cheeks. 'Sorry about that.'

'Let me guess, you had a late night?'

He sniggers. 'Something like that.'

'That's OK. We'll just work through your lunch hour instead.'

He knits his brows. 'No can do. I'm meeting a mate for a bite.'

'*Were*, Nick. Better send a text to say it's off.'

He gives me a sullen shrug. 'Whatever.'

He makes a call and then pulls some files from his bag. He lies back in his chair.

'Do you have a back problem?' I ask.

'No.'

'You seem to have trouble sitting up straight.'

He exhales deeply. 'I'm fine like this, honestly.'

I get up, pull his chair out and instruct him to lie on the floor.

'What?'

'Come on. Let's get you doing some stretching and breathing exercises before we begin.'

The two girls begin giggling.

He reluctantly lies on the floor while I give him instructions. After a few minutes he can't take any more. 'My back's feeling OK now. I can sit up.'

'Great, I say. Let's begin.'

**4 p.m., Caffè Nero, Curzon Street, Mayfair**

Jay is absorbed with his diary while Marilyn takes the floor.

'I appreciate that the guys were all late in today, but they're normally on time.'

'Bethany told me that they have flexi-time arrival before ten.'

She laughs. 'They just make up the rules. That's not true.'

'In that case, don't you think you should set things straight with them?'

Jay clears his throat. 'I think we're to blame. We're usually out most of the morning and I just assume they're there.'

'Don't you call in just to check?' I ask.

Marilyn nods. 'Yep, we must be more disciplined with the kids. This is why merging with a more structured agency like yours will make such a difference.'

'Yes, but it won't work unless we apply the same rules to all staff.'

'Absolutely,' enthuses Jay.

'You've got to realise that in the fashion world nothing happens before eleven,' says Marilyn.

'Yes, but we don't do fashion so the rules have to change.'

'Very true,' says Marilyn. 'All of this we can do. Look, these are just small teething problems. The kids loved the training session this morning.'

It's my turn to laugh. 'Love isn't the word I'd use.'

'OK they said you were a bit scary but they learned a lot. Nick's stuck your press release rule sheet above his desk.'

'He's a difficult nut to crack although, surprisingly, very capable.'

'Exactly, that's why we need you guys,' pleads Jay. 'We've got the resources and once on board with us, you can do all the stuff you enjoy, training and creative input.'

I stare into my cup of green tea. 'I've had serious chats with my own staff and we're not happy about merging before the autumn.'

Marilyn sighs. 'That's a bit disappointing.'

'I think it's the best option for all of us. The clients need time to come to terms with the changes and from what I've seen today, your office needs to develop some new systems. We have very different office cultures.'

Jay shrugs. 'You're probably right. Why rush this through, Marilyn? Better to get things right.'

She pushes her fair hair from her eyes. 'I'd still like us to formally exchange contracts by July.'

'It's possible, providing we agree financial terms and create a new modus operandi in your office.'

'Absolutely,' smiles Jay. 'We'll be guided by you.'

'Together there's nothing we can't do,' says Marilyn emphatically. 'It's your ticket to freedom.'

I study them both. A ticket to freedom or to a whole lot of trouble?

**7.30 p.m., Wild Woods, Chelsea**

The smooth, minimal interiors of the new Wild Woods store seem to have impressed the media present. A feature writer from *House & Garden* runs an appreciative finger along the polished wood of one of the bedsteads.

'These are all your own designs?' she asks.

'We co-design everything with Johannes Vandenbosch. He's the creator of Wild Woods, as you know,' says Serena, reverentially. 'We're just the UK franchise, really.'

'Can I meet him?'

'Of course, come this way.'

I stand at a distance, watching as Serena weaves through the crowd with the feature writer in tow. She eventually reaches Johannes Vandenbosch, who is deep in conversation with the Dutch Ambassador. I had a brief discussion with the God of Wild Woods earlier and decided that he was a deeply unpleasant and arrogant man. Someone raps me on the shoulder. It's my old chum, Frankie Symonds, who is writing a feature on Wild Woods for the *Financial Times* style section.

'He's quite kosher, you know.'

'Really?' I say.

Frankie straightens her Dior glasses before accepting another glass of champagne from a passing waiter. 'Remember some time back you asked me to sniff out anything about him?'

'I do, but you didn't come back to me.'

'Sorry, it slipped my mind at the time. The truth is that he's a ruthless bully who's made a huge amount of money by setting up factories in dirt cheap places. He pays minimum wages but is within the law and he only uses sustainable hardwood.'

'Not a great calling card then.'

She raises her eyebrows a touch. 'No, but he can put on the charm when he chooses, even if he is totally insincere. He's got eyes as tough as marbles. Trouble is, it's hard to pin any dirt on these guys.'

Marcus glides over to us.

'It's all going so well,' he says excitedly. 'The photocall was a triumph. I loved it when that *Evening Standard* photographer got some waiters to carry Anastasia down the street.'

Frankie laughs. 'That bed must have weighed a ton too. You're lucky none of the waiters damaged their backs. 'Elf & Safety would have had a field day.'

'Thank God Elf & Safety hasn't got a hold on Mallorca yet. Mind you, Brussels has already started interfering in the Nit de Foc events.'

'I beg your pardon?' says Marcus with a shrill laugh.

'They're our traditional *fiestas* where devils dance around with fire crackers. You have to hop about to avoid them.'

'Sounds like fun. Not,' he guffaws.

'It's all quite safe. Anyway Brussels wants to ban it of course.'

'That's a shame,' says Frankie. 'Surely the Mallorcans will fight.'

'You bet. They've already had one protest march in Palma,' I reply.

'Good for them. Shame we Brits are so wet about these things.'

Dannie joins us with Yuri who is wearing a black velvet cape and a silver, curly wig.

'You haven't commented on my hair,' he chides.

Frankie peers at him. 'It's very *soignée*.'

'Thank you,' he gives a cheesy smile. 'As it happens, a barrister friend got it for me and I sprayed it silver.'

'Ingenious,' I say.

Dannie gives me a tiny wink. 'Darling, it's been a wonderful evening. Anastasia is on great form. She's being offered a centre page in one of those men's magazines.'

'*Playboy*?' asks Marcus in some surprise.

'No, I think the writer said it was *GQ*. Could be good for her profile.'

Yuri gives a dramatic shrug. 'All thanks to me. My dress has made her, and that's even without the feathers.'

Dannie raises her eyebrows. 'Let's drop the feather issue, Yuri. It all came good in the end. Let's drink to good times and sweet success.' She raises her glass.

'Yes, here's to Wild Woods London,' I say.

'Hear, hear!' says Frankie.

'Are you flying off tomorrow?' I ask Dannie.

She flinches. 'I was, but my astrological adviser has made me alter my arrangements. She said the BA flight was inauspicious.'

Tetley, Dannie's tea leaf reader and astrological adviser thinks every other flight is inauspicious.

'Was it leaving from Heathrow Terminal Five?' asks Frankie with a grin.

'I think so,' she says innocently.

'Then she's probably done you a favour. They seem to be losing a lot of luggage.'

'Oh my, really?' says Dannie.

I make excuses and slip off in the direction of Rachel, who is talking with Anastasia and a young, foppish twenty-something.

His eyes are welded to the Russian's heaving orbs, which seem to be struggling for freedom within a restrictive black bodice.

'So, I say to Yuri, his dream dress is no good with feathers and finally he is seeing sense.'

'So you fancy yourself as a bit of a designer too?' says the young fop.

'I am designer,' she says imperiously. 'I make own swimwear range with Vladimir Lipov in Moscow.'

'Fantastic. You see, that's the sort of photo shoot we'd have in mind. You know, sort of cool minimal beachwear and Jimmy Choos.'

'OK, here is card. Talk to my agent in Moscow.'

He gives her a cheeky boy grin. 'Great to meet you. Always been a big fan. We'll be in touch.'

She takes his hand in hers and gives him a huge smacker on the cheek. He can't believe his luck, and stumbles off in a state of ecstasy and shock.

'Silly boys. All they want is picture of sexy girl, no?'

Rachel gives a tactful shrug. 'I suppose they're just doing their job. Sex sells.'

'Of course, and if price is right, is no problem.'

'It must be a bit frustrating for an intelligent woman like you,' I suggest for want of anything else to say.

She pouts. 'Not really. I have master's degree in biophysics but I earn nothing in Moscow, so instead I take clothes off for magazines and make much money. Is OK with me.'

She takes a massive sip of vodka and bangs the small glass down on a cabinet. A waiter swiftly removes it.

'Another, please,' she says, swishing her fair tresses from her face.

In the light her hair seems to take on a hint of jade, or perhaps it's just my imagination.

Snatching another frosted glass from the waiter, she gives an icy sneer. 'Ha! Look, there is that pig, George. I must talk with him. He owes me money.'

She waves at Greedy George who is in deep conversation with another journalist. He beckons her over.

Rachel and I wait till she's gone before catching up on the evening's events.

I give her a dazzling smile. 'Well done honey, it's been a blast, a triumph, and Anastasia certainly knocked 'em dead.'

She laughs. 'Cut that bloody American accent. You're really beginning to sound just like Dannie now. It's freaking me out. When you let Tetley start changing your flights I'll get seriously worried.'

'What time shall we wrap this all up?' I ask.

'Another hour should do it. At least Marcus and Serena seem happy with the launch, and that weirdo Vandenbosch.'

'He told me he's half-Dutch and half-Belgian so they were both right about his origins.'

'Whatever he is, I'm glad he's back on a plane to Jakarta tomorrow,' she sighs.

'Fancy dinner somewhere afterwards?'

'You bet. I'm starving. Haven't had a minute for a canapé all night.'

'It would be good to chew the fat about my time with Red Hot today.'

She nods vigorously. 'I'm dying to know how you got on. How was the training?'

'Alright, but there's a lot to sort out.'

'That sounds ominous.'

'Not really. We've just got to make sure this is the right deal for us.'

'And what if it's not?'

I take a glug of champagne and shrug. 'Then I suppose we go back to the drawing board.'

'Are you joking?'

I give her a smile. 'Trust me, I've never been more serious in my life.'

# SIXTEEN

# TOAD IN THE HOLE

An agitated, foamy wave dashes against the gnarled honeycomb rock face that juts out at the tip of the old harbour of Colònia de Sant Jordi, on the south-east coast. In the far distance beckons Illa Cabrera, goat island, largest of a small archipelago of nineteen craggy islands and islets that lie some twelve kilometres from Mallorca's rocky headland. Today a fine mist descends and an anaemic sun has risen half-heartedly above a small gathering of ivory clouds, casting cool white light onto the harbour. We are at the southernmost point of the island, a few kilometres from the luscious blonde sands of Platja des Trenc to the west, and on the eastern side, the small town of Santanyí with its dark rat runs and alleys, and tall limestone buildings. Pep wanders up from the jetty where a vessel is moored. His old friend, Xim (pronounced 'Chim') has loaned him his sailing boat for the weekend and we have been persuaded by Pep to join him, Juana and Angel on a sailing trip to Cabrera. To be granted overnight mooring on Cabrera, declared a national park in 1991, is no mean feat given that only fifty moorings are permitted each day, and applications have to be made well in advance to the Institute for the Conservation of Nature. Luckily it's June, so the demand isn't as great as it would be at the height of the summer season. Pep pulls out a *puro* and quickly lights it, shielding the flame with his other hand.

'It's a fine day for sailing. I reckon we should get there comfortably in time for lunch.'

'But it's only ten o'clock. Surely we should make it before then?'

He exhales a small cloud of smoke. 'Yes, but we'll want to visit Sa Cova Blava on the way and have a swim.'

'When I came here on the tourist vessel, they only stopped on the way back.'

He gives an impatient cough. 'That's the beauty of having our own boat. We can do whatever we like. Anyway, we should head off soon.'

I follow him to the ten-metre vessel, which is liveried in racing green. The sails are tightly lashed, no doubt awaiting their moment of liberation, and the deck is glistening white and spotless. We clamber on board and make our way down the narrow vertical stairs to the saloon. Juana is fussing about in the tiny galley into which we earlier attempted to squeeze all the provisions for the trip. I notice Pep slyly peering into one of the lockers, where he has secreted a large quantity of *puros* together with a bottle of Johnny Walker. He winks at me when I raise my eyebrows in disapproval. Ollie and Angel have already bagged the saloon berths, presumably because they are closest to the tiny fridge where they have stashed their private supply of Coke and chocolate, and Alan is lying on a berth in one of the cabins, reading a book. I casually inspect the bathroom. Of course, bathroom isn't quite the word. In Sinbad the Sailor terms it's known as a 'head', and is about the size of a fridge freezer, with a miniscule lavatory, hand basin and a pump shower that presumably drenches everything in sight when in use. The Scotsman calls to me from his cabin.

'We're going to be very cosy in here. Just enough room for us and the sleeping bags.'

I pop my head round the polished wooden door.

'This boat reminds me of my Wendy house when I was about five, although I think I had a lot more space.'

He laughs. 'Come on, it'll be fun. Besides, with your preoccupation for hoofed beasties, I thought you'd be thrilled to be heading for Goat Island?'

'It's the seafaring element I'm worrying about, not the goats.'

'See it as an adventure.'

I give him a frown. 'Remember the last seafaring adventure we went on with Pep and Juana?'

'Yes but that was a whole week. This is just an overnight.'

Pep taps my shoulder. 'Not still complaining about our training course? You had the time of your life.'

I turn and poke his arm. 'It was pure hell from beginning to end. In fairness that's not entirely true. There were two high points: when you and Alan couldn't clamber back on to the boat, and when you fell overboard.'

He shakes his head. 'Very funny. And what about when you sent the sail flying up the pole?'

Juana tuts from behind him. 'Can you stop arguing? We should set sail.'

I look at my watch. 'Come on Pep, you're the skipper. Get to work.'

Alan puts his book down. 'Come on, let's go up on deck and get ready to undo the fenders.'

We all trip upstairs while the boys continue to play a card game and sip at Coke.

'I need you two up here now. *Vamos!*' growls Pep.

They rise to their feet and somewhat reluctantly follow us all up the stairs.

A few minutes later, the boat vibrates as the engine is engaged and Pep begins weighing anchor. We move slowly out of the harbour. There is little wind and Pep seems relaxed at the wheel, puffing on a *puro* and examining the compass before him as he steers through the other vessels. Juana is busy with the anchor windlass. We help the boys undo the fenders and await instructions. Soon we are out on an open sea, enjoying the views while Pep, Juana and the boys fiddle with the mainsail.

'Perhaps we should lend a hand?' asks the Scotsman.

I shake my head. 'Look we're both totally incompetent at this sailing lark so we might as well just let the others get on with it. I'm happy to do all the cooking instead.'

He nods. 'I'll help with the washing up and drink pouring.'

I laugh. 'Yes, that's an important task.'

The sun finally decides to have a dander and the sky is filled with glorious light. A robust wind comes in from the west and soon we are bumping along the waves, a light spume kissing our cheeks. I lie back against the side of the deck and breathe in the briny air. Small craft bob about in the waves, their owners waving as we skim by. An hour into the voyage we can see the scrubby profile of the smaller islands and before long Cabrera, the chunky rock that juts out like an enormous chin on the blue horizon. True to his word, Pep deviates from the route to take in a spectacularly high cave known as *Sa Cova Blava*, the blue grotto, which emits an extraordinarily pure blue light. We sail right into the undisturbed cave, its mouth being at least five times the height of our boat, and dive off into the cool, clear water. It is a deep blue, and as clean and refreshing as a glacier mint. Pep offers a cool beer as we sit on deck draped in towels, dripping salty water all over the pristine floor.

Out on the open sea, the air is warm and a gentle sun caresses our cool, damp skin as we make our final approach towards Cabrera's sheltered harbour, Es Port. We sail round a piece of harsh, brawny headland, its low hills dotted with pines, wild olive and juniper trees, and finally see ahead of us the port and small jetty. We are guided in by one of the nature reserve officials and are surprised to see we are one of only five boats. We drop anchor and help the boys as they put out the fenders.

'Did you both have a nice rest?' asks Ollie in some amusement.

'Yes, thanks. We thought it best to leave you lot to do the work since you're the experts.'

He tuts. 'I haven't got a clue. I just do what Angel and Pep tell me.'

Pep staggers up the bobbing deck with a massive smile.

'Wasn't that simple? No storms, high seas, random sharks, killer whales…'

'No mermaids,' cuts in the Scotsman.

Pep ruffles his grey mane and gives a sniff. 'Yes, that's a shame. We'll have to do better on the way back.'

'Where's Juana?' I ask.

'Chatting up the nature reserve guy, of course. He's quite a stud.'

I get up and stretch my limbs. 'I suppose it's time for lunch. Are you happy for me to cobble something together?'

'You bet!' says the Scotsman. 'I'm starving.'

'And what about another beer or better still a glass of *rosado*?' asks Pep.

Alan follows me towards the ladder. 'Butler service at the ready. Give me a minute, *mon amic*.'

Pep nods cheerfully and, sprawling on some cushions, the sun on his face, he breaks open a pack of *puros*. '*Es la vida!*' he cries in our direction. 'This really is the life.'

It's an idyllic morning, with not the slightest hint of a cloud. Much to my own astonishment, I wake up early feeling refreshed and listen to the sound of the sea birds circling high in the sky beyond my cabin window. I have had a wonderful night's sleep in the cramped berth, rocked into soporific bliss by the gentle swell of the water in whose gigantic hands we lie. After a robust breakfast of eggs, sausages and fried, crispy *serrano* ham, we head off along the wide, dusty track which sweeps up from the harbour towards the castle. This crumbling relic was originally a defence against plundering pirates back in the fourteenth century, and sits up high on a hill. Tofol, one of the nature reserve guides, agrees to accompany us, much to Juana's delight.

'He's so informative,' she coos.

'He's young enough to be your son,' grumbles Pep.

The sun beats down, and soon we are perspiring heavily. We stop on the track and drink from water bottles. Alan takes out his binoculars and studies the skies.

'Would you believe that! There's an Audouin gull, and look – a peregrine falcon.'

We cluster round his binoculars, taking it in turns to scan the sky.

'That's an osprey over there, isn't it?' asks Juana.

'So it is,' says the Scotsman, delighted to see such wonderful bird specimens.

Tofol shrugs his broad shoulders. 'We have many species here, such as the Cory's shearwater and Eleanor's falcon. Don't forget we also have dolphins which we might spot later.'

The two boys sit on the ground fumbling with small plastic bags in their rucksacks.

'What about turtles?' asks Ollie.

'*La tortuga boba* does comes here but it's rare to see one. At certain times of the year the turtles come to lay their eggs on the beach.'

'I'd love to see that,' says Ollie wistfully.

Angel pulls some small pieces of fruit from a plastic bag and places it by some scrub. Ollie does the same. A few seconds later there's a crackling in the bracken and a little green head pops out. Tofol laughs.

'I told the boys to bring some fruit for the lizards.'

'It's got a bluish tummy, look!' cries Angel, leaning down to study it more closely.

'It's the famous Lilford wall lizard,' says Tofol. 'You know, eighty per cent of the world population of Balearic lizards lives in this one park.'

'Is that so?' says Juana, enthralled.

Pep raises his eyes and chortles to himself in Mallorquin. After a few minutes watching the Lilford lizard we begin plodding up the hill to the summit. The castle itself is a bit of a disappointment, being little more than a rocky shell, but the views out to sea are spectacular. Tofol flexes his muscles and begins stretching while Juana looks on appreciatively.

'You know,' he says. 'We had everyone on this island at some time – Romans, Arabs, Talayots, and Berber pirates. I will take you to see the memorial for the prisoners who died here during the Napoleonic wars.'

Pep yawns. 'That sounds like fun.'

Tofol regards him sternly. 'It's a terrible part of the island's history. When the Spanish defeated the French in the battle of Bailén, a reclusion camp was set up here in 1809 to accommodate 9,000 prisoners. Five years later, when peace was declared, only 3,600 were still alive and finally repatriated.'

'Why did so few survive?' asks Ollie.

'Most starved to death,' says Tofol.

'And the others were eaten by giant lizards,' says Pep.

We all snigger but Juana upbraids him.

'Will you quit playing the fool?'

Pep puffs out his cheeks. 'It happened two hundred years ago. What's the point of shedding tears now?'

'It's still tragic,' says Juana.

'So who occupied Cabrera until the time it became a nature reserve?' asks the Scotsman.

Tofol kicks a small stone over the grey rock face.

'The Feliu family had private ownership for a time from the late 1800s and then the Spanish military occupied the island for defence reasons from 1916 until the eighties.'

We walk around the castle grounds, while Pep stays resolutely where he is, lighting up a *puro* and studying the sea with Alan's binoculars.

'Didn't the Roman historian, Pliny, say that Hannibal was born here?' I ask.

'Is that so?' says Tofol, turning to face me. 'There are all sorts of myths about this island.'

'Can we carry on walking up here?' asks Juana, pointing ahead.

'I'm afraid not. We only allow certain routes for the public. Let's head back to the harbour and follow the path to the Napoleonic obelisk. I can also show you the cemetery and memorial to the German soldier shot down during World War Two.'

Pep nearly chokes on his cigar. 'I'd rather see the local lap-dancing club.'

'We haven't installed one of those yet,' says Tofol dryly. 'You don't have to come. You can look for dolphins by the sea if you prefer.'

'Sounds good to me,' says Pep. 'You take Juana and the others on the death tour and I'll protect the boat.'

Juana shoots him a poisonous look, while the rest of us stifle grins. Soon we arrive back in the harbour. Tofol is walking slowly behind everyone else, Juana hanging on his every word. Pep slaps Alan on the back.

'OK, *mon amic*, enjoy your tour. I'll hang out on the boat and see you all in an hour or so.'

Juana puts her hands on her hips. 'Before you go, you might like to hear what Tofol just said?'

'Sorry, what was that?' says Pep, no doubt dreaming of the beer and large *puro* he will reward himself with when back on the boat.

'He was telling me about all the different fauna and flora species on Cabrera.'

Pep throws his arms wide. '*Hombre*! I already know all this.'

She fixes her almond eyes on him. 'Please, do enlighten us all.'

He gives a little smirk and wink in Ollie's direction. 'Now then, there are about five hundred species of plants, two hundred species of fish, more than a hundred species of migrating birds, erm, two hundred species of marine algae...'

'*Muy impresionante,*' says Tofol, clapping his hand together. Very impressive.

Juana's mouth drops open. 'How do you know all this?'

'Natural intelligence, my little vulture.'

He saunters happily towards the jetty while we carry on along the path.

I whisper to Ollie. 'Pep's a dark horse. How do you think he knew all that?'

'Easy, I read out those statistics to him this morning from my Cabrera nature guide.'

'The cheat!' I laugh out loud.

'He didn't exactly cheat,' says Ollie defensively. 'Mind you he got one thing wrong.'

'What was that?'

'There are one hundred and sixty-two species of marine algae.'

I regard my son in some puzzlement, wondering how someone with such a passion for knowledge seems to display so little interest in the majority of his school subjects.

'He also forgot that there are ten subspecies of lizards too.'

'Maybe you should work in a nature reserve when you're older.'

'As long as it's got tennis courts,' he says matter-of-factly.

Alan and Angel beckon us over to see a Lilford lizard scuttling in the dry scrub. We watch as its little grey-green body slithers under a rock. Juana and the guide are far ahead of us.

'Come on chaps, let's get going,' says Alan. 'I'm already thinking about lunch.'

'What are we having?' asks Angel.

'Toad in the hole,' I reply. 'The oven on board apparently works very well.'

'What?' he asks in alarm. 'Toad? Are you joking?'

Ollie tuts. 'It's not a real toad, silly.'

'I'm just going to use up the sausages and *serrano* ham left over from breakfast. It's just a silly recipe name.'

Angel looks doubtful. 'OK, but if I hear one little croak in the boat I'm not eating it.'

Ollie gives me a nudge. 'Thinking about it, that Lilford lizard looks pretty delicious. How about we stick him in the pot too?'

'Toad and lizard in the hole? That's novel,' I reply.

Angel thumps Ollie on the back and laughs. 'You English are disgusting.'

'And what about you Mallorcans? You eat garden snails!'

'At least we don't hunt foxes.'

'But you kill bulls.'

They run up the path together bickering and giggling under the blazing midday sun.

The crossing back to Colònia de Sant Jordi is uneventful. At one stage I only just avoided being hit by the boom but, aside from a few blisters, bumps and bruises, we're all ship shape and in good spirits. We sail slowly into the harbour, Pep at the helm, looking like the original Captain Birds Eye with his grey locks flowing behind him. We drop anchor and spend some time gathering up our final belongings and cleaning the deck. The sun sits like a fat, contemplative Buddha high above us, but soon the dusk will descend. Yawning, we carry our bags and rucksacks to the cars and prepare for the journey back to Sóller. The boys say their farewells.

'You've really caught the sun,' the Scotsman says to me.

'Coming from him, that's rich!' shouts Pep. 'He looked like a Berber pirate before the sun even had a chance to blink at him.'

'You're only jealous of my bronzed, honed body,' quips the Scotsman.

'That's very funny,' says Juana, giving him a friendly push.

He looks somewhat deflated while Pep slaps him on the back.

'*Vale, mon amics*, time to go. I hope you'll come with us on the high seas again. You see, it wasn't so bad.'

'True, it could have been a lot worse,' I say, 'and we only went off course once.'

'What? No we didn't!' protests Pep.

'Only kidding.'

He punches my arm.

'We're thinking of sailing over to Menorca for the Sant Juan festival next year. What do you think?'

'Yes, we'd be up for another adventure,' says Alan.

'Good, let's talk soon.'

We watch as their car draws out ahead of us through the sleepy little harbour and on to the darkening road.

'Did you really mean that?'

'What?' asks the Scotsman, starting the car's engine.

'About going all the way to Menorca with them?'

He shrugs. 'Maybe, after all we seemed to get the hang of it in the end.'

I nod. 'Copious amounts of cava helped.'

He laughs. 'Shall we be off then?'

A sleepy voice comes from the back of the car. 'Aye, aye Cap'n, full steam ahead.'

We set off through the harbour. I'm happy that Ollie's in a drowsy state. Hopefully he can have a kip in the car and won't feel too exhausted for school in the morning. Suddenly his head bobs up. 'Did you know that the largest luxury yacht was owned by the Crown Prince of Dubai?'

'No,' I sigh, 'Now go to sleep.'

He yawns heavily. 'It was called *Platinum* and was a hundred and sixty metres long.'

'Fascinating.'

Alan chuckles. 'Apparently, it was owned by the Sultan of Brunei's brother before he had a few financial problems. I think Sheik Maktoum's rumoured to be renaming it Golden Star but there's supposed to be a new yacht that's nearly two hundred metres long. Isn't that right, Ollie?'

Silence. I turn round, relieved to see that our little boffin has finally fallen fast asleep.

It's a crisp, bright morning. The Scotsman is sniffing the air rather like a deer on the scent. He looks up at the fug forming over the valley and curses.

'You see, this is what happens,' he says flatly.

'What do you mean?' I ask.

'Well today is the last day you can burn bonfires so everyone's gone mad. The air's full of smoke.'

The Scotsman is right. A strong acrid smell clogs the air and a soft white blanket of smoke unrolls like muslin across the sky. We stroll past the blossoming oleanders in their white and rose hues and over to the cattery building which is almost complete.

'It's looking good, isn't it?' I say.

He nods. 'Small and modest, but that's enough for now. Let's see if there's much interest and we can think about something more substantial.'

'What do you mean?'

'In reality, we're not going to be able to have many cats here save those of some chums. It might be worth investing in something official and bigger on some agricultural land.'

'I've thought about that too. Let's see how we get on. Anyway, I hope that order I placed at the Birmingham cat fair comes through soon.'

'They said it would be here this month. Once all that cat kit arrives, Stefan and the guys can finish it off.'

We plod inside the wooden edifice which has a small office and storage area and individual sleeping huts and runs for our cats. There is a comforting smell of wood and newly applied linseed oil on the beams.

'This would make a great storage area for all my tools,' says the Scotsman.

'Don't even think about it,' I warn.

'Well, if all else fails, it's a damned useful storage space.'

We walk over to the corral, where Salvador is spying on us through a chink in the fence. I creep up on the other side and shout, 'Boo!' He jumps back in some irritation and fixing his beady eyes on me, curses loudly in cockerel-speak. Alan pushes my arm.

'You are daft! Come on, let's get going. You've got all that stuff to check for Rachel before we go out.'

'I've also got to finish that marketing document for George. He's signing on the Paris store today and wants my input on the new direction.'

'That's incredible. Havana Leather is cleaning up. What about the Russian store?'

I shake my head. 'I don't really want to think about that. Dannie and Anastasia are involved.'

'I thought he and Anastasia were at war?'

I give a grimace. 'It's a sort of war and peace saga. They're currently in a love-in because he's promised Anastasia she can create a leather swimwear range for the new Moscow store.'

The Scotsman claps his hands together with mirth. 'Leather bikinis! Whatever next?'

We reach the kitchen. He pauses for a moment.

'So what news on the Red Hot PR front?'

'I don't know. They're in the midst of a deal with another fashion agency. Marilyn assures me all is on course.'

He sighs deeply. 'I really think we've got to be careful. There's a lot at stake.'

'I know, but it is a firm offer on the table.'

'There could be others.'

I follow him into the kitchen. 'But when? We could decline this merger and find ourselves out in the cold.'

He puts on the kettle. 'I doubt it. Maybe you've got to have a little more self-belief.'

'If only life were that simple.'

He pulls out the tea caddy. 'Perhaps it's a case of putting out feelers and being more in control rather than just waiting by the phone.'

'Maybe you're right,' I say and, in a pensive mood, ascend the stairs to the office.

A few hours later, we set off to the local supermarket in our battered old car. Our winding streets are as curvy as Sophia Loren and as narrow as a couple of chopsticks, so scraping against rocky walls is an everyday hazard. It's fair to say that our car looks as though its spent half its natural life speeding through a cheese grater, a phenomenon which Vincente, the owner of our local car hire company, cheerfully takes in his stride.

We pull out of our drive and are bumping along the quiet, mud caked lanes towards the town when disaster strikes.

Suddenly the car begins listing on one side. We draw to a halt, put on the hazard light and get out to inspect the problem. In doesn't take long to discover that our front tyre is as flat as a *tortilla*. We find that there's no jack in the boot, so we head off slowly to Vincente's repair shop, luckily only five minutes away. Limping into the garage just after 1 p.m., we are relieved to spot a mechanic in overalls sitting outside the entrance, munching on a *bocadillo* and drinking a beer. The Scotsman calls over to him.

'We've got a puncture, any chance of fixing a new wheel?'

The man sighs but beckons us inside, tossing his lunch onto the bench.

'Sorry to disturb your break,' we mumble in unison.

Pottering about the garage, he makes some tests with an air pressure gauge, announcing that a sharp stone is the culprit. He removes the old tyre and replaces it with the filthy spare lurking in the boot, and carefully winches it into place. Alan offers to help but he waves him away with the words, *'tranquillo, tranquillo'*. When the job is done, he wipes his hands on a cloth, evidently keen to get back to his lunch.

'Fantastic!' beams the Scotsman. 'Thank you so much. Now, one more thing, you couldn't take a quick look at my faulty seat belt?'

Our hero shakes his head. 'I'm sorry, but you're going to have to ask the garage mechanic.'

We gape at him. 'But aren't you Tofol's mechanic?' I ask.

'Me? I own the bicycle shop next door.'

'So you don't work here at all?' Alan quizzes.

'No, I was just having my lunch outside on the bench as I always do.'

'But why on earth did you change our wheel?' I persist.

He shrugs good-naturedly. 'I thought you were tourists needing some help.'

'What can I say?' says Alan. 'Please let me offer you some money.'

He tuts. 'That wouldn't do. It only took me a few minutes.'

We thank him again and tell him our names. He in turn says he is Toni. It transpires that he is used to old and temperamental mountain bikes and we promise to pop by his own store with Alan's misfit of a bike, which is becoming increasingly wayward with age. Toni beckons us to join him on the bench outside until the garage mechanic returns. Within a few minutes he appears, laughing cheerfully about the mistaken identity, and promises to take a look at the errant seat belt. Fifteen minutes later he has rectified the problem and together they wave us off up the road. We assure Toni that we'll be back to share a beer with him on the bench one day – a threat which will probably send the poor man scuttling into the back of his bicycle workshop to hide for evermore.

'Don't people like Toni restore your faith in human nature?' says the Scotsman with gusto, as we head for the supermarket car park.

'They most certainly do.' I reply. 'Without a Toni in our lives, where would we be?'

It's late on Saturday night and, once again, I find myself incarcerated upstairs, staring at my computer screen. Dannie, not to be outdone by Greedy George, has taken a lease on new retail premises in Paris and has urgently asked me to come up with a public relations campaign for the launch period of Miller Magic Interiors. Lying

on the desk next to me is *Discovering Dorothea*. I have reached
chapter fifteen and am desperate to finish it. Deep and low muffled
voices form a hazy background buzz from the room next door,
where Ollie is watching an Indiana Jones adventure. Maddeningly,
by the timbre I can just about separate the different voices but
the volume's too low for me to work out who the characters are.
I upbraid myself for trying to eavesdrop beyond the closed door.
Besides, I have more than enough work to be getting on with. The
frogs offer a more soothing diversion, rhythmically croaking in the
still dark night beyond my open window. Warm, aromatic air wafts
into the room, fusing the dry tang of rosemary with the sweetness
of rose and honeysuckle. On a cushion, Inko sits and purrs, the
sound blending harmoniously with the hypnotic song of my frogs.
I close my eyes and think back to *The Frogs*, a work I once studied
by the Greek comic poet, Aristophanes.

> *Children Of the marshy lake,*
> *Your choral melody awake,*
> *Now let every tuneful throat*
> *Trickling pour the dulcet note,*
> *Koax koax,*
> *Sing the song which most we love*
> *In praise of Bacchus, son of Jove,*
> *The song we sing, when hot with wine*
> *The people crowd to Limnae's shrine-*
> *Brekekekex, koax, koax.*

I sit up in my chair. A new sound rents the air. A harsh croak,
slightly metallic, dull and persistent. With mounting excitement, I
jump up and run from the room.

'What's up?' yells Ollie, turning down the volume to his film.

'I think it's Johnny.'

'You're joking?'

He patters after me in bare feet. Alan greets us at the bottom of the stairs.

'What's up?'

This is beginning to feel like a scene from *Chicken Licken*, except the sky hasn't fallen in and we're on our way to see a toad.

'Are you sure? You really think it's Johnny?'

We carefully open the front door and tiptoe over to the pond. The lads take a break from their crooning as soon as we appear. There's silence. We hardly breathe. Ollie's silhouette gives me a silent shrug, while Alan puts a finger gently to his mouth. We wait. We wait. Then we hear it. A deep, ungainly croak. Something in its tone has a hint of reproach and angst, or am I just hallucinating? I steal up the steps to the side of the pond, listening intently with head half cocked to the intermittent call. Finally my eyes alight on a small patch of mud and weeds, and there, emblazoned in moonlight and peering up at me from inside the deep well of a rock, is Johnny.

'It's Johnny! I'm hooooommme!'

Did he really say that? Ollie is at my side.

'So, can you see anything?' he says excitedly.

I move aside incapable of words.

He gasps. 'It is him. He's really come home!'

Alan jostles to see into the hole. 'My God, who would have believed it? Shall I get a torch?'

I tut loudly. 'Of course not. Johnny needs peace and quiet. He must have been through the wars to get here.'

'But how did he get here?' mutters the Scotsman.

'Thumbed a lift,' says Ollie. 'How else?'

We return to the house, desperate not to frighten him away.

'This is cause for a celebration,' says the Scotsman. 'I'm going to open a bottle of cava.'

He fumbles in the fridge and soon I hear the dull pop of a cork. Ollie holds out his hand.

'OK, a *soupçon* for you too,' Alan says.

He passes me a champagne flute.

'You've got tears in your eyes,' splutters Ollie, mid glug. 'I don't believe it.'

I give him a shove. 'It's a small miracle. Let me have my moment of sentimentality.'

Alan raises his glass. 'To Johnny!'

'To Johnny!' Ollie cries.

'To Johnny,' I say, 'Our little toad who, against the odds, found his way home.'

# SEVENTEEN

# THE CAT'S WHISKERS

Ollie and I are walking through Sóller, laden down with cat provisions. Although my order to a major cattery supplier has arrived, there are still odds and ends to buy before we officially open. We have spent an inordinate amount of time in the local pet shop, sifting through cat accessories and toys and discussing with the owner the benefits of one cat litter over another. He strongly recommends the bulk buying of loose food granules for economic reasons but then frets about the benefits of chicken over beef or vegetables. Will we be accommodating vegetarian or vegan cats? What about oriental and foreign breeds? I hunch my shoulders. Well, if that's the case, what would he recommend and does he, for example, stock a halal cat food range? He hesitates, frowns, then shakes his head. Then there's of course the question of storage and how we keep our rural rodent chums at bay. We walk along the cobbled pavement of Carrer Sa Mar, stopping every now and then to straighten our backs. Javier, from Colmado Sa Luna, our local deli, is walking jauntily along the street.

'Need a hand?'

'*Gracies*, but we're OK. Only another few moments of agony until we reach the car park.'

He laughs. 'Don't forget to come by tomorrow. Your favourite Pyrenees goat cheese has arrived.'

'You and your silly old goats!' exclaims Ollie, placing his bags on the ground to massage his cramped fingers. I stand next to him, wondering why I didn't bring the car nearer the town square. Then I remind myself that it would probably be easier to find a flying pig circling the town church than a free parking space.

'I'm going to have a break for a second,' announces my son. He squats on the stone pavement and rubs his hands. Meanwhile I pace up and down, nosily peering through the glass fronted doors of the elegant terraced houses that give on to the street. All have massive, ancient wooden doors drawn back on either side of the arched doorways. When the occupants are in residence during the daytime they remain open to let in the light and at nightfall are somewhat laboriously closed with the aid of numerous bolts and giant locks from a bygone age. There is something wonderfully voyeuristic about peeping into the dark interiors of these grand old buildings. Rather like a Tardis, a Sóller townhouse has hidden depths. Viewed from the street, it appears lean and tall, and one imagines the rooms to be narrow and perhaps angular, but not a bit of it. Beyond the cobbled *entrada,* the wide front entrance hall, is a labyrinth of whispering hallways and gracious, high ceilinged rooms with polished mahogany doors, vast marble fireplaces and frescoes of breathtaking beauty. The greatest prize of all is the garden. Secreted in walled bliss, a garden of outstanding maturity amazes the visitor's eye. There will be vast and noble plane, lemon and olive trees, small arbours of fruit trees and flowers, exquisite patios and pavilions, ponds, and vine cluttered stone huts, all hidden away in the very heart of the town. An invitation to view such treasures does not come easily, and so the passer-by or tourist must content himself solely with a casual peek at the house courtesy of the splendid *entrada*. This formal space customarily boasts an antique wooden chest, rocking chair with antimacassar, sombre furniture and an assortment of historical family artefacts hanging from rusty nails on uneven white-washed walls. Some *entradas* yawn on to a wide internal corridor that leads directly to the leafy and spacious garden beyond, an unexpected prize for the nosy parker at street level.

Venturing towards a house that has previously escaped my scrutiny, I peer through the old glass fronted door into the gloomy interior. Aside from the usual suspects, upright wicker chairs, chest and armchair, I spy something most peculiar. At first I wonder if it's a trick of the light tugging at an already overstretched imagination but no. There, suspended from a doorframe just beyond the *entrada*, is a goat. I step back and call to Ollie.

'There's a goat in here… I think it's real.'

He shakes his head wearily. 'What are you talking about, mother?'

In some irritation he stumbles over the pile of bloated plastic bags at his feet and stomps up to the house.

He turns to me. 'You know it's very rude to look through other people's front doors.'

'Yes, but it's very boring waiting for you to catch your breath.'

He barges past me and frames his eyes with his hands to see through the glass.

'It's a brown and white goat.'

'See, I told you so!'

'But it isn't a real one, you ninny. It's a full-sized, fake goat.'

He pulls me roughly by the sleeve and walks me back to where our bags are sagging all over the pavement. A slightly disapproving elderly lady steps over them and gives us a stern look as she passes. I mumble '*lo siento*'. Sorry.

'Why would anyone hang a life-sized, fake goat from the door of their *entrada*?' I ask.

He frowns. 'Who knows, or cares for that matter?'

We pick up our load and carry on slowly towards the car park.

'Doesn't it bother you? You see, that will niggle me for hours.'

'That's because you've obviously got nothing better to do.'

I hoist a bag over one shoulder. 'That's not true, Ollie. It's just natural curiosity.'

We reach the car. Depositing his load by the door of the boot, he gives me a sly grin. 'Well all I can say is, just remember what curiosity did to the cat.'

Catalina and I are covered in soap suds. We have been cleaning out the cattery hut, scrubbing the concrete floors, bleaching down surfaces and generally making it clean and habitable. Occasionally a member of the steering committee – Inko, Minky or Orlando – will appear at the door and give a purr of approval or caterwaul of disgust. Salvador and his harem have been regarding our toings and froings with mounting interest, taking it in turns to sidle up to the corral fence to peep furtively through the wooden slats. After a few minutes of spying, one or other will stalk back to the gang to report on progress, whereupon they will natter conspiratorially with much clucking and fussing, no doubt sharing hearty reservations about our proposed venture. Alan appears in the doorway, a dark figure surrounded by fierce sunshine.

'Can you break for a minute?' I've got Rachel on the phone.'

I pull off my pink rubber gloves and take the mobile phone from him.

'How's it going?' says Rachel.

'All on course, thanks, but still a lot more to do.'

'I'm sure. Look, I just wanted to have a quick word. Your chum Fiona has just called to say she's had a call from another company interested in merging with us.'

I walk under one of the lemon trees, out of the sun. 'But it was Fiona who told us about Marilyn and Jay in the first place.'

She gives a sharp cough. 'I know. It seems she's heard about another company keen to merge on a no-strings basis for you.'

'It's a bit late in the day. We're supposed to be signing the contract next week.'

There's a pause on the line.

'To be honest, I have severe reservations about whether Red Hot is the right partner. My instinct's to hold off and speak to a few other companies like this one.'

With the mobile propped against my ear, I twiddle with one of the citrus leaves, finally pulling it off and shredding it into tiny brittle pieces. Given that Rachel and I both have serious reservations about the merger, maybe we should just call it a day and investigate new leads.

'Are you still there?'

'Sorry, Rachel. I'm just mulling everything over. I've got a lot on with the cattery opening this week. Let me talk to Alan about all this.'

'Fiona wants you to call her as soon as possible.'

Placing the mobile in the pocket of my shorts, I pace around the tree for a few moments, considering our options. Our accountant and lawyer are just putting the finishing touches to the contracts with the huge legal and accountancy firms acting for Marilyn and Jay. They're not going to be happy about us pulling out at this stage, but that's too bad – and they'll still get their fee anyway. And what of our clients and staff? At least we haven't confirmed the merger was going ahead. They'll live with it.

'Penny for them?' says the Scotsman, strolling across and cutting a lemon from the tree. He sniffs its skin. 'That pruning I did has paid off. Do you remember how scrawny the branches used to be?'

I laugh.

'What's so funny?'

'It's just that in the middle of a mini crisis, you're talking about pruning.'

He smiles. 'Can't be that much of a crisis if it's work related. Don't tell me Red Hot has called off the deal?'

I repeat my conversation with Rachel. He looks out over the hills and scratches his head.

'Why not give Fiona a call and find out more? You've obviously made up your mind that this merger's not going to work.'

We walk through the orchard, carefully avoiding the spiky and gnarled silvery branches that reach out to touch our skin.

'Besides, just because we have another venture blossoming here doesn't mean we have to race to tie up loose ends in London. Maybe it's better to exercise a little of the old Mallorcan *poc a poc* philosophy.'

'Yes, you're right. I'll have a word with Fiona. Besides, it will take so much pressure off just to take things step by step.'

He folds his arms. 'As it happens, an old colleague runs one of these agencies that puts like-minded companies together for mergers. I could give him a call too. Maybe it's time for us to start calling the shots now.'

We head back to the cattery. 'I'll talk to the clients.'

Alan shrugs. 'Fine, but I doubt they'll be bothered. You told them it wasn't a done deal. Just make sure you put a positive spin on it.'

'George had his doubts.'

He chuckles. 'For all his faults, he's a shrewd operator.'

Catalina comes over, wiping her hand on an old towel. 'Problems at work?'

'We were just discussing the merger.'

She yawns. 'Don't worry, it'll all work out, and if it doesn't something else will turn up.'

'Exactly,' says the Scotsman.

'Now, we need to decide where we put the cat baskets and detergents. I was thinking of the wall cupboards...'

I follow her into the cattery while the Scotsman beats a hasty retreat to his *abajo*.

The night is as dark as a liquorice stick. Ollie is sitting up in bed reading by the light of his bedside lamp. I slope into his room and sit on his rocking horse.

'Hey, don't break Bertie. He's not used to heavy weights.'

I give him a pert smile. 'Thanks a lot, my darling boy.'

He hoists himself up and peers at me.

'You wouldn't believe it, but about eighty per cent of lions do nothing all day long, just sleep and hang out.'

'Is that so? Are they male?'

'Mostly. Believe it or not, a lot of the giant male cats rely on the female to bring up the cubs, find the food and do all the work.'

'So, quite similar to the human world then?'

'Pretty much, I guess,' he says. 'They're not stupid.'

I look out into the orchards, searching for the silent lemon trees heavy with new fruit, but it's too dark. 'Sometimes I wish I was a lion.'

He titters. 'No, you don't. You'd be bored stiff. You're more of a cheetah. They're always running. Did you know a cheetah can accelerate from walking pace to seventy-five kilometres per hour in just two seconds?'

'No. Can we quit University Challenge for a moment?'

He gives me a superior sniff. 'Just trying to educate you.'

'I was wondering about the goat in the doorway.'

He slams down his book. 'Look, it was just a replica goat. Maybe the owner of the house is as mad about goats as you are. What is wrong with you?'

I potter from his room, down the stairs to the *entrada* and out to the pond. The frogs are in fine fettle, leaping about and singing some rowdy number at the tops of their voices. I take a step closer and the revelry stops. Maybe some hidden amphibian conductor clasping a weed baton has whipped it powerfully through the air with the instructive croak of, '*Fin!*' The end!

I search around the old hollow in the rock that Johnny has taken to occupying of late. He isn't there. Bending down, I scrutinise the undergrowth. There's a rustle from the long grass.

'That fooled you. I'm over here.'

The American twang cuts through the eerie silence.

'Johnny, where have you been?'

'Hanging out, catching a few flies and listening to the boys tuning up.'

I sit down on the grass.

'So what's new, Miss Busy Lizzy?'

'The cattery's all shipshape. We have the first three inmates arriving at the end of this week.'

There's a rasp in his throat. 'Jeez. I still can't believe you're going ahead with that crazy scheme. If any of those mogs escape there's gonna be trouble for us boys.'

'Please, I don't need another headache at the moment. But they won't stand a chance of escaping, believe me.'

He puffs out his chest and observes me with a sardonic smile. 'Let's hope you're right, wise guy. So what's with the headache?'

'It's just that I'm about to turn down a potential merger. I feel sorry for the other company.'

He grunts. 'Dry your eyes, for crissakes, and get real! If the deal sucks, dump it.'

'We got quite far down the line so I feel some guilt.'

'But have you signed the piece of paper?'

'No.'

'Then ditch the deal.'

We sit in silence for a few moments and then without warning he dashes out his tongue and catches a passing insect. 'Del-ic-i-ous!'

'That's disgusting.'

'Guy's gotta survive.'

'Talking of survival, I never asked you – how did you cope when our house guest from hell, Bill Spears, dumped you in the Tramuntanas?'

He chews thoughtfully on his insect and then blinks. 'It was a shock, I've gotta tell you. One minute snacking on a fly near the pond, the next stuffed into a plastic box and taken on a nightmare journey.'

He gives a little croak. 'Sorry, got a frog in my throat. So yeah, where was I? That doctor turfs me out of the box, and drives off. I hopped about a bit, got talking to a few *ferrerets* – there's a load of those tadpole-carrying guys up there – and spent some months chilling out. Finally I figured how to get back here.'

'How?'

'A very long hop, skip and a jump, I can tell you.'

'We're glad you're back.'

He laughs. 'Don't go all sentimental on me. I hate schmaltz. Gotta run. I'll be seeing ya!'

He makes a wide leap and disappears into the murky depths of the pond. Ollie is staring at me from the open doorway.

'Talking to your imaginary little friend again?' he asks.

'I was, as a matter of fact. Johnny's still a bit cynical about the cattery.'

Ollie gives an impatient sigh. 'Is he indeed? You really are nuts, mother.'

He patters back into the *entrada*.

'Never did mockers waste more idle breath,' I call after him.

There's a splash from behind a lily pad. Johnny bobs up, his face glistening in the moonlight.

'I like that quote. Good old Helena in A Midsummer Night's Dream.' He submerges his body once more. 'And that's my last word.'

I get up and brush myself down. How my son can possibly think I'm a few *centimos* short of a euro, I just cannot guess.

A fat slice of sunlight falls on to the work surface. I have just finished bottling lemon curd and am about to have a well-earned coffee break. It's been a productive morning altogether, in which I have spoken with my friend Fiona and informed our clients that we won't be merging with Red Hot. The response was wholly favourable. With that behind me I feel more confident about facing Red Hot. Alan walks into the kitchen.

'That was a useful call. My old chum, Paul, is keen to meet up with you next week in London. He's got a few companies on his books looking to merge.'

I look up, licking the sticky lemon curd from my fingers. 'Shall I call to fix a meeting?'

'Absolutely. I'll give you his number. What did Fiona have to say earlier?'

I rinse my hands under the tap. 'She's excited about this other company she's found. I told her we were going to bow out of the Red Hot PR deal.'

He puts on the coffee machine. 'How did she take it?'

'She seemed totally laid back. Said that it was only the first offer on the table.'

'You see how things work out. The clients have all been supportive, so all you have to do now is speak to Marilyn and Jay.'

I bite my lip. 'Yes, I'm not looking forward to that call.'

'It will be fine,' he says distractedly as he attempts to master the coffee machine. I nudge him out of the way and set it in motion. He saunters over to the kitchen door and picks up a trug overflowing with artichokes.

'Last of the season. Anyway, I've just planted the French beans so we'll have those to look forward to.'

I pounce on the artichokes. 'Fantastic! I shall do them with vinaigrette for supper.'

Alan picks up the coffee cups. 'Let's go and sit in the sun.'

We pull out chairs on the patio and sit basking in the warm sunlight. The Scotsman takes a hefty sip and smacks his lips together.

'Isn't this bliss? Just look at the mountains.'

'They're unbelievably beautiful with the halo of the sun behind them. The novelty still hasn't worn off.'

'How can it?' he says dreamily. 'when every day you have paradise on your doorstep?'

A gentle breeze ruffles through the silvery leaves of the olive tree and soft light the colour of maize blanches the rocks on the old stone walls of the courtyard. Spilling across the valley, the bright sun throws hills, orchards and sleepy town into sharp relief against an aquamarine sky. Catalina and I are sweeping and tidying the front porch in anticipation of welcoming our very first feline guests to the cattery. Minky and Orlando stand like sphinxes on either side of the pond while Inko sprawls on the path in the sun with twitching tail and a murderous look in her eye. There's a deep rumbling along the track. Catalina taps my arm.

'It must be Mrs Talbot. She's very early.'

I stare at her. 'Why Judy Talbot? It could be the couple from Valldemossa.'

She shakes her head impatiently. 'No, they said they had a small car. Mrs Talbot has a Range Rover. Listen, that's a big car coming along the track.'

Her suspicions are borne out when a glossy black vehicle with darkened windows tears into the courtyard, coughing up a pile of gravel. We wait until the dust has settled and walk along the path to greet our guest. No sooner have we reached the driver's door when it flies open and Greedy George jumps out. Catalina and I step back in surprise.

'George! What on earth are you doing here?'

He turns to me. 'That's a nice greeting, I must say! I come all the way over to help you inaugurate your cat hospice and that's all the thanks I get.'

'It's just such a surprise.'

I give him a peck on the cheek. Catalina does likewise then shakes a finger at him.

'You naughty man. Why didn't you tell us you were coming?'

He gives me a quick wink. 'To be honest, your old Scotsman was in on it.'

'Was he indeed? I shall deal with him later.'

'Anyway, guv, got a little launch gift for you. It'll be here in a minute.'

Catalina gives me a questioning look.

I shrug. 'What do you mean, George?'

There's a wild tooting and a small white van draws into the drive. Catalina looks at her watch.

'Do you think it's the couple from Valldemossa?'

A swarthy Mallorcan gets out of the van and heads towards us, a massive smile on his face. What is going on?

'Watcha Ignacio! Got stuck at the lights?' bawls George. 'I was just coming over the tram tracks and the lights changed. I lost you after that.'

'*Si*, I had to stop at the lights but I found the house easily enough.'

'I'm very confused,' I say wearily.

Greedy George walks off conspiratorially with Ignacio and they pull open the back doors to the van. An almighty bleating pierces the air and, a second later, a little fawn and white kid with a red ribbon round its neck half skips, half stumbles out of the van. Ignacio has it tethered to a piece of rope and leads it over to me.

'George went to a lot of bother to get you this little guy. His staff found out about my farm on the Internet and ordered it months ago.'

I bend down to stroke the little creature. It lets out a plaintive 'maaaaaaaaaa!'

'It's beautiful, George. Thank you. I'm not sure what to say. I mean, I hadn't envisaged keeping a goat.'

He gives a sniff. 'It's a *macho* of course. I've christened him Bill in deference to our mutual pal Vice Admiral Mason.'

I laugh. 'How on earth do you know about Bill the Goat?'

'I told you, there's nothing I don't know about goats. By coincidence old Admiral Mason and I both happened to have ozone appointments with Doc Zimmerman in Wimpole Street and we got talking about goats, as you do.'

I shake my head.

'So he told you all about Bill the goat at the Maryland Naval Academy?'

'He certainly did but I told him something he didn't know. He was talking about a flock of goats and I explained to him that the correct collective was a trip.'

'Or tribe,' butts in Ollie, who has slunk along the porch and now squats down to fondle the little kid.

'Well if it isn't my favourite little smarty pants. OK then, where does the word trip come from?'

Ollie looks vague. 'No idea. Maybe from troop?'

George tuts. 'No one knows its real origin but it apparently dates back to the fourteenth century.'

'I didn't know that,' says Ollie.

'Stone the crows. I've actually caught you out.'

He tousles Ollie's hair and signs a delivery note from Ignacio.

'He's from good stock,' says Ignacio. My farm is just outside Sineu and we breed very healthy goats.'

'Good,' I reply. 'Let's hope he thrives here. What do we feed him?'

'Goats eat most things really and your field will be perfect for him. I've got some notes on goat care for you in Mallorcan dialect. Is that OK?'

'I suppose it's good to practice. Anyway, Catalina will translate if I get stuck.'

We wave as he slowly makes his way back down the track.

Catalina, ever practical, takes the goat by the rope and takes him down into the field with Ollie following close behind her. Greedy George and Alan are in deep conversation when another car arrives. It's getting like Piccadilly Circus. A Range Rover nestles closely next to George's sleek motor, and a large lady in enormous shades jumps out.

'I'm Judy. I've come with Mr Jakes, as agreed.'

We shake hands and there are general introductions all round.

'Who's Mr Jakes?' yells George. 'Putting your old man in the cattery while you go on vacation?'

Judy Talbot gives a wry laugh. 'No, silly! I got rid of my old man years ago. Mr Jakes is my Persian. He's staying here for two weeks while I'm in the States.'

George gallantly takes the wicker cat basket that she pulls from the back of the car.

'Where are you from in the States?'

'Boston.'

'Know it well.'

She seems delighted, and gives him an approving smile. 'We must chat.'

'Sure,' he enthuses. 'Now where do I take Mr Jakes?'

'Follow me,' says the Scotsman. 'We'll have some cava once the others have arrived.

We're just awaiting one other arrival, a young Siamese from Valldemossa.'

I watch as they all set off down to the field. It's turning out to be a surreal morning. A few minutes later John and Isabella Perry arrive with their Siamese and together we join the others in the spanking new cattery block. We give a brief guided tour of the building and help settle in the first two inmates.

'It's so sweet and cosy,' says Judy Talbot. 'I know Mr Jakes will love the tranquillity.'

'Flopsy will too,' enthuses Isabella Perry. Her husband gives a nod but seems more interested in the view outside.

'You called her after the bunny in Beatrix Potter?' I ask.

Isabella touches my arm. 'So you remember the Flopsy and Mopsy bunnies?'

'Of course. I was a great fan as a child. Still am, as a matter of fact.'

She smiles and returns to her Siamese's run where it is sniffing the cat toys and generally familiarising itself with its surroundings. Her husband yawns and stands in the sunshine admiring the view of the Tramuntanas.

'Nice spot. Damned lucky cats if you ask me.'

'What I want to know is where you're going to sell all my cat gear?' bellows George, stomping around the small office area.

I give an exasperated sigh. 'I doubt many of our mountain cats will be looking for bondage gear in temperatures of forty degrees.'

'Bondage gear?' coos Judy Talbot. 'George is obviously a man after my own heart.'

Heaven help us. I must keep this pair at arms length otherwise who knows what it might lead to?

I retreat to the kitchen area where the Scotsman is pulling some bottles of cava from the mini fridge we have installed.

There's a series of pops as he unleashes the corks. 'Everyone for a drink?'

Amid murmurs of approval, Catalina hands everyone a glass just as George clears his throat.

'I hereby declare Tom Gingers, exclusive holiday home for spoilt mogs, officially open!'

We chink glasses and Ollie runs round taking pictures with his digital camera.

'It's such a beautiful day too,' says Judy Talbot. 'The gods must be on your side.'

'I do hope so,' says the Scotsman.

There's a sound of footsteps and Rafael together with Catalina's husband, Ramon and her brother, Stefan, appear. 'Are we too late?'

'Come in!' calls the Scotsman. 'Have a drink.'

'The rest of the builders are on their way.'

This is going to be some topping out ceremony. I slip out of the merry throng, now clustered around the doorway, to check up on little Bill the Kid. He is chomping on a wild clump of grass under a lemon tree, his glossy coat shining in the golden rays of the sun. I crouch down on my knees, ignoring the inquisitive ants, and stroke his thick wiry hair. It is such a perfect day. The mountains are a fiery bronze and the fields are bathed in dazzling light. After so many months of planning, disappointment and uncertainty we have finally been able to realise our plans. It may just be the first small step towards a bigger scheme, but for now it will do. I close my eyes for a second, at which auspicious moment Judas begins bleating. With difficulty I extract the mobile from the back pocket of my shorts, observing that it's a UK number. Who could possibly be calling me on a Sunday?

'Hi! It's Marilyn here. I've just flown back from Milan. We were doing a fashion shoot.'

Marilyn Hughes. Why now? I feel my pulse race. Bill stops munching and gives me a quizzical look, followed by a little 'maaaaa'.

I clear my throat. 'Good to hear from you. I was going to call you tomorrow.'

'Right. About signing the deal?'

'Yes.'

'Are we still on board?'

A pause. It's now or never. Johnny's face swims before me, his steely, croaky little voice cutting through the knife edge silence – 'ditch the deal'. I take a deep breath and, with as much compassion as I can muster, reply, 'I'm afraid not, Marilyn. I've had a change of heart.'

The Scotsman stands in the kitchen doorway, admiring the Tramuntanas. He sips on a glass of cold water.

'What a perfect day. Everything went off without a hitch.'

'True, although Marilyn's call wasn't that welcome.'

He gives a little guffaw. 'Not the best timing, admittedly, but at least you got it all over with.'

I pull a chair out from the table and face him. 'She was amazingly reasonable about it, in fairness.'

Alan nods. 'I wonder if her heart was really in it at all. She seemed to be juggling too many balls.'

'Yes, she was always flying around and never really seemed to have a clue what was going on in her own office.'

I get up and wander over to him. 'It's so good to look out at the hills. Somehow it puts everything into perspective. So what are our plans for tonight?'

He potters on to the patio. 'George is having a stroll around the field and then I suppose we should get changed and head off for Es Turo for supper. He can only stay tonight.'

'That's enough! I love little Bill the goat. How did George persuade you to let me have him?'

He laughs. 'Between you and me, I did have my reservations but if we give him a fenced off area so that he keeps away from my trees and plants, it'll be OK.'

There's the sound of discordant whistling, and George appears at the top of the steps leading from the field. Beaming, he makes his way over to us across the patio and strides into the kitchen. 'Can't believe it's so hot at this time of the afternoon. What a fun day, eh, guys?'

We follow in his wake.

'It sure was. Everyone seemed to have a good time and little Bill the goat was the cat's whiskers,' I say.

'It was good that Marilyn whats-er-name called and you could tell the dozy cow where to stick her deal.'

'I wouldn't have phrased it quite like that. She was really very nice about it.'

'Yeah, and the rest. Anyway, now you can concentrate on my new Paris shop and selling my cat gear over here.'

'You don't give up, do you?'

He chortles to himself and sitting down at the table grabs at a chunky paperback lying by a heap of old newspapers.

'Hey, guv, is this the book you were talking about? *Discovering Dorothea*?'

I walk over to him. 'Yes, the biography of the lovely Dorothea Bate. I've just finished it.'

'Can I borrow it?'

'Sure, but you're not seriously thinking of mounting some bizarre Myotragus exhibition in your stores?'

He breaks into a mischievous grin. 'I'll keep you posted. By the way, young Bill seems to be making himself at home in your field. He's found himself a nice bush of thistles to chew on.'

The Scotsman smiles genially and then suddenly frowns. 'Did you say thistles?'

'Yes, there's a big bush of the blighters. Like bleeding triffids. Lucky I got you Bill.'

'Those aren't thistles!' exclaims the Scotsman in some frustration. 'He must be munching on my prized Cardoons!'

'Your what?'

In a flash, the Scotsman has sprinted across the patio, disappearing down the steps to the field.

Greedy George rises to his feet. 'That's got his goat.'

We cross the patio and look down into the field where the Scotsman appears to be wrestling with little Bill as he hangs on to a Cardoon for dear life.

'I feel a whole new chapter starting in our lives,' I say to George with a grin.

He laughs raucously. 'Well Gov, let's hope you haven't bitten off more than you can chew.'

We hear a loud, triumphant 'maaaaa' from the field and, with much ado, several towering Cardoons, together with the Scotsman and Bill, go tumbling in a messy heap to the ground.

Have you enjoyed this book? If so, why not write a review
on your favourite website?

Thanks very much for buying this Summersdale book.

# www.summersdale.com